Digital Tools for Computer Music Production and Distribution

Dionysios Politis
Aristotle University of Thessaloniki, Greece

Miltiadis Tsalighopoulos
Aristotle University of Thessaloniki, Greece

Ioannis Iglezakis
Aristotle University of Thessaloniki, Greece

A volume in the Advances in Multimedia and Interactive Technologies (AMIT) Book Series

Information Science REFERENCE
An Imprint of IGI Global

Published in the United States of America by
Information Science Reference (an imprint of IGI Global)
701 E. Chocolate Avenue
Hershey PA 17033
Tel: 717-533-8845
Fax: 717-533-8661
E-mail: cust@igi-global.com
Web site: http://www.igi-global.com

Library of Congress Cataloging-in-Publication Data

Names: Politis, Dionysios. | Tsaligopoulos, Miltiadis, 1949- | Iglezakis, Ioannis, 1965-
Title: Digital tools for computer music production and distribution / Dionysios Politis, Miltiadis Tsaligopoulos, and Ioannis Iglezakis, editors.
Description: Hershey PA : Information Science Reference, [2016] | Includes bibliographical references and index.
Identifiers: LCCN 2016003159| ISBN 9781522502647 (hardcover) | ISBN 9781522502654 (ebook)
Subjects: LCSH: Information storage and retrieval systems--Music. | Music--Computer network resources. | Interactive multimedia. | Copyright--Music. | Cochlear implants.
Classification: LCC ML74 .D53 2016 | DDC 780.285--dc23 LC record available at http://lccn.loc.gov/2016003159

This book is published in the IGI Global book series Advances in Multimedia and Interactive Technologies (AMIT) (ISSN: 2327-929X; eISSN: 2327-9303)

British Cataloguing in Publication Data
A Cataloguing in Publication record for this book is available from the British Library.

Advances in Multimedia and Interactive Technologies (AMIT) Book Series

ISSN: 2327-929X
EISSN: 2327-9303

Mission

Traditional forms of media communications are continuously being challenged. The emergence of user-friendly web-based applications such as social media and Web 2.0 has expanded into everyday society, providing an interactive structure to media content such as images, audio, video, and text.

The **Advances in Multimedia and Interactive Technologies (AMIT) Book Series** investigates the relationship between multimedia technology and the usability of web applications. This series aims to highlight evolving research on interactive communication systems, tools, applications, and techniques to provide researchers, practitioners, and students of information technology, communication science, media studies, and many more with a comprehensive examination of these multimedia technology trends.

Coverage

- Multimedia Services
- Digital Communications
- Digital Technology
- Multimedia technology
- Social Networking
- Digital Images
- Web Technologies
- Digital Games
- Gaming Media
- Digital Watermarking

IGI Global is currently accepting manuscripts for publication within this series. To submit a proposal for a volume in this series, please contact our Acquisition Editors at Acquisitions@igi-global.com or visit: http://www.igi-global.com/publish/.

The Advances in Multimedia and Interactive Technologies (AMIT) Book Series (ISSN 2327-929X) is published by IGI Global, 701 E. Chocolate Avenue, Hershey, PA 17033-1240, USA, www.igi-global.com. This series is composed of titles available for purchase individually; each title is edited to be contextually exclusive from any other title within the series. For pricing and ordering information please visit http://www.igi-global.com/book-series/advances-multimedia-interactive-technologies/73683. Postmaster: Send all address changes to above address.

Titles in this Series

For a list of additional titles in this series, please visit: www.igi-global.com

Trends in Music Information Seeking, Behavior, and Retrieval for Creativity
Petros Kostagiolas (Ionian University, Greece) Konstantina Martzoukou (Robert Gordon University, UK) and Charilaos Lavranos (Ionian University, Greece)
Information Science Reference • copyright 2016 • 388pp • H/C (ISBN: 9781522502708) • US $195.00 (our price)

Emerging Perspectives on the Mobile Content Evolution
Juan Miguel Aguado (University of Murcia, Spain) Claudio Feijóo (Technical University of Madrid, Spain & Tongji University, China) and Inmaculada J. Martínez (University of Murcia, Spain)
Information Science Reference • copyright 2016 • 438pp • H/C (ISBN: 9781466688384) • US $210.00 (our price)

Emerging Research on Networked Multimedia Communication Systems
Dimitris Kanellopoulos (University of Patras, Greece)
Information Science Reference • copyright 2016 • 448pp • H/C (ISBN: 9781466688506) • US $200.00 (our price)

Emerging Research and Trends in Gamification
Harsha Gangadharbatla (University of Colorado Boulder, USA) and Donna Z. Davis (University of Oregon, USA)
Information Science Reference • copyright 2016 • 455pp • H/C (ISBN: 9781466686519) • US $215.00 (our price)

Experimental Multimedia Systems for Interactivity and Strategic Innovation
Ioannis Deliyannis (Ionian University, Greece) Petros Kostagiolas (Ionian University, Greece) and Christina Banou (Ionian University, Greece)
Information Science Reference • copyright 2016 • 378pp • H/C (ISBN: 9781466686595) • US $195.00 (our price)

Design Strategies and Innovations in Multimedia Presentations
Shalin Hai-Jew (Kansas State University, USA)
Information Science Reference • copyright 2015 • 589pp • H/C (ISBN: 9781466686960) • US $225.00 (our price)

Cases on the Societal Effects of Persuasive Games
Dana Ruggiero (Bath Spa University, UK)
Information Science Reference • copyright 2014 • 345pp • H/C (ISBN: 9781466662063) • US $205.00 (our price)

Table of Contents

Detailed Table of Contents

and over report some trouble hearing. One in eight people in the United States (13 percent, or 30 million) aged 12 years or older has hearing loss in both ears, based on standard hearing examinations. About 2 percent of adults aged 45 to 54 have disabling hearing loss. The rate increases to 8.5 percent for adults aged 55 to 64. Nearly 25 percent of those aged 65 to 74 and 50 percent of those who are 75 and older have disabling hearing loss. These figures depict the impact on patients' quality of life and the necessity for early and accurate diagnosis and treatment. It is important to mention that congenital hearing loss and deafness is also a condition that requires early diagnosis and hearing aiding in order to develop normal speech. Profound, early-onset deafness is present in 4–11 per 10,000 children, and is attributable to genetic causes in at least 50% of cases.

The ordinary user of cochlear implants is subject to post-surgical treatment that calibrates and adapts via mapping functions the acoustic characteristics of the recipient's hearing. As the number of cochlear implant users reaches indeed large numbers and their dispersion over vast geographic areas seems to be a new trend with impressive expansion, the need for doctors and audiologists to remotely program the cochlear implants of their patients comes as first priority, facilitating users in their programmed professional or personal activities. As a result, activities that need special care, like playing sport, swimming, or recreation can be performed remotely, disburdening the recipient from traveling to the nearest specialized programming center. However, is remote programming safeguarded from hazards?

Human senses enable humans to perceive and interact with their environment, through a set of sensory systems or organs which are mainly dedicated to each sense. From the five main senses in humans hearing plays a critical role in many aspects of our lives. Hearing allows the perception not only of the immediate visible environment but also parts of the environment that are obstructed from view and/or that are a significant distance from the individual. One of the most important and sometimes overlooked aspects of hearing is communication, since most human communication is accomplished through speech and hearing. Hearing does not only convey speech but also conveys more complex messages in the form of music, singing and storytelling.

Section 2
Audiovisual Tools for Rich Multimedia Interaction

The evolutional course of music through centuries has shown an incremental use of chromatic variations by composers and performers for melodies' and music sounds' enrichment. This chapter presents an integrated model, which contributes to the calculation of musical chromaticism. The model takes into account both horizontal (melody) and vertical chromaticism (harmony). The proposed qualitative and quantitative measures deal with music attributes that relate to the audience's chromatic perception. They namely are: the musical scale, the melodic progress, the chromatic intervals, the rapidity of melody, the direction of melody, music loudness, and harmonic relations. This theoretical framework can lead to semantic music visualizations that reveal music parts of emotional tension.

The playing of a musical instrument is one of the most skilled and complex interactions between a human and an artifact. Professional musicians spend a significant part of their lives initially learning their instruments and then perfecting their skills. The production, distribution and consumption of music has been profoundly transformed by digital technology. Today music is recorded and mixed using computers, distributed through online stores and streaming services, and heard on smartphones and portable music players. Computers have also been used to synthesize new sounds, generate music, and even create sound acoustically in the field of music robotics. Despite all these advances the way musicians interact with computers has remained relatively unchanged in the last 20-30 years. Most interaction with computers in the context of music making still occurs either using the standard mouse/keyboard/screen interaction that everyone is familiar with, or using special digital musical instruments and controllers such as keyboards, synthesizers and drum machines. The string, woodwind, and brass families of instruments do not have widely available digital counterparts and in the few cases that they do the digital version is nowhere as expressive as the acoustic one. It is possible to retrofit and augment existing acoustic instruments with digital sensors in order to create what are termed hyper-instruments. These hyper-instruments allow musicians to interact naturally with their instrument as they are accustomed to, while at the same time transmitting information about what they are playing to computing systems. This approach requires significant alterations to the acoustic instrument which is something many musicians are hesitant to do. In addition, hyper-instruments are typically one of a kind research prototypes making their wider adoption practically impossible. In the past few years researchers have started exploring the use of non-invasive and minimally invasive sensing technologies that address these two limitations by allowing acoustic instruments to be used without any modifications directly as digital controllers. This enables natural human-computer interaction with all the rich and delicate control of acoustic instruments, while retaining the wide array of possibilities that digital technology can provide. In this chapter, an overview of these efforts will be provided followed by some more detailed case studies from research that has been conducted by the author's group. This natural interaction blurs the boundaries between the virtual and physical world which is something that will increasingly happen in other aspects of human-computer interaction in addition to music. It also opens up new possibilities for computer-assisted music tutoring, cyber-physical ensembles, and assistive music technologies.

While many scientific fields loosely rely on coarse depiction of findings and clues, other disciplines demand exact appreciation, consideration and acknowledgement for an accurate diagnosis of scientific data. But what happens if the examined data have a depth of focus and a degree of perplexity that is beyond our analyzed scope? Such is the case of performing arts, where humans demonstrate a surplus in creative potential, intermingled with computer supported technologies that provide the substrate for advanced programming for audiovisual effects. However, human metrics diverge from computer measurements, and therefore a space of convergence needs to be established analogous to the expressive capacity of musical inventiveness in terms of rhythm, spatial movement and dancing, advanced expression of emotion through harmony and beauty of the accompanying audiovisual form. In this chapter, the new era of audiovisual effects programming will be demonstrated that leverage massive participation and emotional reaction.

The industry of video games has rapidly grown during the last decade, while "gaming" has been promoted into an interdisciplinary stand-alone science field. As a result, music in video games, as well as its production, has been yet a state-of-the-art research field in computer science. Since the production of games has reached a very high level in terms of complication and cost (the production of a 3-d multi-player game can cost up to millions of dollars), the role of sound engineer / composer / programmer is very crucial. This chapter describes the types of sound that exist in today's games and the various issues that arise during the musical composition. Moreover, the existing systems and techniques for algorithmic music composition are analyzed.

Cloud computing offers internet users the fulfillment of the dream of a Celestial Jukebox providing music, films or digital books anywhere and when they want. However, some activities done in the Cloud, especially file-sharing, may infringe copyright law's exclusive rights, like the right of reproduction or the making available right. The purposes of the present chapter are to briefly examine how digital technology like p2p systems or Cloud computing potentiate new distribution models, how they allow unauthorized uses of copyright protected works and to point out solutions to reconcile the interests of rightholders and consumers so that the benefits from digital technology can be enjoyed by all the stakeholders in a legal and balanced way.

Preface

The instructional approaches presented in this book are not oblivious to the advances in our networked society. Indeed, audiophiles around the globe, plunging into oceans of music clips and hearings, are intimately accustomed with the digital substrate of computer music production and distribution. Terms and notions for the subject domain of digital audio, like synthesis techniques, performance software, music editing and processing systems, algorithmic composition, musical input devices, MIDI, karaoke, synthesizer architectures, system interconnection, psychoacoustics, music libraries, song competitions and voting systems, are more or less on the lips of the average music surfer.

Without a doubt, computer music not only succeeded in replacing big, cumbersome and expensive studios by computer oriented hardware and software that in most cases can produce and distribute music, but also, has directed the average listener in hearing music via his/hers computer, tablet or smartphone. And it should be noted, that virtually all residents of this planet indulge into music synaesthesia at least for a while every day.

Taking into account that mobile devices are crafty in recording audiovisual proceedings, with unprecedented accuracy and proximity, multimedia social networks become capable of delivering a multitude of music renditions in vast webcasting repositories. Therefore, it could be claimed that nearly every noteworthy music event produced in the synchrony of this world, ranging from amateur performances up to niche festivities, has significant opportunities to be part of a huge mosaic that imprints the collective memory of humanity. Gigantic repositories, acting as interactive multimedia libraries, mold the mood for the design of a new paradigm for producing, distributing and hearing music. New software modules come up, along with promotional web architectures, biased by a strong and prolific industry hidden behind.

Concomitantly, privacy concerns arise for inner core surveillance practices that penetrate the sphere of anonymity, which most people account for their social movements.

This book is written with an interdisciplinary orientation. It probes into the main actors for this march of events: the listeners, the producers-distributors, and the regulators.

For that reason, the book is divided into three sections:

In section 1, titled Hearing and Music Perception, the substrate for properly listening to music is explored. Hearing aids and bionic devices are analyzed in an attempt to outline the new frontiers for scientific resources on listening comprehension.

The second section, titled Audiovisual Tools for Rich Multimedia Interaction, dips into the theory, the technology, and the tools that reshape what links music with visual, kinetic and sensory-intensive robotic interaction.

The last part, Legal Action and Jurisprudence, gives a proscriptive norm on how the world-wide Internet screen can cope with matters of confidentiality, protection of intellectual property, and after all human integrity, as far as digital audio is concerned.

Overall, an international culture of listening streamlined music has commenced to prevail. As a result, the human factors that leverage enactment in music are emphatically promoted. The same time, the hurling, insulting abuse of the private sphere of communications via public channels is behaviorally abjured, especially when social networks are intermingled.

Acknowledgment

This book would not be possible if the editors did not enjoy the all heartedly support of the publisher, IGI Global. A chain of credible, helpful consultants, whose first link was Ms. Jan Travers and last Ms. Courtney Tychinski, walked with us the 18 month long bumpy way of forming the unstructured incoming material of interrelated articles to a thematic concatenation with strong cohesiveness and sturdy orientation. For the history of this book, it should be noted that the instigation force to proceed with such enthusiasm to new methods and experimental ideas was Dr. Mehdi Khosrow-Pour, with whom the editing team has shared, for quite some time, eagerness, commitment, and constructive feedback in driving the preclusive joy of research advancements to a handy perpetuation in printed matter.

In closing, we wish to express our deep appreciation to our families, to whom this book is devoted to, for providing us the needed inspirational resources to balance our careers and family trajectories.

Dionysios Politis
Aristotle University of Thessaloniki, Greece

Miltiadis Tsalighopoulos
Aristotle University of Thessaloniki, Greece

Ioannis Iglezakis
Aristotle University of Thessaloniki, Greece

Section 1
Hearing and Music Perception

Chapter 1
Oral and Aural Communication Interconnection:
The Substrate for Global Musicality

Dionysios Politis
Aristotle University of Thessaloniki, Greece

Miltiadis Tsalighopoulos
Aristotle University of Thessaloniki, Greece

ABSTRACT

Speech science is a key player for music technology since vocalization plays a predominant role in today's musicality. Physiology, anatomy, psychology, linguistics, physics and computer science provide tools and methodologies to decipher how motor control can sustain such a wide spectrum of phonological activity. On the other hand, aural communication provides a steady mechanism that not only processes musical signals, but also provides an acoustic feedback that coordinates the complex activity of tuned articulation; it also couples music perception with neurophysiology and psychology, providing apart from language related understanding, better music experience.

DOI: 10.4018/978-1-5225-0264-7.ch001

INTRODUCTION

Phonetics and speech science have been incorporated into our discourse for quite some time. These terms refer to how the phonetic instrument, within its anatomic formations, contributes to the global substrate of our everyday sonification.

Human language is studied intensively by IT systems and it is a focal point for global communication in its synchrony and diachrony; it is estimated that currently some 7,200 languages are spoken daily, and many of them are voiced not particularly changed for centuries or even millenniums (Anderson, 2012; Langscape, 2015) Moreover, some 75% of music heard day-to-day arranges speech elements alongside orchestration, bringing the ability to express thoughts and feelings as a direct outcome of speech communication to the forefront. Therefore, music becomes a multilayered activity that combines instrumental sounds, with whatever this may seem to mean, along with vocal hearings that produce as a final outcome an activity characterized by the beauty of its form.

Indeed, the musical revolutions of the 21st and 20th centuries have increased the potential for music perception: most of the music heard daily is reproduced music and not a live performance. However, music is no longer a synonym of only listening melody and tune, but it incorporates within its reproduction systems theatrical activity, like dancing or audiovisual interaction, not contrived to stage managed effects but ranging up to sequences of moving images. Undeniably, the most thematic contingently produced music is the kind that accompanies motion pictures; TV and the cinematographic industry seem to be a major instigating force that produces music to new frontiers of expression, dynamics and motif impression (Cox & Warner, 2007).

Although images and tunes have more or less a global awareness, the linguistic content of music is limited by the neurophysiological understanding of its sonic content; the distinct conceptuality of the wording is achieved to a high degree when understanding of the language or family of languages for the lyrics performed is attained.

And yet, while most people in this planet enjoy a reasonable understanding of English, thus making music more or less driven by the English language mentality, the mother tongue of a specific region designates the preeminent prosody characteristics that have been contrived for many centuries in the semantics and semiotics of the written form. The scientific study of language phenomena tries to intermingle the study of signs and symbols with biological, social, cultural and historic folds that have shaped the development of each language.

Furthermore, not all people can perform music instrumentally; as a matter of fact, the ones that have a substantial knowledge of orchestrated music reproduction are rather few. Therefore, it comes in handy to seek measurement of aural perception via its conjugate musical linguistic performance. In this case, we do not seek to detect merely the speech disorders, like hesitations, false starts or phonetic errors; on the contrary, we elevate the measurements to the level of interdisciplinary science, where strong anatomical and physiological components are involved. The nature of musicality then is dependent on the anatomical structure of the vocal tract, indeed a complex and highly coordinated process that exerts delicate motor control on articulation. Phonation by itself is dependent on the listening channel, i.e. the ability to dip into the musical codes, dependent on the spectrum of sounds heard, and predominantly, on the way they are "translated" as a cerebral activity. In fact, it is still dark on certain points of the higher cortical functions that organize human language. It is also obscure how intricate muscular commands control at the high end the vocal tract and allow thought to be transformed to recognizable speech and melodious accomplishment in music (Colton & Estill, 1981).

Physical, mathematical and computer models have been engaged in the attempts to decipher the astute nature of perceptive musicality, but at best these practices are still approximations. It seems that hearing mechanisms and the process of perception, as it is typically recognized now, have inaugurated a correlation between neurophysiology and psychology. Indeed, in recent times our knowledge of the interior mechanisms that stimulate speech production and the physiology of hearing has increased a lot; as a matter of fact, inner core operations are performed as a daily routine. Furthermore, the developments in speech technology advance our understanding of music perception. Computer technology does not merely allow a more analytic approach of musical processing; it associates inner core procedures with technology, as is the case of cochlear implants that insert a speech processor in contact with the acoustic nerve.

However, the microchip revolution comes at a cost. Advances in silicon technology provide essential machinery to practically realize the desktop metaphor implanted in our skull, and not only. Cochlear implants are not merely cranial extensions of the inner ear to the brain. They are highly sophisticated "wearable" mobile devices that constitute a very sensitive interface of sensory impulses with the outside world. Moreover, they have the potential of Internet connection, in pursuit of interoperability for remote sensing, indicating uncontrolled and unrestrained possibilities for inner core data leakage (Politis et al., 2014).

In historical terms, the landmarks for what we call Western civilization musicality and linguistics are traced some 2500 years ago, and even further. Hindu grammarians had given then surprisingly accurate descriptions of speech sounds, and laid the foundations the Indo-European languages. Their unattested, reconstructed ancestor, Proto-Indo-European, is considered as spoken well before 3000

BC in a region somewhere to the north or south of the Black Sea (Harris, 1993). In contemporary terms, most of the languages we speak in our synchrony were molded phonetically during the 16th or 17th century, and this formation yielded the vastly spread languages

- English (in fact Germanic - including Dutch, Saxon, Gothic, and the Scandinavian languages offsprings like Norman), mingled with Celtic and French
- Spanish, Portuguese, Catalan and French (in fact the Italic branch of the Indo-European family of languages, coming from Latin and the Romance Languages)
- Indic (including Sanskrit and its descendants)
- Slavic (including Russian, Polish, Czech, Slovak, Slovenian, Bulgarian, and Serbo-Croatian)

and various smaller in expansion languages like Iranian, Greek, Armenian, Albanian (possibly descending from Illyrian), Baltic, Anatolian (an extinct group including Hittite and other languages), Tocharian (an extinct group from central Asia), etc.

A special mention is dedicated to Greek, since its grammarians devised an alphabet that is phonetically rational (Devine & Stephens, 1994), not to mention that it enjoys systematic grammar, syntactic and phonological treatment for millenniums and therefore it is proffered for diachronic comprehension. Indeed, the Ancient Greek syntax with accents and "breath" spirits gave to its syntax and morphology phonological inflections and semantics that are very close to the prosodic elements of vocal music (Barbour, 1972). Some of these elements survive with a remote distinctness in modern French, and coherently in Byzantine Music (Gianellos, 1996).

As a result, the Ancient Greek culture was permeated with music (Gombosi, 1944). Even the etymology of music comes as an offspring of that background: the muses were the daughters of Zeus and Mnenosyne (=remembrance) and their specialization demonstrates what is the breadth of music as a social, artistic and scientific phenomenon[1].

Surprisingly, contemporary scientists come to the same conclusions, not of course when studying one language, like Ancient Greek, but when coping with the polymorphism and complexity of our contemporary linguistic and musical intuitive knowledge (Williamson, 2014). As trained musicians exhibit finer-grained auditory skills and higher (music) *memory* capacity, in a collective level, spoken languages demonstrate through the years musical fidelity, clarity and imagery at different levels of their complicated continuum in terms of form, structure and music complexity.

To start with familiar historic trajectories, it is true that we know very little about Ancient Greek Music primarily because we have no actual recordings or hearings and secondly because sources about Eastern Music, a successor of Ancient Greek Music, are scattered and not thoroughly indexed as is the case with its counterpart, Western Music. Fortunately, researchers and pioneers like West (1992) and Pöhlmann (2001) have managed to collect and organize a very large amount of documents and actual music scores and have given a scientific insight for a music system over 2000 years old. On the other hand, performers and scientists like Halaris (1999), Harmonia Mundi (1999), and D' Angour (2013), have recreated hearings of that period, so, it is not so unfamiliar to our senses anymore.

Additionally, it is difficult for researchers with a profound musical education in Western Music and culture, well advanced in diatonicism and tempered scales to understand the chromatic and enharmonic background of Ancient Greek Music (Barsky, 1996). It should be noted, that all this vast area, from the "Western" world to India is not historically unified in terms of musicology. As Barsky states, there is an eminent historical rift: North-West Europeans, and therefore "Westerners", tend to progress with diatonicism, polyphony and orchestration, while "Easterners" more actively encourage chromaticism, vivid vocalizations and more passionate stage performances (Politis, 2015). There seems to be a reasonable medical explanation why people living for centuries in cold climates have developed different phonation and musicality practices in comparison to their counterparts in warm regions that have elaborated in their behaviorism an outward sociolinguistic, communal and cultural demeanor. So, in medical terms the rift is not "West" - "East", but rather "North" - "South".

As a result, while Russian music culture for instance tends historically to be at the Eastern side of the cultural rift, its musical substrate progresses more easily with "Western" diatonicism than with "Eastern" music chromaticism, rooted traditionally in Byzantium and Middle East. Surprisingly so, Italian or Spanish music, although though to be rooted in the "Western" side of the rift, are closer most of the times to the "warm" flux of "Eastern" chromaticism. This is emphatically sonorant in contemporary Latin American music. Even further, jazz music, characterized by improvisation, syncopation, and generally forceful rhythm, did not only serve as a precursor for the revolution of rock and pop music that characterizes the explosive music forms introduced after the 1950s, but also mingled the "southern" colorful, emphatically energetic performance of black American artists with the "northern" obstructed and disciplined music of the USA.

As West and East fervently mix via massive migration and cultural influx via globalized broadcasts, music recordings, and Internet multimedia exchanges (Cox & Warner, 2007), listeners discover colored pieces for the global mosaic of musicology. Thus, they unearth the diverse elements of our synchrony, and amazingly, by diachrony, their coherent historic roots.

For instance, there is evidence from antiquity that "Easterners" where gamboling in circular dances clicking castanets with their fingers as a rhythmic accompaniment. Although most contemporary people would link castanets with passionate Spanish dances in Europe and predominantly within the Americas, the original dance has survived as well (Figure 1). It has been sung and danced uninterruptedly in Cappadocia, an ancient region of central Asia Minor, north of Cilicia towards the Euphrates river. As Turkic populations started moving from central Asia to Europe, Turkish, Azerbaijani, Kazakh, Kyrgyz, Uighur, Uzbek and Tatar people have adapted the dance, now being a part of their vivid tradition for more than a 1,000 years. The same time, this very clearly identified dance promulgated

Figure 1. Left: Ancient Greek dancer with castanets – sketch from original lekythos in the British museum, cropped from www.carnival.com. Right: Singing and dancing Greek women from Sementra, Cappadocia, Ottoman Empire, circa early 20th century. Center for Asia Minor Studies.

to Slavic populations and it is part of the ethnic folklore, for countries from the Balkans up to Ukraine and Russia. However, the difference in musicality, i.e. the arrangement of pitch distributions is clearly sensed according to the discernible arrangement of the previously mentioned pattern rift.

What is the future in this prolonged historical evolution? There is high level of activity in speech and music technology that wants to take advantage of the high level advances in IT arenas in an attempt to solve fundamental issues on associated areas of science investigating the structure and processes of language-related and music-related human cognition.

THE PRINCIPLES FOR SPEECH PRODUCTION

Phonation and Anatomy of Sound Sources

Human speech and singing are considered to be acoustic signals with a dynamically varying structure in terms of frequency and time domain. Generally speaking, voice sounds are in the broader sense all the sounds produced by a person's larynx and uttered through the mouth. They may be speech, singing voices, whispers, laughter, snorting or grunting sounds, etc.

No matter how these sounds are produced and what communication purposes they may serve, they are categorized to:

1. Voiced sounds that are produced in a person's larynx with a stream of air coming from the lungs and resonating the vocal cords. This stream continues to be modulated through its passage from the pharynx, mouth, and nasal cavity, resulting to an utterance in the form of speech or song.
2. Unvoiced sounds. Singing or utterance would be incomplete if unvoiced sounds where not produced. They do not come as a result of a vibration from the vocal cords, but as partial obstruction of the airflow during articulation.

The human ability to communicate relies on our capacity to coherently set up sequences of sounds that encode acoustically logical propositions. When voicing produces musical or singing sounds, then the articulated sounds of speech communication are enriched with phonation tuned up to melodic, definite pitches that are called notes or tones.

Not all people however produce the same notes in a uniform manner. A particular quality may be observed that gives the timbre of our voicing. Since the voice channel of each individual varies in morphology, and each subject may uniquely control its internal characteristics, virtually each one of us is capable to produce music with a unique quality, apart from its pitch and intensity. Even further, any malfunction or disease that affects the human organ, not to mention ageing, has impact on our ability to produce prosody or melody. Since the voice organ consists of the breathing apparatus, the vocal cords and nasal-oral passages, it is obvious that the process of phonation is a rather complex and multi-parametric phenomenon.

As seen in Figure 2, the lungs provide the air supply, the primordial energy source for phonation. In medical terms, the lungs consist of two spongy sacs situated within the rib cage, consisting of elastic bags with branching passages into which air is drawn, so that oxygen can pass into the blood and carbon dioxide be removed. The volume of the lungs is controlled by the surrounding rib-cage and the underlying diaphragm muscle. When the ribcage is expanded by the muscular system, and the diaphragm is contracted, the volume of the thorax increases, and inhalation takes place, inflating the lungs.

The mechanism for vocalization is better understood from an acoustic point of view by considering a set of variable sound sources, coupled together to form the complex structure seen in Figure 3, right. For programming purposes, a simulation of this multi-muscularly driven region that plays a key-role in the

Figure 2. Schematic representation of the vocal tact in coronal cross section. Left: The respiratory system and the upper vocal tract mechanism for phonation, in medical terms, from Wikimedia commons. Right: A computer programming simulation for synthetic musical vocalization. Sonification comes as output from both the nasal and oral cavities.

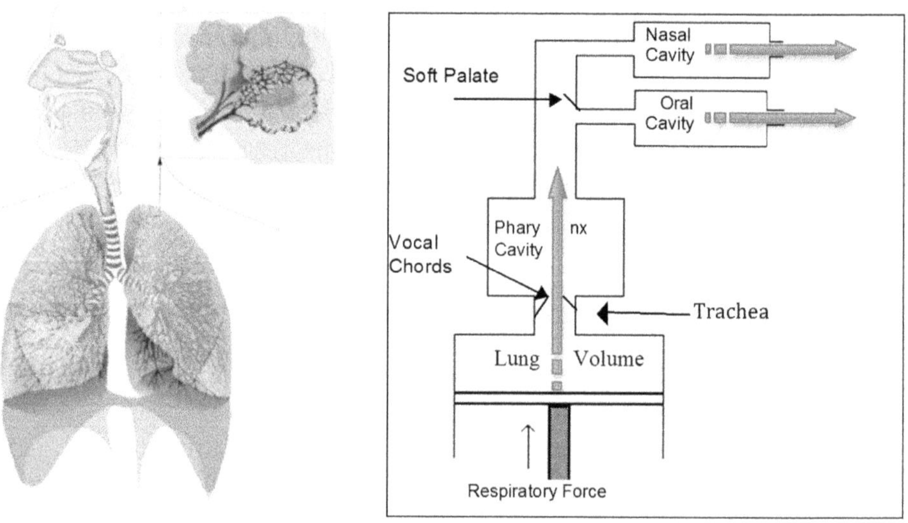

Figure 3. Left: Sequences of the breathing mechanism, denoting the relative position role of the diaphragm and is role for the formation of airflow directed to the vocal box. Right: The Trachea and Larynx sections analytically.
Pictures cropped via public domain Wikimedia commons.

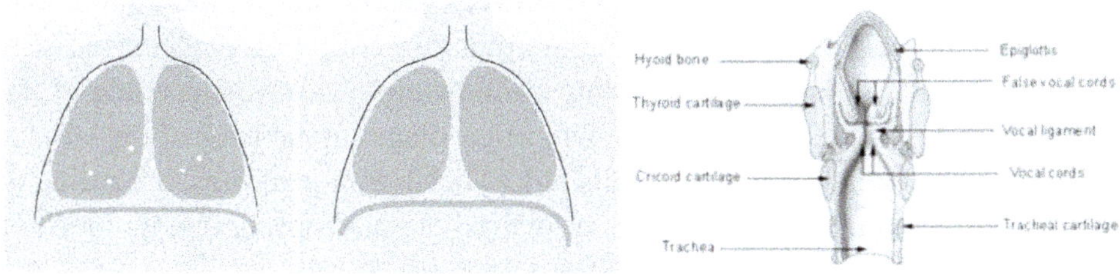

dynamic formation of the vocal tract activities is shown in Figure 2, right (Politis et al., 2007). The model used there is the source and filter model, which gives a rather sustainable approximation of the speech production process from an articulatory perspective. However, as we describe with more details the ways in which the anatomical structures of the voicing mechanism are developed, controlled, forcefully shaped, or dynamically changing position, we devise better models describing in motor command terms the vocal track muscular movement that serves as the motive force.

The process that provides the energy source lies within the lungs, while the primary sound source is positioned within the voice box, i.e. the larynx.

In detail:

The air within the lungs can be kept for long. The conjugate of inhalation is exhalation: the ribcage is contracted by its muscular system, the diaphragm is expanded and raised, expiration of air from the lungs takes place, and breathe out in a deliberate manner eventuates. Indeed consciously and intentionally deliberate, since the majority of speech sounds (in the case of English or Greek, all) are produced during this phase.

Of course, exhalation and inhalation are not only linked with phonation; more importantly they are integral parts of the life-supporting respiratory cycle with which living organisms produce energy from the oxidation of complex organic substances.

Once the controlled breath-out is triggered, the airflow passes via the larynx, a hollow muscular organ forming an air passage to the lungs and holding the vocal cords in humans and other mammals. Its basic biological function is a fast-acting valve that can interrupt and control the encountered airflow by asserting muscular control over the membranous tissue of the vocal cords. This way, the effective aperture of the airway through the larynx is altered, a slit is formed across the glottis in the throat and the airstream starts to produce sounds (Figure 3).

The motor functions of phonation at this level are performed by muscular movement of the cricoid, a ring-shaped cartilage of the larynx, the thyroid cartilage which forms the Adams apple, the epiglottis, a flap cartilage at the root of the tongue, which is depressed during swallowing to cover the opening of the windpipe, and finally the arytenoid, a pair of cartilages at the back of the larynx.

The flow of air in this region results in localized drop pressures, according to the Bernoulli effect, i.e. the principle of hydrodynamics stating that an increase in the velocity of an airstream results in a decrease in pressure. As a result the vocal chords snap shut. This process continues in a rather pseudo-periodic manner with the muscles setting vocal chord position and tension to appropriate levels so to adjust efficient respiratory force that maintains greater air pressure bellow the vocal chords than above them.

In conclusion, the vibratory action of the vocal chords takes place due to the combined action of muscular settings, vocal chord elasticity that unfortunately decreases with ageing, differential air pressure exerted across the epiglottis, and application of aerodynamic forces.

Once the airflow leaves the voice box, the overall energy source for phonation, it is directed via the pharynx to the oral and nasal cavities. As expected, the shape of the larynx and pharynx, along with its variable size play a primordial role for the production of speech sounds. It is this part of the body that controls the range of pitch or the type of tone that a person can produce.

Indeed, the periodicity with which the edge of the vocal cords vibrates in the airstream is mainly responsible for pitch of the singing voice (Sundberg, 1987). The bigger the vocal folds, the more bass sound is produced; the less lengthy the vocal chords are (as is predominantly the case of women and children) the degree of highness of the uttered tone is increased.

Indicatively, when speaking, the phonation frequency of an adult man is ranging between 100 Hz and 150 Hz; Women are easily within the 200 Hz - 300 Hz band, while children have an area of variation between 300 Hz and 450 Hz. However, when it comes to singing, male bass performers are sonorous from 65 Hz (note C_2) up to 330 Hz (note E_4), while baritones range from 110 Hz (note A_2) to 440 Hz (note A_4), and tenors can climb up to 523 Hz (note C_5). For women and children, contraltos, mezzo-sopranos and sopranos extend their pitches from 260 Hz (note C_4) up to 1320 Hz (note E_6).

Figure 4. Left: Transverse section of the vocal chords. Right: Vibrating sequences for the membranous tissue, in transverse view, depicting pressure flow and resistance.

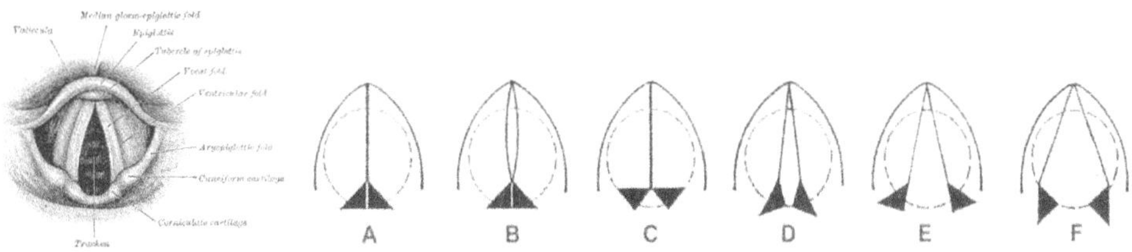

Recent research has also shown that this part of the human body is not only responsible for the resonance of the vocal chords according to singing voice patterns (such as soprano, tenor or bass); The elasticity and vigorousness with which this complex neuro-muscular structure corresponds to the pitch array of musicality prescribes the idiosyncratic speed with which the performer conveys a specified impression as a distinctive time quality.

Indeed, this valve mechanism seen in Figure 4 is responsible for several physical concepts related with phonation. Apart from the phonation frequency, which was described beforehand, some other factors that set the conditions for the vocalization activity are:

- **The Subglottic Pressure:** It is the pressure below the closed glottic slit. It builds up as air keeps concentrating and it causes vocal chords to vibrate rapidly. Apart from determining the voice loudness, it is also the pressure of air transferred to the mouth cavity. How this airflow is modulated by the organs of the mouth will be examined further on. Typical values are about $10cmH_2O \approx 1kPa$, i.e. roughly the same with the lung pressure when speaking loudly[2].
- **The Loudness of Phonation:** It is a rather subjective quantity since the sense of audible sounds varies with frequency. Sounds with the same sound level are easier perceived when their pitches are between 1,000 Hz and 3,000 Hz. Around this hotspot, sounds are heard attenuated.
- **The Airflow Through the Slit Like Opening of the Glottis:** Through extraction or contraction, as seen in Figure 4, the modulation of the airflow characterizes good singing. Although not the only parameter for well tuned continuous and regular vibrations, steady air flow in small quantities - for the sake of economizing stored air within the lungs, like 0.5 liters/s is typical for good singing, taking into account some 5 liter average lung capacity.

- **The Glottal Resistance:** The ratio of subglottic and transglottal airflow, characterizes the resistance to airflow passing via the glottis. Although varying considerably rather than being a uniform or steady bodily condition, it provides a distinguishable measure for what is referred to as "breathy" phonation when a comparatively high air consumption is involved (Sundberg, 1987). Regulated by the laryngeal muscles it provides a measure of the acoustic impedance, which is in a tube proportional to the air density and the speed of sound, and inversely proportional to the area of the tube's cross section. Therefore, glottal resistance is infinite when the glottis is fully shut, and zero when it is wide open.
- **The Articulation Parameters:** Before reaching the oral cavity, airflow is dependent on the size, shape and elasticity of the vocal track length. Not only length but also the area function of this tube-like structure along with the sound transfer function, i.e. the ability to transfer as intact as possible the sound vibrations from the glottis to the lips, determine phonation.

The mechanism that was previously described acts as a fast acting valve that can interrupt and control airflow in many ways. Muscular control exerted over the vocal chords is primarily aiding the respiratory system by refraining foreign objects from entering to the lungs via the trachea. This medical aspect is of some importance, since it gives to researchers incentive on how motor control is achieved over the sound generation process. Furthermore, after the musical revolutions of the 20th and 21st centuries, musicology extends significantly further than melody and tune; it incorporates art and theater, listening via amplified speaker or wearable apparatus, and of course intense bodily activity. For instance, bass reflex speaker systems transduce low frequencies over the body, and acoustic waves of the lowest range interact with the skeletal and muscular human structure.

As seen in Figure 2, the airflow continues after the "voice box" of larynx to the large cavity of pharynx. The pharynx is a membrane-lined cavity that extends to the nose and mouth, connecting them to the esophagus. The back wall of pharynx is formed by a series of small bones, the cervical vertebrae, while its shape is altered by the encircling pressure exercised to its walls by the constrictor muscles. The shape of this tubular structure varies considerably during articulation as an indirect consequence of the tongue movement. The part of pharynx below epiglottis has a rather complex geometry.

The tongue, which is supported by a U-shaped bone in the neck, the hyoid bone, is composed by a number of muscles. The root of the tongue convolves well bellow the upper flap of the epiglottis, a cartilage which is depressed when swallowing so to protect the larynx and lungs from food and drink. At the upper part of the pharyngeal tube is placed the velum, which along with the epiglottis and the root

Figure 5. Passive and active articulators: Sagittal section, distributed via Wikimedia Commons [link].
https://commons.wikimedia.org/wiki/File:Places_of_articulation.svg
1. Upper and Lower lip 2. Endo-labial part 3. Upper teeth 4. Alveolar ridge 5. Post Alveolar 6. Pre-palatal 7. Hard Palate 8. Velar 9. Uvula10. Pharynx wall 12. Epiglottis 13. Tongue Root 14. Back of the 15. Front of the tongue 16. Tongue blade 17. Tongue tip 18. Under the tongue. At the upper part, the Nasal cavity with the nostrils.

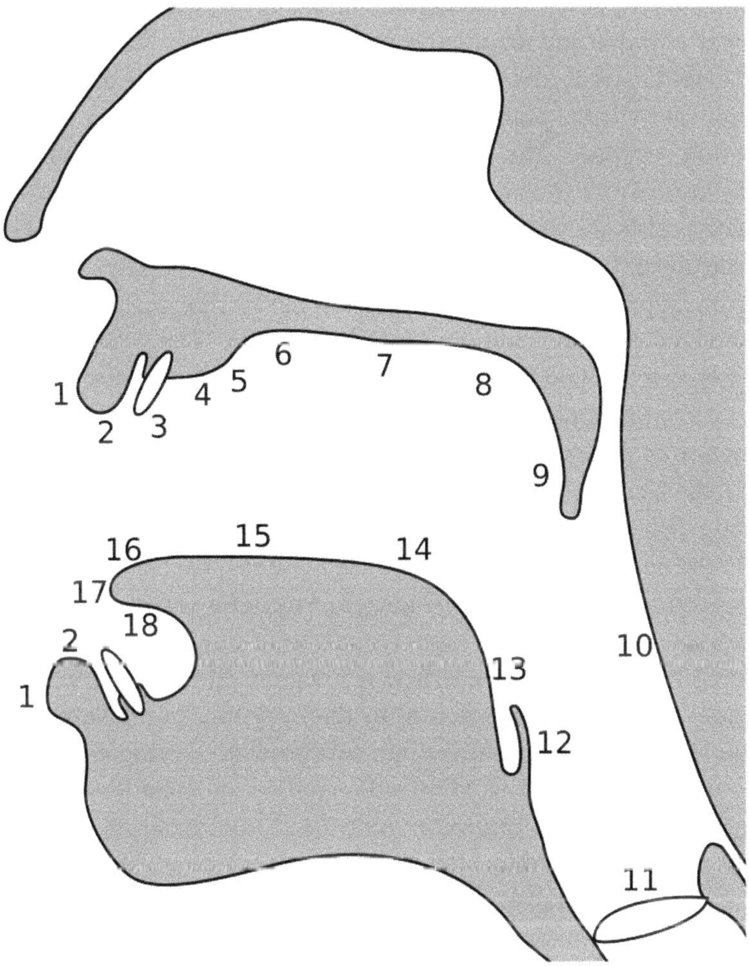

of the tongue determine the phonetic quality of voicing, i.e. its formants. Indeed, vowels are linked with resonator frequencies, which radiate high amplitude sound waves. This happens when a comparatively open configuration of the vocal tract is formed, accompanied with vibration of the vocal cords but without audible friction. As a result, the whole tubular cavity resonates to specific frequencies, the formant frequencies. At these frequencies the sound system generates waves with high energy that determine predominantly the color and timbre of phonation. It is the point where airstream starts to become sound.

After the pharyngeal tube, airflow is inserted into the oral cavity from the back of the tongue, and directly above it into the nasal cavity.

In linguistic terms, the oral cavity provides the primary source of variability for the acoustic properties of phonation. The lower surface of this cavity is floored by the lower jawbone and the tongue structure. The upper surface comprises the teeth, the maxillary arch, the bony extension of the hard palate and the soft palate.

The oral cavity is the place where typically the tongue is mainly in operation for phonation purposes. The tools assigned for that task are called articulators. Two kinds the are: active and passive.

The active ones move to produce vocalizations, and the most influential of them are the lower lip, the tongue, the uvula, and the lower jaw. Accordingly, the most prominent passive articulators are the upper lip, the teeth, the upper jaw, the maxillary arch (with the upper jaw) and the pharynx. The soft palate at the roof of the mouth is a class of its own, being active and passive the same time, in the sense that it can lower it self, or the tongue can come in touch with it influencing the production of palatal and nasal sounds.

Indeed, the nasal cavity plays its role in the production of phonemes, i.e. the perceptually distinct units of sound. The airflow from the pharynx can be variably directed to the nasal cavity by the fleshy, flexible soft palate, in conjunction with the correspondent vertical move of the pharynx. The soft palate acts as a flap, and having not negligible dimensions (for an adult it is 4cm long, 2 cm wide and 0.5 cm deep) it forms the characteristic resonations for phonemes /m/, /n/, etc.

The nasal cavity, in contradiction to the oral one, has steady geometry. A diaphragm splits the rhinal passage into two nostrils, serving simultaneously as breathing and olfactory organs. More or less it has a standard length slightly more than 10 cm, while it's total volume is some 20-25 cm^3. Its cross section varies up to 2 cm^2 at the end of the rhinal canal, where at the nostrils the resonation function of the nasal cavity radiates the airstream. Being a pathetic resonator means in practice that the phonation coming out of this source is irregular and aperiodic. Indeed, by no means the nasal cavity can compete with the variability of the oral cavity in shaping the prosodic musicality; however, albeit the lack of profound motor command control, nasalization is a fervently wanted and difficulty achieved quality mastered by well trained singers.

The singing mechanism, along with speech communication, uses vowels and consonants set at a tune. Vowels provide the normal basis for syllable structure in both cases. They are produced by the combined action of the articulators that were described thus far, but without any audible constriction or obstruction that would cause turbulence in the airflow through the vocal tract. Along with the consonants they form compounds that bear the linguistic information. Both are necessary for speech intelligence and perception, but it is evident that in the case of singing, and musicality in general, that vowels are the carriers of phonetic energy and melodic contours.

Acoustically, vowels are distinguished by each other by their energy peaks, or formants, that indicate how the phonation energy is distributed through the acoustic spectrum. They are produced at the end of the laryngeal part of the vocal tract, and they utilize the resonant properties of the tube system for phonation. The resonance patterns are rendered acoustically by tongue position and shape along with jaw and lip movement that control the airflow out of the oral cavity nozzles like a scoop.

Consonants on the other hand are basic speech sounds for which the airflow through the tract is at least partly obstructed. Apart from appreciable constriction, their other main characteristic is that they use as primary sound source the region above the larynx. The resultant acoustic signals bear greater complexity, but of course their energy content is significantly reduced in comparison to vowels. Furthermore, in most languages, they do not form autonomous meaningful morphological units, and they are combined in various forms with vowels.

As a result they are parallelized with aperiodic and unmusical sounds, like noise, that are conceived as non contributing elements to the musicality of prosodic forms. However, as "noise-like" music is entering our continuum with cinematic and radio productions, sonically investing extreme thematic designs, scientists commence to realize the contribution of "harsh" sounds to sonic sensory cognition. After all, in practice, nations speaking languages that are lacking musical expression are distinguished for their achievements in music. Furthermore, nasalization, which is eminent in musical languages like French, has started to be examined for its controlled contribution to prosodic enrichment and "colorization" of the singing voice.

Conclusively, for vowel production the larynx provides the sound source and the vocal track shapes its tubular structure by controlled movement that collectively provide the energy and the melodic contours of phonation. For consonants, the various organs of the oral and nasal cavities provide the obstructive matter to the inner tube that control the blockage of airflow.

The phonic components of speech are of various kinds. These are:

- **Musical Tones:** Especially related with the articulation of vowels. However, some times consonants, like the approximants, may contribute to the melodious content of verbal communication or singing.

- **Harmonic Waves:** Produced by vibrating parts of the body. They are week sounds, felt as vibrations of the skull, nose, lips, and parts of the chest. They may however, have rhythmic occurrences (half note, quarter note, eighth note ...) either deliberately provoked or as a result of the natural body functions that accompany phonation, as is for instance breathing. It is an interesting part of ongoing research how human senses respond to ultra bass sounds, heard by loudspeakers, and how they influence awareness in synaesthetic musicality.
- **Noise:** Present when most of the consonants are uttered.

Even the articulation mechanism does not have invariant characteristics per person. From infancy, the absence of teeth plays a role for incomplete capacity to properly articulate phonation. Even further, the size and the stage of development for the articulators starts getting its final status during adolescence, and quickly the voice mechanism, especially for boys, develops to its adult stage. For girls, the mutational voice change occurs in lesser extent.

After mental and somaesthetic maturity, however, both the oral and aural sensors gradually degrade: dental health degrades, and at the end teeth may be missing or replaced, bones (including the jaw) lose their osseous mass and hardness, muscles are progressively losing their ability to contract along with their elasticity, and as we will see in coming chapters, the hearing mechanism fails in its auditory stimulations, especially in the upper frequency spectrum, and unfortunately, not only. Otologic and pathologic disorders affect various bands of the hearing spectrum, along with environmental degradation. To this natural decay, empirically studied for ages, newly sensed disturbances admix, not previously experienced to such an extent: excessive urban noise, pandemonium or wild listening conditions when attending blaring, loud speaker amplified harsh sounds, like heavy-metal, or even, when for reasons of discretion listeners blow-up their ears with the prolonged use of earphones.

Therefore, organic or functional disorders that take place in great extend due to altered living conditions affect neurologically and aesthetically the oral and aural canal coupling, and alter the normal limits of musical perception.

Models of Speech Production

Although researchers have been focusing on this topic for quite a while, and amidst rapid technological advances in computer machinery along with visualizing apparatus that operates on inner core anatomical details, it seems that the phonation mechanism in a truly comprehensive manner has not been yet achieved.

It is true that the circulation of multimedia clips in excess around us has given much incentive for a more global perspective and of course a deeper understanding of intonation contours and linguistic phonation variability. However, the true cerebral activity that causes this substantial variability is just now convolving out of a mechanism of enormous complexity, musical variability and speech intelligibility.

Articulatory Models

These reproduction schemes take into account a midline cross-section of the vocal tract in which the complex range of movements is interpreted as a set of inputs that controls tongue, lips and jaw. As medical imaging gives more detailed representations of the moving parts responsible for phonation, more articulators are taken into account: glottis, teeth, velum, palate, and recently, the nasal cavity.

The progenitors of these approaches are Fant (1960) and Flanagan (1970). Such research group attempt to define all the possible positions of the basic articulators using pairs of orthogonally related coordinates. The tongue position, the tongue tip, the soft palate structure along with the lip aperture and protusion provide a rather vivid explanation of how the bodily mechanism with its moving parts renders phonation. There is an increase in the variety of these models coming up recently. They are developed by studying the behavior of the corresponding parts of the vocal tract, using X-Rays, MRI, Ultrasound imaging and video imaging of the vocal tube. This approach provides means to test the validity of the model, by comparing the articulatory configuration predicted for a given utterance with the one that medical imaging has given for a normal speaker.

Thus, in Figure 6, we can see the sequence of cross-sagittal analyses predicted by a computer model for the utterance of the word "Kyrie" sung in a Dorian mode.

Most articulatory models quantify given articulatory configurations. They take into account vocal tract cross sectional areas taken at equal incremental distances over its length from lips to glottis. The more cross sections taken into account, the more accurate quantitative representation the model gives.

It is commonly known as an area function analysis and the number of these used is typically around 50. The computer program analyses the recorded utterances and proceeds in estimating vocal tract

Acoustic Models

The basic acoustic model for speech production was anatomically depicted earlier, when the phonation mechanism was presented. The vocal tract is perceived thus as a filter which shapes the excitation source seeking to produce a musical sound

Figure 6. Physical modeling of speech production. Reverse modeling from the utterance of /Ki:/ sung in mode A (Dorian), estimated by D. Politis.

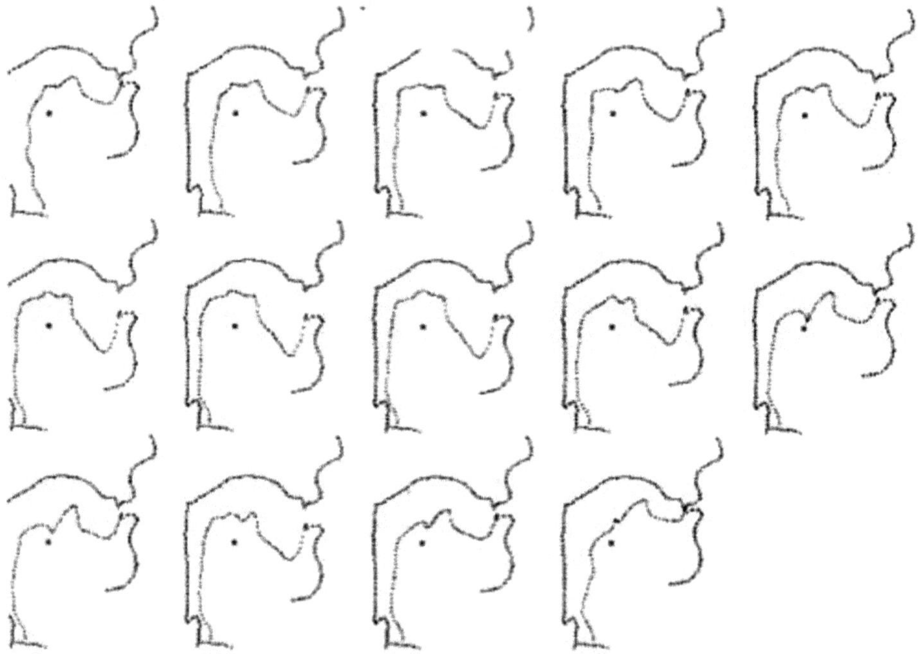

that has the characteristics of the desired phonation. A small set of parameters provides the characteristics of the filter array that shapes the output in such a way, so to have a comparable spectrum match with utterances cropped out of natural speakers (Figure 7).

Figure 7. Source and filters acoustic model

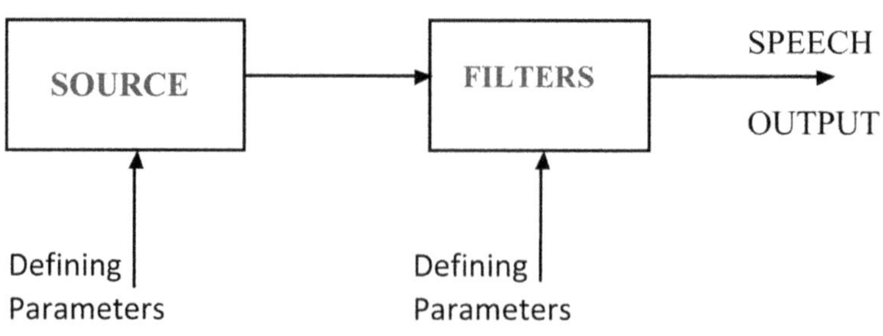

The most economic and commonly accepted solution, in terms of complexity, relays to define the lower frequency formant structure. It is generally agreed, that three or four lower resonances of the musical utterance have to be well described so to give the essential information so to reproduce synthetically the utterance with adequacy.

Usually this model focuses on simulating the phonation mechanism by the spectral properties of the utterance without giving much emphasis on the physical characteristics of the articulation. However, recently, the phonation waveform of the larynx may be taken into account, enhancing the primary sources of phonation, i.e. intensity and fundamental frequency.

As a result, Articulatory to Acoustic Transformation models emerge, that take into account the anatomical parameters of phonation before coping alone with the signal processing attributes of speech and music. The articulatory configuration has inherent connection with the definition of the acoustic properties of the vocal tube. In simulation terms, each part of the tube, depending on the function analysis performed over its area function, can be approached as either a short acoustic resonator or a single section of a lumped constant electrical transmission line. Although a rather laborious process, the frequency response of this array of resonators, filters and transmission lines may be estimated, and the formants of the melodious voice result as a rather expected requisite of the shape and position of the articulators. However, this approach dips well into perplexity, and in linguistic terms has inability to handle the complicated or unaccountable multitude of various languages; therefore, it yields good results for a specific language or a set of phonetically linked human communication patterns.

Process Models

Nomologically, the articulatory and acoustic models lead to a functional modus operandi of the human mechanism for producing speech and singing. Musical sounds with voice engage extended vocal techniques that are associated with a rather complex approach in terms of motor commands, synaesthesia, and even bodily functions. Therefore, process models are involved in an attempt to encode how ideas, and in the case of music melodious singing voices, tune-up by conveying messages to motor commands which make articulators to move and ultimately produce acoustic output from the vocal tract.

Feedback is provided through various pathways. For instance, when the tongue is touching the upper part of the oral cavity, the receptors in the muscles that provoke the movement give information about the degree of contraction. The same time, the auditory system via its aural sensors provides facts about what after all has been produced as an acoustic wave. Of course, the interconnection of the

Figure 8. The process type speech production model basics
According to Raphael, Borden and Harris, 1997

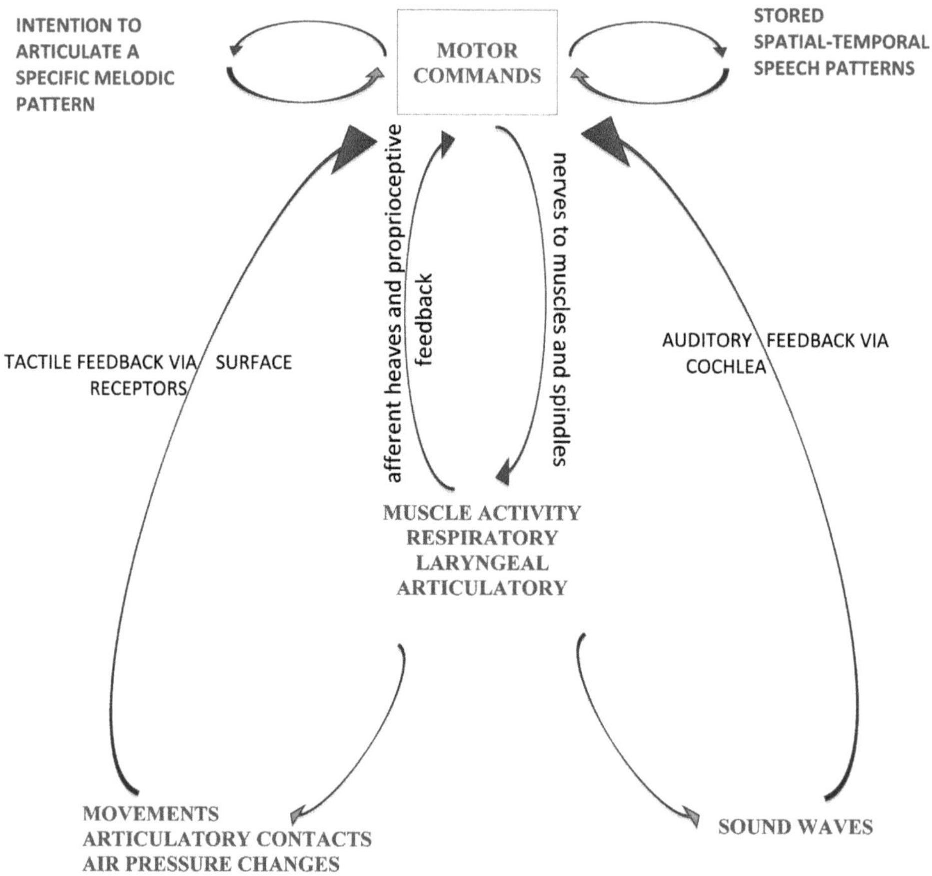

oral and aural canals via tubular ducts, like the Eustachian tube, or the vibrations of the cranial bones give a slightly altered perception of the sounds uttered, but in any case, we hear the sounds we produce ourselves clearly enough to provide feedback to the articulation mechanism (Figure 8).

In any case, the models that try to simulate so complicated and perplexed processes are generally confined within the limits of the vocal tract behavior. The degree of simulation extents to reproducing the articulatory or acoustic domains demonstrating as much fidelity as possible without getting involved in neuroanatomical indiscriminate haphazard that may deregulate obvious principles of organization (Raphael, Borden, & Harris, 2007).

It is vital for scientists to understand the poly-parametric perplexity of how the human body interacts with its own articulatory music production and perception before trying to study how vocal or instrumental sounds combine to produce the beauty of form, harmony, and expression of emotion that is collectively defined as musicality.

AURAL, SPEECH, AND MUSIC PERCEPTION

In the practice of everyday communication a listener receives a multiple of aural signals that trigger the sensory mechanisms for hearing. Although music seems to be the most prominent triggering mechanism in terms of form, harmony and emotional arousing, it is evident that speech communication and singing provide the active coupling mechanism for multilayered message exchange at a constant rate. Indeed it is a truly complicated mechanism, since in a chaotic world with 7,200 spoken languages, apart from mass migration of people, scientists contemplate a rapid convolving phenomenon where long spoken dialects are vanishing, languages are systematically conveyed according to institutional or political bias, and musical patterns that correspond to historical periods of long inhabiting people vigorously fade into oblivion. Cultural hegemony and colonization seems to be affecting the collective musical memory of countries, ethnicities and nations, driving remarkable intellectual achievements to parochialism, marginalization and disdain.

However, this despondent situation sets in motion research on vocal communication, since it seems that the linguistic message is constrained in an ill-fated expedition of the oral-aural communication channel.

Figure 9. Left: Anatomy of the ear. Apart from the aural anatomy, clearly indicated are the balance organs. Right: The curves of equal sensitivity for the hearing spectrum of human perception.

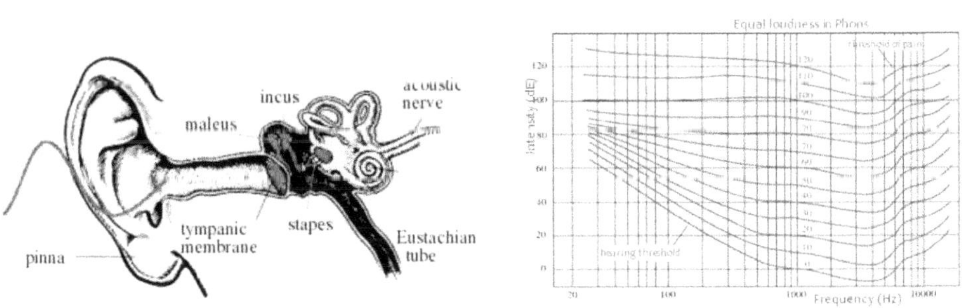

The Auditory System

The ear consists of the external ear, the middle and the inner ear. In the external ear clearly identifiable are the auricle and the external auditory meatus. The cartilaginous framework, to which the skin is tightly applied, separated only by the perichondrium, mainly molds the auricle or pinna. On the other hand, the external auditory meatus has a 3.7 cm long S-shaped course, ending to the tympanic membrane. The outer 1/3 is cartilaginous, while the inner 2/3 are osseous, having the skin closely adherent to the osseous part. The tympanic membrane or eardrum consists of 3 layers, has an oval shape and is normally translucent. Points of interest on the tympanic membrane are the pars tensa, which is the largest part of the membrane, the pars flaccid, which is a small, lax triangular area above the lateral process of the malleus, the umbo, the light reflex, the handle and the lateral process of the malleus. The middle ear or tympanic cavity is a narrow cavity in the petrous part of the temporal bone and contains mainly the auditory ossicles. Anteriorly, the middle ear cavity communicates with the pharynx by the Eustachian tube, a 3.7 cm long bony and cartilaginous tube (Figure 9).

Emphasis is paid on the dimensions of the tubular structure of the ear, the external auditory meatus and the Eustachian tube, since their dimension, and primarily the geometry of the former, heavily influence the frequencies and the sensitivity of hearing. And, surprisingly, many other functions that influence cerebral activities (Updhayay, 2015).

The effect of the outer ear is to increase the intensity of sounds, acting as a tube that increases the oscillation of incoming sounds. Indeed, as seen in Figure 9, right, the frequency range is enhanced by about 10 to 15 dB, for frequencies ranging from 1.5 kHz up to 7 kHz, as a result of the resonant characteristics of the hollow part of the pinna and the auditory canal. The three auditory ossicles of the middle ear, the maleus (“hammer”), incus (“anvil”) and stapes (“stirrup”), further increase the sound level some 20 dB, around 2.5 kHz due to the force transfer characteristics of the ossicular chain.

The combined action of the outer ear, flap-like structure, and the air-filled middle ear cavity, is to increase the amount of amplification for frequencies that are effectively transmitted to the dense fluids of the inner ear. The inner ear is a complex fluid-filled labyrinth that consists of the spiral cochlea (the primary organ for hearing, where vibrations are transmitted as impulses of sensation to the brain) and the three semicircular canals (forming the organ of balance). As a result, the acoustic system in humans, as is the case with most mammals, is coupled with the vestibular system which provides the quality and ability to coordinate movement with balance when sensing spatial orientation and acceleration.

Figure 10. Left: The curving of the spiral cavity within the cochlea, projected in a transverse (axial) plane. It establishes the cochlear frequency tuning curve based upon the threshold and frequency equalization of individual neuron cells. Right: The neurophysiologic arrays and sensory pathways of the inner ear, that contribute to hearing and balance.

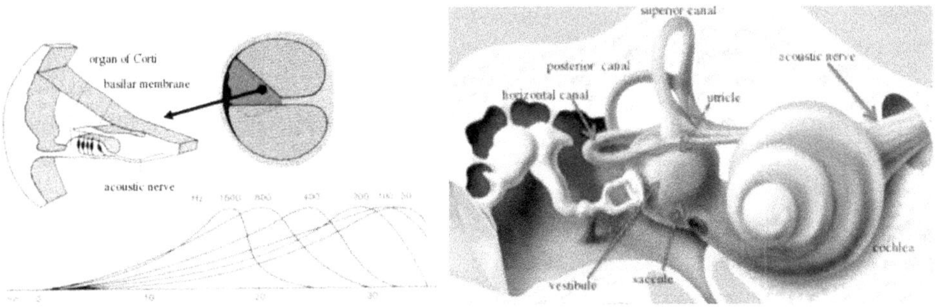

Actually, to start with the acoustic sense, the cochlea is a fluid filled spiral cavity, containing hair cells, and the organ of Corti. Sounds reach the cochlea as vibratory patterns, which provoke mechanical response to both the organ of Corti and the basilar membrane within the cochlea. Each point along the basilar membrane is set to motion, vibrating according to the intensity and the frequency characteristics of the stimulus. The amplitude of the membrane vibration is not uniform; it resembles travelling waves over the fluids of the inner ear, which are directed by the ossicular chain. The hair cells that are positioned at different locations within the cochlea partition respond differentially to frequency and cause encoded auditory information to be transmitted from the synapses of the cochlea with the VIIIth cranial nerve to the auditory cortex of the brain (Figure 10).

Essentially, the eighth pair of cranial nerves, conveys the sensory impulses from the organs of hearing and balance in the inner ear to the brain. This vestibulocochlear nerve on each side branches into the vestibular nerve and the cochlear nerve.

Therefore, indeed the inner ear is an intricate arrangement embedded in the temporal bone, whose diverse organs, like the utricle, saccule, cochlea and three semi-circular canals. While the cochlea, as it has been described, serves as a neurotransmitter for the junction of electromechanical vibrations of fluids, membranes and elastic solids with the synapses of the acoustic nerve, the vestibular structures highly influence the sense of balance for the whole body.

For instance, the utricle, the larger of the two fluid-filled cavities of the labyrinth within the inner ear, contains hair cells and otoliths that send signals to the brain concerning the orientation of the head. With it the brain senses when the human body changes its position horizontally. This happens during physical activity, or abundantly, when people assume a horizontal, retiring position while resting on a supporting surface, like bed. The saccule, the smaller of the two fluid-filled cavities, encloses another region of hair cells and otoliths that send signals interpreting the orientation of the head as vertical acceleration; For example, when listening to highly rhythmic music, with strong bass frequencies that vibrate our body, we may perceive a feeling similar to moving within a fast elevator.

Apart from the labyrinth that functions in a way that regulates body balance, there is also present a fluid in the membranous labyrinth, the endolymph that attributes its movement according to the force of gravity. The vestibular system uses tiny hair cells, as is the case of the auditory system, with the modification that they are triggered somewhat different. It seems that the five vestibular receptor organs (utricle, saccule, and the three semicircular canals) respond not only to linear acceleration and gravity, but also sense with their neurons rotation, along with angular acceleration and deceleration (Boundless, 2016).

It is impressive that this geospatial and stabilization information is also using the auditory nerve in order to become cerebral activity. Therefore, it seems that hearing or sensing music is not irrelevant to the process of moving body parts or bodily feelings like dizziness. To a great extend, music provokes conditioned reflective movement, like dancing, which is dependent on the rhythmic and resonating, especially at low frequencies, nature of music.

Transformations and Perception within the Peripheral Auditory System

Although extensive research has been focused on the middle and inner ear that has revealed a lot about the way that the cochlea is processing sound, there is still significant difficulty around the cerebral activity of music perception. Indeed, the scientific findings about the processes of the cochlea have lead to astounding achievements, like the cochlear implants that transcend some form of "bionic hearing" to people with severe loss of hearing, or even total deafness.

However, when it comes to deciphering individual hair cell action at the synapses of the acoustic nerve, little is known on how the central auditory nervous system interacts with speech or music. The advances on cochlear implantations have provided, however, the first significant psychoacoustic data, giving hope that a backdoor to cerebral auditory transformations has been found.

The available evidence collected thus far indicates that the frequency domain of incoming sounds is processed in the cochlea. Its function is similar to a filter-bank where the filters, i.e. the synapses of hair cells with the bundle of fibers from the

Figure 11. Left: M. Tsalighopoulos examines post surgically a cochlear implant receiver stimulating hearing with the 7th frequency band. On the corners of the video screen have been transferred the videos from the head display, monitoring eye movement and reaction, while the computer measurements are depicted in another corner. The patient communicates by stirring her fingers. Measurements and eye movement monitoring crosscheck patient's subjective assertions. Center: Left eye. Superimposition of the first and last video frame of an ocular movement. Solid arrow: pupil at the first frame, before the start of the movement. Dashed arrow: pupil at the last frame, after the end of the movement. White arrows indicate the downward and counter-clockwise direction of the movement. Right: Superimposition of the first and last video frames of the body's movement. Solid arrow first frame, at the start of the forward movement. Dashed arrow last frame, showing the end-position of the forward movement of the body.

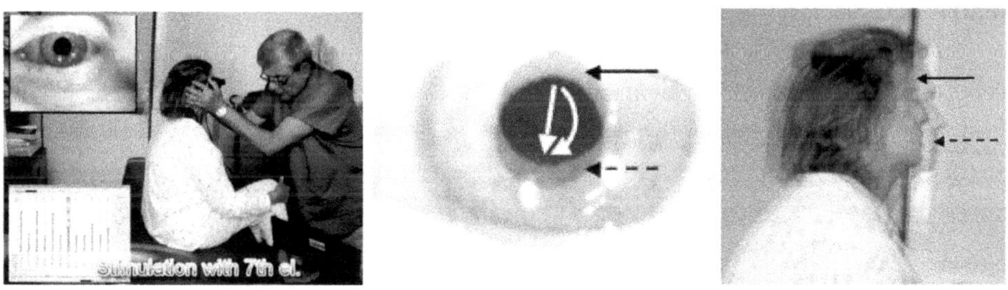

acoustic nerve, provoke impulses that reach the brain. Indeed, electromechanical filters are formed acting on narrow frequency ranges, and this very idea is leading the function of cochlear implantations that are programmed to work with up to 22. The amplitude of the sounds is processed by a log transformation of these filter outputs so to confine the range of the amplitude values while maintaining a quite dynamic range. The processing that occurs within the cochlea also preserves and even further, enhances, the temporal aspects of speech including duration and relationships between sequences.

Neurophysiological studies have investigated the output of the cochlea at the VIIIth nerve (i.e. the auditory nerve) and the cochlea nucleus for speech sounds. These studies provide complementary intelligence about the way that the cochlea functions in addition to data from psychological studies. Together they detail aspects of the frequency, amplitude and temporal processing conveyed by the peripheral auditory system on the speech waveform.

Recently, new tools have been added to the quiver of neurologists. Cochlear implants are electronic devices reconstituting the hearing potential of damaged inner ears. This is done by a delicate microsurgical procedure that stimulates electrically the remaining auditory nerve fibers with codified sound information inserted via a an electrode array implanted into the recipients head.

Cochlear Implants can be applied in adults and children with bilateral, severe to profound sensorineural hearing loss, who have not benefited by the use of powerful hearing aids and have not improved their oral communication skills by specific speech therapy. This is because early stimulation of the acoustic Central Nervous System, especially in preschool ages, leads to improved acoustic memory and sound discrimination.

The training processes that follow-up cochlear implantations reveal a lot about the way that cerebral activity encompasses musicality. They even reveal how close is sonic perception to kinetic activities and balance (Figure 11).

CONCLUSION

Why we "rock" when we hear music? What causes our bodies to move gently from side to side, apart from exciting "sensor emotional" reactions to the beauty of form and melodic expression in music perception? How the auditory stimuli relate to the musical revolutions of the last century, culminating in multimodal, kinetic and predominantly sparkling bodily sensations? How speech signal variability is related with musicality and sonorous perception? Which stimuli evoke functional reaction in organic matter and provoke motor commands? Does selective adaptation, so idiomatic to speaking some of the 7,200 active languages bias musicality? How balance, acceleration and position intermingle with the perceived complexity and accomplishment for music?

This introductory chapter presents the functional characteristics of the phonation mechanism intermingled with the psychological assumptions that after all provide information coding and musical intelligibility. This human-centered approach will be very useful for understanding in the chapters that follow how modern musical expression is mastered and how its audiovisual indicators lead to tactile devices and research.

REFERENCES

Anderson, S. (2012). *Languages - a Very Short Introduction*. Oxford University Press. doi:10.1093/actrade/9780199590599.001.0001

Barbour, J. M. (1972). *Tuning and Temperament: a Historical Survey*. New York: Da Capo Press.

Barsky, V. (1996). *Chromaticism*. Harwood Academic Press.

Boundless. (2016). The Vestibular System. *Boundless Biology*. Retrieved from https://www.boundless.com/biology/textbooks/boundless-biology-textbook/sensory-systems-36/hearing-and-vestibular-sensation-208/the-vestibular-system-786-12022/

Colton, R. H., & Estill, J. A. (1981). Elements of voice quality: Perceptual acoustic, and physiologic aspects. In J. Lass (Ed.), *Speech and Language: Advances in Basic Research and Practice* (Vol. 5, pp. 311–403). Academic Press. doi:10.1016/B978-0-12-608605-8.50012-X

Cox, C., & Warner, D. (2007). *Audio Cultures. In Readings in Modern Music*. Continuum.

D' Angour, A. (2013). *Oxford classicist brings ancient Greek music back to life*. Academic Press.

Devine, A. M., & Stephens, L. D. (1994). *The Prosody of Greek Speech*. New York: Academic Press.

Fant, G. (1960). *Acoustic theory of speech production*. The Hague, The Netherlands: Mouton.

Flanagan, J., Coker, C., Rabiner, L., Schafer, R., & Umeda, N. (1970). Synthetic voices for Computers. *IEEE Spectrum*, *7*(10), 22–45. doi:10.1109/MSPEC.1970.5212992

Gianelos, G. (1996). La musique Byzantine. L'Harmatan.

Gombosi, O. J. (1944). New Light on Ancient Greek Music. *International Congress of Musicology*. New York: Academic Press.

Halaris, C. (1999). *Music of Ancient Greece.* booklet and CD.

Hardcastle, W. J., Laver, J., & Gibbon, F. (2010). *The handbook of phonetic sciences.* John Wiley & Sons. doi:10.1002/9781444317251

Harmonia Mundi. (1999). Musique de la Grece Antique. Booklet and CD, HMA 1951015, France.

Harris, R. (1993). *The linguistics wars.* Oxford University Press.

Langscape - Maryland Language Center. (n.d.). University of Maryland.

Laver, J. (1994). *Principles of phonetics.* Cambridge University Press. doi:10.1017/CBO9781139166621

Pöhlmann, E., & West, M. L. (2001). *Documents of Ancient Greek Music.* Oxford, UK: Academic Press.

Politis, D., Margounakis, D., Tsalighopoulos, G., & Kyriafinis, G. (2015). Transgender Musicality, Crossover Tonality, and Reverse Chromaticism: The Ontological Substrate for Navigating the Ocean of Global Music. *International Research Journal of Engineering and Technology, 2*(5).

Politis, D., Tsalighopoulos, M., Kyriafinis, G., & Palaskas, A. (2014). Mobile Computers, Mobile Devices, Mobile Interfaces: … Mobile Ethics?. In *Proceedings of the6th International Conference on Information Law and Ethics ICIL'14.* University of Macedonia.

Raphael, L., Borden, G., & Harris, K. (2007). *Speech Science Primer - Physiology, Acoustics and Perception of Speech.* Williams & Wilkins.

Sundberg, J. (1987). *The Science of the Singing Voice.* Northern Illinois University Press.

Updhayay, N. (2015). *Do You Have A Body Balancing Problem?* Your Ears Can Make You Look Drunk.

West, M. L. (1992). *Ancient Greek Music.* Oxford, UK: Academic Press.

Williamson, V. (2014). *You Are the Music: How Music Reveals What it Means to be Human.* Icon Books Ltd.

KEY TERMS AND DEFINITIONS

Cochlear Implant: A cochlear implant is an electronic device that replaces the auditory system, mainly the sensory capillary cells in the organ of Corti in the cochlea. A modern cochlear implant is composed of two parts: one is the cochlear implant that is surgically implanted in the recipient and the second is the speech processor that is commonly worn behind the ear and communicates with the implant via an RF transmitter. In order to successfully stimulate the auditory nerve so that the recipient can perceive sound, sound waves must be transformed to electric pulses. This process begins at the speech processor where the sound wave is collected through a microphone. Afterwards sound waves are converted into an electric sound signal that is filtered, encoded and transformed through a very specific procedure. This signal is channeled through the speech processors transmitter to the implants receiver via an RF link.

Neurons: Most often simply referred as nerve cells, responsible for transmitting nerve impulses. They are the basic information processing structures in the human nerve system. Sensory neurons transmit electrochemical messages from the sensory receptor cells to the brain. Motor neurons transfer information to the muscles. Interneurons undertake the communication between nervous cells in a unique way.

Synaesthesia: Literally, it refers to a "union of the senses". It is a neurological oddity, in which a sensation of one of the senses triggers involuntarily and automatically a parallel sensory or cognitive pathway. It is a focal point of recent research in acoustics, relating chromatic reconstruction with musical impression.

Vestibular System: A system relating to a vestibule, in otorhinolaryngology that of the inner ear, which is linked to the sense of balance. Its stimuli are associated with linear acceleration (gravity) and angular acceleration/deceleration. Gravity, acceleration, and deceleration are detected by evaluating the inertia on receptive cells in the vestibular system. Gravity is detected through head position, while angular acceleration and deceleration are expressed through turning or tilting of the head. In neurological terms the vestibular system is linked with the acoustic system.

ENDNOTES

1 The Muses are generally listed as Calliope (epic poetry), Clio (history), Euterpe (flute playing and lyric poetry), Terpsichore (choral dancing and song), Erato (lyre playing and lyric poetry), Melpomene (tragedy), Thalia (comedy and light verse), Polymnia (hymns, and later mime), and Urania (astronomy).

2 A pressure of 1 cm H_2O has the similar effect with 100 Pascal, that is 1/1,000 of normal atmospheric pressure.

Chapter 2
Diagnosis and Evaluation of Hearing Loss

Marios Stavrakas
Aristotle University of Thessaloniki, Greece

Georgios Kyriafinis
Aristotle University of Thessaloniki, Greece

Miltiadis Tsalighopoulos
Aristotle University of Thessaloniki, Greece

ABSTRACT

Hearing disorders are quite common in our days, not only due to congenital causes, environmental factors abut also due to the increased rate of diagnosis. Hearing loss is one of the commonest reasons to visit an ENT Department both in the clinic and in the acute setting. Approximately 15% of American adults (37.5 million) aged 18 and over report some trouble hearing. One in eight people in the United States (13 percent, or 30 million) aged 12 years or older has hearing loss in both ears, based on standard hearing examinations. About 2 percent of adults aged 45 to 54 have disabling hearing loss. The rate increases to 8.5 percent for adults aged 55 to 64. Nearly 25 percent of those aged 65 to 74 and 50 percent of those who are 75 and older have disabling hearing loss. These figures depict the impact on patients' quality of life and the necessity for early and accurate diagnosis and treatment. It is important to mention that congenital hearing loss and deafness is also a condition that requires early diagnosis and hearing aiding in order to develop normal speech. Profound, early-onset deafness is present in 4–11 per 10,000 children, and is attributable to genetic causes in at least 50% of cases.

DOI: 10.4018/978-1-5225-0264-7.ch002

ANATOMY OF THE EAR

The ear consists of the external ear, the middle and the inner ear (Figure 1). The external ear comprises the auricle and the external auditory meatus. The auricle or pinna is mainly formed by the cartilaginous framework to which the skin is tightly applied, separated only by the perichondrium. The external auditory meatus has a 3.7 cm long S-shaped course, extending to the tympanic membrane. The outer 1/3 is cartilaginous while the inner 2/3 are osseous, having the skin closely adherent to the osseous part. The tympanic membrane or ear drum consists of 3 layers, has an oval shape and is normally translucent. Points of interest on the tympanic membrane are the pars tensa, which is the largest part of the membrane, the pars flaccid, which is a small, lax triangular area above the lateral process of the malleus, the umbo, the light reflex, the handle and the lateral process of the malleus. The middle ear or tympanic cavity is a narrow cavity in the petrous part of the temporal bone and contains mainly the auditory ossicles. Anteriorly, the middle ear cavity communicates with the pharynx by the Eustachian tube, a 3.7 cm long bony and cartilaginous tube. Posteriorly it communicates with the mastoid antrum and the mastoid air cells. Conduction of sound through the middle ear is by way of the malleus, incus and stapes. The malleus is the largest of the auditory ossicles. It has a handle which is visible in otoscopy attached to the tympanic membrane, a head which articulates with the incus and a lateral process. The incus has a head, a short and a long process, which articulates with the stapes, the latter having a head a neck and a base which is fixed in the oval window. Two muscles are associated with the ossicular chain and are useful in damping high frequency vibrations. These muscles are the stapedius, attached to the neck of the stapes and the tensor tympani, inserted into the handle of the malleus (Kullar et al., 2012).

The internal ear consists of the bony labyrinth made up of a central vestibule, which communicates posteriorly with three semicircular ducts and anteriorly with the spiral cochlea (Figure 2). The cavity encloses the membranous labyrinth, comprising the utricle and the saccule which communicate with the semicircular canals and the cochlear canal. In each part of the membranous labyrinth there are specialized sensory receptor areas (maculae of utricle and saccule, ampullary crests of the semicircular canals, organ of Corti in the cochlea). The organ of Corti contains the auditory receptor cells. These are the outer and inner hair cells and they are surrounded by other structural and supporting cells (Roland et al., 2000; Kyriafinis, 2005).

Figure 1. Anatomy of the ear: The ear consists of the external ear, the middle and the inner ear. The main elements of each part are pointed with arrows.

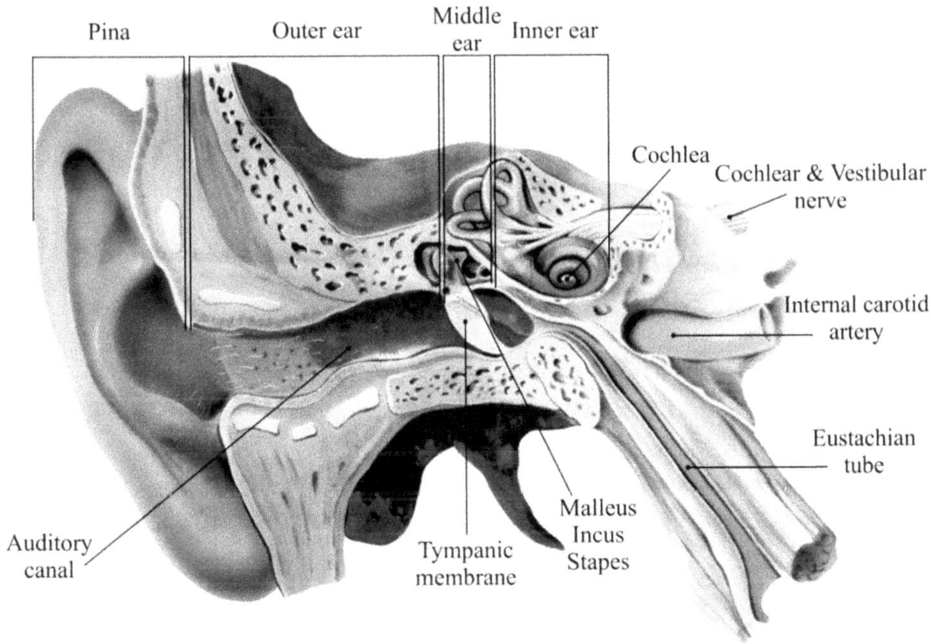

Figure 2. Cross section of the cochlear duct. Scala tympani and scala vestibule are depicted as long as their relationship with the organ of Corti.

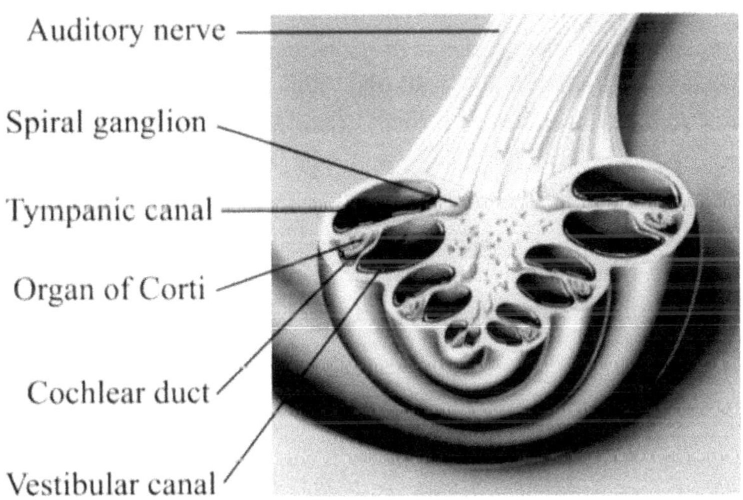

Auditory Pathway

As seen in Figure 3, the auditory pathway consists of:

1. Eighth nerve
2. Cochlear nucleus
3. Superior olivary nucleus
4. Lateral limnescus
5. Inferior colliculus
6. Medial geniculate body
7. Superior temporal gyrus

In the paragraphs that follow, it will be examined how acoustic signals evoke memorable responses, especially for musical instrument sounds, and some insight will be given on how the human hearing intermingles with the (musical) brain. Emphasis will be given on how hearing loss or other neuro-otological damages affect music perception and cognition.

FUNCTION OF THE EAR AND SOUND TRANSMISSION

The auricle collects sound waves and directs them to the tympanic membrane through the external auditory meatus. Its shape helps to localize sound direction and amplification. The middle ear transduces sound waves, amplifies them through the ossicular chain system and passes them to the cochlea. There is also a protective mechanism from loud noise, consists of the stapedius and tensor tympani muscles and is activated by loud sounds (>80 dB). The cochlea, part of the inner ear, is the organ of sound transduction. It turns sound waves into electrical signals that pass to the brain. The cochlea has a tonotopic representation, which means that different areas are frequency specific. High frequencies are dealt with at the start or at the base of the cochlea. Low tones are dealt with at the cochlea apex. The electrical signals from the cochlea are then transmitted to the auditory cortex via the auditory pathway (Kyriafinis, 2005). Figure 4 summarizes the basic concepts of sound transmission.

Types of Hearing Loss

Hearing loss can be divided into two main categories, depending on the affected parts of sound transmission (Lalwani, 2008; Lin et al., 2011):

Figure 3. Auditory pathway: Transmission of the stimulus from the inner ear (receptor organ) to the acoustic area of the cortex
(Source: EmCAP, 2008)

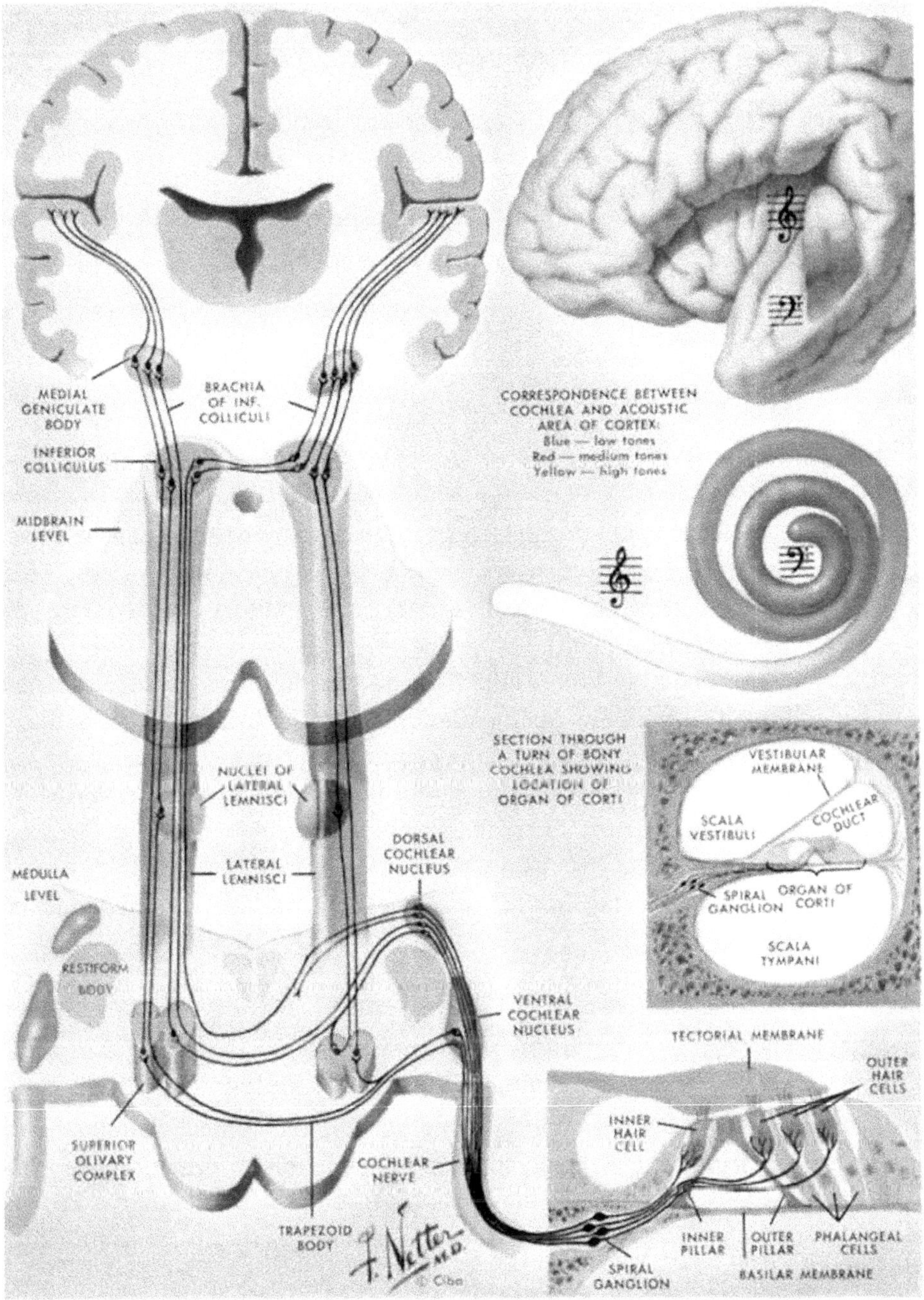

Figure 4. Sound transmission

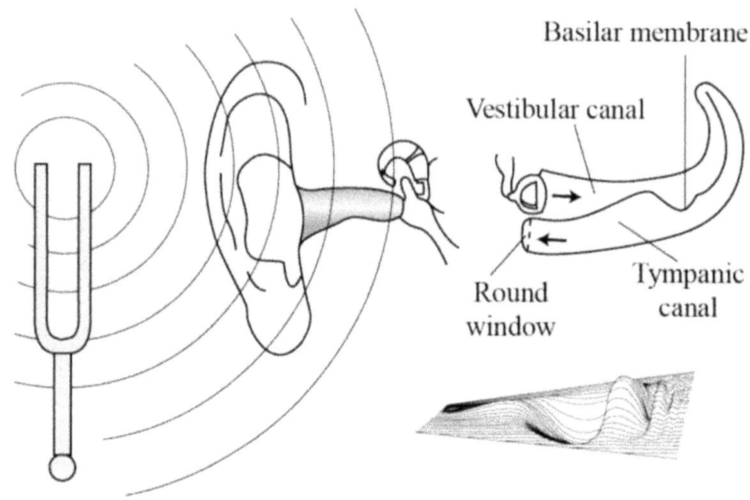

1. Conductive hearing loss results from any disruption in the passage of sound from the external ear to the oval window. It can be caused by pathologies involving the external and middle ear (external auditory meatus, tympanic membrane, ossicular chain).
2. Sensorineural hearing loss results from disruption of the passage of sound beyond the oval window. Such pathologies can be located to the auditory receptor cells of the cochlea and the eighth cranial nerve.
3. Mixed hearing loss represents a mixture of both conductive and sensorineural hearing loss.

In a nutshell, the hearing loss causes that influence active perception are sumarized in Table 1.

CLINICAL EXAMINATION OF HEARING

Good history taking is very important when starting the clinical examination of the ears and hearing. The ENT doctor can gain valuable information about the type of hearing loss, the duration, the causative mechanisms and other associated medical conditions. It is always the first step to a targeted clinical examination and successful diagnosis.

Table 1. Causes of hearing loss

Conductive Hearing Loss	Sensorineural Hearing Loss
Wax impaction/foreign body	Presbyacousis
Inflammatory swelling	Infections
Tympanic membrane perforation	Noise injury
Immobile ossicles	8th CN/cerebellopontine angle tumours
Stapes fixation by otosclerosis	Syndromes
Syndromes	Perilymph fistula
Otitis media	Ototoxic medication
Eustachian tube dysfunction	Sudden onset hearing loss
Trauma	Trauma

Ear and hearing examination is an integral part of a complete head and neck examination (Kullar et al,. 2012) . We can start with inspection of the external ear, paying attention for deformities, scars from previous surgery, infections or skin problems (Warner et al., 2009). Otoscopy with a portable otoscope or a microscope will allow the examination of the external auditory meatus and tympanic membrane. Areas to comment on are the external auditory meatus (infections, discharge, wax impaction), the pars tensa of the tympanic membrane (perforations, retraction pockets, ossicles, presence of ventilation tubes) and the pars flaccid of the tympanic membrane (attic retraction pockets, cholesteatoma). Pneumatic otoscopy or the Valsalva manoeuvre can help the examiner assess the tympanic membrane mobility. One can perform the fistula test when indicated. This can be achieved by applying tragal pressure and watching the eyes for nystagmus with a fast phase away from the diseased side. Free field testing can give a rough estimation of hearing, especially in a setting where audiological examination is not available. The non test ear is masked with tragal pressure and the patient's eyes are shielded to prevent any visual stimulus. The examiner then whispers three two-syllable words or bi-digit numbers from 60cm from the test ear. If the patient gets two out of these three correct then the hearing level is 12 dB or better. If there is no accurate response, use a conversational voice (48 dB or worse) or a loud voice (76 dB or worse). Then the examiner can move closer and repeat the test at 15 cm. Here the thresholds are 34dB for a whisper and 56dB for a conversational voice. Tuning fork tests can give valuable information about a possible hearing loss and its characteristics (Warner et al., 2009). The most frequently performed tests in a routine examination are Weber and Rinne tests (Figures 5 and 6). A 512Hz tuning fork is used, as it gives the best balance between time of decay and tactile vibra-

Figure 5. Weber test. A 512 Hz tuning fork is preferred. The examiner places the vibrating tuning fork in the midline forehead or the vertex. The patient is asked whether they hear it loudest in the right, the left or the midline.

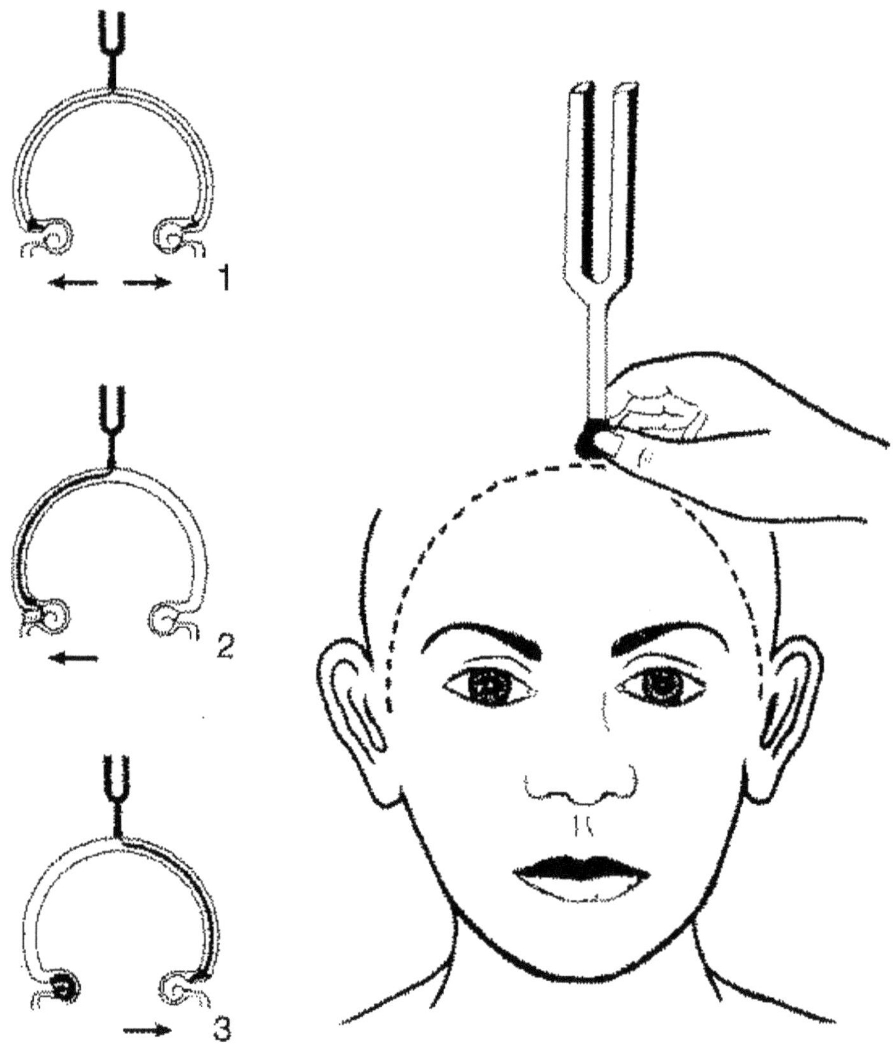

tion. In order to perform Weber's test, the examiner places the vibrating tuning fork in the midline forehead or the vertex. The patient is asked whether they hear it loudest in the right, the left or the midline. Rinne's test is performed by placing the vibrating tuning fork on the patient's mastoid process until they stop hearing it. Immediately the tuning fork is placed in front of the ear and the patient is asked

Figure 6. Rinne test. A 512 Hz tuning fork is preferred. Rinne test is performed by placing the vibrating tuning fork on the patient's mastoid process until they stop hearing it. Immediately the tuning fork is placed in front of the ear and the patient is asked whether they hear it loudest in front or behind the ear.

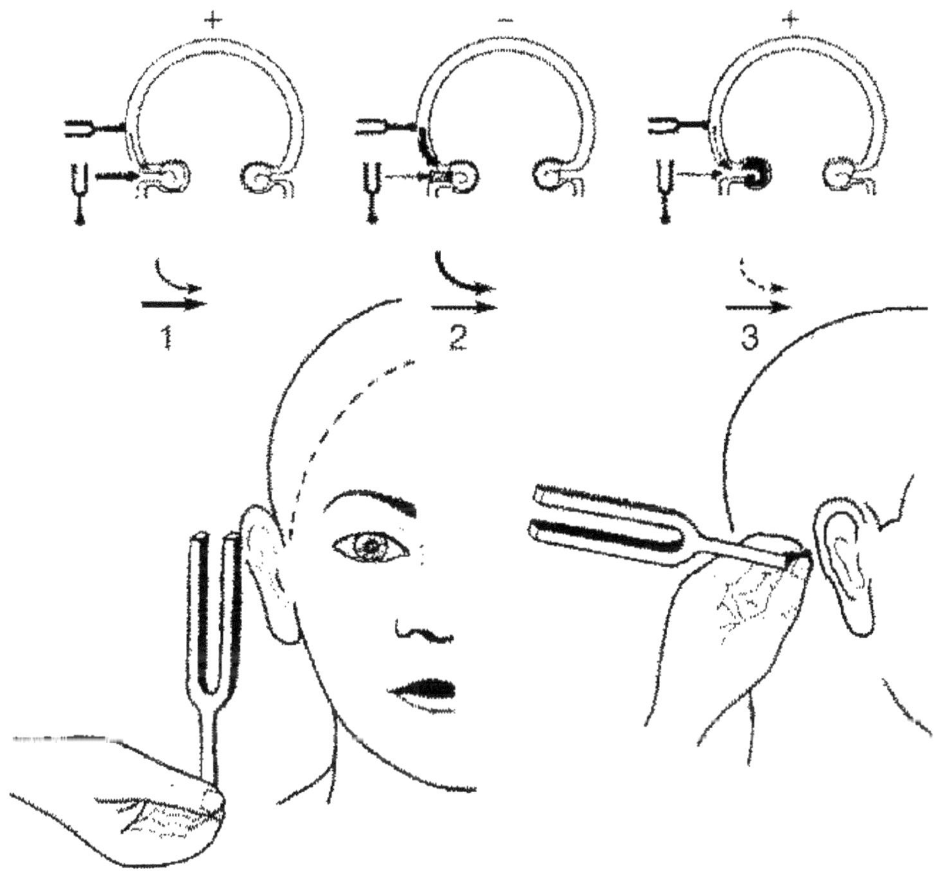

Table 2. ENT examination results

	Weber lateralises left	Weber lateralises right
Rinne positive both ears AC>BC	SNHL in right	SNHL in left
Rinne negative left BC>AC	CHL in left	SNHL in left
Rinne negative right BC>AC	SNHL in right	CHL in right

whether they hear it loudest in front or behind the ear. The possible results and their interpretation are summarized in Table 2 where:

SNHL=Sensorineural hearing loss,
CHL=Conductive hearing loss,
AC=air conduction, and
BC=bone conduction.

After completing the above mentioned tests, one can examine the cranial nerves, paying attention to the facial nerve, and the postnasal space for the sake of completion.

PURE TONE AUDIOMETRY

Pure tone audiometry is a subjective test that aims to establish hearing thresholds (Blackwell et al., 2014). This means that the quietest sounds the patient can perceive form a graphic representation of the patient's hearing ability which is then compared to an established "normal" value.

Sounds are measured in decibels in an audiogram, with the decibel hearing level scale (HL) being the most frequently used. A decibel is a logarithmic unit, and the decibel scale was created with the 0 dB designated for each frequency representing the median value of the minimal audible pure tone in a group of healthy individuals. In other words, although normal hearing thresholds are different in various frequencies, a reference of 0dB HL conventionally represents normal hearing across the entire frequency spectrum. Some basic thresholds are the following:

- Threshold of hearing 0 dB
- Whisper from 1m distance 30 dB
- Normal conversation 60 dB
- A shout 90 dB
- Discomfort 120 dB

A different scale represents the exact amount of energy at each frequency. This is the decibel sound pressure level (dB SPL) scale and is a physical scale. It is not widely used as it produces a U-shaped audiogram, making abnormalities difficult to identify.

Table 3. Hearing loss audiometry

<20dB HL	Normal hearing
20-40dB HL	Mild hearing loss
40-60dB HL	Moderate hearing loss
60-80dB HL	Severe hearing loss
>80dB HL	Profound hearing loss

The other axis of the audiogram has the frequency values. The human ear detects sounds between 20 and 20,000 Hz. The speech frequency spectrum is 400-5000 Hz and the audiometric test typically assesses frequencies between 20 and 8000 Hz.

Pure tone audiometry is performed in an audiometric test room, where the subject's face should be clearly visible to the tester. When the test is observed from outside the audiometric test room the subject should be monitored through a window or a TV monitor. Excessive ambient noise can affect test results, thus it is recommended not to perform the test if the ambient noise is >35 dB. Both ears are tested for air conduction firstly at 1000 Hz and then at 2000 Hz, 4000 Hz, 8000 Hz, 250 Hz and 500 Hz. In case there is a 40 dB difference between the left and right ear, masking with background noise in the non-tested ear is required (Rule 1 of masking). After testing the air conduction thresholds, the examiner proceeds in the same way to test bone conduction, applying a bone vibrator over the mastoid process of the patient. Rule 2 of masking suggests that masking is needed if the not masked bone conduction threshold is more acute than the air conduction level of either ear by 10dB or more. Rule 3 of masking needs to be applied where rule 1 has not been applied but where the bone conduction threshold of one ear is more acute by 40 dB or more than the not masked air conduction threshold attributed to the other ear. Masking is a method to overcome the cross-hearing, which is observed when the difference in the thresholds of the two ears is greater than the transcranial transmission loss.

The interpretation of the audiogram provides information not only for the quality of any potential hearing loss (conductive, sensorineural or mixed) but for the level of hearing loss as well (Lin et al., 2011). Generally, normal hearing is considered to be >20 dB (Marazita et al., 1993). Hearing thresholds and degrees of hearing loss are summarized below, in Table 3.

Conductive hearing loss has the characteristic air-bone gap in the audiogram while different ontological pathologies have specific audiogram patterns which help differential diagnosis. (Figures 7, 8, 9, 10)

Figure 7. Normal hearing

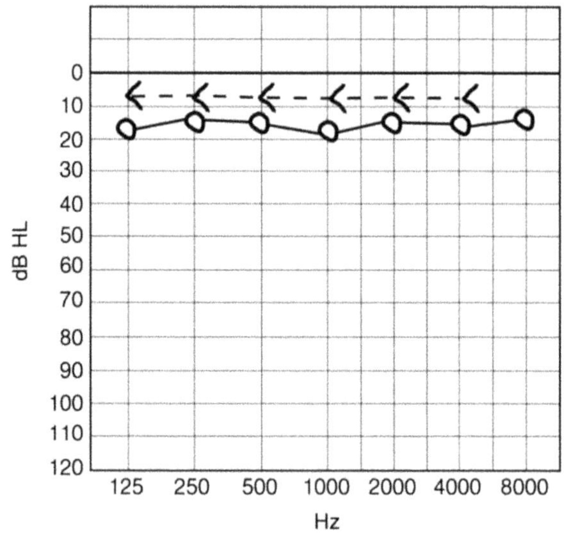

Figure 8. Conductive hearing loss. There is an obvious air-bone gap in the pure tone audiogram.

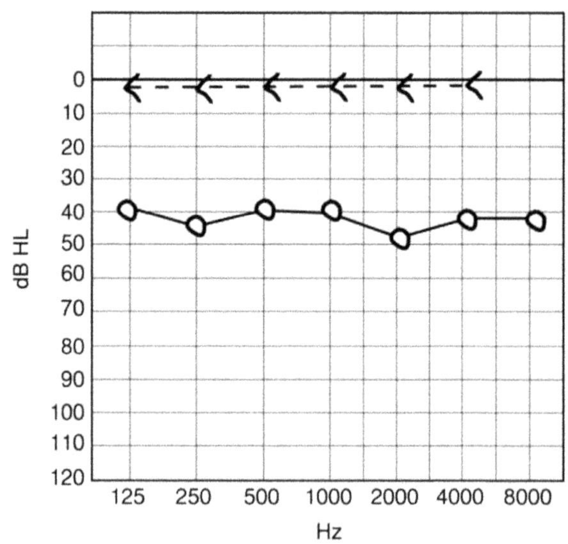

Figure 9. Sensorineural hearing loss

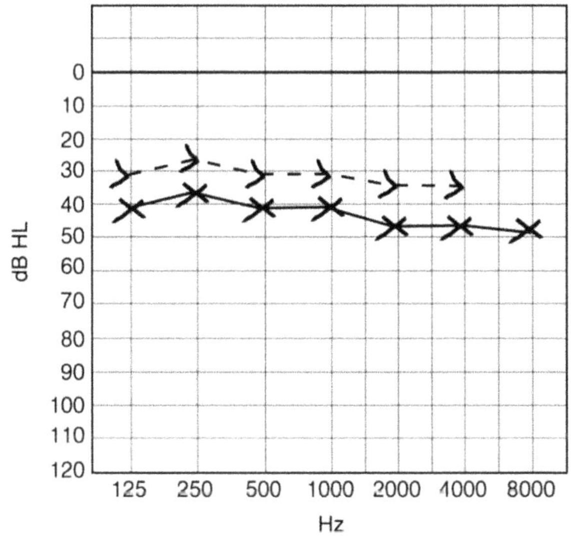

Figure 10. Mixed hearing loss

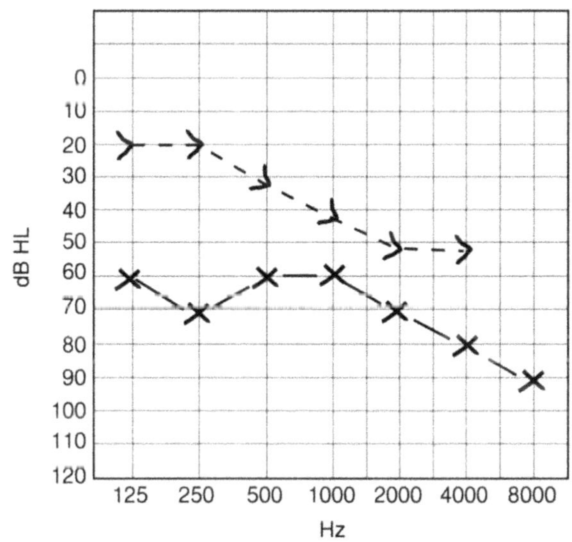

Figure 11. Speech audiogram patterns. Retrocochlear lesions can be identified by the "roll-over" phenomenon.

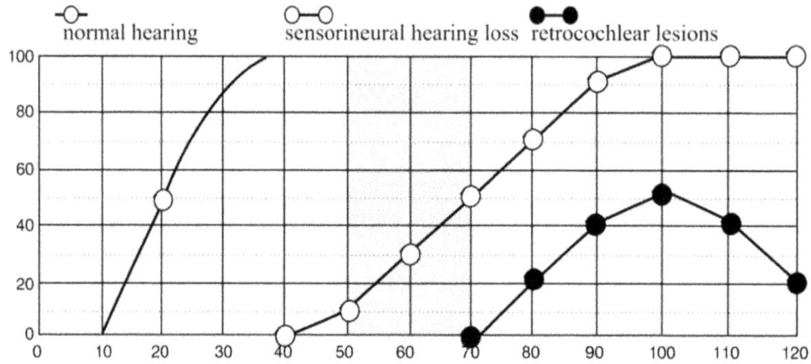

SPEECH AUDIOMETRY

Speech audiometry is a method that offers a more realistic representation of an individual's hearing as it involves single-syllable words rather than pure tones. The patient repeats each word and the score is determined according to the percentage of the words that are correctly identified. In other words, speech audiometry is a method to assess auditory discrimination (Lalwani, 2008).

It is delivered to only one ear through headphones or free-field to both ears. The optimum discrimination score (ODS) is the highest score achieved (maximum is 100%). The speech-reception threshold (SRT) is the sound level at which the individual obtains 50% of the score. The half peak level (HPL) is the sound level at which the individual obtains his/her ODS. Half peak level elevation (HPLE) is the difference between the HPL of the tested individual and normal individuals.

Normally a sigmoid curve is obtained. In conductive hearing loss the curve is displaced towards the right and in sensorineural hearing loss, speech discrimination deteriorates with increased sound levels ("roll-over" phenomenon - Figure 11).

TYMPANOMETRY

Tympanometry is part of acoustic impedance testing along with acoustic reflexes. It is an objective test that measures the mobility (compliance) of the tympanic membrane and the middle ear system. The sound transmission from the external ear to the middle ear is optimal when the pressure in the ear canal is the same

Figure 12. Various types of tympanograms. Type A is divided into A_s and A_d. Type B represents a flat tympanogram and type C shows a peak in the negative pressure range. It is further divided into C1, C2 and C3.

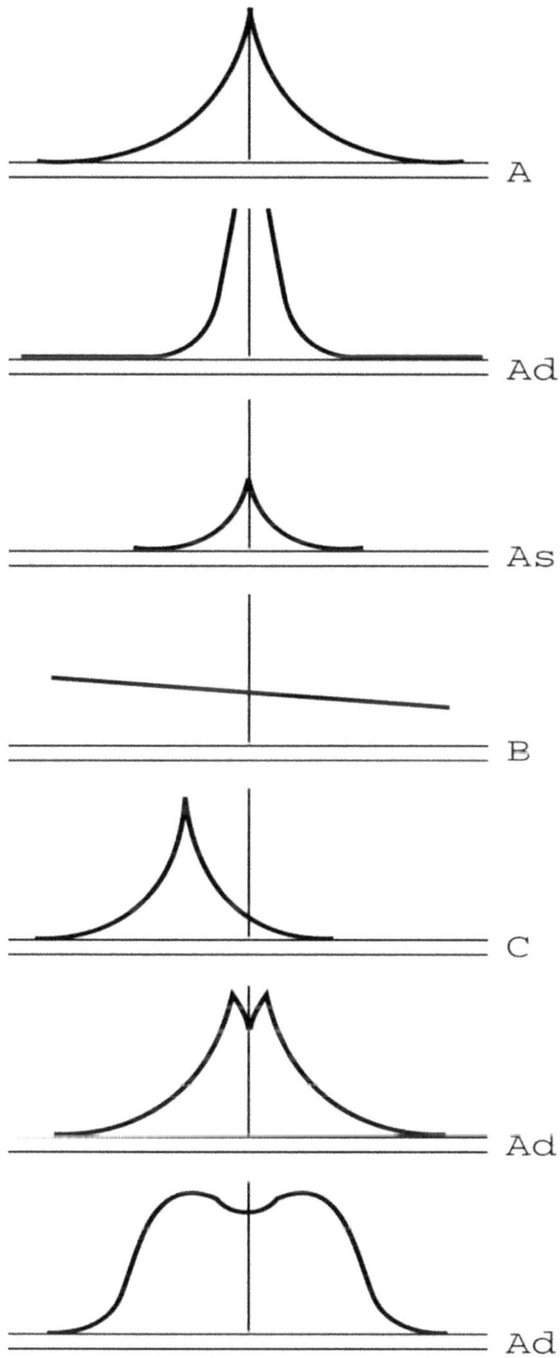

as the middle ear. The compliance of the tympanic membrane is measured as a function of mechanically varied air pressure in the external auditory meatus and so the middle ear pressure is indirectly measured (Roland et al., 2000).

The test is performed by putting a probe to the external auditory meatus, achieving air-tight seal. Air pressure is manipulated into the space bound by the probe, the external auditory meatus and the tympanic membrane. The air pressure is gradually raised to +200 mm HgH_20 and then reduced to -200 mm HgH_20. The compliance is measured by measuring the amount of sound energy reflected. The maximum compliance is achieved when there is no difference of pressure across the tympanic membrane. In addition, the ear canal volume is measured. An increase in this value represents either a tympanic membrane perforation or a very large pars tensa retraction.

There are several types of tympanograms, each one associated with one or a group of pathologic characteristics:

Type A: Normal
Type A_s: Tympanic membrane is stiffer than normal (lower compliance) → otosclerosis
Type A_d: Tympanic membrane is more flaccid than normal (higher compliance) → ossicular discontinuity
Type B: Immobility of tympanic membrane as in middle ear effusion or perforation ("flat" tympanogram)
Type C: Tympanic membrane shows a peak in the negative pressure range → Eustachian tube dysfunction. Further divided into C_1, C_2, C_3, according to the pressure range of the peak. (Figure 12)

ACOUSTIC REFLEXES

The acoustic reflex has an ipsilateral and a contralateral pathway, with the majority of neurons running through the ipsilateral pathway (Blackwell et al., 2014):

- **Ipsilateral:** Cochlea → 8th cranial nerve → cochlear nucleus → trapezoid body → superior olivary complex → facial motor nucleus → ipsilateral stapedial muscle
- **Contralateral:** Crosses the brain at the superior olivary complex → opposite cochlear nucleus → trapezoid body → contralateral olivary complex → facial motor nucleus → contralateral stapedial muscle

Figure 13. Acoustic reflexes. Tests 2 and 3 show that the acoustic reflexes are present.

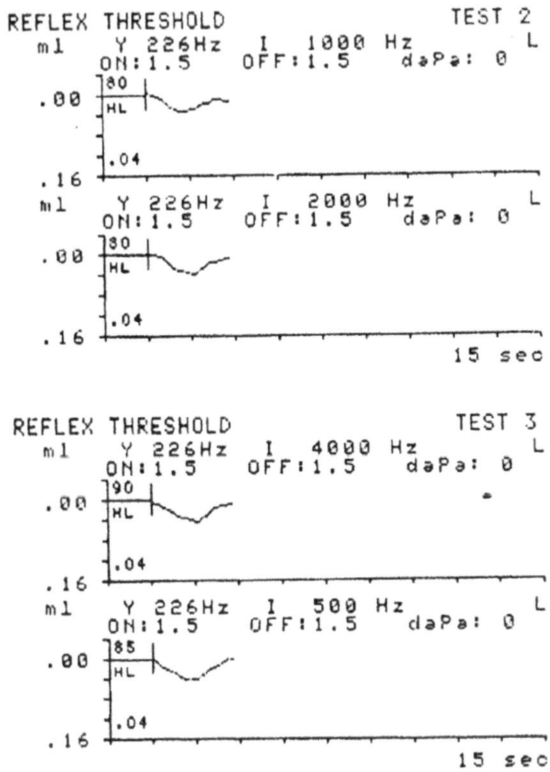

The equipment used is the same as in tympanometry. Pure tones are produced in order to stimulate stapedial reflexes. This is achieved with pure tones about 70-100dB above the hearing threshold.

Stapedial reflex assessment provides valuable information in case of facial paralysis, otosclerosis and also helps differentiate retrocochlear lesions. Figure 13 depicts a normal acoustic reflex test.

OTOACOUSTIC EMISSIONS

Otoacoustic emissions are sounds produced by the outer hair cells in the cochlea. They are low level sounds (about 30 dB SPL loud) that are produced following acoustic stimulation and provide an assessment of the function of the cochlea.

The acoustic stimulus varies from click stimuli to tones and the nature of the stimulus determines which part of the cochlea is stimulated. Each individual has his/her own characteristic repeatable otoacoustic emissions. Reproducibility is used to verify the response.

Several categories of otoacoustic emissions are used, mainly divided into two main groups: Spontaneous and evoked. Evoked otoacoustic emissions are further divided in transient evoked, stimulus frequency and distortion product otoacoustic emissions.

Their clinical applications vary. They are useful in neonatal screening, sudden hearing loss, loud noise, ototoxicity, acoustic neuroma re- and postoperatively, suspected non-organic hearing loss and research.

Figure 14. The resulting electrical response in the auditory nerve and brainstem is recording in vertex positive waves. The waveform peaks are labeled I-VII. These waveforms normally occur within a 10-millisecond time period after a click stimulus presented at high intensities.

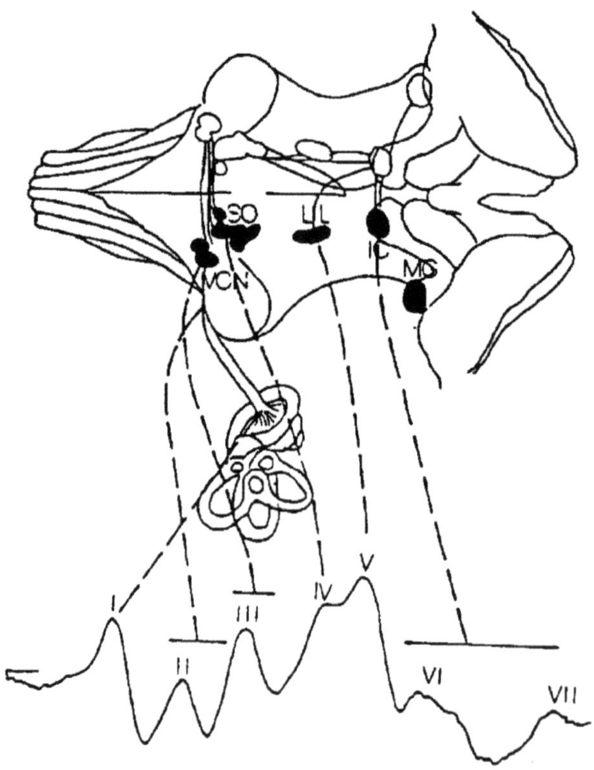

Their role is still important in neonatal screening. A pathological response demonstrates cochlear dysfunction and will require further testing of the auditory pathway (Lalwani, 2008).

AUDITORY BRAINSTEM RESPONSE

This test examines the electrical response in the auditory nerve and brainstem. Clicks are used and eventually the hearing thresholds can be determined in groups such as young children or in adults who are not able to give accurate behavioral results.

The examiner puts electrodes on the scalp (active electrode, reference electrode, ground electrode) and masking is applied. A series of clicks are delivered to the patient and when a signal stimulates the ear, it elicits a series of small electrical events that are identified by the electrodes. This is amplified and depicted on a waveform with five latency-specific peaks. The latency of each wave peak corresponds to an anatomic structure in the auditory pathway (Figure 14).

Clinical applications include acoustic neuroma diagnosis, threshold determination especially in children and intraoperative testing during acoustic neuroma surgery.

REFERENCES

Blackwell, D., Lucas, J., & Clarke, T. (2014). Summary Health Statistics for US Adults: National Health Interview Survey, 2012. *Vital and Health Statistics. Series 10, Data from the National Health Survey*, (260), 1–161. PMID:24819891

EmCAP. (2008). *Emergent Cognition through Active Perception*. FP6-IST project for Music Cognition (Music, Science and the Brain). Retrieved from http://emcap.iua.upf.edu

Kullar, P., Manjaly, J., & Yates, P. (2012). *ENT OSCEs: A Guide to Passing the DO-HNS and MRCS (ENT)*. Radcliffe Pub, UK: OSCE.

Kyriafinis, G. (2005). *Cochlear implantation*. Publish City.

Lalwani, A. (Ed.). (2008). Current Diagnosis & Treatment in Otolaryngology: Head and Surgery. McGraw-Hill Medical.

Lin, F., Niparko, J., & Ferrucci, L. (2011). Hearing loss prevalence in the United States. *Archives of Internal Medicine*, *171*(20), 1851–1853. doi:10.1001/archinternmed.2011.506 PMID:22083573

Marazita, M., Ploughman, L., Rawlings, B., Remington, E., Arnos, K., & Nance, W. (1993). Genetic epidemiological studies of early-onset deafness in the US school-age population. *American Journal of Medical Genetics*, *46*(5), 486–491. doi:10.1002/ajmg.1320460504 PMID:8322805

Roland, N., McRae, R., & McCombe, A. (2000). *Key topics in Otolaryngology*. Taylor & Francis.

Warner, G., Thirlwall, A., Corbridge, R., Patel, S., & Martinez-Devesa, P. (2009). *Otolaryngology and head and neck surgery*. Academic Press.

Chapter 3
Cochlear Implant Programming through the Internet

Georgios Kyriafinis
Aristotle University of Thessaloniki, Greece

Panteleimon Chriskos
Aristotle University of Thessaloniki, Greece

ABSTRACT

The ordinary user of cochlear implants is subject to post-surgical treatment that calibrates and adapts via mapping functions the acoustic characteristics of the recipient's hearing. As the number of cochlear implant users reaches indeed large numbers and their dispersion over vast geographic areas seems to be a new trend with impressive expansion, the need for doctors and audiologists to remotely program the cochlear implants of their patients comes as first priority, facilitating users in their programmed professional or personal activities. As a result, activities that need special care, like playing sport, swimming, or recreation can be performed remotely, disburdening the recipient from traveling to the nearest specialized programming center. However, is remote programming safeguarded from hazards?

DOI: 10.4018/978-1-5225-0264-7.ch003

COCHLEAR IMPLANTS

A cochlear implant is an electronic device that replaces the auditory system, mainly the sensory capillary cells in the organ of Corti in the cochlea (Kyriafinis, 2005). A modern cochlear implant is composed of two parts: one is the cochlear implant that is surgically implanted in the recipient and the second is the speech processor that is commonly worn behind the ear and communicates with the implant via an RF transmitter. In order to successfully stimulate the auditory nerve so that the recipient can perceive sound, sound waves must be transformed to electric pulses. This process begins at the speech processor where the sound wave is collected through a microphone. Afterwards sound waves are converted into an electric sound signal that is filtered, encoded and transformed through a very specific procedure. This signal is channeled through the speech processors transmitter to the implants receiver via an RF link. This signal contains the sound signal, the mapping of the T and C Levels, the amplitude and electrical pathway for each electrode passes the signal to the auditory nerve, as well as information regarding the decoding of the input signal. There is also communication from the implant to the speech processor that mainly includes the functioning state of each electrode and the impedance that is measured at each one. The speech processor apart from the data mentioned above also supplies the implant with the power required in order to function. The implant converts the incoming sound signal into electric signals that reach the cochlear nerve through an array of electrodes ranging from 12 to 22 depending on the implant model and brand. These electric signals stimulate the nerve in a way that simulates the normal function of the cochlea. From this point on the auditory signal follows the natural course to the primary auditory cortex on the cerebral cortex. This series to steps allows the recipient to perceive sound.

The process of converting the sound waves into an auditory signal is as mentioned above very specific an happens through specialized hardware and software in the sound processor as well as the implant. For every cochlear implant recipient the auditory nerve and brain respond differently to the electrical stimulus that is produced by the electrode array. As such one configuration cannot be applied to all recipients. Differences lie in the amplitude of the sound where a normal audio level for one patient can be perceived as painful for another. Sound amplitude is demonstrated in cochlear implants as the amplitude of the electric signal. Differences also lie in frequency. Frequency is demonstrated as channels that are respective to a single electrode in the electrode array. In the case of frequency differences the amplitude of each frequency must be adjusted for each recipient, and the correct channel levels must be selected.

Every channel has three main characteristics that are:

- The Threshold or T Level, which is the lowest electrical level that causes an auditory response to the recipient
- The Comfortable or C Level, which is the highest electrical level that causes a loud auditory response to the recipient while still being pleasant and
- The Dynamic Range which is simply the difference between the T and C Level.

It is important to note that the specific value of the T and C Levels as well as the Dynamic Range value is not important. What is most important is that these values provide the auditory response that is ideal for each recipient. The procedure of setting the above levels to their values is called mapping or programming of the cochlear implant (Kyriafinis, 2005).

REMOTE COCHLEAR IMPLANT PROGRAMMING

In order to correctly program the cochlear implant it is usually required that the recipient visits a programming center. In these programming centers, programming of the cochlear implant is most commonly done by a doctor or audiologist but other suitably trained professionals can take part under the supervision of a doctor. The programming session is usually conducted by constantly receiving feedback from the cochlear implant recipient in order to correctly set the T and C Levels. It is also required that the doctor cooperates with other specialists especially in the cases of toddlers, children and other recipients that require special care. During the programming sessions specialized software and hardware are required that will enable the doctor to communicate with the implant and successfully achieve the desired result.

With the increasing number of cochlear implant recipients and their distribution over a large geographic area a new trend arises that enables doctors and audiologist to remotely program the cochlear implants without the recipient traveling to the specialized programming center. This is possible due to the recent advances in Internet communications. More specifically the wide availability of high speed internet links such as the Asymmetric Digital Subscriber Line (ADSL) with a downstream transfer rate ranging from 8.0 Mbit/s for ADSL to 52.0 Mbit/s for ADSL2++ and the Very-High Speed Digital Subscriber Line (VDSL) networks with a downstream rate from 55.0 Mbit/s for VDSL to 100.0 Mbit/s for VDSL2.

These high speed networks are enabled by optical fibers, and have allowed doctors to simultaneously interact with the recipient through commercially available video conferencing software and also with the cochlear implant through the required hardware and software.

In the case of local fitting all parties including the cochlear implant recipient, the doctor and/or audiologist as well as other professionals that support the programming procedure are located in the same office. Other professionals are especially required in the cases of infants, children and other patients that require special care. During the local fitting session, the recipient's implant is checked with the use of a specialized transmitter that is connected via dedicated hardware to the computer. This hardware provides a programming interface between the cochlear implant and the software that runs on the computer. This software is custom for the each brand of cochlear implants and also keeps a database of the recipients that are programmed through this program. After the functionality of the implant has been reassured, then the speech processor is connected with the programming interface hardware and is also connected to the implant as it would be during normal operation. After this step, the programming session continues by setting the appropriate values of T and C Levels with each party communicating directly with the others.

In comparison with the local cochlear implant programming, remote programming of cochlear implants requires some extra steps as well as supporting personnel, software and hardware in order to make remote programming feasible such as video cameras and a microphone. Remote programming is almost identical to the local fitting session with regards the actions that can be performed (Ramos et al., 2009). As in the local session, the clinician is able to perform measurements to check the integrity of the implant as well as read the electrode impedances. It is also possible to take objective measurements regarding the condition of the speech processor and implant as well as the auditory nerve. Furthermore the clinician is able to view the history of T and C Levels, in order to have a complete picture about the recipients progress with the implant. The clinician can also program new parameters into the speech processor and activate it in live mode as in a local session. Thereafter the clinician can also offer consultation to the recipient on the best ways he can use the new settings in his speech processor. Two are the basic setups (Wesarg et al., 2006) that are usually used in remote programming which are analyzed in more detail below. In both cases a support clinician or specialist must be available in the remote location. He will be responsible for initiating and testing the connection with the fitting center before the fitting session, and also support the recipient. This specialist must be trained to connect the speech processor with the hardware interface and allow the fitting center clinician to remotely control the computer running the remote control software. Another responsibility is to support the recipient in any case that he may require during the fitting session.

The first remote fitting setup, which is graphically show in Figure 1, requires the following hardware: one computer in the clinician's and/or audiologists cochlear implant fitting room and another computer in the room where the recipient and other professionals, including a properly trained monitoring clinician to establish a connection between the two computers and support the recipient if necesary. The connection pod is also required in the remote location that will allow the speech processor to be connected with the computer so that the fitting session can take place. An Internet connection is also required in order for the two remote systems to communicate with one another. The bandwidth of the connection is a vital parameter for the success of the remote fitting session. Researchers suggest a minimum of 512 kbit/s (Wasowski et al., 2010; Wesarg et al., 2010). Although modern communication system have surpassed this minimum an order of magnitude it is crucial that the connection is uninterrupted and has a steady speed to avoid lagging. Although in most systems a small amount of lagging is acceptable, lagging that occurs during the fitting session, especially while increasing the T Levels, can cause uncomfortable situations for the recipient. If the clinician increases a T level and this is not immediately shown in the remote software, the clinician may increase it again beyond the threshold that is comfortable for the recipient. Other hardware include a video camera in both locations so that all parties can visually communicate with each other. The resolution of the video camera is also an important factor during the session. Although modern cameras may offer high definition video (HD: 1080x720, FullHD:1920x1080) transmitting a live video feed at these resolutions is not viable especially in the case of slow or unsteady connections. As such the resolution must be adjusted in the video conferencing software to the value that offers acceptable image quality, while not causing delays in the connection between the two computers. Visual communication is required

Figure 1. Local cochlear implant programming setup

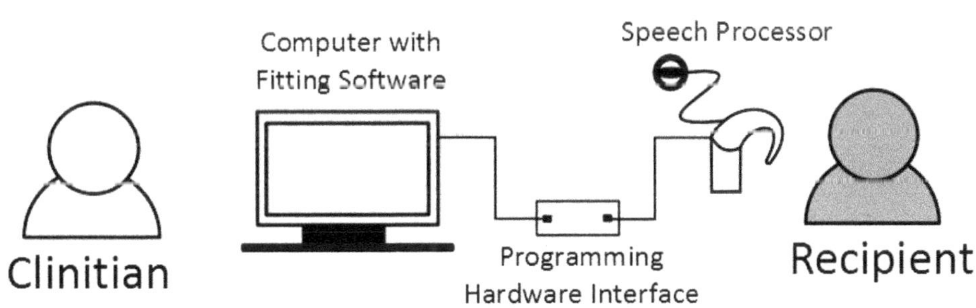

so that the clinician is able to see the reactions of the recipient to the new mapping of his implant and also communicate visually with the monitoring clinician in the remote location. Furthermore a set of good quality speakers must be available in both locations so that all parties can communicate verbally. The clinician as in a local fitting can ask for feedback from the recipient about the T and C Levels as well as if he has any problems with the new mapping.

Apart from the hardware a set of software is also required to successfully complete a fitting session. In the clinicians fitting room a remote control software is required. This software will enable the clinician to remotely control the computer in the remote location on which the recipients speech processor is connected. In the remote location the computer an installation of the cochlear implant programming software must be available. Apart from the above software, both computers must have video conferencing software that will enable the clinician and recipient to communicate through the Internet. There is a number of video conferencing applications that are commercially available. Whilst selecting one the clinician must take into account the cost of such software, although the majority is available free of charge, the compatibility with the operating system on each computer, the ease of use and learn ability of the conferencing software as well as the robustness of the software. This means that the software will not lag often and will also have a small chance of crashing and terminating the connection. Other features may also be helpful such as the ability to communicate with text messages, the ability to share a screen and also the option of filesharing. Although these features are not required they may appear helpful as secondary communication methods. While setting such a session it is also necesary to make sure that the proper drivers are installed that will support all the hardware connected to the computers, including the speaker system and microphone that are usually connected through the computers sound card. It is advised that the connection between the clinicians fitting room and the remote location is initiated before the recipient arrives for the fitting. This will save time and frustration for the recipient and any problems that may occur can be addressed before the beginning of the session.

An issue that might arise for the clinician in the fitting center is the small size of the video conferencing software and the remote control software if on the same screen. This may make reading the recipients visual cues difficult or even impossible. A simple solution for this problem is the use of two computer screens/monitors. The majority of modern graphic cards support at least two monitors. The setup is usually very simple and consists of simply tethering both monitors on the graphics cards and using the second one to extend the primary screen. This allows to view the video conferencing software on one screen and the remote control software on the other. As a result the clinician will have a whole screen dedicated to each software and lack of screen space will not be an issue. The number of software used during a remote fitting session may cause one of the computers to overload with processing task that may even lead to the operating system crashing and requiring a reboot. This problem can be solved by using a computer with better performance that is able to handle the workload imposed by the various applications running at the same instant. Another problem that may arise is the different operating system between the two computers in the clinicians fitting room and the remote location. This may cause serious compatibility problems that must be addressed by selecting the appropriate software and drivers or using computers with the same or similar operating system. A third problem could be network congestion and safety. As mentioned above a robust connection is needed to avoid any frustration for the recipient but also for the clinician. Lagging and unreliable connections can make the remote fitting session tiresome and lengthy. This issue cannot be immediately solved. If there is no option for higher bandwidth or reliability the fitting sessions can bc programmed at times of low network usage to minimize lagging as far as possible. The issuc of safcty is also very important. Although connections established via remote control software and video conferencing software are considered secure there is always a risk when data is transferred through the Internet. Consulting a network specialist and correctly setting the inbound and outbound rules in the firewalls between the two computers can help lower the risk of any data being compromised. The issue of safety must be addressed and discussed with the recipient and he must understand that there is a small possibility that some or all of his session's information might be available to a third unauthorized party.

The second remote fitting setup, shown in Figure 2, seeks to solve some of the before mentioned problems especially the ones regarding the lack of screen space and computer workload. This setup requires the use of two computers on each end. Two computers in the clinicians fitting room and two in the remote location. The logic is to split the workload between two computers to minimize the probability of a lagging or unresponsive operating system. In both locations one computer will be dedicated to achieving and maintaining a remote control connection so that the clinician can connect and interact with the cochlear implant. The second computer will handle the video conferencing software. With this setup the hardware necessary for video conferencing are all connected to one computer removing this workload from the other one that is free to simply handle the remote control software. This setup however does not reduce the network load if both computers are connected to the same internet connection. It does make the system more reliable in the sense that if one computer stops responding only half of the work needs to be done to continue the remote fitting session. If the computer handling the remote control software crashes the clinician can still

Figure 2. Remote cochlear implant programming setup

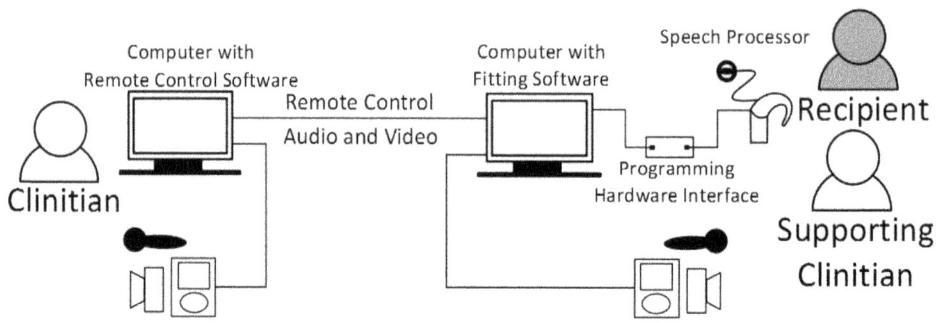

communicate with the recipient. In the case where the computer that handles the video conferencing stalls the clinician can still make minor adjustments until the video communication link is reestablished.

In this setup if two computers are not available in both locations this part can be filled with the use of a mobile device. Modern mobile devices are equipped with a Wi-Fi connection that allows them to connect to the Internet. Although smartphones may not be ideal due to small screen size that will hinder visual communication tablets are ideally sized for multimedia sharing. As a result they can be used to replace a more expensive computer system that might not be available. If screen size is still an issue, the tablet's screen can be mirrored on a bigger computer screen or a smart television making the video conference perhaps easier than in the case where a computer is used. The use of mobile devices does not apply however to the programming software since common tablet operating systems are not supported.

The two setups above are the ones that are most commonly used in research regarding the remote fitting of cochlear implants. This area of research has grown in the last years mainly due to the number of cochlear implant recipients as well as their geographical distribution.

Remote fitting has many benefits that are focused mainly on the recipient. One of the major benefit is the reduction of travel costs and time. Travel costs can be significant for the recipient and his family especially if he lives a long distance from the fitting center. Apart from the cost and time that the recipients spend to reach the center they are usually tired, especially children, and as such the recipients cannot perform optimally during the programming session. This may lead to delays in the hearing rehabilitation process since the T and C Levels cannot be optimally set. Distance is also a barrier for the communication between the specialists that monitor the recipient at his location and the clinician at the fitting center. This communication is crucial so that the two parties can coordinate in order to achieve the best possible hearing rehabilitation, which can be part of the remote fitting session.

The drawbacks of remote cochlear implant programming are not very prominent and mainly emerged in the cases where the connection was not reliable or the bandwidth was not the required minimum. It has been reported that remote fitting sessions usually take longer than local fittings by about 10 minutes, which is especially a problem in the cases of children that may grow tired and unwilling to further cooperate. It is possible that if clinicians and monitoring clinicians acquire more experience with the remote system this time difference can be minimized. In the case of unreliable Internet connections delayed feedback may cause the programming clinician to increase levels unintentionally to too loud stimulation which may be uncomfortable for the recipient. Low audio and video quality may also be a problem in the case of low bandwidth. Low video quality may hinder lip reading by the programming clinician and low audio quality can make the session tiring and increase the frustration of the recipient. In a very small number of cases it was reported that the recipient thought that remote fitting would negatively affect his relationship with the clinician.

The aims of a remote fitting system include among others to provide versatile care for cochlear implant recipients using a complex method of hearing rehabilitation focused on the recipients individual need, without the need to travel long distances. Some recipients may require multiple programming sessions in one year, especially in the period right after the implantation, which would be very difficult to achieve. Remotely the clinician can cater to such needs without the extra cost of travel and without the recipient having to lose time during trips to the fitting center. A second aim is the coordination of the hearing rehabilitation process, in order for the recipient to develop sound perception and interpretation abilities. Through systematic training the recipient will eventually develop the skills to verbally communicate with other people. The coordination must take place between the specialized fitting center and the professionals that attend to the recipient's needs closer to his home location. Such a system also aims to allow the recipient to develop social, educational and professional skills by informing him about the programs available to his disposal, through the professionals in the fitting center. Another aim is to transmit and spread the knowledge about cochlear implant and the hearing rehabilitation process of the recipients, as well as the difficulties that these patients face in their everyday lives. This will help family members, friends and supporting professionals to better support the recipient during the time of the rehabilitation process. Furthermore a remote fitting system allows the clinician to assist the recipient in case of an emergency where a local fitting would be impossible or extremely difficult to take place. If for some reason the previous fitting causes discomfort for the recipient an emergency session can be scheduled in a short time maybe in the same day in order to reprogram the sound processor so that the recipient can resume his normal activities.

RESEARCH REVIEW ON REMOTE PROGRAMMING

Beyond the benefits of remote fitting sessions it is important to discuss the results of such a session. From these results, crucial decisions can be made regarding the safety and efficiency of a remote fitting session. The results obtained during the remote fitting sessions not only encompass the programming of the new parameters in the speech processor and setting the T and C Levels, but also include the satisfaction of all parties that take part in the remote session. In most research scenarios, the remote session was linked with a local session, that happened shortly after or before the remote session, and the parties where asked to compare the two. In order to measure the satisfaction of clinicians, recipients and other personnel a questionnaire is usually handed to each party specific for their role in the fitting session. The responders in each case where asked about the quality and reliability of the communication between the recipient and clinician through the video conferencing software. Major issues where covered by questions that concerned the performance, effectiveness and safety of the remote fitting session and how comfortable the new settings where for the recipient. Another question posed regarded the time difference between the local and remote sessions and if the time difference was considered acceptable. Furthermore, other questions inquired about the comfort level of the clinicians and recipients during the remote sessions and benefits regarding travel time, travel costs and overall effort for each session.

In one study (Wasowski et al., 2010) of 29 individuals it was reported that 26/29 (89.7%) recipients agreed that the remote fitting session was an efficient alternative to local fitting sessions, while 25/29 (86.2%) of individuals believed that the method of remote fitting would make their lives easier. The result of the remote session was considered satisfactory by 25/29 (86.2%) recipients while 1 recipient disagreed with the above statement. In the case of the fitting specialists all of them agreed that remote measurement was safe for the recipient and the system used in the study was easy to use, while 25/29 (86.2%) sessions where comparable to a local session.

In a second multicenter study (Wesarg et al., 2010) 70 recipients undertook both a local and remote fitting, while one fitting could not be completed. Half the recipients had the remote fitting first and the local fitting second, while the reverse was true for the rest of the recipients. The time period between the two fittings was set to a maximum of two days.

This study reported that the majority of the recipients (43/69, 62.3%), was able to effectively communicate with the clinician through the remote fitting system, but on average this was more difficult compared to the local fitting session. In the case of remote fittings 16 recipients (23.2%) reported that they had problems with lip-reading the clinicians face compared to 4 recipients (5.8%) in the local fitting. A similar increase was observed when the recipients were asked to rate the fluency of the conversation. One recipient disagreed having a fluent conversation locally while this number increased to 13 (18.8%) in the case of the remote fitting. Moving to the quality of the communication between the recipient and the clinician in the fitting center 51 recipients (73.9%) agreed that the tone quality of the clinicians voice was good and 67 recipients judged the remote clinicians image on screen as clear. For remote fitting most recipients (54/69, 78.3%), felt comfortable communicating with the audiologist through a computer screen and loudspeakers, 65 of the recipients (94.2%) felt comfortable with the remote technology around them and 64 (92.8%) considered the duration of the remote fitting session acceptable. Most recipients were happy with the quality of treatment received in the remote sessions and the vast majority of recipients agreed that the clinician understood their hearing problem both in the local session (68/69, 98.6%) and in the remote session (67/69, 97.1%). There was a difference concerning the satisfaction with the new program between the local and remote sessions. While 64 recipients (92.8%) were satisfied in the local session, 59 recipients (85.5%) were satisfied in the remote fitting. Concerning the relationship between the recipient and the clinician, 41 of the recipients (60.3%) did not think that the relationship would be influenced negatively if their programming was to be performed remotely in the future, but 15 of the recipients (22.1%) were afraid that remote fitting might affect their relationship with the clinician. The majority of recipients responded that remote fitting is an efficient alternative to local fitting (57/69, 82.6%) and 54 (78.3%) of the recipients thought that a remote session could save travel time for them.

Clinicians were asked to answer to questions apart from the quality of communication and overall satisfaction concerning the clinical usability of the remote fitting system. In 62 of the cases (89.9%) they agreed that the remote system was easy to use and that the remote measurements displayed an acceptable performance in 56 (81.2%) of the cases. Furthermore it was noted that in 44 (63.8%) of the cases the remote system was comparable with the local fitting system. It was noted that in 37 of the cases the remote fitting session prolonged working time but these times where considered as acceptable for a remote fitting session. The clinicians opinions where split in the following areas regarding, in 30 (43.5%) cases the time for feedback on stopping stimulation, in 33 (47.8%) of the cases, the time delay to display stimulus indicators and in 37 (53.6%) of the cases the time delay to drag CL sliders. In the cases above the time delay was not considered acceptable for clinical use. In the majority of cases (66/69, 95.7%) the clinicians agreed that the remote measurements were safe for the recipient. However in 13 sessions (18.8%) they saw risks with remote fitting, related to remote connection reliability and the emotional distance due to the spatial distance between the recipient and clinician. In 30 sessions (43.5%) the clinicians recognised benefits during the remote fitting session. Regarding the quality of communications for most sessions that the sound (61/69, 88.4%) and the video (64/69, 92.8%) quality were acceptable for clinical use.

Questionnaires were also filled by the supporting clinician in the remote location in this study. They reported that in the majority of cases (65/69, 94.2%) the remote programming system was easy to use and in 66 (95.7%) of the cases the performance level of the remote measurements was acceptable and that the sound quality was adequate for effective communication with the clinician. Few where the problems during the session and included low sound and video quality, and in three cases the need to re-establish the connection with the fitting center and the re-connection of the speech processor. In 2 cases the programming software had to be restarted and in one case the computer in the remote location had to be rebooted. Apart from the subjective data in the above study the programming parameters where analysed statistically. Based on the statistical analysis presented in the study it was reported that the T and C Levels obtained during the remote session where comparable to those obtained during the local session. This conclusion was also reached by Ramos et al. (2009) a study conducted on 5 adult recipients in a single center.

From the results in the above studies a number of conclusions can be reached. Taking into account the subjective feedback from the clinicians, recipients and supporting professionals it can be inferred that remote cochlear implant fitting is a viable alternative to a local fitting session. The majority of recipients felt comfortable during the remote fitting session and the new programming of their implant was satisfactory as in the case of local programming. The level of comfort also encompasses the remote fitting environment, and the communication with the clinician which in some cases was problematic especially if the recipient was highly relying on lip-reading and as such some recipients requested assistance by the monitoring clinician at the remote location. In one reported case the fitting could not be successfully completed due a severe facial nerve stimulation (FNS) on many electrodes. This results hints to the limitations of remote fitting in the cases where recipients may display additional problems and disabilities e.g. excessive FNS, blind patients or patients with mental disabilities. However, in Wesarg et al. (2010) a total of 13 paediatric recipients were successfully fitted remotely, with the youngest one being one year of age.

CONCLUSION

Concluding, it can be said that remote cochlear implant fitting is a very useful and safe way acceptable by both clinicians and recipients and is a viable alternative and comparable to a local fitting. Commercially available remote control and video conferencing software and hardware allow an effective and in most cases reliable operation ofremote fitting systems. They also provide sufficient audio and video quality for most recipients and clinicians. Crucial parameters for the success of a remote session are available network and internet connections that must have a bandwidth of a least 512kbit/s. A remote fitting session can minimize travel time and cost for recipients that have to travel large distances to reach the fitting center and recipients can have easier access to cochlear implant services and fittings in very brief periods of time. Therefore a number of fitting centres taking part in the above studies have decided to incorporate the remote fitting approach in their clinical routine.

REFERENCES

Kyriafinis, G. (2005). *Cochlear implantation*. Publish City.

Ramos, A., Rodríguez, C., Martinez-Beneyto, P., Perez, D., Gault, A., Falcon, J. C., & Boyle, P. (2009). Use of telemedicine in the remote programming of cochlear implants. *Acta Oto-Laryngologica*, *129*(5), 533–540. doi:10.1080/00016480802294369 PMID:18649152

Wasowski, A., Skarzynski, P., Lorens, A., Obrycka, A., Walkowiak, A., & Bruski, L. (2010). Remote Fitting of Cochlear Implant System. *Cochlear Implants International*, *11*(Supplement 1), 489–492. doi:10.1179/146701010X12671177318105 PMID:21756680

Wesarg, T., Kröger, S., Gerber, O., Kind, H., Reuss, S., Roth, J., & Laszig, R. et al. (2006). Pilot Study of Remote Measurement and Fitting of Cochlear Implant Recipients. In *8th EFAS Congress / 10th Congress of the German Society of Audiology*. Heidelberg, Germany: EFAS.

Wesarg, T., Wasowski, A., Skarzynski, H., Ramos, A., Gonzalez, J., Kyriafinis, G., & Laszig, R. et al. (2010). Remote Fitting in Nucleus Cochlear Implant Recipients. *Acta Oto-Laryngologica*, *130*(12), 1379–1388. doi:10.3109/00016489.2010.492480 PMID:20586675

Chapter 4
Cochlear Implants and Mobile Wireless Connectivity

Panteleimon Chriskos
Aristotle University of Thessaloniki, Greece

Orfeas Tsartsianidis
Aristotle University of Thessaloniki, Greece

ABSTRACT

Human senses enable humans to perceive and interact with their environment, through a set of sensory systems or organs which are mainly dedicated to each sense. From the five main senses in humans hearing plays a critical role in many aspects of our lives. Hearing allows the perception not only of the immediate visible environment but also parts of the environment that are obstructed from view and/ or that are a significant distance from the individual. One of the most important and sometimes overlooked aspects of hearing is communication, since most human communication is accomplished through speech and hearing. Hearing does not only convey speech but also conveys more complex messages in the form of music, singing and storytelling.

DOI: 10.4018/978-1-5225-0264-7.ch004

INTRODUCTION

Human senses enable humans to perceive and interact with their environment, through a set of sensory systems or organs which are mainly dedicated to each sense. From the five main senses in humans hearing plays a critical role in many aspects of our lives. Hearing allows the perception not only of the immediate visible environment but also parts of the environment that are obstructed from view and/or that are a significant distance from the individual. One of the most important and sometimes overlooked aspects of hearing is communication, since most human communication is accomplished through speech and hearing. Hearing does not only convey speech but also conveys more complex messages in the form of music, singing and storytelling.

HEARING AIDS

The importance of hearing can be also stressed by the number of devices that have been invented in order to assist individuals hard of hearing (Howard, 1998; Levitt, 2007; Mills, 2011). In modern times one of the simplest forms of hearing aid dates to the 17th century known as the ear trumpet. Ear trumpets were tubular or funnel-shaped devices that gather acoustic waves and lead them to the user's ear. Due to the large size of the opening of the device, compared to the human ear, more sound waves were guided into the ear, which result in a stronger vibration of the eardrum and thus allowing a stronger in magnitude perception of sound.

Ear trumpets where usually large, cumbersome, awkward to use and aesthetically unappealing devices. This changed drastically with the advent of the 19th century and hearing aids became devices that could be incorporated or concealed in everyday items of even in articles of clothing or jewelry (Beckerexhibits, 19th century). This led to an increase in the number of hearing aid users, since the hearing aid new design and appearance could conceal the devices' true purpose. Worn or handheld devices included among others, acoustic headbands, concealed in a hat or in an elaborate hairstyle, acoustic fans, commonly used by women, acoustic canes, used by men, sound receptors designed to be concealed in hair or under a beard, as well as, acoustic hats that concealed ear trumpets under or in the hat with earpieces held in place by springs. In 1819, F. Rein, was commissioned to design an acoustic chair for King John VI of Portugal. In the same period similar chairs were designed and where meant to aid royalty, judges, lawyers and merchants in their everyday business. Other everyday items that were used to conceal hearing aids where vases. Such devices were commonly used on a table. They had multiple openings in order collect sounds, mainly the voice of the others seated, from many directions and lead them to the user's ear through a long flexible hearing tube. The above devices apart from aiding those hard of hearing also provided concealment in an effort to secrete the user's hearing problem.

Further progress in the field of hearing aids had to wait until the late 19th century when the invention of the microphone and telephone enabled the alteration of acoustic signals (Mills, 2011). One of the first hearing aid was created by Miller Reese Hutchison in 1898 called the Akouphone. The sound signal was amplified using an electric current through a carbon transmitter. Siemens in 1913 developed an electronic hearing aid that was portable and consisted of a speaker that fit in the ear. In 1920 Earl Hanson developed a hearing aid called Vactuphone using vacuum tubes that used a telephone transmitter to convert sound to electrical signals that were amplified and then passed on to a telephone receiver. In 1927 Acousticon Model 28 was released (Beckerexhibits, 20th century). This large device consisted of multiple carbon components rendering it and hard to carry especially with the batteries of the time that were large in size and weight. Due to the limitations in size and weight many hearing aids were camouflaged to resemble table top radios or concealed in large handbags. With the reduction in the size of vacuum tubes and batteries in the 1930's and 40's the size of hearing aids allowed them to be concealed under articles of clothing or strapped on the body with the use of harnesses.

After the development of transistors in 1948 by Bell Laboratories a new era begun in the field of hearing aids and later allowed the development of cochlear implants (Mills, 2011). The first hearing aids implemented using solely transistors were the Microtone Tansimatic and the Maico Transit-ear offered in 1952. In 1954 hearing aids where integrated in eyeglasses and by 1959 this type of hearing aid accounted for about 50% of the total market (Beckerexhibits, 20th century). The minimization of transistor and battery size led in the mid 1950's to the first behind the ear (BTE) hearing aids. Advances in technology led to the demise of the transistor with the development of integrated circuits in 1958 by J. Kibly at Texas Instruments. This was the choice for developing hearing aids until the 1970s when the introduction of the microprocessor allowed high speed signal analysis and processing. In this period the size of hearing aids declined even more and many models appeared as in the ear (ITE) or in the canal (ITC) and finally led to completely in the canal (CIC) models. Microprocessors coupled with amplitude compression developed by E. Villchur enabled the separation of frequency bands that allowed parallel processing of these bands. The first real-time digital hearing aid was developed in 1982 at the City University of New York.

COCHLEAR IMPLANT HISTORY

Despite the above advances hearing aids simply assisted people hard of hearing by increasing the intensity of the sound around them but did not in any way aid people with deafness. This was accomplished by cochlear implants that have a somewhat briefer history but have a large impact on the lives and wellbeing of deaf individuals.

A first successful attempt to restore hearing in a deaf patient took place in 1957 by A. Djourno and C. Eyries (1957), who restored hearing in a deaf patient by electrically stimulating acoustic nerve fibers in the inner ear. Their observations lasted only a few weeks since the device they used stopped functioning in less than a month. Their observations where published in the French journal Presse Médicale. Until 1965 W. House using the first surgical microscopes of the time, implanted a single channel cochlear implant he had developed earlier (Eshraghi et al., 2012). This simple and durable device stimulated the auditory nerve fibers in unison and as a result the recipient could only recognize the rhythm of the speech. The next year, 1966, B. Simmons (1966) performed the first temporary human implantation of a multichannel device but not in the cochlea but rather in the auditory nerve itself. The multichannel approach allowed the perception of different frequencies. This was also shown by a team in Paris led by C. H. Chouard and P. Macleod by using devices with 8 to 12 electrodes isolated from one another. These electrodes where placed in parts of the scala tympani and allowed the recipients to perceive different frequencies (Mac Leold et al., 1975). The first implant took place at the Saint Antoine Hospital in Paris on September 22 1976 and was performed by C. H. Chourad assisted by B. Meyer (Chouard et al., 1977). The patient recovered his hearing the next day and another five patients were also implanted. After a short period from the implantation, the recipients were able to recognize some words without lip-reading.

In 1975 in Vienna, K. Burian began the development of the first Austrian cochlear implant with work on single channel cochlear stimulation and then on multichannel stimulation (Hochmair et al., 1979). His work was extended by Ingeborg and E. Hochmair whose work led to the world's first microelectronic multi-channel cochlear implant in 1977 and was implanted by K. Burian. The implant had 8 channels and a stimulation rate of 10k pulses per second for each channel on a flexible electrode (22-25 mm) implanted in the cochlea. In 1979 a recipient with an implant from the above team received a body worn speech processor. After a modification in March 1980 this patient was the first individual to shown speech understanding without lip-reading using a mobile speech processor (Hochmair, 2013). This work led to the establishment of the Med El Company in 1990 and one year later in 1991 the world's first behind-the-ear audio processor was presented by the same company. The same year MXM-Neurelec (Chouard et al., 1995) presented their first fully digital multichannel implant that could be adapted to an ossified cochlea. Expanding their expertise, in 1994, Med-El (2015) presented the world's first electrode array capable of stimulating the entire length of the cochlea to allow a more natural hearing and in 1996 presented the world's first miniaturized multichannel implant at 4 mm. Another pioneering act by Med El was the first bilateral implantation for the purpose of binaural hearing. From that point on the capabilities of cochlear implants increased constantly leading to modern cochlear implants that coupled with their speech processors utilize wireless communication technologies to allow connectivity with various devices. Cochlear implants role is to override part of the natural auditory path described next.

HUMAN HEARING

Being one of the major senses, hearing (Kyriafinis, 2005; Alberti, 1995) is the process that transduces pressure gradients from sound vibrations, into neuro-electrical signals transferred to and recognized in the central nervous system. All these are made possible through the special anatomic futures and the ultra-labyrinthal physiology of the ears (Figure 1).

Figure 1. " The Anatomy of the Ear"
Image credits: Blausen.com staff. "Blausen gallery 2014" Wikiversity Journal of Medicine. DOI:10.15347/wjm/2014.010. ISSN 20018762. (Own work), via Wikimedia Commons.

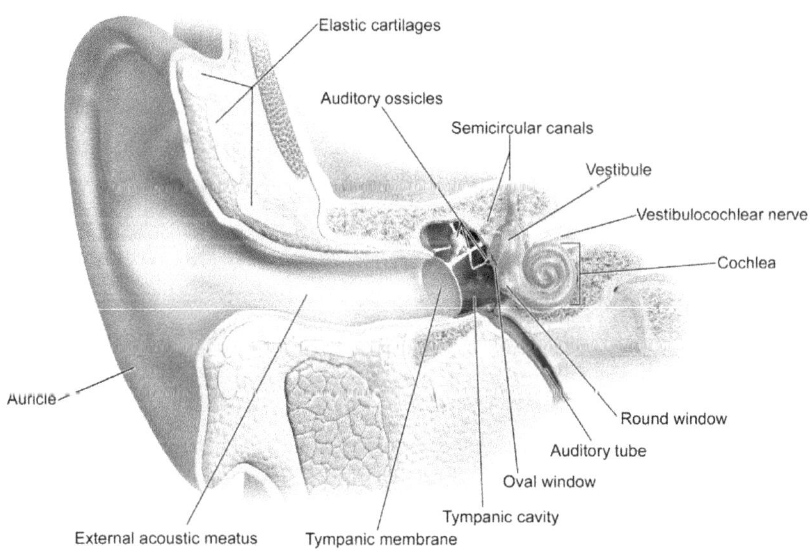

Ears are paired organs positioned on each side of the head and each one is anatomically divided into three portions: the Outer ear and the Middle ear conduct sound to the Inner ear which is engraved into the temporal bone and transforms the mechanical movements into electrical signals.

- Outer ear is consisted of the pinna and the external auditory canal. Pinna is cartilaginous and protrudes in order to collect the sounds preferably from the front side of the head, helping this way to localize sound of higher, mainly, frequencies. The ear canal has a protecting role for the sensitive inner structures having hairs, sweet and oily sebaceous glands which together form the ear wax, a disinfectant and a protective barrier. It has a functional role, too: it has a shape of a loudspeaker cone and transmits sounds from pinna to the tympanic membrane which separates outer from middle ear.
- Middle ear is a space covered with respiratory epithelium and it is connected with pharynx by the Eustachian tube (a long and thin tube with cartilaginous and muscular walls, that provides equilibrium between air pressure of the middle ear and atmospheric pressure, thus protecting the tympanic membrane) and with Mastoid process. It contains three tiny bones malleus, incus and stapes, articulated to one another, which transfers movements created by sounds waves from the tympanic membrane to the inner ear.
- Inner ear is enclosed into the bony cochlea which has the shape of a snail shell with two and a half turns and it is called membranous labyrinth due to its complexity. It consists of three membranous spaces the Scala Vestibuli, the Scala Media or Cochlear Duct and the Scala Tympani. The first and the last are connected with each other by an opening near the apex of cochlea, called helicotrima and they are filled with a liquid called perilymph. The first is connected with the oval window, a small opening in the bonny wall of the middle ear where stapes' foot plate is attached, and the last ends in the round window, a smaller opening closed with a membrane, just under the oval one. In that way, they function as a closed circuit, filled with a practically uncompressed fluid, with a pressure equalizing mechanism, that transmits movements to the medial part, the Scala Media, which is filled with another liquid called endolymph, contains about 30,000 hair cells and about 19,000 nerve fibers and is the main organ for conception, transformation and transmission of the sound produced signals. On the basilar membrane, the barrier between the scala media and scala tympani, the placement of the hair cells form a triangular structure known as the Corti tunnel. Any movement of the Corti tunnel results in consequent movements of the hair cells and these movements generate an electric impulse that travels to the brain through the afferent nerve fibers which join altogether in the cochlear part of the vestibu-

locochlear nerve. Basilar membrane has many parallel fibers enclosed in gelatinous substance. These fibers resonant in a progressively lower frequency as the sound created liquid movements travel from the base to the apex of the cochlea. A certain wave travels till it reaches the point that corresponds to the specific frequency and no more.

The labyrinth is connected with the vestibular labyrinth, the organ of balance and a small projection of it protrudes through the temporal bone into the CSF cistern.

Audible sound has a range from 16-32 Hz to 16,000-20,000 Hz with greater sensitivity among 128 Hz and 4,000 Hz, numbers that diminish with age. In order to hear a sound, it should get caught by the pinna first.

Human head is big enough to act as a barrier between the ears and, in this way it helps in the side localization of the sound. The pinna to head ratio in humans is smaller in comparison with the other animals but pinna has an efficient shape to catch higher frequency sounds and drive them into the ear canal. Ear canal acts as a resonating tube. Thus it amplifies sounds of 3,000 to 4,000 Hz and increase the sensitivity of the ear to these frequencies. But sounds are amplified with other futures, too. Pinna has a large surface and it funnels sound in a relatively smaller surface, that of the tympanic membrane. And after that, this surface is getting even smaller in the staples' footplate. It works like a hydraulic amplification all the way through the ossicular chain. The total amplification of the sound through the outer and middle ear is almost 30 dB.

The inner ear transduces vibrations to electric signals. At the same time it analyzes the frequency and intensity of the sound. It had already been discussed that there are specific areas along the basilar membrane for each sound frequency. The 1 kHz point is located at about its middle. Frequency components lower than 1 kHz has to travel further and those higher stop somewhere before it. In this way only specific areas in the brain are stimulated and thus it is made possible to distinguish and recognize various sounds (music, deferent musical organs, noise, voices etc). A problem that emerges from this set-up is that low frequency information has to travel through the high frequency one and, in that way, the brain has some difficulty to distinguish higher from lower frequency sounds which simulate ears at the same time.

Ears have to deal with sound intensity, too. They are able to cope with a huge range of sound intensity; so huge that it has to be expressed as logarithm. The normal range is from 0 to 100 dB; after that sound becomes uncomfortable. There are some processes on the basilar membrane and its hair cells that make it possible for the ears to transmit the right impulses and create the right stimulus in the brain in order to perceive the sound intensity and give the orders for the right reactions (avoiding movements, head turn to the right direction of a low intensity sound etc).

COCHLEAR IMPLANTS

A cochlear implant is a high fidelity electronic device that replaces the auditory system, mainly the sensory capillary cells in the organ of Corti in the cochlea (Kyriafinis, 2005). This device bypasses the natural hearing process transferring the converted auditory signal directly to the cochlea . A modern cochlear implant is surgically implanted in the recipient under the skin behind the ear and sometimes anchored on the temporal bone. Since the implant does not have a power source, in order to function properly it must be coupled with an external unit known as a speech processor. This device is commonly worn behind the ear, provides power to the cochlear implant and communicates with the implant via an RF transmitter (Figure 2).

Both cochlear implants and their speech processors are mobile devices that interact with the user via a brain-computer interface, other devices, as well as, with the environment around them, altering their signal output depending on the environmental conditions. Cochlear implants are highly robust and precise implanted mobile devices that interact with a coupled speech processor and the recipient (Kyriafinis, 2005). Cochlear implants are composed of three basic parts. As seen in Figure 1 at the top is the coil that is used as an RF link, and the coil magnet that paired with the coil magnet of the speech processor keep the coil in place through the skin. The middle part of the implant is known as the body contains the electronics that convert the input signals to electrical stimuli to stimulate the auditory nerve. The final part of the implant is composed of one or more "tails" one of which is implanted in the cochlea and is equipped with a number of electrodes to stimulate the auditory nerve.

Figure 2. Left: Cochlear™ Nucleus 6 Speech Processor. Right: A typical Cochlear™ Implant.

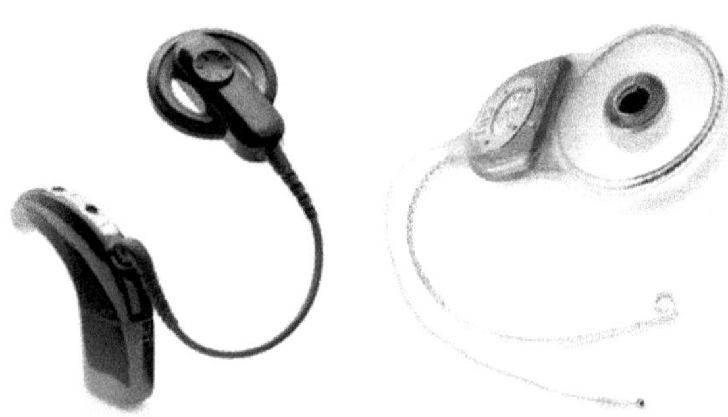

During the communication with the speech processor cochlear implants, send and receive data to and fro the speech processor. Data input contains a processed version of the audio signal captured by the speech processor. This signal is then converted to electrical signals, that after the required processing are utilized to stimulate the auditory nerve, in order to allow the recipient to perceive sound. The process of converting the input to electrical signals is unique for each individual and varies greatly between different brands and is achieved through a digital signal processor with mapping parameters, that are set during the programming of the cochlear implant. The cochlear implant also transmits data either to the speech processor or other dedicated equipment used in the programming of the implant. Output data include diagnostics concerning the functionality of the different parts of the implant, power consumption and requirements, and the nerve response of the recipient. All of these data can be used to assess the needs of the recipient and the condition of the implant itself, and can be utilized by a monitoring clinician to provide for the needs of the recipient. One interesting characteristic of cochlear implants is that they are not fitted with a power source and must rely on the speech processor for power. The two devices are linked with an RF transmitter, that allows wireless power and data transfer between the two devices. All of the above are contained in the main body of the implant that is not actually implanted in the cochlea (Figure 3). The part that is implanted in the cochlea is an electrode array with the number of electrodes ranging from 12 to 22, depending on the model and brand.

Figure 3. Cochlear Implant and Speech Processor schematically (not to scale)

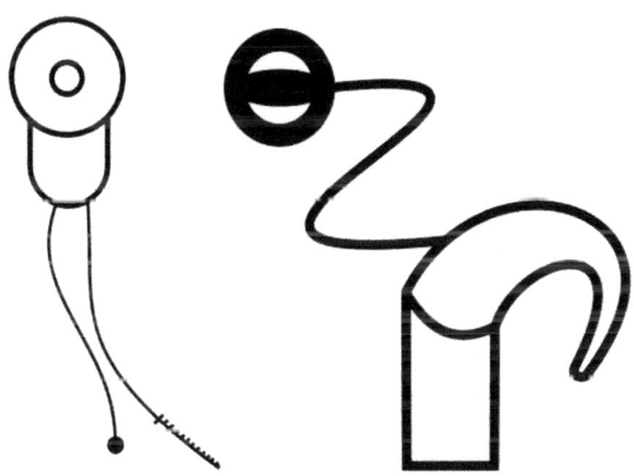

SPEECH PROCESSOR

Speech processors are wearable mobile devices that interact with the environment, the cochlear implant and also the user. Speech processors are consisted of three main parts. The largest part is at the bottom and is composed of the battery compartment. These batteries can be either disposable or rechargeable batteries supplied by the manufacturer. The coil allows connection with the cochlear implant and is composed of the coil cable, the coil magnet and coil. Similarly with the cochlear implant, the coil is used as an RF link and the coil magnet keeps the coil in place (Kyriafinis, 2005). The cable is used to transmit the data from the processing unit to the coil. The processing unit is the most important part of the speech processor. It is responsible for capturing environment sounds, achieved through microphones whose number varies typically from one to three. In the case of multiple microphones, their orientation also varies, i.e. for three microphones one is oriented to the front of the user, one to the back and one oriented to capture the sounds above the user. These microphones are of adjustable sensitivity which can be changed by the user. After the sound signal has been captured it is converted into electrical signals that are then conveyed to the cochlear implant through the RF link. The cochlear implant recipient can personalize the functions of the speech processor by using either the buttons on the speech processor itself or by using a remote controller that is supplied by the cochlear implant manufacturer. The parameters that the user can set are, among others, microphone sensitivity, volume level, connections and select the various programs available to the user. These programs alter the process of converting sound to electrical stimulations specific for different environments and hearing conditions. As devices, speech processors contain a analog to digital converter responsible for transforming the input sounds to digital signals, and a digital signal processor used as an intermediate step before the processing conduced in the cochlear implant. Speech processors communicate with various devices such as the cochlear implant and a remote controller, and are battery operated. Modern speech processors, apart from their traditional connectivity options, are 2.4 GHz enabled enabling communication with a wide range of devices as will be discussed later.

COCHLEAR IMPLANTS AND WIRELESS COMMUNICATIONS

Cochlear implants and their coupled speech processors have long enabled their users to be able to verbally communicate and perceive the world around them. The speech processors however did not at first have the capability of connecting to other devices except from the implant and the specialized mapping interface usually connected to a personal computer. This limitation became apparent with the advent of mobile telephony and especially smartphones. Modern mobile devices such as smartphones, tablets, multimedia players and global positioning system devices have advanced wireless connectivity capabilities that could not be easily utilized by the cochlear implant recipient. Wireless connectivity is also evident in other appliances such as personal computers, smart televisions, home entertainment centers, gaming consoles and stereo systems also offer plenty wireless connection functions. Connection to some of the above devices was achieved, and can still be achieved as a secondary solution, with the use of a set of cables and connectors that the user had to carry along. Apart from the need to carry these aids to connect to other devices problems also arose along with incompatibility issues between the different connector types found in the various devices, that sometimes rendered these devices unusable by the recipient. To allow easier connection to the aforementioned devices the manufacturers of speech processors chose the 2.4 GHz band to communicate with other devices. This specific band is the basis of the Bluetooth and Wi-Fi wireless protocols that are commonly found in devices today.

Bluetooth

Bluetooth (Fast-Facts, 2015; Bluetooth, 2015) is global wireless standard technology that enables connection and data transfer between two to eight devices using UHF radio waves in the frequency band between 2.4 and 2.485 GHz. This frequency band is available and unlicensed in most countries. There are two main types of Bluetooth communication protocols known as Bluetooth BR/EDR (basic rate/enhanced data rate) and Bluetooth Low Energy (BLE). The first type is commonly found is Bluetooth headsets and Bluetooth BLE in devices that have a limited power supply. Bluetooth was developed in 1994 by Ericsson, in order to replace RS-232 cables. Bluetooth was designed to transfer data within the users Private Area network or PAN with a maximum range of 100 meters. The networks between Bluetooth devices are known as a piconets. Piconets are dynamic networks that connect and disconnect devices as they move in or out of range. In such a network, one device has the role of the master, while all other devices act as slaves. In terms of security, Bluetooth technology offers three modes of security (Padgette et al., 2012). In Security Mode 1, no authentication or encryption is used. this mode is commonly used by devices such as a Bluetooth wireless mouse. Modes 3 and 3 use security and differ in the level security is applied, with the Mode 2 taking place in the service level and Mode 3 in the link level. These levels can be selected in order to achieve different levels of secure and private connections.

Bluetooth networks were adopted by mobile phone companies to transfer data between devices and to connect to peripheral devices such as Bluetooth headsets and smart-watches. This was also one of the first applications of wireless technologies in cochlear implant speech processors directly linking the speech processor to the device, or with the use of an accessory to manage the wireless communication. Communication can be achieved with other Bluetooth devices beyond mobile and smart-phones such as the ones mentioned above.

Wi-Fi

Wi-Fi (PCmag 802; PCmag Wi-Fi; BBC, 2012) is a wireless local area networking technology that enables the connection between multiple devices mainly using the 2.4 GHz and 5 GHz frequency bands. The roots of Wi-Fi are part of a "a failed experiment to detect exploding mini black holes the size of an atomic particle" developed by Australian radio-astronomer Dr John O'Sullivan of Commonwealth Scientific and Industrial Research Organisation (CSIRO). Wi-Fi was first standardized by the Institute of Electrical and Electronic Engineers (IEEE) as standard 802.11, whose first version was released in 1997 and provided up to 2 Mbps link speeds. This link speed has increased significantly with modern devices supporting up to 1 Gbps. Wi-Fi has become synonymous to the term Wireless Local Area Network or WLAN, since the majority of WLANs are based on Wi-Fi technology. Devices can connect to a Wi-Fi network via wireless network access points that have a range of about 20 meters indoors. Due to security issues various encryption technologies where added to the Wi-Fi technology in order to make it more secure. This technology has been adopted by numerous devices that have been mentioned above. Another feature that makes Wi-Fi ideal for wireless communications is the advanced security options that it offers (Wi-Fi Org, 2015). Modern Wi-Fi networks use the WPA2 security protocol in order to secure personal data, providing privacy and security. The above algorithm employs the Advanced Encryption Standard (AES) for encryption, which is considered as one of the most secure encryption algorithms.

The introduction of wireless communication technologies in speech processors enabled cochlear implant recipients to make better use of this era's technology (Figure 4).

Figure 4. Left: Cochlear™ Wireless Mini Microphone. Center: Cochlear™ Wireless Phone Clip. Right: Cochlear™ Wireless TV Streamer.

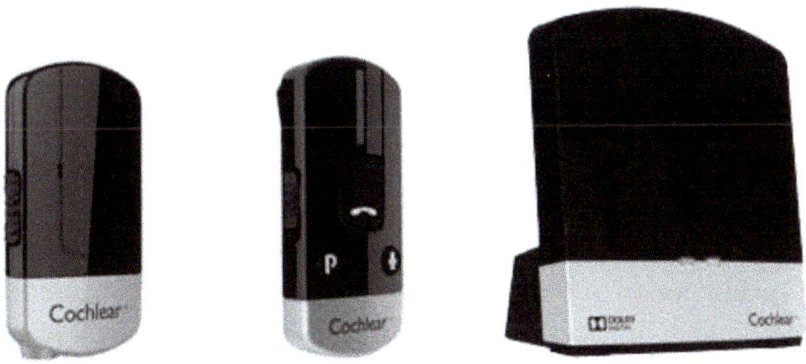

CONNECTIVITY USES

Connection through the 2.4 GHz band using Bluetooth or Wi-Fi between the speech processor and various devices can be achieved directly or through specialized accessories. The leading companies (Cochlear Nucleus, 2015; Medel Sonnet, 2015, Cochlear, 2015) in the field of cochlear implants and their respective speech processors, have developed or are in the process of developing various accessories that enable the connection between the speech processor and other commonly used everyday devices. Examples of such accessories include a device that allows wireless Bluetooth connection with smartphones. This device acts as an intermediary between the smart-phone and the speech processor, allowing call handling and voice control functions. Another speech processor peripheral device is a mobile microphone. This microphone connects wirelessly with the speech processor and can be used in large rooms, such as lectures halls. This microphone can be placed closer to the speaker or worn by the speaker, such as the teacher at school, and provide clear and sound with less noise for the recipient. In the same category another device allows connection with smart televisions, allowing the cochlear implant recipient to adjust the volume without disturbing the other spectators. Another wireless connection that has be already been mentioned is the wireless remote controller for the speech processor. The remote controller has many functionalities, such as adjusting microphone sensitivity and sound volume. It is possible that in the future this controller will also have smart phone functionalities, such as call handling and internet connectivity. The aforementioned devices connect with the speech processor though a secure, private and robust connection reducing privacy concerns and increasing the ease of use.

Beyond the devices above, there is a growing number of devices that have wireless connection capabilities. Such devices include Bluetooth headsets, smart-phones and tablets, Global Positioning Systems, MP3 players or Stereo Systems, smart televisions, personal computers and laptops. It is therefore possible for the cochlear implant recipient to connect directly with one or more of the above devices. This connectivity can transfer sound directly to the cochlear implant recipient with minimal noise and the best possible quality without other interferences. however the device mentioned above, are just a few examples of everyday devices that already support wireless communication standards. However with the ever-growing notion of the Internet of Things, it is certain that other devices, such as household appliances, will in the future be wirelessly enabled. These devices certainly will allow many new functions to the speech processor and other accessories that have been or are being developed will certainly further extend the number of devices a cochlear implant recipient can connect and interact with, aiding the recipient in everyday life (Figure 5).

Figure 5. Connectivity with 2.4 GHz enabled speech processors

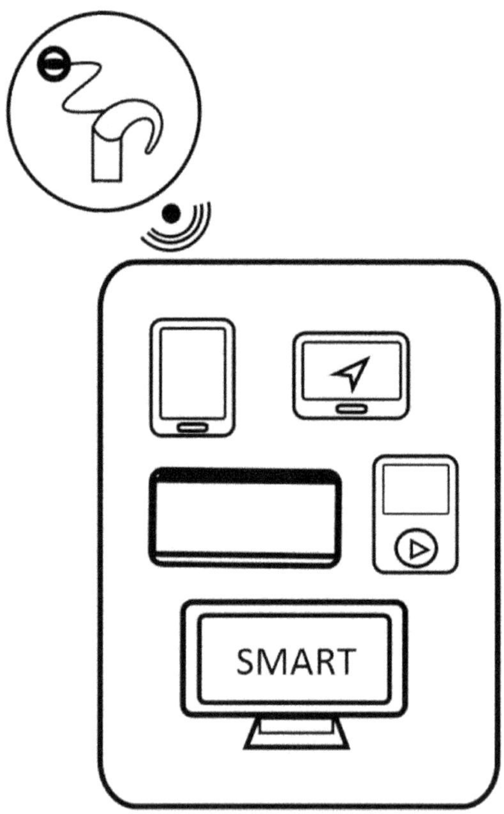

REFERENCES

Alberti, P. (1995). *The anatomy and physiology of the ear and hearing*. University of Toronto Press.

BBC. (2012). *Wi-fi, dual-flush loos and eight more Australian inventions*. Retrieved from http://www.bbc.co.uk/news/magazine-20071644

Beckerexhibits, 19th century. (n.d.). Concealed Hearing Devices of the 19th Century. *Deafness in Disguise.*

Beckerexhibits, 20th century. (n.d.). Concealed Hearing Devices of the 20th Century. *Deafness in Disguise.*

Bluetooth. (2015). *Bluetooth Technology Basics.* Academic Press.

Chouard, C., Mac Leod, P., Meyer, B., & Pialoux, P. (1977). Surgically implanted electronic apparatus for the rehabilitation of total deafness and deaf-mutism[in French]. *Annales d'Oto-Laryngologie et de Chirurgie Cervico Faciale*, *94*, 353–363. PMID:606046

Chouard, C., Meyer, B., Fugain, C., & Koca, O. (1995). Clinical results for the DIGISONIC multichannel cochlear implant. *The Laryngoscope*, *105*(5), 505–509. doi:10.1288/00005537-199505000-00011 PMID:7760667

Cochlear. (2015). *True wireless freedom.* Academic Press.

Cochlear Nucleus. (2015). *The breakthroughs continue with the Nucleus® 6 System.* Retrieved from http://www.cochlear.com/wps/wcm/connect/us/home/treatment-options-for-hearing-loss/cochlear-implants/nucleus-6-features

Djourno, A., & Eyries, C. (1957). Auditory prosthesis by means of a distant electrical stimulation of the sensory nerve with the use of an indwelt coiling. *La Presse Medicale*, *65*(63), 1417. PMID:13484817

Eshraghi, A., Nazarian, R., Telischi, F., Rajguru, S., Truy, E., & Gupta, C. (2012). The cochlear implant: Historical aspects and future prospects. *The Anatomical Record*, *295*(11), 1967–1980. doi:10.1002/ar.22580 PMID:23044644

Fast-Facts. (2015). *Bluetooth Fact or Fiction*. Author.

Hochmair, E., Hochmair-Desoyer, I., & Burian, K. (1979). Investigations towards an artificial cochlea. *The International Journal of Artificial Organs*, *2*(5), 255–261. PMID:582589

Hochmair, I. (2013). "The importance of being flexible" (PDF), Laske Foundation. *Nature Medicine, 19*(10), 1–6. PMID:24100995

Howard, A. (1998, November 26). Hearing Aids: Smaller and Smarter. *New York Times.*

Kyriafinis, G. (2005). *Cochlear implantation.* Thessaloniki, Greece: Publish City. (in Greek)

Levitt, H. (2007). Digital hearing aids: Wheelbarrows to ear inserts. *ASHA Leader, 12*(17), 28–30.

Mac Leold, P., Pialoux, P., Chouard, C., & Meyer, B. (1975). Physiological assessment of the rehabilitation of total deafness by the implantation of multiple intracochlear electrodes. *Annales d'Oto-Laryngologie et de Chirurgie Cervico Faciale, 92*(1-2), 17–23. PMID:1217800

Med-El. (2015). *The hearing implant company.* Retrieved from http://www.medel.com/about-Med-el/

Mills, M. (2011). Hearing Aids and the History of Electronics Miniaturization. *IEEE Annals of the History of Computing, 33*(2), 24–44. doi:10.1109/MAHC.2011.43

Padgette, J., Scafone, K., & Chen, L. (2012). *Guide to Bluetooth Security. NIST Special Publication 800-121, Revision 1.* National Institute for Standards and Technology.

PCmagazine Encyclopedia. (n.d.). *Definition of 802.11.* Retrieved from http://www.pcmag.com/encyclopedia/term/37204/802-11

PCmagazine Encyclopedia. (n.d.). *Definition of Wi-Fi.* Retrieved from http://www.pcmag.com/encyclopedia/term/54444/wi-fi

Simmons, F. (1966). Electrical Stimulation of the Auditory Nerve in Man. *Acta Oto-Laryngologica, 84*(1), 2–54. PMID:5936537

Wi-Fi Alliance Org. (2015). *Discover Wi-Fi Security.* Retrieved from http://www.wi-fi.org/discover-wi-fi/security

Section 2
Audiovisual Tools for Rich Multimedia Interaction

Chapter 5
Music in Colors

Dimitrios Margounakis
Aristotle University of Thessaloniki, Greece

Dionysios Politis
Aristotle University of Thessaloniki, Greece

Konstantinos Mokos
Aristotle University of Thessaloniki, Greece

ABSTRACT

The evolutional course of music through centuries has shown an incremental use of chromatic variations by composers and performers for melodies' and music sounds' enrichment. This chapter presents an integrated model, which contributes to the calculation of musical chromaticism. The model takes into account both horizontal (melody) and vertical chromaticism (harmony). The proposed qualitative and quantitative measures deal with music attributes that relate to the audience's chromatic perception. They namely are: the musical scale, the melodic progress, the chromatic intervals, the rapidity of melody, the direction of melody, music loudness, and harmonic relations. This theoretical framework can lead to semantic music visualizations that reveal music parts of emotional tension.

DOI: 10.4018/978-1-5225-0264-7.ch005

INTRODUCTION

This chapter presents the concept of *chromaticism* in music, which is analyzed based on different interpretations. According to its semantic definition that covers the aspects of chromaticism in a multicultural level, a theoretical framework, upon which methods for chromatic musical analysis can be structured, is presented.

The concept of *chromaticism* in music, which is a high-level cognitive concept, has been extensively investigated (Barsky, 1996) and redefined many times through the centuries. Taking into account only the simplified Western standards, chromaticism is at the moment poorly defined, as Western music theory omits crucial chromatic elements. According to the *New Grove Dictionary of Music and Musicians* (2004), chromaticism in music generally refers to notes marked with accidentals foreign to the scale on which the piece is written on.

In this research, the concept is extended through microtonal fluctuations (typical to "non- Western" musical sounds) into measurable quantities that can be applied across the spectrum of world music. The modeling of microtonal deviations led to an algebraic metric that allows among others: the identification of chromatic elements in music melody, the comparison between scales of various genres, the comparison of different kinds of music and the application of music information retrieval (MIR) functions (searching, sorting, finding duplicates, etc). The visualization of musical chromaticism allows the musicologist to explore chromatic variations and can even be used as a digital signature for music. This implementation reveals the "hidden" musical dimensions of chromaticism, which undoubtedly influences the listener's perception.

This research extends into MELIRIS, a musical imaging tool that analyzes audio files and visualizes the chromaticism of music. The tool implements specially designed algorithms to perform chromatic indexing of music, by assigning chromatic description to psychoacoustic phenomena. The generated chromatic description can be used for classification, identification, making queries based on emotion and characterization of the style of an artist. The latest version of MELIRIS is a stand-alone media player for Windows operating systems only, which allows the user to store the chromatic results of any analyzed audio file in a local database. This database can further be used for Music Information Retrieval (MIR) to perform comparison, pattern recognition, melodic sequence prediction, and color-based searching.

THE QUALITATIVE NATURE OF CHROMATICISM

An important attribute of a musical composition is its *chromaticism*, defined first in Ancient Greek Music (West, 1994). According to that musical system, there were three genuses: the "diatonic", the "chromatic", and the "enharmonic". From these concepts, the separation in "chromatic", "harmonic", "melodic" and "diatonic" entities has evolved for the Western music paradigm. Furthermore, additional musical phenomena have been detected in Oriental music, in Byzantine music and in prosodic vocal phenomena, which cannot be exactly categorized with these predicates for tonal distributions (Politis et. al., 2002).

Whereas the term *chroma* is widely used, especially in comparative musicology, there is not yet a clear definition for "musical chroma". That is the reason why music chromaticism is yet an open research problem (both practical and theoretical). There is a great deal of many considerations and approaches from many different points of view. For instance, in the expression "European chroma, Oriental or Greek chroma" the differentiation is associated with cultures, uses of sounds and feelings. Shepard (1999) has defined with chroma the note's position within the octave and has created a nonlogarithmic pitch helix, the *chroma circle* that clearly depicts octave equivalence. This has led to rather complex pitch-space representations in which the chromatic tone scale, the circle of fifths, octave circularity and other properties are all accounted for. This approach perceives chroma as extension to the concept of tonality. It has been argued that the dimension of tone chroma is irrelevant in melodic perception (Idson & Massaro, 1978).

From antiquity the term "*chromatic*" was used to determine the coordinates of diversification in terms of psychoacoustic perception of music, and it yielded relatively recently the chromatic scale as a fine-tuning aberration of Western music to acoustic polymorphism. Barsky (1996) states that the translation of the Greek term diatonic is "running through tones" (the whole tones). This definition is closer to the etymology of the word, and also implies indirectly that the term chromatic deals with intervals different from whole tones (since "diatonic" and "chromatic" are often treated as mutually exclusive opposites, concerning common practice music).

"Chromaticism in music is the use of notes foreign to the mode or diatonic scale upon which a composition is based. Chromaticism is applied in order to intensify or color the melodic line or harmonic texture" (Barsky, 1996; Jacobs,

1980). Chromatic elements are considered to be "elaborations of or substitutions for diatonic scale members" (Brown, 1986). According to Meyer (1956): "Chromaticism is almost by definition an alteration of, an interpolation in or deviation from this basic diatonic organization" [1]

Musical instruments, like the classical piano, can execute a particular melody with limited (little) chromaticim. This extracts from the fact that the piano can only produce discrete pitches of sound (12 pitches per octave), so the chromaticism produced by the piano is specified only in terms of unrelated to the specific scale notes. Consequently, in this case the concept of chroma coincides with the terminology of Western music. What happens, however, in the case of the violin or the great "instrument" of human voice? Things here are much more complicated, since the violin or human voice can produce continuous sound frequencies without limitations. Moreover, the intervals between notes can be of any distance, not just multiples of the half-tone, as with the piano. These special intervals affect the chromaticism of music (Figure 1).

Figure 1. The musical human computer interface of chromaticism in staff notation, in haptics, and its fundamental frequency perception

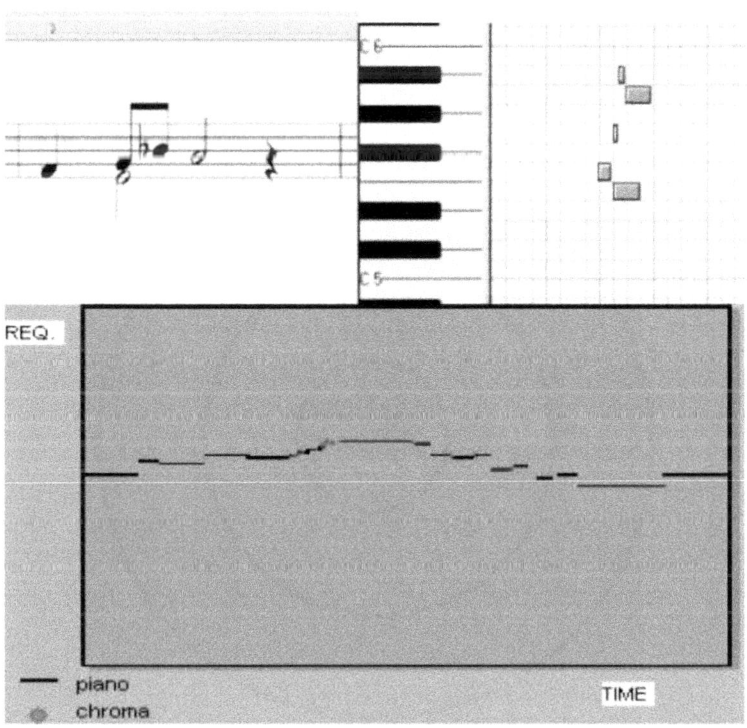

Our research focuses on musical hearings from all around the world and therefore the western approach of chromaticism is not sufficient. Non-western music recordings (e.g. oriental or Byzantine) define different modes and sounds. Therefore, a general definition of "musical chromaticism" is needed: As "chromatic" is defined any sound with pitch irrelevant to the discrete pitches of the scale. In proportion to the distance of the interval, that this sound creates with its "neighbors" (previous and next sound), it can be estimated, how much chromatic this sound is.

An additional issue is that the characterization of music as chromatics or not is also affected by its correlation with psychoacoustic phenomena, e.g. a particular artist may "color" a song with his voice, while another may not (Sundberg, 1999). While listening to a melody, it can be intuitively assumed that the more chromatic it is, the more emotional tension it causes to the listener. This hypothesis has been examined in (Margounakis & Politis, 2012).

Based on the previous discussion, we can distinguish three levels of music presentation, with each of them adding quality of chromaticism to the previous level:

1. The transcription (notation staff),
2. The recording (processed audio with digital media) and
3. The audio-visual live performance (recorded or not) (Figure 2).

Figure 2. Levels of Music Presentation. The outer circles embed more chromaticism compared to the inner circles.

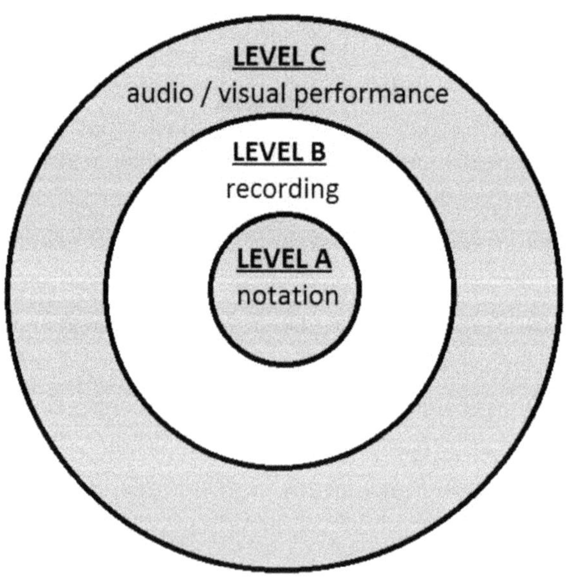

The chromaticism of level A coincides with the Western definition. However, in level B, more chromaticism is added in relation to level A, depending on singer's voice, instruments' deviations and extra phenomena. Finally, in level C, all players (singers, instrument players, conductor etc.) use emotional techniques (pitch deviations, embellishments, even improvisation). The result is an even more chromatic performance than level B, and (usually) an absolutely different auditory performance from level A.

For chromatic determination there is need to clarify:

- The musical elements that turn a musical piece "chromatic" during performance
- The way a computer music transcription may reveal these elements
- The factors that categorize a musical piece according to its chroma

The current chapter explores the aforementioned factors and limitations, in order to produce quantitative measures of music chromaticism and develop a software tool that calculates and visualizes the chromaticism of melodic lines. The developed tool (MEL-IRIS) uses specially designed algorithms for musical data analysis and is presented in the second part of this chapter.

Chromaticism in music has been studied by several researchers (Perttu, 2007; Katsanevaki, 2011). In the case of Perttu a simplified model for counting the notes that do not belong in the scale music pieces of Western classical composers have been written has been used. Perttu's research is limited in only notation staff of classical Western composers.

AN INTEGRATED MUSIC CHROMATICISM MODEL

The study of several aspects of chromaticism in music resulted in the modeling of a theoretical framework that calculates the factors of music chromaticism by the authors. The model, which is shown in Figure 3, covers the attributes that affect the chromaticism in the melodic and harmonic structure of a musical piece, without taking into account the music dimension of timbre.

As Figure 3 demonstrates, the scale, in which a musical piece is written to, comprises the first benchmark in analyzing the chromatic nature of musical pitch (Tenkanen, 2008). Moreover, the calculation of horizontal and vertical chromatic relations prerequisites the knowledge of the music piece's scale. Each scale (or mode) bears a Scale Index (SI), which determines the inherent chromaticism of the scale according to its intervallic structure. For example, a music piece in Hijaz / Rast (SI = 2.096) is naturally more chromatic than one written in C-Major

Figure 3. The factors that affect music chromaticism in a framework

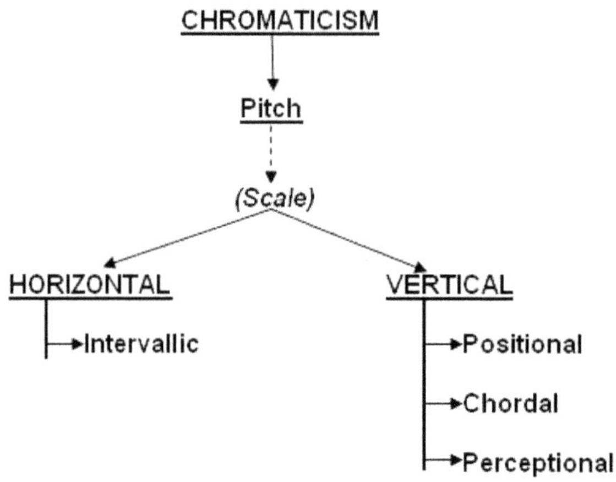

(SI = 1.286). More about the chromaticism of musical scales and the calculation of SI can be found in (Politis & Margounakis, 2003). In the case where a mode is deployed in more than one scales, then, the exact scale is detected, and a Scale Base Indicator (SBI) is calculated. Aspects of horizontal and vertical chromaticism will be discussed throughout this chapter, since calculations can be directly applied to music notation.

Horizontal (Intervallic) Chromaticism

An extended study on chromaticism of intervallic nature has been presented in the past. The interested reader is prompted to refer to (Politis & Margounakis, 2003; Politis & Margounakis, 2010; Margounakis et. al., 2009) for a comprehensive description. Intervallic chromaticism is expressed by a running variable χ_i. In general, the value of χ is greater at times when music produces greater chromatic phenomena of intervallic nature. Figure 4 demonstrates an example graph of χ over time.

Vertical Chromaticism

Most of the time, chromatic pitches change the harmony of a given musical passage. Chromatic harmony means harmony (chords), which uses notes that do not belong to the key the music is in (they are not in the key signature).

In tonal music, most chromatic harmony falls into one of the following categories:

Figure 4. An exemplar graph of χ over time for an analyzed musical file

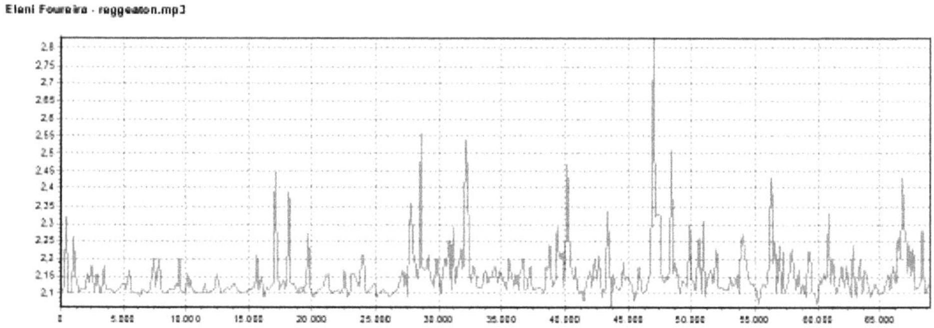

- Secondary Dominants
- Borrowed Chords (Mode Mixture)
- The Neapolitan Sixth Chord
- Augmented Sixth Chords
- Altered Dominants
- Linear Harmony

Concerning chromatic harmony, things are more complicated since chromaticism depends on inflected chords (regarding the music scale, see Figure 5). A value of chromaticism for each chord should be separately calculated in order to achieve chromatic evaluation. A rather simple way to calculate χ_h (harmonic chroma) would be the ratio of the altered notes in the chords of a segment to the total amount of the segment's notes (Equation 1). Another, still simple but more accurate, way would be the ratio of the altered chords in a segment to the total amount of the segment's chords (Equation 2). In both cases, notes that belong to the melodic line are not taken into account. These simple approaches can reveal some preliminary clues about the chromatic harmony of a musical piece.

$$\chi_{h1} = \frac{\# n_{alt}}{\# n_{tot}} \tag{1}$$

$$\chi_{h2} = \frac{\# c_{alt}}{\# c_{tot}} \tag{2}$$

Figure 5. A chromatic passage (m. 130-138) from Tchaikovsky's "The Waltz of the Flowers" (from The Nutcracker). Chromatic phenomena occur both in melodic and chordal level.

Figure 6 presents the meters 5-7 from Tchaikovsky's "The Waltz of the Flowers" (from The *Nutcrucker*). This segment contains no melodic intervallic chromaticism as it is obvious from the melodic line. However, the flattened B in meter 6 creates chromaticism in the chordal level. Equations (1) and (2) for this segment result in 0.1 and 0.22 respectively. By listening to the segment, one could possibly feel that the emotional tension of the chromatic phenomenon affects more than 10% of the segment implied in the first equation. Thus, the chord approach is considered to be more accurate.

However, if we try to read into the actual chromaticism that a single altered note of a chord creates, then we realize that four coexistent auditory relations should be examined. Three of them are actually written in the music notation, while the fourth one is subconscious and is perceived by the listener's music cognition.

Figure 6. Meters 5-7 from Tchaikovsky's "The Waltz of the Flowers" from "The Nutcracker"

The arrows in Figure 7 denote the four aforementioned relations, which will be then discussed using the terms of the model in Figure 1. In this example, only monophonic melodic progression and harmonic triads are used in order for the discussion to be more comprehensible. The music phrase of Figure 7 is considered to belong in a music piece written in C major.

- **Positional Chromaticism:** As it can be seen in Figure 7, the first two relations under consideration concern the intervals that are created by the altered note of the chord and the corresponding notes of its adjacent chords. Relations 1 and 2 are horizontal. Consequently, the same chromatic index χ, which is used for calculating the chromaticism of the melodic line, can be used as a metric of positional chromaticism.
- **Chordal Chromaticism:** The third relation pertains to the association between the melodic note and the accompanying chord. Two cases can be distinguished here:
  a. Both the chord and the melodic note belong to the scale of the musical piece and, therefore, comprise a non-chromatic tetrad, and
  b. The melodic note is chromatic in regard of the accompanying triad.

  In case (a) no more harmonic chroma is added, and the value of chromaticism is zero.

  In case (b), where the accompanying triad is non-chromatic, chromaticism is caused only because of the melodic note. This note, however, affects already the index of intervallic chromaticism (see section 2.1) at the horizontal level

Figure 7. Vertical chromatic relations

of the melody. Therefore, the greatest chromatic weight in this case is accredited in melodic indices. At the chordal level, an extra chromatic value is added, which is equal to the difference of semitones between the chromatic note and the corresponding non-chromatic note of the accompanying chord (considered to be in the same octave).

There are two more cases of chromaticism in a chord:

c. Some note of the accompanying chord is chromatic in regard of the triad that is created by the melodic note and the other two notes of the accompanying triad, and

d. Two or more notes out of the complete tetrad are chromatic.

Both of these cases fall into the category of perceptual chromaticism, which is explained below.

- **Perceptual Chromaticism:** Finally, the fourth relation is associated with musical expectancy and is very important since it affects emotional responses. The benchmark for the comparison in this case is not written in the music score. It is rather "stored" in the mind of the listener. Perceptual chromaticism is measured in semitones of difference between the chromatic chord and the chord that the listener would rather expect (a non-chromatic chord comprised with notes of the scale). In the example of Figure 6, the expected chord (IV) is shown under the bass stave. Its perceptual chromaticism is $\chi_p = 1$. It should be noted here that the closest non-chromatic chord containing the rest of the chord notes (except for the altered one) is considered as the expected one. In our example, where both II and IV are suitable, the choice of the IV chord is stronger since it belongs to the basic harmonic pattern (I-IV-V).

If two or more notes of the chord are chromatic, then the calculated perceptual chromaticism should be greater. Therefore, the equation for measuring perceptual chromaticism (χ_p) of a chord is:

$$\chi_p = \#ch\_notes \cdot \sum_{i=1}^{i=\#ch\_notes} D_i f_i \qquad (3)$$

where #ch_notes is the total amount of chromatic notes in the chord and $D_i f_i$ is the semitones' difference between the chromatic note and its counterpart in the expected non-chromatic chord

Example of chords, which are built on the degrees of the scale and are used in rock and popular music, are the augmented sixth chord and the Neapolitan chord (Perttu, 2007). These chords are presented in Figure 8. According to Equation (3), both of them bear a chromatic perceptual index χ_p equal to 4.

Figure 8. An Italian sixth is moving to V at the first meter, while a Neapolitan resolves to the V at the second meter

QUANTITATIVE MEASURES OF HORIZONTAL CHROMATIC ANALYSIS

The approach of chromatic analysis, which is used in this research, consists of five stages:

1. Extraction of melodic salient pitches (for audio files) or notation for MIDI files,
2. Matching a scale to the music piece,
3. Segmentation,
4. Calculation of the chromatic elements, and
5. Visualization of Chromaticism using colourful strips.

The main methods of the five stages are presented below. The reader can refer to (Margounakis et. al. 2009) for the fundamental concepts and algorithms of chromatic analysis. Also several discussions can be found in (Politis & Margounakis, 2003; Margounakis & Politis, 2006; Politis et. al., 2004).

The extraction of melodic salient pitches from a musical piece is the first step in chromatic analysis. Acquiring this series of values is an easy task when dealing with MIDI files, since the notation can be easily extracted by a text parser. However, in the case of audio files, this stage is a bit more complicated (see Section "Music in colors: A digital tool for the visualization of chromaticism in music performances").

Afterwards, three different algorithms are applied in these two files:

1. The Scale Match algorithm associates the melody with a scale, and thus determines the "Scale Base Indicator" χ^0,

2. The Segmentation algorithm fragments the musical piece and produces the file segments.mel, which determines how many consecutive notes comprise a segment, and
3. The Mini Conv algorithm.

The latter reduces the files conv1.mel and times1.mel, because of the fact that the initial sampling of the FFT is applied on very short intervals (Margounakis et. al., 2009).

It is really necessary to know, in which scale the musical piece being analyzed, is written because its SBI χ^0 is used as a benchmark. The Scale Match algorithm scans the whole sequence of frequencies that resulted from melody extraction and writes down how many times each note has been played on a space of an octave. From the notes, most frequently played, it is fetched which note spaces predominate on the musical piece. Sliding the values of cents 6 times (one interval at a time) it creates 7 possible modes. If one of them matches perfectly with a mode of the "Scale Bank", the melody automatically corresponds to that mode ("Scale Bank" is a database that contains scales and modes, each of which is expressed in terms of its individual attributes). "Scale Bank" contains more than 100 scales, which can be classified in categories like: Western, Oriental, Byzantine etc. The database structure supports the enrichment with more "unusual" scales and modes, like African or Thai scales. If there is not an exact match, the closest mode to the interval sequence is considered. Essentially, the scale that yields the minimum error rate (calculated from the absolute values of the differences between the several combinations of spaces) is chosen.

The first basic factor that characterizes a musical piece either as chromatic or non-chromatic is the scale on which it is written. It is not incidental that major scales in Western mode comprise an expression of happiness, livelihood, strength, and cheerfulness while compositions in minor scales express grief, lamentation, weakness, melancholy, sorrow etc (Margounakis et. al., 2009). Although these associations are not absolutely intrinsic, at this stage of research they are assumed to be true for the sake of computability. This verbal-conceptual approach of music (joint with the observation that feelings like pain and grief are usually stronger and more stressful) leads to the conclusion that minor scales should score higher in our chroma measure than major ones in order to reflect the psychological validity of the metrics. This means that the minor Scale Base Indicator (SBI) is greater than the major one. This can also be noticed from the intervals of minor scales (1½-step, different accidentals while going up and down the scale). In the same manner, the Hijaz scale of Oriental music bears a greater SBI than Western music scales, since it contains 1½ and ¾-steps. A proposed algorithm for the metrics of the chromatic index for a specific scale is the following:

Let a tone correspond to 200 cents, as usual. Therefore, a half-tone corresponds to 100 cents, a quarter-tone to 50 cents etc.

- For each interval *i* in the scale calculate K_i:

$$K_i = 200/c_i \quad c_i \le 200 \tag{4}$$

$$K_i = -0.0002 \cdot c_i^2 + 0.12 \cdot c_i - 15 \quad 200 < c_i \le 400 \tag{5}$$

where ***c*** is the interval cents

- *SBI* is equal to

$$\mathrm{SBI} = \left[\left(\sum_{i=1}^{n} K_i\right) + j\right] \Big/ n \tag{6}$$

where *n* is the number of whole tone steps in the scale (number of notes – 1) and *j* is the amount of the extra accidentals on the scale notation, different from the accidentals at the key signature.

Lemma: If $c \to 0$ then $\chi \to \infty$

Explanation: The smaller the interval, the more chroma is added to a melody. However, a historically accepted threshold of about 30 cents (2 echomoria) is defined as the least interval of two distinguishable tones (Margounakis & Politis, 2006).

Proof: Obvious, if Equation (4) is considered. Figure 9 depicts the chromatic contribution of very small intervals.

As one can observe on Figure 9, the smaller the intervals are, the more chromatic they are [Lemma (7)]. Also, the 2nd order polynomial applied on values 200-400 cents creates a peak in the middle (300 cents). This explains the chromatic nature of 1½ steps, as it was previously mentioned. The non-linear attitude of the polynomial is based on the fact that non-western scales contain intervals that are not exact multipliers of the semitone. For example, the 1½ step of Hijaz

Figure 9. Contribution of intervals (up to two tones) to the "Scale Base Indicator"

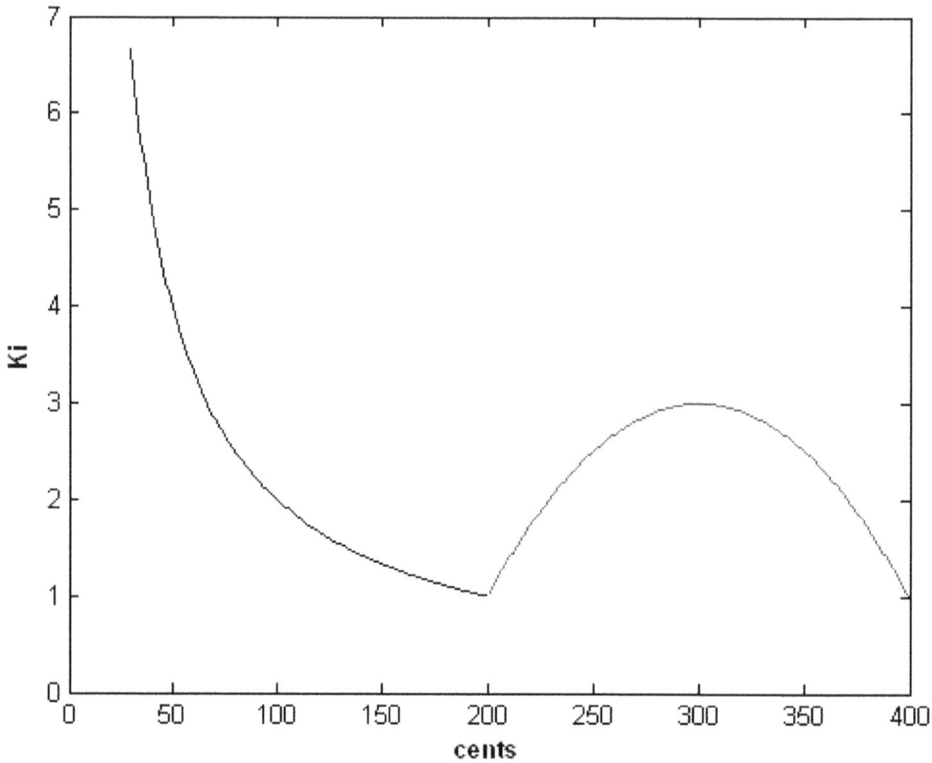

is slightly bigger than 300 cents. The smoothing of the peak on the graph allows such intervals to be measured according to their real chromatic perception. The same also stands for Plagal 2nd of Byzantine Music. The reader is prompted to refer to Politis and Margounakis (2010) for examples of calculating SBI (from worldwide scales: Western, Oriental, Byzantine etc.).

Segmentation of the musical input is done automatically using clues from several proposed algorithms in literature. Also, some possibility rules from Lerdahl and Jackendoff (1983) and some heuristic rules are used. These rules apply some constrains on the way the algorithm splits the melodic sequence of a song into segments. Some rules the segmentation algorithm uses are:

- IF (time >1 sec) AND (NO sound is played) THEN split the segment at exactly the middle of the silence time
- IF a melodic interval is bigger than the previous and the following one, THEN this interval may represent the splitting point.
- Segments that contain less than 10 notes are not allowed, etc.

Figure 10. Colour grades for chromatic analysis

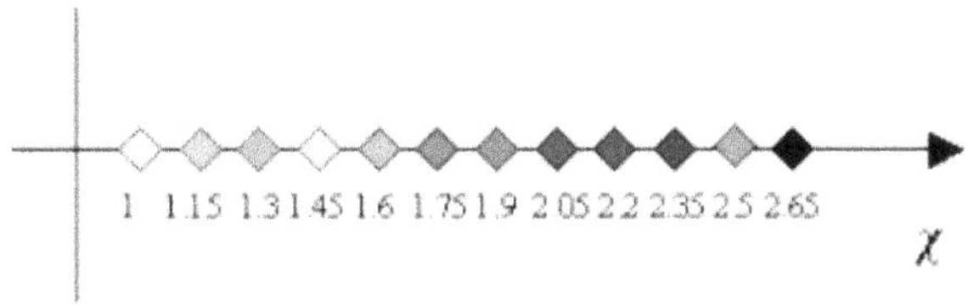

The output of the algorithm is a series of time stamps for defining the segments of the piece. The segments are finally represented in colorful bricks (see Figure 11). For the needs of various composers' analyses, we moved on manually creating larger patterns out of groups of segments, as it will be discussed at the second part of this chapter.

After the segmentation, χ values of the melodic progression are calculated. Table 1 shows 10 basic rules for chroma increment and decrease. These rules are related to the use of notes that do not belong to the chosen scale, and therefore cause the notion of chromaticism.

A discussion of the mathematical modeling of calculating chroma χ for each segment follows. Let a segment contain n musical units[2] $(m_1, m_2, \ldots, m_n)$. Each musical unit is assigned to a chroma value χ_{m_i} (for $i=1,2,\ldots,n$) based on the interval which is created from the previous musical unit (according to the rules of Table 1). The chromatic index of brick j (χ_j) is equal to the musical units' χ_{m_i} $(i=1,2,\ldots,n)$ average it contains:

$$\chi_j = \frac{\sum_{i=1}^{n} \chi_{m_i}}{n} \tag{7}$$

Figure 11. Exemplar chromatic walls

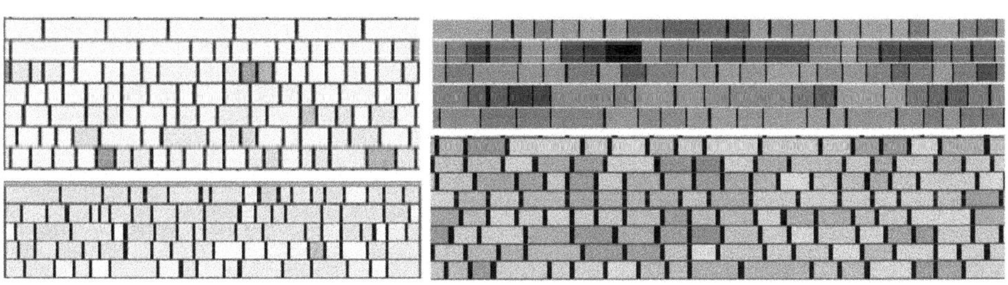

Table 1. Intervallic relation to Chromaticism in music

Rule	Intervals	χ transition	Constraints
1	Chromatic semitones	*1.01	-
2	Chromatic 3/2-tone	*1.03	-
3	Chromatic quarter-tones	*1.04	-
4	Part of chromatic scale (N notes, N≥3)	*(1+0.01*N)	-
5	Chromatic integer multiples of tone	%1.005	-
6	Chromatic tones	%1.01	-
7	Retraction of chroma	%1.01	$\chi \geq \chi^0$
8	Retraction of chroma (3/2-tone)	%1.015	$\chi \geq \chi^0$
9	Same note repetition	% 1.02	
10	Accepted Scale Intervals	-	-

However for each χ_{m_i} *(i=1,2,,...,n)* stands

$$\chi_{m_i} = f(\chi_{m_{i-1}}) \tag{8}$$

and more specifically:

$$\chi_{m_i} = \chi_{m_{i-1}} k_i \tag{9}$$

where

$$K_i = 1 + 0.01 \bullet N_i \ (N_i \in Z^+ - \{2\}) \tag{10a}$$

if it is about the rules 1-4 of Table 1, or

$$k_i = \frac{1}{1 + 0.005 \cdot N_i} (N_i \in \{1,2,3,4\}) \tag{10b}$$

if it is about the rules 5-9.

The sum of χ_{m_i} is equal to:

$$\sum_{i=1}^{n} \chi_{m_i} = \chi_{m_1} + \chi_{m_2} + \chi_{m_2} \cdots + \chi_{m_n} \tag{12}$$

SBI of the selected scale comprises the value, around which the chroma values of music events wrap. Each segment *j* bears the average chroma value χ_j (Equation 7). For visualization purposes, we match each of these values to a specific colour, so as to create the chromatic wall. Therefore, a twelve color-grade has been designed. The order of the colours with their corresponding χ values is: white (1.00) / sky blue (1.15) / green (1.30) / yellow (1.45) / orange (1.60) / red (1.75) / pink (1.90)/ blue (2.05)/ purple (2.20) / brown (2.35) / gray (2.50) / black (2.65). The actual color of each segment is characterized from the combination of the R–G–B variables (Red–Green–Blue). The values of R–G–B for a particular segment are calculated from linear equations. A set of three equations has been designed for each of the intervals between the basic grades. For example, a χ value of 1.96 is assigned to the color with RGB values $\{R= -1700\chi + 3485, G=0, B=255\} \rightarrow \{R=153, G=0, B=255\}$, while a χ value of 1.65 is colored as $\{R=255, G= -850\chi + 1487.5, B=0\} \rightarrow \{R=255, G=85, B=0\}$.

Colors in this scale are ranged beginning from white (=absence of chroma) and ending to black (=greatest chroma). Equations lead χ to correspond to darker colors while ascending. Each color grade differs from the previous one by a χ distance of 0.15. This distance proved to be ideal for identifying significant chromatic differences. These metrics allow the visual observation of significant χ deviations on the piece's chromatic wall. Exemplar parts of chromatic walls are shown in Figure 11. Moreover, these grades serve our previous calculations concerning music scales. The Major SBI (1.286) is located on grades of low chroma, the Minor SBI (1.857) on grades of medium chroma, while some Byzantine and Oriental scales (SBI > 2.1) on grades of high chroma values. The association of relative degrees of emotional state to chroma χ is currently under research. The experimental results are to be published soon.

CHROMATICISM AND MUSIC PERCEPTION

The general conclusion is that the *intervals* and *melodic structure* is indeed critical sentiment factors. The color indicator χ calculates continuous tonal relations in a sequence of tonal heights of melody. Therefore, this metric is certainly related partially to the emotional background of a song (with rhythm and expressiveness). Regarding the terminology of anticipation, color (as defined in this study) shows the "unexpected", since its increase is due to non-diatonic (foreign in scale) notes of the melody in microtonal deviations and cases of tonal instability . Broadly, greater χ means more intense emotional impact (always concerning the melody), which proved to be experimental (Margounakis & Politis, 2012).

An interesting phenomenon, which is related to the issues of musical perception is that in real musical performances there are variations from what is prescribed in music notation (Juslin, 2000). According to the Seashore (1937), these deviations from the exact data (timing, dynamics, timbre and pitch) are the means for conveying emotions. By applying the proposed chromatic analysis on a sound performance, we can "capture" the microtonal variations and deviations. In the light of chromaticism, the musical manipulations of expression are clearly chromatic and reveal the intention of the performer to give emotions to the audience. In contrast, when analyzing an equally-tempered melodic sequence (the case of MIDI files), which unequivocally follows the denominations of notation, the chromatic indicator χ can manifest only chromatically melodic patterns associated only with the intentions of the *composer*.

The color indicator χ and also detects intervals more extensive or more limited range in sound performances, e.g. a compressed third major (more "coordinated") in a string quartet from the related equally-tempered intervals. If such an event is detected individually at some points of a track, it then adds color to the music. If, however, these particular sounds continuously displayed during the track (that is the rule rather than the exception), no color is added, since the spaces created by these sounds have already been calculated in the SI (in our example the distorted vocal sound would have been considered part of the calculated level of the track). At this point should be made clear that the concept of the color indicator χ encompasses:

1. The chromatic impact of the *scale* (SI),
2. The impact of *chromatic interval patterns* (considered chromatically depending on the underlying key / scale), and
3. The impact of *microtonal deviations* created to live musical performances.

The (1) and (2) relate to the impact of particular music tracks, while (3) is related to the impact of specific embodiments.

MEL-IRIS HISTORY

MEL-IRIS tool was developed during our research on chromaticism in music. "MEL-IRIS" derives from the words Melodic Irida. Iris is the name of the goddess Irida, as it is pronounced in the ancient Greek language. Irida is associated with colors, as she is said to be the Greek goddess of the rainbow.

The main task of MELIRIS is to chromatically analyze music files (MIDI, WAV, and MP3). It provides a unique method of classification, identification, and visualization of songs and can be applied in large song databases as well as in web applications. MELIRIS is designed for processing musical pieces from audio servers, creating a unique chromatic index for each of them, and classifying them according to the chromatic index. Each chromatic index results to a colorful strip, which can serve as a signature as well as a classifier for a song. The fundamental background of chromatic analysis has been described previously in this Chapter.

The first version of MEL-IRIS (Politis et. al., 2004) provided an integrated environment for chromatic analysis of MIDI mainly audio files. MEL-IRIS v1.0 was also supporting other kind of audio pieces provided that MATLAB sonogram analyzer was used to process the audio files and separate the melody from them. The extracted melody was then analyzed similarly to the MIDI audio files, where a unique chromatic index was created for each of them and finally they were visualized based on this unique chromatic index. MEL-IRIS v1.0 was mainly developed in Borland C++ Builder and used the Paradox database to store any chromatic information.

The second version of MEL-IRIS (Margounakis & Politis, 2012) is explicitly improved with regard to the previous version. There are improvements both in design and the kernel of the application in terms of musical pieces analysis. Apart from the new algorithms, the old algorithms have been redesigned in order to succeed a more effective and correct approach of chrominance in music. The application's design was lionized in order MELIRIS to turn into an easy-to-use program, without remising its substantial proposal in computer music. A simple user auditor can treat MEL-IRIS as his/her default Media Player, with which he/she can organize and monitor all his/her music collections in an easy and effective way, and also listen to the music while watching this prototypal way of music visualization. On the other hand, the music analyst/composer/researcher can work with MEL-IRIS in his music analyses, since it provides an integrated environment for chromatic analysis and extracts useful statistics from large music collections.

The latest MEL-IRIS version 3.0, presented in the rest of the chapter, comes in two versions: a stand-alone PC version and a network-based version which aimed at the organization and manipulation of large music collections on the Internet.

MEL-IRIS v3.0

Processing

MEL-IRIS v3.0 supports directly the following file formats: .midi, .wav and .mp3. Similarly to previous version stand-alone version AUDIO analysis is only invoked in wave files. Thus if the input to the application is an MP3 file, this will automatically be converted to a .wav file. Then, it will be analyzed as a wave file and finally this intermediate file will be erased from disk.

The diagram in Figure 12 shows analytically the whole chromatic analysis process of a wave file from MEL-IRIS. All the intermediate produced results can be seen in the diagram. The legend shows what each shape stands for. An observation here is that the text files, which are marked as XML, are those that contain analysis data that are finally exported in XML format. All the intermediate files are automatically deleted after the end of the analysis (however their data can be retrieved, since they are stored in the database).

Initially, an FFT (Fast Fourier Transform) is applied on the .wav file. The FFT algorithm is followed by an embedded process for predominant frequencies extraction, so as to arise a table, which (in a satisfactory percentage) contains the fundamental frequencies of the piece's melody. Since pitch is normally defined as the fundamental frequency of a sound, this process executes melody pitch tracking. The resulting values are stored in the files conv1.mel (frequency values) and times1.txt (duration of the frequencies in milliseconds).

In these two files are afterwards 3 different algorithms applied:

1. The Scale Match algorithm that corresponds the melody to a scale and, in extension, determines the "Scale Chroma by Nature" χ^0,

Figure 12. Implementation of Chromatic Analysis in MEL-IRIS

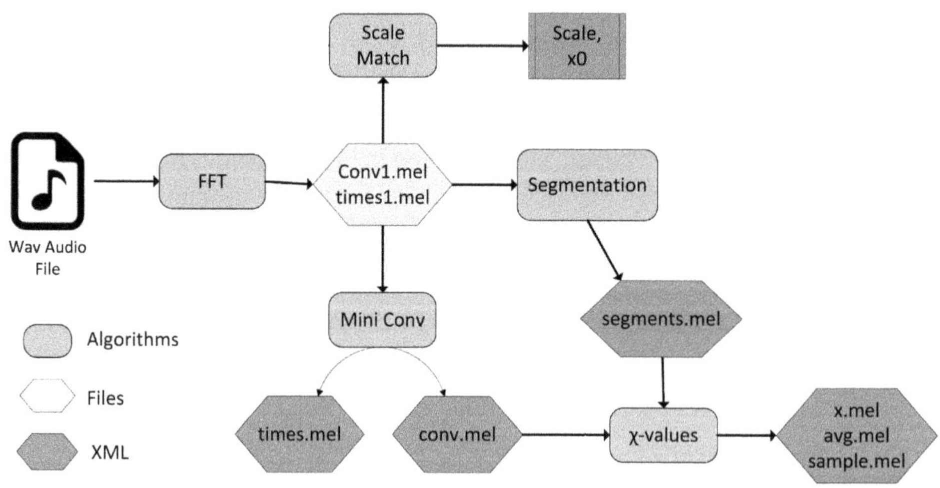

2. The Segmentation algorithm that fragments the musical piece and produces the file segments.mel, which determines how many consecutive notes comprise a segment, and
3. The Mini Conv algorithm.

The latter condenses the files conv1.mel and times1.mel, based on some rules, because of the fact that the initial sampling of the FFT is applied on very short intervals. For example, if we take a sample every 200 milliseconds and the note A4 lasts 2 seconds, the result of the sampling would be ten A4 notes, which is not correct (the default sampling in MEL-IRIS is applied every 20 milliseconds, which is a typical frame length in sound analysis). The algorithm diminishes the melodic sequence by producing two new files: conv.mel and times.mel.

The new conv.mel as well as segments.mel are inputs to the algorithm of chromatic elements mining (a series of rules and controls regarding the chromatic variation), which results in the χ sequence (how the chromatic index is altered during the melodic progression over time) in the file x.txt and the avg.mel, which contains the chromatic average values for each segment. Finally, sample.mel contains the appropriate information, which is needed for the visual chromatic diagrams to be produced on screen.

Database Handler

MEL-IRIS database handler stores all the information about chromatic elements and the songs in the "MELIRIS" database, which is structured on an SQL server. The database handler does all the operations required on the database (e.g. querying, update and addition of data). The use of Borland Database Engine provides support for different database management systems, also supporting different engines, from MySQL to Microsoft SQL Server or Oracle or any other Open Data Base connectivity (ODBC) protocol.

Database diagram is shown in Figure 13, in which the Scale Bank holds a variety of scales and modes taken from Western, Balkan, Arabic, Oriental, Ancient Greek and Byzantine music that each of them has a unique "chroma" value. SongList table holds the list of all analyzed songs and SongsDetail holds the categorization of each song based on the ScaleBank, as well as its chromatic category. Inside SongKaliscope exist the chromatic indices for each segment, that will be visualized in the MELIRIS player.

Figure 13. MELIRIS database diagram

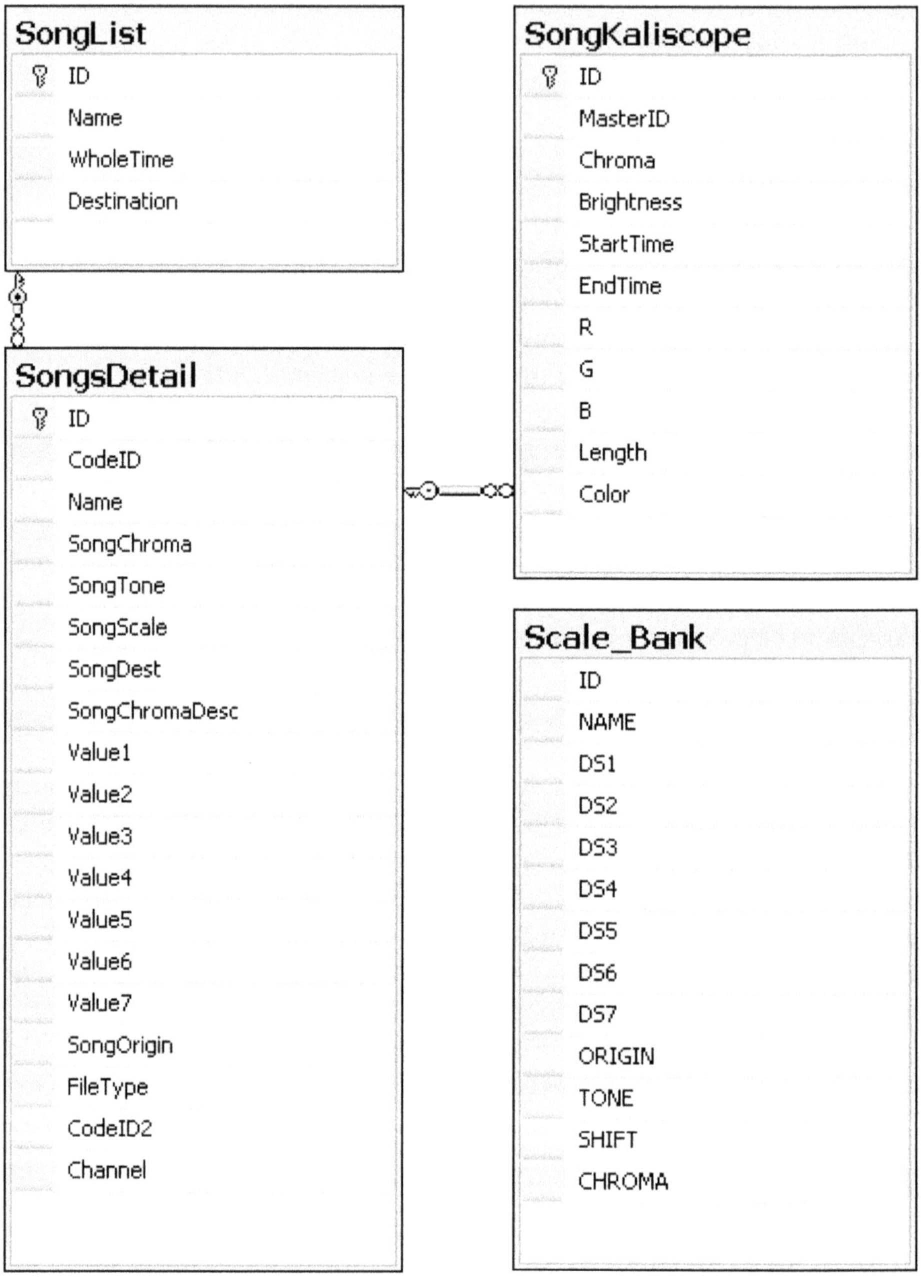

MEL-IRIS Client Application

The client application (MEL-IRIS stand-alone PC version) was developed using Borland C++ Builder 6 platform, and uses Windows Media Player to play any music files. However, analysis is only performed on specific file types: mid, wav, and mp3. It supports both playlist generation, along with more basic features, such as playing a selected song, see its details or checking the chromatic distribution of the songs.

The basic controls of MEL-IRIS are:

1. **Play Functions:** Figure shows the basic operating area. It holds the controls to play, stop, pause, rewind and fast-forward a track, each represented by symbols similar to other media players.
2. **Seeking Bar:** To change position within a song or track that is playing, drag the “seeking bar” right or left (Figure 16).

Figure 14. MELIRIS v3.0 (standalone)

Figure 15. Play functions

Figure 16. Seeking bar

3. **Volume**: The long slider bar above the seeking bar controls volume. This controls the volume output from MEL-IRIS itself (Figure 17).
4. **PL Toggle Button:** Playlist window open and close (Figure 18).

Playlist and dedicated controls are:

1. **Play List:** The playlist allows you to save, edit and arrange groups of audio files, or playlists, by using the dedicated buttons shown in Figure 19.
2. **Reports:** Click and hold "Reports" button. Four options appear:
   a. **Statistics Table 1:** This option reports the statistics of all analyzed songs (Figure 20). Report could be exported to excel.

Figure 17. Volume

Figure 18. PL toggle button

Figure 19. Playlist dedicated buttons

Figure 20. Statistics of all analyzed songs (Statistics Table 1)

MEL-IRIS statistics

Date : 18/6/2015
Time : 11:22:59 μμ

Amount of analysed songs : 1

STATISTICS TABLE

Song No	Name	Scale	Xo	Lower x	high x	dev+	dev-	AVG
1	01. SOLDIER OF FORTUNE.mp3	Todi	1,5	1,46	2,01	0,51	0,04	1,55023830538392

TOTAL X avg : 1,56

b. **Statistics Table 2:** This option reports the chromatic diagram of all songs (Figure 21). Report could be exported to excel.

c. **Statistics Table 3:** This option reports the dominant color of all analyzed songs (Figure 22). Report could be exported to excel.

d. **Other Reports:** This option allows the user to search songs based on song details (Figure 23) or average chromaticism (Figure 24). By clicking on a song MELIRIS will automatically play the selected song.

Figure 21. Chroma diagram of all songs (Statistics Table 2)

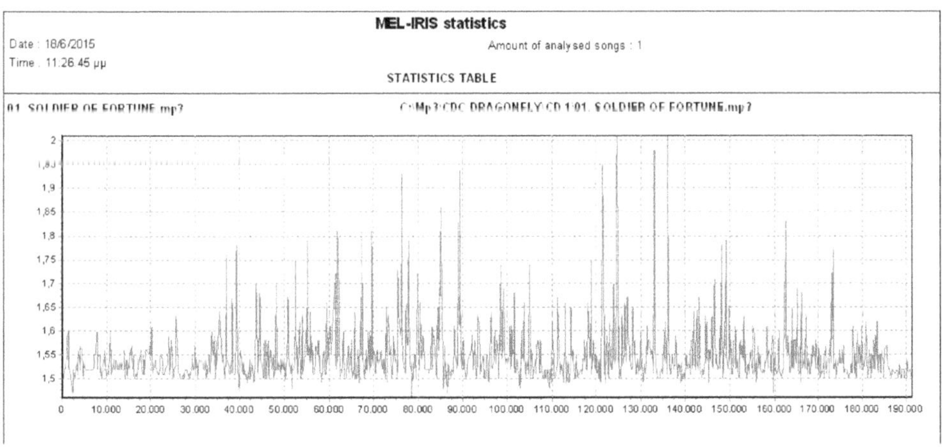

Figure 22. Dominant color (Statistics Table 3)

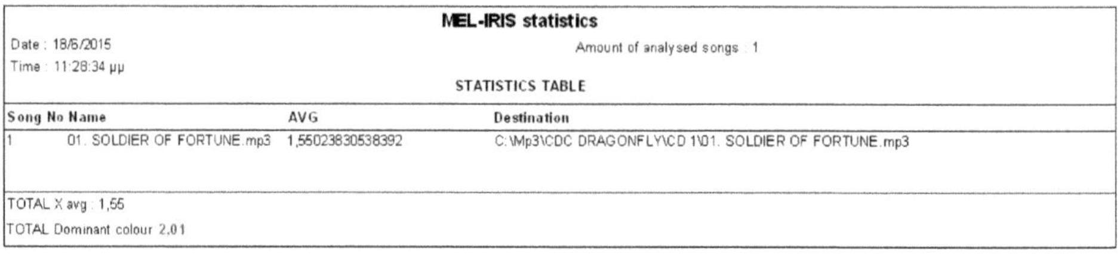

Figure 23. Search songs based on song details (Other Reports)

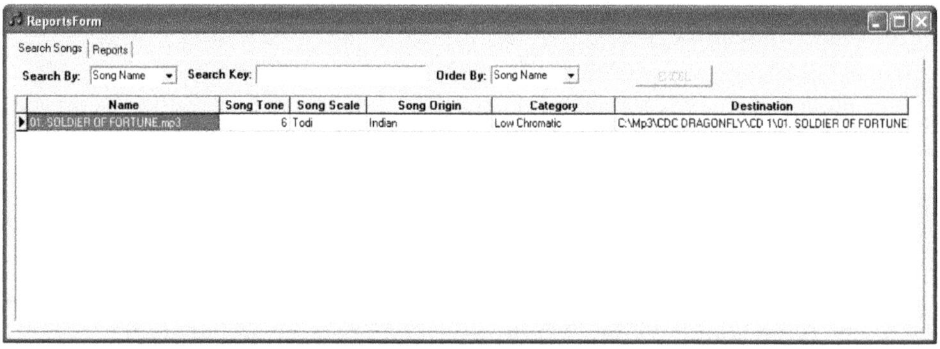

Figure 24. Search songs based on average chromaticism (Other Reports)

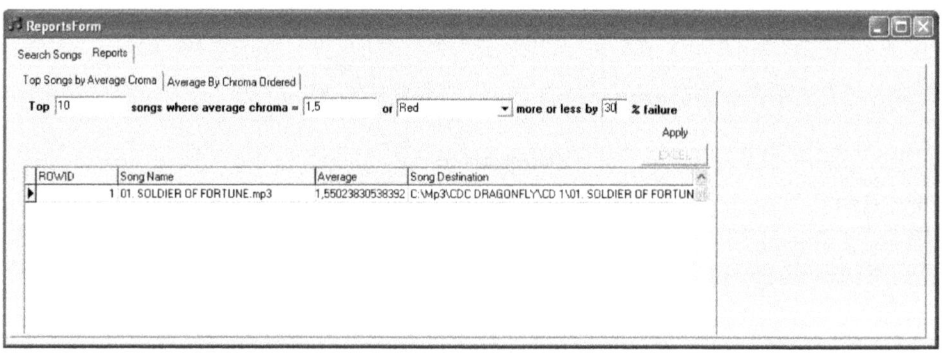

MEL-IRIS Server Application

The function of the server is to receive all the requests from the client and provide the correct responses to that requests. Also, it interacts with the database and processes audio files.

The MEL-IRIS system's architecture is shown in Figure 25. The main mechanism of statistical analysis and storage exists in a central server, to which several client machines are connected. The server contains the main database of the system as well as numerous stored MP3 files (Cs—Server MusicCollection). An easy-to-use graphical interface and a smaller (in terms of capacity) local database (C1—Cn) are installed on each client.

Authorized users may take advance of the several functionalities of MEL-IRIS from the client machines. To begin with, users can listen to the musical pieces that are already stored in the server and/or watch their visualization and examine the results of the chromatic analysis. Clients have access to all the pieces in the music collection of the server. Moreover, they are able to load their own music files either only for listening to (audio player function) or for chromatic analysis. In the second case, the extracted statistics are stored both in the local client database and the central server. This means that if client 1 analyzes the file x.mp3, then client 2 is also able to retrieve the corresponding statistics from his terminal and listen to the piece, since this exists in the server and can be downloaded in his/her personal computer. This is the case where client 1 has uploaded his music for analysis on the server. The gathering of the statistics, which are the result of the analyses of all the clients, aims at a massive data collection for further processing and data mining. These data are accessible from all the users of the system. This means that each user may choose any number of pieces, which have been chromatically analyzed, as a sample for his/her research. Moreover, each user can

Figure 25. MEL IRIS client/server architecture
(from Margounakis et. al., 2009)

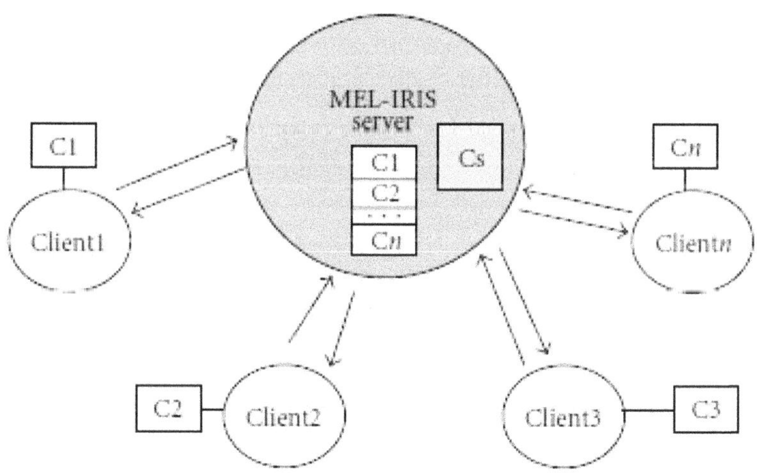

create locally his/her own profile, so as to interfere on the variable attributes of chromatic perception, for example, the colors emotions correspondence and the way of the final results visualization. Finally, each user is able to use the MIR (Music Information Retrieval) functions of the systems, through queries to the database.

EXPERIMENTAL RESULTS

Table 2 shows summarized statistics for each of the 12 genres of the sample. Although some genres contain only a few songs and are therefore not recommended for general conclusions, we can make some observations on the numbers.

Taking into account the genres that contain over 30 songs, we can observe that the most chromatic genre is classical music. In Figure 26, we can see that there is a great variety of chromaticism in the classical songs of the sample.

In contrast, the hip hop genre (the less chromatic from the considered genres) shows no such variation with the most of the tested songs belonging to an orange tint of about $\chi = 1.6$. This is normal, because hip-hop music is more rhythmic and less (or not at all) melodic and creates static little chromatic impression to the audient. Figure 11 also shows the songs distribution of ecclesiastical chants, which

Table 2. Summarized statistics for a song collection (sample)

Genre	Number of songs	Ch. Avg
Classic	75	2,413
Dance	7	1,888
Hip Hop	44	1,890
Metal	13	1,856
Pop	51	2,127
Rock	15	1,869
Greek Old Classics	15	2,517
Greek Traditional	4	2,232
Rebetico	53	2,085
Instrumental	50	2,083
Ecclesiastical	47	2,196
Ethnic	33	2,061
TOTAL	407	2,2

Figure 26. Songs distribution from the chromatic analysis

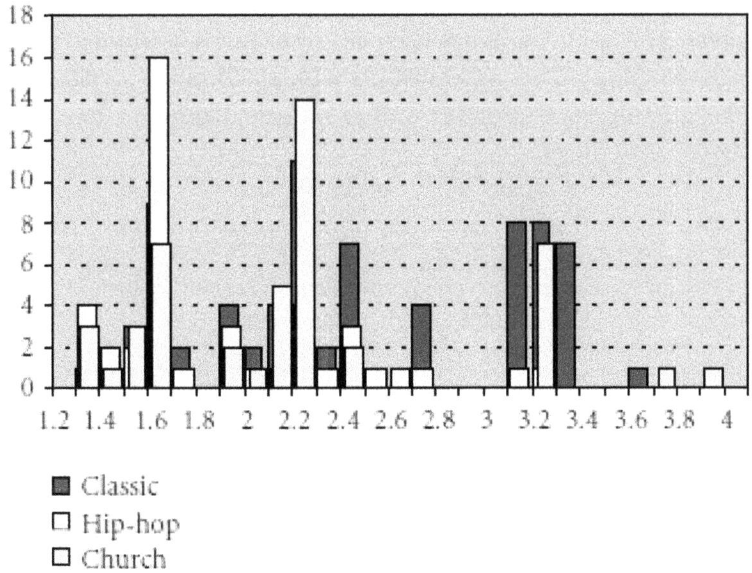

is a very chromatic genre. We can note here that it was the only genre, where chromatic averages greater than 3.5 appeared (with an exception of a 3.7 occurrence in classical music).

CONCLUSION

An integrated model that takes into account all the factors, which create emotional tension because of musical chromaticism, has been presented. Both qualitative and quantitative measures of chromaticism in music have been explained throughout the chapter. The applied metrics on musical pieces can result to useful data for representing musical chromaticism in semantic visualizations. Calculating musical chromaticism can be a tool for in-depth music analysis.

MEL-IRIS, which has been presented in this chapter, is a digital tool for the visualization of chromaticism in music performances. The tool can be used for classification, identification, making queries based on emotion, characterization of the style of an artist, or as a simple media player for the average user. The analyzed data can be used for Music Information Retrieval (MIR) to perform comparison, pattern recognition, melodic sequence prediction, and color-based searching.

Together with the stand-alone version of MEL-IRIS, a network-oriented client-server edition has been developed and this specific architecture has been presented in this chapter. The application has been designed in C++ Builder and uses MS-SQL server technology. The system works with all common sound files as input and outputs color representations as well as statistical numeric data, useful to the community of musicology.

REFERENCES

Barsky, V. (1996). *Chromaticism*. Harwood Academic Publishers.

Brown, M., & Schenker, . (1986). The Diatonic and the Chromatic in Shenker's theory of harmonic relations. *Journal of Music Therapy*, *30*(1), 1–33. doi:10.2307/843407

Idson, W. L., & Massaro, D. W. (1978). A bidimensional model of pitch in the recognition of melodies. *Perception & Psychophysics*, *24*(6), 551–565. doi:10.3758/BF03198783 PMID:751000

Jacobs, A. (1980). *The new Penguin dictionary of music*. Penguin.

Juslin, P. (2000). Cue utilization in communication of emotion in music performance: Relating performance to perception. *Journal of Experimental Psychology. Human Perception and Performance*, *26*(6), 1797–1813. doi:10.1037/0096-1523.26.6.1797 PMID:11129375

Katsanevaki, A. (2011). Chromaticism – A theoretical construction or a practical transformation? *Muzikologija*, *11*(11), 159–180. doi:10.2298/MUZ1111159K

Lerdahl, F., & Jackendoff, R. (1983). *A generative Theory of Tonal Music*. Cambridge, MA: MIT Press.

Margounakis, D., & Politis, D. (2006). Converting images to music using their colour properties. In *Proceedings of the 12th International Conference on Auditory Display* (ICAD2006).

Margounakis, D., & Politis, D. (2012). Exploring the Relations between Chromaticism, Familiarity, Scales and Emotional Responses in Music. In *Proceedings of the XIX CIM Music Informatics Symposium* (CIM 2012). Trieste: Conservatory of Music "Giuseppe Tartini".

Margounakis, D., Politis, D., & Mokos, K. (2009). MEL-IRIS: An Online Tool for Audio Analysis and Music Indexing. International Journal of Digital Media Broadcasting. doi:10.1155/2009/806750

Meyer, L. (1956). *Emotion and Meaning in Music*. Chicago: University of Chicago Press.

Perttu, D. (2007). A quantitative study of chromaticism: Changes observed in historical eras and individual composers. *Empirical Musicology Review*, *2*(2), 47–54.

Politis, D., Linardis, P., & Mastorakis, N. (2002). The arity of Delta prosodic and musical interfaces: A metric of complexity for "vector" sounds. In *Proceedings of the 2nd International Conference on Music and Artificial Intelligence* (ICMAI2002).

Politis, D., & Margounakis, D. (2003). Determining the Chromatic Index of music. In *Proceedings of the 3rd International Conference on Web Delivering of Music* (WEDELMUSIC '03).

Politis, D., & Margounakis, D. (2010). Modeling musical Chromaticism: The algebra of cross-cultural music perception. *International Journal of Academic Research*, *2*(6), 20–29.

Politis, D., Margounakis, D., & Mokos, K. (2004). Visualizing the Chromatic Index of music. In *Proceedings of the 4th International Conference on Web Delivering of Music* (WEDELMUSIC '04).

Sadie, S., & Tyrell, J. (Eds.). (2004). *New Grove Dictionary of Music and Musicians*. Grove.

Seashore, H. (1937). An objective analysis of artistic singing. In University of Iowa Studies in the Psychology of Music: Objective Analysis of Musical Performance (vol. 4). University of Iowa.

Shepard, R. (1999). Pitch, perception and measurement. In P. Cook (Ed.), *Music, Cognition and Computerized Sound*. Cambridge, MA: MIT Press.

Sundberg, J. (1999). The perception of singing. In D. Deutch (Ed.), *The Psychology of Music* (2nd ed.). London: Academic Press. doi:10.1016/B978-012213564-4/50007-X

Tenkanen, A. (2008). *Measuring tonal articulations in compositions*. MaMuX Computational Analysis Special Session, Paris, France.

West, M. L. (1994). *Ancient Greek Music*. Oxford, UK: Clarendon Press.

KEY TERMS AND DEFINITIONS

Chomaticism: A compositional technique interspersing the primary diatonic pitches and chords with other pitches of the chromatic scale (in Western music terminology). Chromaticism is in contrast or addition to tonality or diatonicism (the major and minor scales). Diatonic music uses only the notes available within the scale, and chromaticism uses notes outside of the members of a key's scale. The stem of the word, Chromaticism, comes from Greek and it means intensity or shade of colors.

Client-Server Model: A distributed application structure that partitions tasks or workloads between the providers of a resource or service, called servers, and service requesters, called clients.

Microtonal Music: Music using tones in intervals that differ from the standard semitones (half steps) of a tuning system or scale.

Music Information Retrieval (MIR): The interdisciplinary science of retrieving information from music. MIR is a growing field of research with many real-world applications. MIR uses knowledge from areas as diverse as signal processing, machine learning, information and music theory.

Music Perception: The research area of perceptual and cognitive aspects of the psychology of music, with special emphasis on underlying neuronal and neurocomputational representations and mechanisms. Basic perceptual dimensions of hearing (pitch, timbre, consonance/roughness, loudness, auditory grouping) form salient qualities, contrasts, patterns and streams that are used in music to convey melody, harmony, rhythm and separate voices. Perceptual, cognitive, and neurophysiological aspects of the temporal dimension of music (rhythm, timing, duration, temporal expectation) are also explored by music perception.

Pitch: A perceptual property of sounds that allows their ordering on a frequency-related scale, more commonly, pitch is the quality that makes it possible to judge sounds as "higher" and "lower" in the sense associated with musical melodies.

ENDNOTES

1. These definitions accept the major and minor scales as the diatonic scales, although this is not generally acceptable by all authors.
2. The term "musical units" is used instead of "notes", because certain rules apply to more than a note.

Chapter 6
Natural Human-Computer Interaction with Musical Instruments

George Tzanetakis
University of Victoria, Canada

ABSTRACT

The playing of a musical instrument is one of the most skilled and complex interactions between a human and an artifact. Professional musicians spend a significant part of their lives initially learning their instruments and then perfecting their skills. The production, distribution and consumption of music has been profoundly transformed by digital technology. Today music is recorded and mixed using computers, distributed through online stores and streaming services, and heard on smartphones and portable music players. Computers have also been used to synthesize new sounds, generate music, and even create sound acoustically in the field of music robotics. Despite all these advances the way musicians interact with computers has remained relatively unchanged in the last 20-30 years. Most interaction with computers in the context of music making still occurs either using the standard mouse/keyboard/screen interaction that everyone is familiar with, or using special digital musical instruments and controllers such as keyboards, synthesizers and drum machines. The string, woodwind, and brass families of instruments do not have widely available digital counterparts and in the few cases that they do the digital version is nowhere as expressive as the acoustic one. It is possible to retrofit and augment existing acoustic instruments with digital sensors in order to create what are termed hyper-instruments. These hyper-instruments allow musicians to interact naturally with their instrument as they are accustomed to, while at the same time transmit-

DOI: 10.4018/978-1-5225-0264-7.ch006

ting information about what they are playing to computing systems. This approach requires significant alterations to the acoustic instrument which is something many musicians are hesitant to do. In addition, hyper-instruments are typically one of a kind research prototypes making their wider adoption practically impossible. In the past few years researchers have started exploring the use of non-invasive and minimally invasive sensing technologies that address these two limitations by allowing acoustic instruments to be used without any modifications directly as digital controllers. This enables natural human-computer interaction with all the rich and delicate control of acoustic instruments, while retaining the wide array of possibilities that digital technology can provide. In this chapter, an overview of these efforts will be provided followed by some more detailed case studies from research that has been conducted by the author's group. This natural interaction blurs the boundaries between the virtual and physical world which is something that will increasingly happen in other aspects of human-computer interaction in addition to music. It also opens up new possibilities for computer-assisted music tutoring, cyber-physical ensembles, and assistive music technologies.

INTRODUCTION

Music today is produced, distributed and consumed using digital computer technology in each of these stages. In a typical scenario the process starts with musicians recording individual tracks using their respective instruments at a recording studio. These tracks are stored as digital waveforms which are then mixed and processed using digital audio workstation (DAW) software by one or more recording engineers. The resulting music track is then digitally distributed typically through either streaming services like Spotify and Pandora or online music stores like the Apple iStore or Google Play. Finally music listeners hear the music typically using their computers or smart phones. Despite these amazing advances in technology that have made practically all music accessible to anyone with an internet connection, the way musicians typically interact with computers is still primitive and limited in many ways especially when contrasted with how musicians interact with each other.

These limitations in human-computer interaction (HCI) in the context of music making can be broadly be classified as being caused by two factors. The first is related to hardware and is that we still mostly interact with computers using a keyboard and a mouse. The situation in music is not much different with the primary digital instruments being keyboards (the music kind) and other essentially digital controllers such as sliders and rotary knobs. The amount of control and expressivity these digital control afford is nowhere close to that afforded by acoustic instruments. The other major factor limited natural HCI in the context of music making is that computers process music signals as large monolithic blocks of samples without any "understanding" of the underlying content. When musicians listens to music especially when interacting with other musicians in the context of a live music performance they are able to extract an enormous amount of high level semantic information from the music signal such as tempo, rhythmic structure, chord changes, melody, style, and vocal quality. When working with a recording engineer it is possible to say something along the lines of go to the 4th measure of the saxophone solo and she will be able to locate the corresponding segment. However this level of understanding is currently impossible to achieve at least in commercial software systems. Natural human-computer interaction in music will only be achieved when musicians are able to use their instruments to convey performance information to computer systems and that way leverage their incredible abilities and long time investment in learning their instruments. In addition the associated computer systems should be able to "understand" and "listen" to music in similar ways to how human listeners and especially musicians do.

In this chapter an overview of current efforts in creating novel ways of musical human-computer interaction is provided. These efforts have been supported by advances in two important research communities to this work. The first research area is Music Information Retrieval (MIR) which deals with all aspects of extracting information from musical signals in digital form. Although originally the primary focus of MIR was the processing of large collections of recorded music in recent years several of the techniques developed in the field are starting to be used in the context of live music performance. These techniques include monophonic and polyphonic pitch detection, melody extraction, chord recognition, segmentation and structure analysis, tempo and beat tracking, and instrument classification. The second research area is New Interfaces for Musical Expression (NIME) (Miranda & Wanderley, 2006) which deals with new technologies and ways for creating music enabled by computing technology.

The string, woodwind, and brass families of instruments do not have widely available digital counterparts and in the few cases that they do the digital version is nowhere as expressive as the acoustic one. It is possible to retrofit and augment existing acoustic instruments with digital sensors in order to create what are termed hyper-instruments. These hyper-instruments allow musicians to interact naturally with their instrument as they are accustomed to, while at the same time transmitting information about what they are playing to computing systems. This approach requires significant alterations to the acoustic instrument which is something many musicians are hesitant to do. In addition, hyper-instruments are typically one of a kind research prototypes making their wider adoption practically impossible. In the past few years researchers have started exploring the use of non-invasive and minimally invasive sensing technologies that address these two limitations by allowing acoustic instruments to be used without any modifications directly as digital controllers. This enables natural human-computer interaction with all the rich and delicate control of acoustic instruments, while retaining the wide array of possibilities that digital technology can provide.

The remaining chapter is structured as follows. A section on related work provides an overview of existing work in this area and the background technologies needed to support it. This is followed by a section on current sensing technologies and algorithmic techniques that can be used to build natural music HCI systems. A section describing some case studies from the work of my group in more detail is also provided. The chapter ends with a speculative section on future directions.

RELATED WORK

The field of music information retrieval (MIR) has a history of about fifteen years. The main conference is the International Conference of the Society of Music Information Retrieval (ISMIR). A good tutorial overview of MIR has been written by Orio (2006) and described important techniques developed in this field such as audio feature extraction, pitch representations, and automatic rhythmic analysis. The excellent book of Robert Row "Machine Musicianship" (Rowe, 2004) describes how musicianship can be modeled computationally mostly in the symbolic domain and includes information about how to implement musical processes such as segmentation, pattern recognition and interactive improvisation in computer programs. The majority of work in MIR has focused on processing large audio collections of recorded music. More recently, the importance of MIR techniques in user-centered scenarios and using multimodal input has been suggested (Liem et al, 2011). A prophetic paper about the limitations and potential for more natural music HCI was written by the late David Wessel and Matt Wright in 2002 (Wessel & Wright, 2002). Techniques from the HCI have also been used to evaluate new interfaces for musical expression (Wanderley & Orio, 2002). The importance of intimate control in the design of new interfaces for musical expression was identified as early as 2004 (Fels, 2004). The term hyperinstruments has been used to describe acoustic instruments that have been augmented with digital sensing technologies but are still playable in their traditional way (Machover, 1991). The most common use of hyperinstruments has been in the context of live electro-acoustic music performance where they combine the wide variety of control possibilities of digital instruments such as MIDI keyboards with the expressive richness of acoustic instruments. A less explored, but more interesting from a musicological perspective, application of hyperinstruments is in the context of performance analysis. The most well known example is the use of acoustic pianos fitted with a robotic sensing and actuation system on the keys that can capture the exact details of the player actions and replicate them. Such systems allow the exact nuances of a particular piano performer to be captured so that when played back on the same acoustic piano with mechanical actuation they will sound identical to the original performance. The captured information can be used to analyze specific characteristics of the music performance such as how timing of different sections varies among different performers (Goebl et al, 2005; Bernays & Traube, 2013). Hyperinstruments opened new possibilities as they combined the flexibility and enormous potential of digital control with the control and expressiveness of acoustic playing. However their adoption was limited due to two factors:

1. The need to invasively modify the actual acoustic instrument,
2. Their limited availability as in most cases they were (and still are) one of a kind instruments created as proof-of-concept prototypes and frequently only played by their creator.

These limitations can be addressed by leveraging MIR techniques and also advances in embedded computing, digital sensors and 3D printing. More recently the use of sophisticated audio feature extraction and machine learning technology has enabled the non-invasive sensing of music performance gestures (Tindale et al, 2011; Perez-Carrillo & Wanderley 2015). An alternative is to have minimally invasive and reversible sensing in which the actual acoustic instrument is not modified but simply augmented when needed. The EROSS trumpet system described in more detail below is such as an example (Jenkins et al, 2013) in which a 3D printed attachment can be easily added to (and removed from) an acoustic trumpet to provide digital sensing of the displacement of each valve.

Musicology has traditionally been focused on having musical scores as the primary representation used to analyze music despite the fact that the majority of music throughout history has not been notated. In addition to musical scores, more recently audio recordings in conjunction with signal processing techniques such as spectrograms have also been used in musicology and especially computational ethnomusicology (Tzanetakis et al, 2007). An audio recording captures information about the end results of making music but makes it hard to analyze the actual process or the cultural aspects of making music. The use of non-invasive sensing in acoustic musical instruments enables us to capture the nuances of the actual creation of music something particularly interesting in oral and improvised music traditions.

SENSING TECHNOLOGIES

Sensing technologies in the field of new instruments for music expression can be divided into two broad categories:

1. Direct sensors are directly and physically attached to the instrument and used to convert various types of physical quantities into electrical signals that can then be digitized and used to control computer processes. The associated digital signals are then typically directly utilized for mapping and control purposes.
2. Indirect sensors also convert various physical quantities into electrical signals that are digitized but can do so without being attached to the instrument or sound source. Indirect acquisition requires the use of digital signal processing techniques and in some cases machine learning in order to extract the desired gesture information from the player (Traube et al, 2003).

Examples of direct sensors include accelerometers, gyroscopes, force sensing resistors, capacitance sensing as well as various types of controls such as knobs, sliders, and buttons. The most common indirect sensors are microphones, cameras and 3D depth structured light cameras such as the Microsoft Kinect (Zhang, 2012). The Kinect was first made commercially available in 2010, and shipped as part of the Microsoft Xbox platform. A version for Windows development was first released in 2012, which consisted of an adapter to plug the unit into a computer, and a comprehensive SDK that allowed for access to body tracking functionality.

CASE STUDIES

In this section a number of case studies of new interfaces for musical expression that enable natural HCI in the context of music playing are described. They are roughly ordered in terms of increasing use of non-invasive and minimally invasive sensing technologies. They are representative examples of the type of research that is currently conducted in this area done by the author and his students and collaborators. They are by no means an exhaustive list but were chosen because of familiarity with the work. The following section discusses applications of these technologies such as automatic music transcription, computer-assisted music tutoring and assistive computer music technology in which natural music HCI is crucial.

E-Sitar

The sitar is a 19-stringed, pumpkin shelled, traditional North Indian instrument. Its bulbous gourd (shown in Figure 1), cut flat on the top, is joined to a long necked hollowed concave stem that stretches three feet long and three inches wide. The sitar contains seven strings on the upper bridge, and twelve sympathetic strings below. All strings can be tuned using tuning pegs. The upper strings include rhythm and drone strings, known as chikari. Melodies, which are primarily performed on the upper-most string and occasionally the second copper string, induce sympathetic resonances in the twelve strings below. The sitar can have up to 22 moveable frets, tuned to the notes of a Raga (the melodic mode, scale, order, and rules of a particular piece of Indian classical music) (Bagchee, 1998).

It is important to understand the traditional playing style of the sitar to comprehend how our controller captures its hand gestures. Our controller design has been informed by the needs and constraints of the long tradition and practice of sitar playing. The sitar player uses his left index finger and middle finger to press the string to the fret to play the desired swara (note). The frets are elliptically curved so the string can be pulled downward, to bend to a higher note. This is

Figure 1. E-Sitar and associated thumb sensor and network of fret resistors

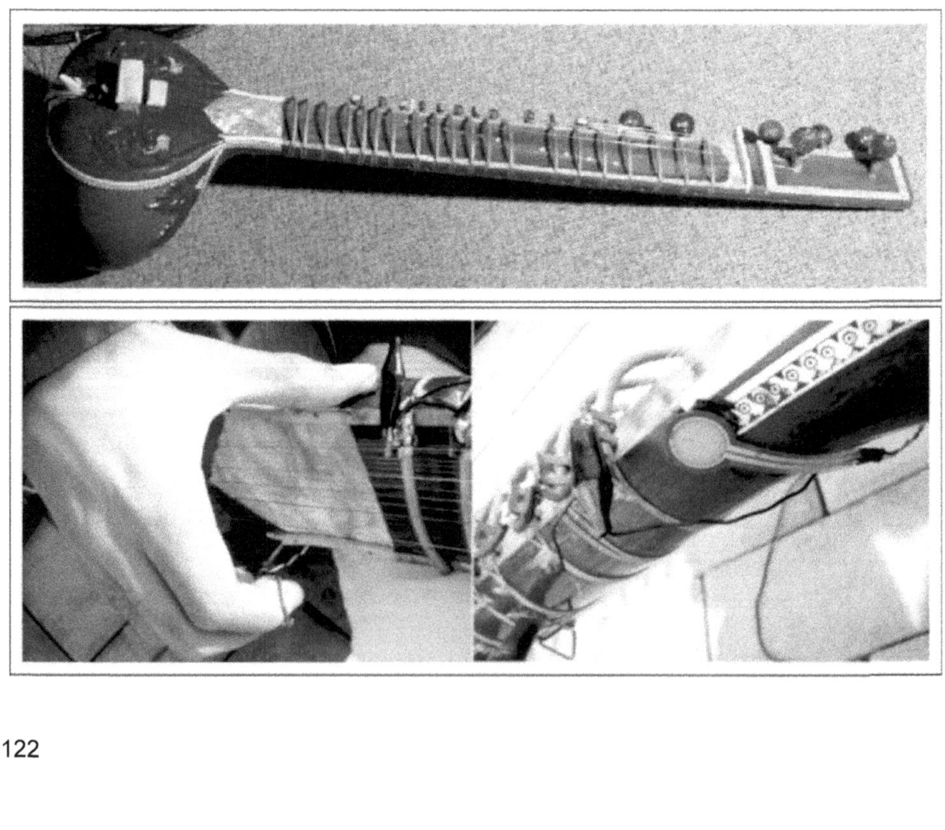

how a performer incorporates the use of shruti (microtones) which is an essential characteristic of traditional classical Indian music. On the right index finger, a sitar player wears a ring like plectrum, known as a mizrab. The right hand thumb, remains securely on the edge of the dand (neck) as the entire right hand gets pulled up and down over the main seven strings, letting the mizrab strum the desired melody. An upward stroke is known as Dha and a downward stroke is known as Ra (Bagchee, 1998). The two main gestures we capture using sensors and subsequently try to model using audio-based analysis are: 1) the pitch/fret position and 2) the mizrab stroke direction.

The E-Sitar was built with the goal of capturing a variety of gestural input data. A variety of different sensors such as fret detection using a network of resistors are used combined with an Atmel AVR ATMega16 microcontroller for data acquisition. The fret detection operates by a network of resistors attached in series to each fret on the E-Sitar. Voltage is sent through the string, which establishes a connection when the string is pressed down to a fret. This results in a unique voltage based on the amount of resistance in series up that that fret. The voltage is then calculated and transmitted using the Music Instrument Digital Interface (MIDI) protocol. The direct sensor used to deduce the direction of a {\it mizrab} stroke is a force sensing resistor (FSR), which is placed directly under the right hand thumb, as shown in Figure 1. The thumb never moves from this position while playing, however the applied force varies based on the mizrab stroke direction. A Dha stroke (upward stroke) produces more pressure on the thumb than a Ra stroke (downward stroke). We send a continuous stream of data from the FSR via MIDI, because this data is rhythmically in time and can be used compositionally for more than just deducing pluck direction.

The E-Sitar (Kapur et al, 2004) is an example of a canonical hyper-instrument that is an acoustic instrument that has been heavily modified to add digital sensing capabilities. One interesting and creative use of these digital sensing capabilities is the idea of creating a surrogate sensor (Tindale et al, 2011). In this approach the augmented instrument with direct sensors is used to capture gesture information. For example in the case of the E-Sitar we can consider the thumb pressure data. Subsequently that data is used as ground truth to train a machine learning model (regression) that is able to predict the thumb pressure data from audio features extracted from the audio signal captured by a non-invasive microphone. That way the direct sensing apparatus is used for training the surrogate sensor but once the indirect surrogate sensor performs well enough it is not needed any more. The same approach was used to derive using indirect acquisition the position of striking a drum surface in the case of the E-Drum (Tindale et al, 2011). When a human listens to the sound of a snare drum it is possible to determine with reasonable accuracy how close the striking position is to the rim. However performing the direct signal processing for deriving this position from analyzing the audio would be extremely challenging. By using an instrumented snare drum for ground truth it is possible to build a machine learning model that takes as input audio features of the microphone captured signal and produces as output an accurate estimate of the striking position.

Range Guitar

The RANGE guitar is a minimally-invasive hyperinstrument incorporating electronic sensors and integrated digital signal processing (DSP). It introduces an open framework for autonomous music computing eschewing the use of the laptop on stage. The framework uses an embedded Linux microcomputer to provide sensor acquisition, analog-to-digital conversion (ADC) for audio input, DSP, and digital-to-analog conversion (DAC) for audio output. The DSP environment is built in Puredata (Pd) (Puckette, 1996).

Electric guitar players have utilized audio effects since their inception. An extensive variety of DSP guitar effects are offered commercially, some of which even provide a code environment for user modification of DSP algorithms; however, in most cases the functionality of these devices is specific and their programmability is limited. These commercial audio effects are typically implemented either as foot pedals or as separate hardware devices. An alternative is the use of a laptop and audio interface to replace the dedicated guitar effects. This approach is generic in the sense that any audio effect can be implemented as long as the computer is fast enough to calculate it in real-time. Using a laptop is also completely open, flexible, and programmable. However such a setup requires more cables, more power, and is cumbersome to transport and awkward on stage. In both of these cases (dedicated hardware or laptop) the control of the effects is separated from the actual guitar playing as shown in Figure 2.

Figure 2. Traditional ways of controlling electric guitar effects

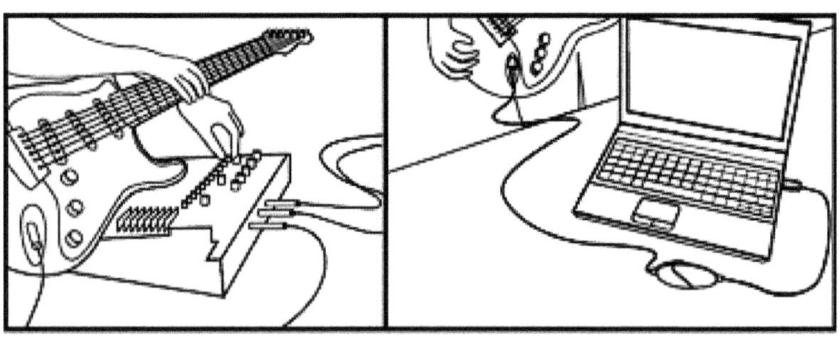

There has always been a union of guitar and effect despite a separation of guitar playing and effect control. To address this issue, we have integrated minimally invasive sensors on the body of the guitar to allow natural and intuitive DSP control. The RANGE system was designed for use in performance contexts to allow guitar players more expressivity in controlling DSP effects than conventional pedal controllers provide. The proximity of the sensors to the guitarist's natural hand position is important, as it allows the guitarist to combine DSP control with traditional guitar playing technique. Like the Moog Guitar, the sensors sit flat on the guitar body, eliminating any interference with a guitarist's performance technique. Further, we have reduced the hardware dependencies, cabling, and power requirements to a minimal footprint. Design goals were motivated by the desire to shift away from the cumbersome and distracting laptop on stage in exchange for a smaller, open architecture. This framework is designed to take advantage of low-cost electronic components and free open-source software, facilitating reconfiguration and adaptation to the specific needs of different instruments and musicians. Figure 3 shows the RANGE system.

Figure 3. Schematic of RANGE

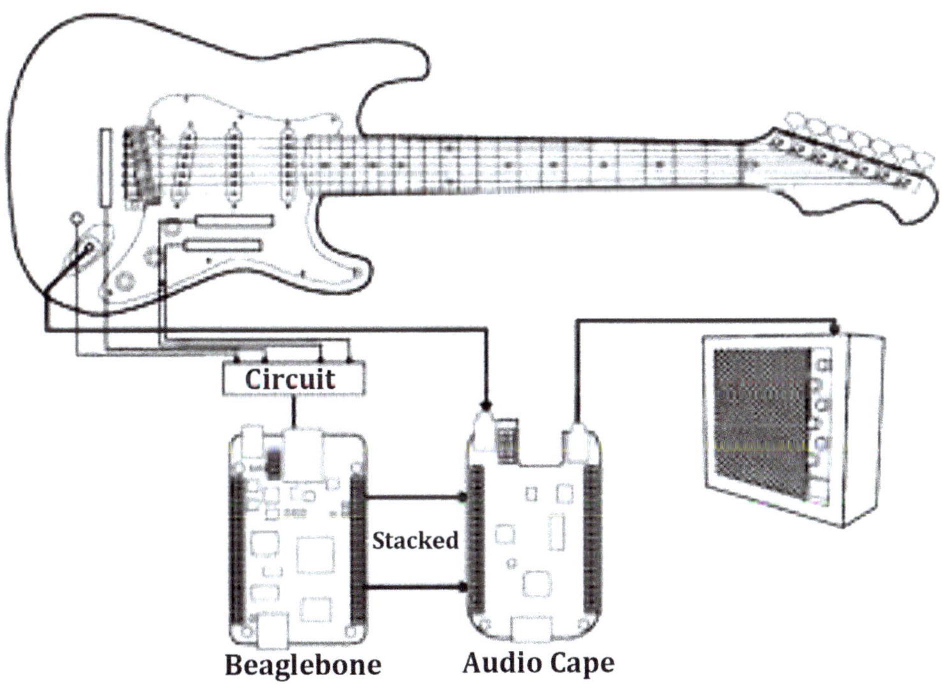

Figure 4. EROSS mounted on a trumpet

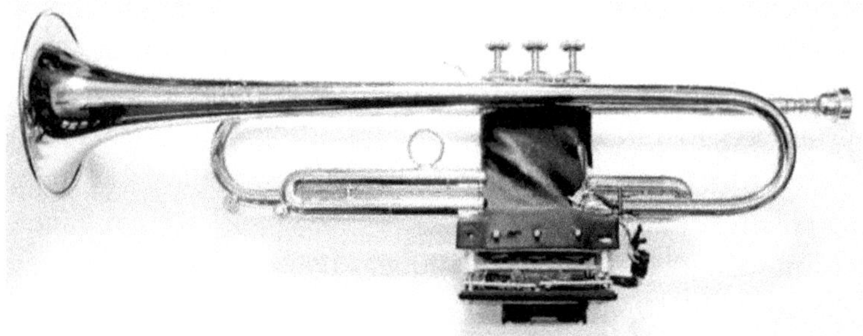

EROSS

One of the problems with many hyperinstruments is that they require extensive modifications to the actual acoustic instrument in order to install the sensing apparatus. EROSS (Jenkins et al, 2013) is an Easily Removable, Wireless Optical Sensor System that can be used with with any conventional piston valve acoustic trumpet. Optical sensors are utilized to track the continuous position displacement values of the three trumpet valves. These values are transmitted wirelessly to a host computer system. The hardware has been designed to be reconfigurable by having the housing 3D printed so that the dimensions can be adjusted for any particular trumpet model. Figure 4 shows the EROSS system mounted on a trumpet. Although strictly this is still direct sensing the ease with which the attachment can be applied and removed makes it more flexible and potentially easier to adopt.

Pitched Percussion

In addition to microphones and direct sensors another possibility is to utilize image sensors for capturing music performance gestures. These include traditional digital cameras as well as 3D depth sensors such as the Microsoft Kinect. Pitched percussion instruments are a family of acoustic instruments that are played using mallets striking bars and produce a full set of well-defined pitches. Members include the xylophone, marimba, and vibraphone as well as traditional variants such as the African Gyil. By utilizing computer vision techniques it is possible to track the positions of the mallet tips in 3D space which enables fascinating possibilities of control that is seamlessly integrated with traditional playing. For example the space above the bars can be used for controlling various types of audio effects and digital processes. Figure 5 shows how this process can work.

Figure 5. Mapping performance gestures to digital control using a Kinect and a vibraphone

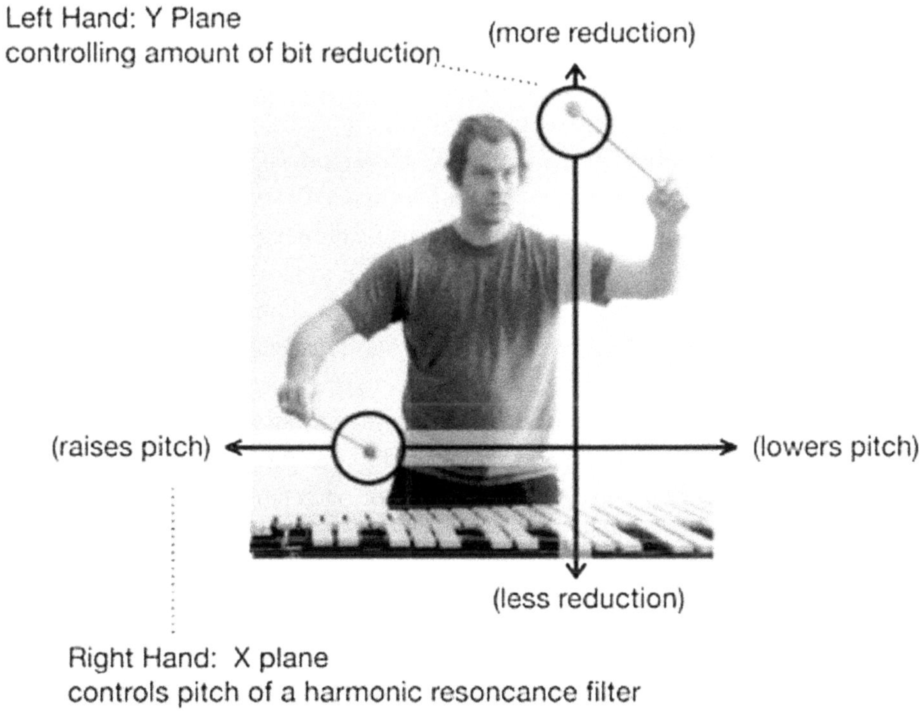

By utilizing the Kinect for tracking the mallets any vibraphone can be used and no modification is required (Odowichuck, 2011).

APPLICATIONS

In this chapter a background on new interfaces for musical expression (NIME) and music information retrieval (MIR) was provided, followed by an overview of sensing technologies and a list of cases studies describing different architectures, instruments, and systems. In this section we describe how these systems can be used to enable new paradigms of interaction between humans and computers that is more natural than existing approaches. Again the examples are drawn from the work of the author and collaborators because of familiarity and are representative of general work in this area.

Transcription

Automatic music transcription is a well-researched area (Klapuri & Davy, 2006) and is typically based on analyzing an audio recording. The novelty of this work is that it looks beyond the audio data by using sensors to avoid octave errors and problems caused from polyphonic transcription. In addition, it does not share the bias of most research that focuses only on Western music. The sitar is a fretted stringed instrument from North India. Unlike many Western fretted stringed instruments (classical guitar, viola de gamba, etc) sitar performers pull (or "bend") their strings to produce higher pitches. In normal performance, the bending of a string will produce notes as much as a fifth higher than the same fret-position played without bending. In addition to simply showing which notes were audible, the system also provides information about how to produce such notes. A musician working from an audio recording (or transcription of an audio recording) alone will need to determine which fret they should begin pulling from. This can be challenging for a skilled performer, let alone a beginner. By representing the fret information on the sheet music, sitar musicians may overcome these problems.

Figure 6. Fret data, audio pitches, and the re- sulting detected notes. The final three notes were pulled.

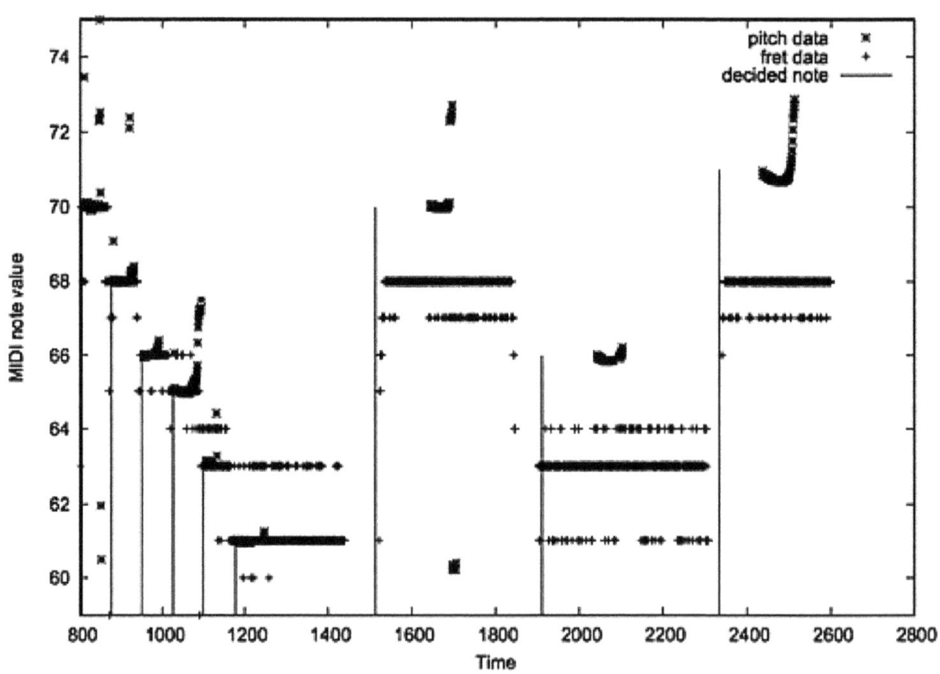

The E-Sitar was the hyperinstrument used for these experiments. Automatic pitch detection using an autocorrelation-based approach was utilized with adaptive constraints (minimum and maximum pitch) based on the sensor fret data from the E-Sitar. To compensate for noisy fret data median filtering in time is utilized. To get an accurate final result, pitch information from the audio signal chain is fused with onset and pitch boundaries calculated from the fret signal chain. The fret provided convenient lower and upper bounds on the pitch: a note cannot be lower than the fret, nor higher than a fifth (i.e. 7 MIDI notes) above the fret. Using the note boundaries derived from the fret data, we find the median value of the pitches inside the boundaries supplied by the fret data. These are represented by the vertical lines in Figure 6, and are the note pitches in the final output.

Assistive Computer Music Technologies

Computer technologies have played an increasing role in improving the lives of people with various disabilities. The speech synthesizer utilized by Stephen Hawkins is a canonical example. When it comes to music-making until recently the technology to enable people with disabilities to make music has been relatively limited, consisting primarily of mechanical approaches. With new developments in computing, including the Microsoft Kinect, touchless sensors are providing a new way for people with disabilities to interface with instruments in novel ways. Touchless musical instruments are a particularly interesting case. The first touchless musical instrument was the Theremin which first appeared in 1920, made by Leon Theremin (Glinsky, 1992). When playing the Theremin, the left hand controls a frequency oscillator, while the right controls amplitude. Theremins often come in a kit and require some setup before they can be played. Hence they are normally used by people who are familiar with electronic musical instruments. Also, the Theremin requires a lot of dexterity and fine motor movements, making it only useful for able-bodied players. Still, the Theremin brought in a new age of touchless musical sensors, and the makers of the Soundbeam cite the Theremin as a major influence.

The Soundbeam is a touchless adaptive musical instrument that emits a sonar beam, and detects when the beam is obstructed, which triggers MIDI notes (Swinglerm, 1998). It is the size and shape of a flashlight, and plugs into a MIDI controller for sound output. The Soundbeam was initially developed for dancers in a large space as early as 1989, but has become popular as an adaptive musical instrument in the 90's and beyond because it can be played without physically grasping anything. It has evolved to be a popular instrument for people with a variety of disabilities, but primarily for movement impairment. The Soundbeam has a number of modes that each trigger MIDI events differently. For example, in one setting, when the player approaches the Soundbeam the notes played increase in pitch, and when the player moves away, the notes decrease in pitch. In another mode, the Soundbeam is pre-programmed with a MIDI melody, and each time the beam is obstructed it plays one note. The flexibility of the instrument allows for it to be played by both beginner and experienced player, and allows for a smooth transition between settings. A wider overview of computer assistive and adaptive music technologies can be found in (Graham-Knight & Tzanetakis, 2015a).

We have used the Kinect sensor to explore creating musical interfaces for assistive purposes (Graham-Knight & Tzanetakis, 2015b). One of the biggest challenges is dealing with the latency of the Kinect which is not ideal. One particular application has been developing a system for a guitar player who has not been able to play music after developing multiple sclerosis. By moving his arm he is able to trigger samples of different chords. Our goal is to develop truly expressive interfaces that like actual music instruments provide expressivity and control whereas previous work has focused on simply music generation.

Computer-Assisted Music Tutoring

Learning musical instruments is one of the most challenging tasks especially for young children. Early attempts at using multimedia for computer-assisted music tutoring mostly targeted remote instruction and replacing the role of the traditional music lesson with a teacher. More recently it has been argued that it is important to focus on the daily practice routine as that is where most of learning takes place and typically little feedback is provided. The assessment of a music instrument performance is challenging and can not be done by simply checking the right answer as for example is the case for learning multiplication as there is no clear-cut "correct" and "incorrect" answer. The author fondly remembers how as a beginner after he played a particular saxophone piece correctly in terms of notes and rhythm his saxophone instructor played it again making it sound significantly better. By performing pitch estimation and note segmentation, we can judge that a particular note was unacceptably out of tune (every note is "out of tune" to some degree). However, this fact may not be obvious to a music student, even after informing the student that the note was incorrect. We must employ visualization techniques to ensure that the student understands why the note was not sufficiently "in tune". In addition, learning a musical instrument involves a great deal of physical control. Since musicians are rarely covered in sweat while performing, non-musicians seldom consider musicians to be athletes, but in reality musicians must perform physical activities (finger movement, exhaling, adjusting lips) within very tight tolerances. A music student may know perfectly well that he made a mistake; the problem was purely physical. By analogy, consider an athlete training for a long jump or lifting weights: the athlete knows how to perform the actions – he knows the optimal distance to begin running, he can pace his footsteps such that his jump always begins within the allowable limit, or he understands that he should lift with his legs instead of his back – but this does not guarantee that the athlete can jump seven meters or lift two hundred kilograms. After a certain point, the athlete has all the knowledge he needs; the only problem is training his body so that it can perform the actions. The sensing technologies described in this chapter enable computer systems to monitor all the physical processes that take place while performing and provide valuable feedback.

A good example of the possibilities for computer-assisted music tutoring is The Digital Violin Tutor (DVT) (Jun et al, 2005) provides feedback in the absence of human teachers. DVT offers different visualization modalities – video, "piano roll" graphical displays, 2-D animations of the fingerboard, and even 3-D avatar animations. We present an example of this interface in Figure 7. The student's audio is transcribed and compared to the transcription of the teacher's audio. If mistakes are detected, then the proper actions are demonstrated by the 2-D fingerboard animation, video, or the 3-D avatar animation. The music transcription system in DVT is customized for use with violins in student's homes. This audio is quite noisy – the microphone will be quite cheap, it will not be placed in an optimal position, and the recording levels will not be expertly set. The transcriber must be quite robust against such problems.

Figure 7. Screenshot of the Digital Violin Tutor

We identified daily individual practice as having particular need of assistance, and the most productive way to enhance practice is to increase the motivation and efficiency of technical exercises. This motivation may take several forms, but we feel that many students would benefit from edutainment games which provide object analysis of the student. Musical instrument edutainment games present some special challenges: first, we do not want students to be sitting in front of a computer with traditional HCI tools; they should be playing their instrument as much as possible. Second, we must use novel visualization techniques to provide intuitive feedback for the students. Recently Yousician has been a company that has been successful commercializing a game approach to music education. Finally, the potential for online collaborative learning is an extremely exciting area that should be investigated.

FUTURE DIRECTIONS

The ideas of natural music human-computer interaction are currently a topic of active research and there is a lot of potential for future work. Currently only a small subset of the traditional western musical instruments have been explored in this context and if one includes instruments from musical cultures from around the world this subset becomes even smaller. Driven by technologies such as smartphones and the internet of things digital sensors are constantly becoming more accurate, smaller, and cheaper. The associated embedded computing systems have much more computational power and therefore are able to perform more sophisticated processing. So expanding interaction to all musical instruments and improving sensing and processing are clearly directions for incremental advances. Probably the most exciting new directions is the integration of virtual and augmented reality technologies. One can envision that not too far in the future a budding musician could wear an augmented reality headset such as the Microsoft Hololens and pick up their violin. Using indirect acquisition through a microphone the computer would be able to extract the played pitch, dynamics, bow position and velocity, string number, and finger position. This information could be used for real-time computer accompaniment using a virtual string quartet that would also be visible as 3D avatars in the augmented vision of the Hololens. This would provide a very close experience to playing with a real string quartet and would leverage several of the technologies and ideas explored in this chapter. To summarize currently there is a lot of interesting activity in making the human computer interaction in the context of music playing more seamless and natural by blurring the boundaries between the physical and virtual world and the best is yet to come.

ACKNOWLEDGMENT

The author would like to thank the National Sciences and Engineering Research Council (NSERC) and Social Sciences and Humanities Research Council (SSHRC) of Canada for their financial support. The case studies described in this chapter have been done in collaboration with many people include Ajay Kapur, Peter Driessen, Leonardo Jenkins, Duncan MacConnell, Steven Ness, Gabrielle Odowichuck, Tiago Tavares, Shawn Trail, and Andrew Schloss.

REFERENCES

Bagchee, S. (1998). *Understanding Raga Music*. Ceshwar Business Publications Inc.

Bernays, M., & Traube, C. (2013). Expressive Production of Piano Timbre: Touch and Playing Techniques for Timbre Control in Piano Performance. In *Proceedings of the 10th Sound and Music Computing Conference (SMC2013)*, (pp. 341-346). Stockholm, Sweden: KTH Royal Institute of Technology.

Fels, S. (2004). Designing for intimacy: Creating New Interfaces for Musical Expression. *Proceedings of the IEEE*, *92*(4), 672–685. doi:10.1109/JPROC.2004.825887

Glinsky, A. V. (1992). *The Theremin in the Emergence of Electronic Music*. (PhD thesis). New York University, New York, NY.

Goebl, W., Bresin, R., & Galembo, A. (2005). Touch and Temporal Behavior of Grand Piano Actions. *The Journal of the Acoustical Society of America*, *118*(2), 1154–1165. doi:10.1121/1.1944648 PMID:16158669

Graham-Knight, K., & Tzanetakis, G. (2015a). Adaptive Music Technology: History and Future Perspectives. In *Proceedings of the International Computer Music Conference*.

Graham-Knight, K., & Tzanetakis, G. (2015b). Adaptive Music Technology using the Kinect. In *Proceedings of the 8th ACM International Conference on PErvasive Technologies Related to Assistive Environments*.

Jenkins, L., Trail, S., Tzanetakis, G., Driessen, P., & Page, W. (2013). An Easily Removable, Wireless Optical Sensing System (EROSS) for the Trumpet. In *Proceedings of the 2013 Conference on New Interfaces for Musical Expression NIME2013*.

Kapur, A., Lazier, A., Davidson, P., Wilson, R. S., & Cook, P. (2004). The Electronic Sitar Controller. In *Proceedings of the 2004 conference on New interfaces for musical expression*.

Liem, C., Müller, M., Eck, D., Tzanetakis, G., & Hanjalic, A. (2011). The Need for Music Information Retrieval with User-Centered and Multimodal Strategies. In *Proceedings of the 1st International ACM Workshop on Music Information Retrieval with User-Centered and Multimodal Strategies*. doi:10.1145/2072529.2072531

MacConnell, D., Trail, S., Tzanetakis, G., Driessen, P., & Page, W. (2013). Reconfigurable Autonomous Novel Guitar Effects (range). In *Proc. Int. Conf. on Sound and Music Computing (SMC 2013)*.

Machover, T. (1991). *Hyperinstruments: A Composer's Approach to the Evolution of Intelligent Musical Instruments*. Organized Sound.

Miranda, E., & Wanderley, M. (2006). *New Digital Musical Instruments: Control and Interaction Beyond the Keyboard*. Middleton, WI: AR Editions.

Odowichuk, G., Trail, S., Driessen, P., Nie, W., & Page, W. (2011). Sensor Fusion: Towards a Fully Expressive 3D Music Control Interface. In *Proceedings* of the *Communications, Computers and Signal Processing 2011 IEEE Pacific Rim Conference (PacRim)*. doi:10.1109/PACRIM.2011.6033003

Orio, N. (2006). *Music Retrieval: a Tutorial and Review*. Boston, MA: Now Publishers Inc.

Perez-Carrillo, A., & Wanderley, M. (2015). Indirect Acquisition of Violin Instrumental Controls from Audio Signal with hidden Markov Models. *IEEE/ACM Transactions on Audio, Speech, and Language Processing*, *23*(5), 932–940.

Puckette, M. (1996). Pure Data: Another Integrated Computer Music Environment. In *Proceedings of the Second Intercollege Computer Music Concerts*.

Rowe, R. (2004). *Machine musicianship*. Cambridge, MA: MIT Press.

Swingler, T. (1998). The Invisible Keyboard in the Air: An Overview of the Educational, Therapeutic and Creative Applications of the EMS Soundbeam™. In *2nd European Conference for Disability, Virtual Reality & Associated Technology*.

Tindale, A., Kapur, A., & Tzanetakis, G. (2011). Training Surrogate Sensors in Musical Gesture Acquisition Systems. *IEEE Transactions on Multimedia*, *13*(1), 50–59. doi:10.1109/TMM.2010.2089786

Traube, C., Depalle, P., & Wanderley, M. (2003). Indirect Acquisition of Instrumental Gesture based on Signal, Physical and Perceptual Information. In *Proceedings of the 2003 Conference on New Interfaces for Musical Expression NIME2003*.

Tzanetakis, G., Kapur, A., Schloss, A., & Wright, M. (2007). Computational Ethnomusicology. *Journal of Interdisciplinary Music Studies*, *1*(2), 1–24.

Wanderley, M., & Orio, N. (2002). Evaluation of Input Devices for Musical Expression: Borrowing Tools from HCI. *Computer Music Journal*, *26*(3), 62–76. doi:10.1162/014892602320582981

Wessel, D., & Wright, M. (2002). Problems and Prospects for Intimate Musical Control of Computers. *Computer Music Journal*, *26*(3), 11–22. doi:10.1162/014892602320582945

Yin, J., Wang, Y., & Hsu, D. (2005). Digital Violin Tutor: an Integrated System for Beginning Violin Learners. In *Proceedings of the 13th annual ACM International Conference on Multimedia*. ACM. doi:10.1145/1101149.1101353

Zhang, Z. (2012). Microsoft Kinect Sensor and its Effect. *IEEE MultiMedia*, *9*(2), 4–10. doi:10.1109/MMUL.2012.24

Chapter 7
Interactive Technologies and Audiovisual Programming for the Performing Arts:
The Brave New World of Computing Reshapes the Face of Musical Entertainment

Eirini Markaki
Aristotle University of Thessaloniki, Greece

Ilias Kokkalidis
Aristotle University of Thessaloniki, Greece

ABSTRACT

While many scientific fields loosely rely on coarse depiction of findings and clues, other disciplines demand exact appreciation, consideration and acknowledgement for an accurate diagnosis of scientific data. But what happens if the examined data have a depth of focus and a degree of perplexity that is beyond our analyzed scope? Such is the case of performing arts, where humans demonstrate a surplus in creative potential, intermingled with computer supported technologies that provide the substrate for advanced programming for audiovisual effects. However, human metrics diverge from computer measurements, and therefore a space of convergence needs to be established analogous to the expressive capacity of musical inventiveness in

DOI: 10.4018/978-1-5225-0264-7.ch007

terms of rhythm, spatial movement and dancing, advanced expression of emotion through harmony and beauty of the accompanying audiovisual form. In this chapter, the new era of audiovisual effects programming will be demonstrated that leverage massive participation and emotional reaction.

INTRODUCTION

It was inevitable that the awakening of digital technology as a substrate for global progression would have its ramifications influencing all sectors of human activity. In the space of arts and visually striking performances the tendencies of modern-day technologies would guarantee the creation of original and impressive spectacles asserting accomplishment in music, whether these advances concern the awareness of music and rhythm or the musicality of stage performances in general. The growth of computer systems and the developments in computer music offer the possibility of producing more and still more ostentatious works that bolster the theatrical-like character of live performances with significantly lower costs.

The term "performing arts" is used interchangeably for the description of a wide category of events of human expression: it may indeed engulf performance in the flesh, with the artists seen on stage, but it may also include a perforated event, where some parts of the musical scene are prerecorded or performed by automata, while the remaining rest is indulged with live enactment of artists, technicians, DJs or the participating public itself (Cox, 2003).

In this sense musicality is considered to be a basic axis for theatrical enactments since every major performing activity, from voguish fashion exhibitions up to the movies, relies on the arousal of fantasy that influences the audience's strong emotions. With this manner spreads out a tree-like lineage of spectacles that indomitably promote its ritualistic essential substance, even though sometimes in its modern expression globalized forms of music masquerade this persistent underground. Despite the big differences that occur in music performances in the synchrony of our world, the common denominator is the presence of a live public, which vibrates and reacts according to the streamed or performed music. (Figure 1).

The participation of the public during a performance is of vital importance for its own success story. Every stage incarnation initiates a unique relationship between the artist and its audience, and this relation (in computer science terms: a transaction) yields the human interaction to the event. In case some kind of machinery is involved, which is duly prompted nowadays, then we have

Figure 1. The participatory climax of audiovisual events for small audiences. Left: Professional dancers performing choreographic music in a club, commencing the show. Right: The clubbers' carousal, spontaneous "ignition", after 2-3 hours of audiovisual meditation: they dance and sing.

Human-Machine Interaction (or its subpart Human-Computer Interaction) elaborating on the subaudition of the performance. In audiovisual arts terminology reciting is transformed to a virtual screenplay that emphasizes on act instructions and scene directions (Cox & Warner, 2007).

Even if we lacked the modern computer technology which is accountable for the technological transformation of the performing stage and scene, the panorama of contemporary renditions includes in its evolving strategies the reactions of the public: indeed, the audience is a factor that has to be subjugated to a desirable physiological response ranging from a warm applaud up to getting "wild", as is the case, for example, in heavy metal recitals. In any case, what is taken into account is the timeline of events, which includes tokens and slots for the public interactions. Since most of these events are televised, it is basic to have tactical plans for carefully directing the huge assembly of spectators so that the strict timing criteria for telecasting are met. Sometimes, although striking, it is more important to comply with the strict lapses of the televised time offered than to tame the spectators (Figure 2).

The role of the public in situ is so crucial, even for televised events, because the thousands that gather in concert places will put the context for the response of millions who watch the event. Therefore, researchers look up for methods that accurately record all the information concerning the correspondence of the crowd. Simultaneously, the organizers of the event provide stimuli and leverage to the spectators aiming to activate their participatory interaction.

Figure 2. The spectators' point of view. From huge audiences (±100,000 assembled spectators). Left: To global audiences. Right: Formatting new ways for mass participation. The former mold the mood, the latter follow through and in some occasions, as is the Eurovision song contest, vote.

With the continuous development of technological means the organizers have become the predominant benefactor in experimenting with new ways of interaction between music production systems and the new, multimedia oriented ways of expression and communication (Ouzounian, 2007). This tendency to enhance creativity leads to the exploitation of interactivity: Artists foresee new methods for performing, researchers make full use of technological advances to explore remote interfaces, producers capitalize on new media that penetrate massive broadcasting, the industry sees that the necessary items enabling user participation are timely scattered to the stores' shelves, managers finance futuristic events by setting benefits against the cost of maintenance of massive build-up systems[1], and of course huge amounts of data circulate via the Internet creating mash-ups the propel the multimedia industry to enormous figures both in big data volumes, fiscal value and global penetration.

Indeed, the use of sound and pictures is found to have deep roots in the history of theatre and spectacle. Undoubtedly, in the 20th century it became the main benefactor of leisure time and entertainment provision. In the 21st century, it has promoted itself as the main activity for receiving significant on-line and off-line participation. Various applications, like YouTube, Daily Motion, Vimeo, iTunes, Facebook and Twitter (Dahl et al., 2011) subsidize the computer industry by promoting event group videos, sounds and photos that mingle interchangeably with the computer industry networks. As a result, we can no longer differentiate classic TV and radio broadcasting from the electronic mass media industry that has been set up on huge on-line repositories (Margounakis & Politis, 2011; Politis et al., 2015a).

Consequently, digital technology and computing machinery have essential influence to the nature of things to come. They have given increased control to complex arrays for natural movement and the setting of lights, revolutionizing the way with which stage performers handle sound and insinuate motion. In a lot of cases, it has changed the way with which the stage designers, whether organizers, performers, or technical assistants attest, develop, present and distribute their work.

This way we could say that the space within which the performance is staged becomes an imminent human-machine interface. Everything the performer or the stage technician touches and uses produce elaborate results: in one-way or another the whole stage, and even its online "extensions" conveys to means of expression. It is recognized by theatre and art people that sound expression and motion are adjusted to the demands of the performing space; this space by it self dictates some, perhaps unwritten-rules. As the audience perceives the performing environment as its natural habitat, audiovisual engineers take advantage and regulate accordingly scene and lighting design to express the collective mood of the gathering (Cangeloso, 2012).

However, the variety of systems deployed produce so many audiovisual controls that the live presentation and handling becomes somewhat fuzzy, not to say problematic (Figure 3). Therefore, computerized systems and programming languages have commenced to appear deployed for the flow control of lighting, video streams and sound channels. Prerecorded sequences and programmed loops reduce overload and allow musicians using keyboards, along with video jockeys (VJs) and disc jockeys (DJs) that master multimedia streams, to produce in real time skillful performances. As a result, the last few years have started to appear computerized systems that facilitate the control and smooth flow of audiovisual effects. In addition, a new perspective has been introduced that entangles stage directors and audiovisual engineers in reshaping the potential for scenery action, enhancing the creativity of musicians, entertainers and actors. Innovation meets intuition, and by any means, computerized feedback enhances productivity.

Advances in electronic equipment are not really newly received information. For the past decades, both engineers and spectators, we are experiencing a pivotal recreation in our audiovisual things and conditions for entertainment provision. What is a really new substantial innovation is the increased level of control that Human-Machine Interaction offers between electronic lighting devices, sound dispatching equipment, and computing machinery of all kinds, which collectively produce distinctive audiovisual streams by promoting pioneering ways of interaction. For instance, the ability to interpret human motions and indicative signs is a sheer, unmitigated increase in the degrees of communication exerted over music production. It introduces a behavioral communiqué that introduces bodily patterns in the incorporeal of music perception (Figure 4).

Figure 3. The artist's point of view. Renowned musician Yanni combining live performances along with computer based electroacoustic technology and audio-visual effects. Images cropped from Yanni's YouTube channel.

Figure 4. Various performing styles based on laser technology and MIDI based Digital Musical Intrument representation. A: The Laser Harp in a Science Museum in Malaysia, G. Hill performing on his YouTube channel. B: The Laser Man Show performed by the Playzer band in Israel, again available on YouTube.

a. 

b. 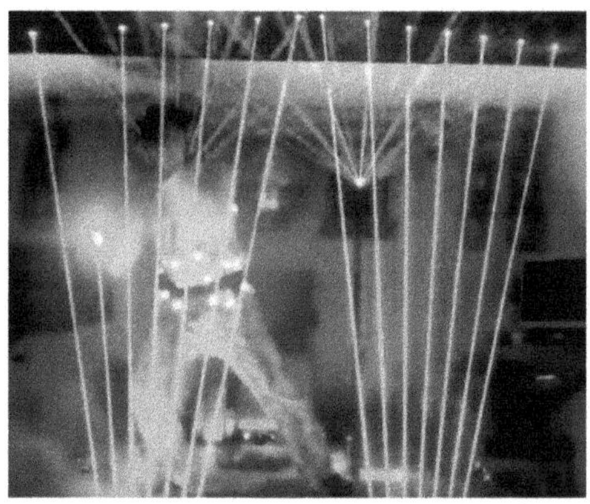

These pioneering ways of control are not any more a privilege of the elite. Although laser-sensing equipment is rather unusual for our everyday music habitat, computerized control systems are finding their way to the appliances of ordinary music stations and bars (Figure 5).

Indeed, music performance involves the concretization of notes, signs, neumes. The interpretation of a bodily language was more or less involved long ago, for instance as the conveyance of the conductor to the orchestra he directed. Nonetheless, innovative technology offers new possibilities that drive creativity beyond the boundaries of musical formal semantics (Cox & Warner, 2007). This human activity, however, is subject to restrictions. Robotic systems have a very small

Figure 5. The degree of interaction in music club "Plan B" in Thessaloniki, Greece. The DJ reshapes dynamically the audiovisuall environment as a one man show using robotic audiovisual effects.

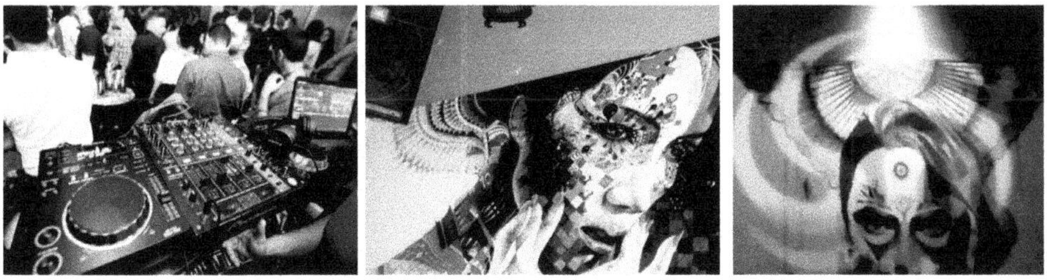

response time compared to human reactions; therefore, the synchronization of movements between performers and machinery is crucial for the naturalness of musical entertainment.

This notion is of extreme importance for the computer industry: the use of bodily functions is the object of communication for devices with large penetration to the public. As this culture of music synaesthesia gets more promulgation, handling systems like Xbox with Kinect becomes more learnable, and vice versa (Zhang, 2012; Graham-Knight & Tzanetakis, 2015). On the whole, people are accustomed to communication with body, voice and gestures. Handling our bodily movement leads to expressing our emotions via the production of sense impressions. One sense or part of the body consequently is triggered, along with the performing environment, and as a result a new feedback is repulsed by the stimulation of another sense.

This is the entry point for digital technology to reshape and promote its functionality, via computing languages and interfaces along with advanced robotic machinery. Gradually, the electronics and robotics world that controlls audiovisual entertainment, becomes a virtual space that simulates the stage events.

Modeling performable action means linking singing, dancing and acting with the stage's digital habitat: video cameras, action cameras, decorative illuminations, low frequency sound radiations, image metamorphoses, brighter or paler surroundings imitating natural light impressions, interconnected mobile devices to streaming media, and advanced optoelectronic circuitry (Fox & Kemp, 2009).

At this point, the prospect to develop programming languages not only simulating the interface of control knobs, but even further, giving the possibility to interconnect devices that stream different kind of data, not interconnected thus far.

For how interconnection is achieved when music is involved, a retrospect into MIDI, the milestone of computer music industry may help.

MUSIC TECHNOLOGY ADVANCES IN A NUTSHELL

The Music Instrument Digital Interface (MIDI): An Unfinished Revolution

Before commencing to deploy the potential of MIDI in audiovisual performances, it is important to point out some basic characteristics that musical instrumentation bears as quality of servicing.

The MIDI protocol started evolving around this concept: a very important aspect in music synchronization is the note played and the exact timing of when this event is triggered on, and when the musician decides, it is turned off (Field-Selfridge, 1997).

Musicians always wanted to have interconnection between their digital instruments along with some remote sensing. This way a musician, who normally plays one instrument each time, can combine and "chain" more instruments. For example, a musician performs with a saxophone, but he wants to combine some more instruments that are homophonous, and as result merge a more dense, a more intrinsically rich sound. Under normal circumstances, this tactics was not feasible unless a small orchestra was employed.

Alternatively, a musician may want to use one keyboard that produces multiple sounds. Although this image is familiar nowadays, some decades earlier it was not even thinkable.

Each digital instrument had its own keyboard, which, apart of its own physical properties, produced a series of control signals destined for the sound generating unit it hosted. The whole process was cumbersome, expensive and not compatible with other similar devices produced by other manufacturers (Figure 6).

Figure 6. The evolution of species in time series. Left: An original sequencer - synthesizer with its own keyboard, circa 1970's. Center: The equivalent iPad virtualization with multitouch capabilities. Right: A new concept for multisensor music reproduction – a "virtual" compact disc surface enabling the DJ to perform cueing effects with his hands.

From the aspect of usability, the query was set as follows: can we play multiple digital instruments using *one* keyboard? And the answer did not delay to come. Every acoustic instrument was simulated by a "box" capable of producing digitized sounds by the modulation of electrical signals, correlated with a specific instrument or family of instruments. Another "box" was assigned to stringed musical instruments for the violin family, another for wind instruments, a different one for the piano and so on.

The first revolutionary step was that all these "boxes" shared an interchangeable keyboard that served as a synchronization unit as well. Thrillingly, the *synthesizer*, the sound-making electronic device for most of our everyday music was devised, allowing a large degree of control over sound output. A *sampler* was an expedient variant using prerecorded sounds (potentially any sound, not just other people's records) and playing them back as sequences of pre-arranged different notes. The *vocoder* on the other hand was mixing two or more audio signals, one of which is usually a voice, to produce special effects such as talking wind, etc.

The second step was to provide these electronic devices with programmable memory for storing sequences of musical notes, chords, or rhythms and transmitting them when required to an electronic musical instrument. Usually these devices where intermingled with a synthesizer, so the revolutionary decade of the 1970's amalgamated in the sweeping sequencer-synthesizer module. A new era in music had just began, reshaping the formation and the environment of music. For instance, pop music started to mean in our ears something entirely different from what our grand - grand parents for centuries though of it (Aikin, 2003).

The third and most crucial step took place in 1983. All these loosely hanging innovations were combined in a communication protocol, the Musical Instrument Digital Interface. The versatility of this novelty laid not only in its communication capabilities within digital instrumentation, where it facilitating synchronization and exchange of musical information and playback, but in its ability to interconnect musical instruments with computers. Gradually this led to the awakening of computer music and the creation of advanced programming languages and interfaces that gave composers the potential to create synthesized sounds, multimedia presentations or computer games.

Most importantly, the new hi-tech substrate acts as a technology enabler in music, since it is "also adding an unbelievable variety of new timbres to our musical store, but most important of all, it has freed music from the tempered system, which has prevented music from keeping pace with the other arts and with science" (Cook, 1999). Western music theory and practice is many times insufficient to explain the uniqueness and the richness of the melodic structures and the metric structures that have emerged in contemporary music scenes (like that of Eurovision) as an amalgam of traditional Eastern music.

Figure 7. The progressive advancement to microtonality in software (with multitouch capabilities for mobile implementations) and its equivalent hardware realizations, the Hπ Tonal Flexus™

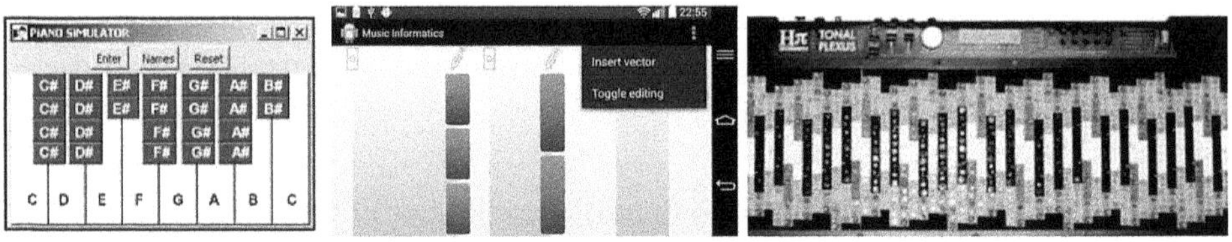

Indeed, in Eastern music traditions performers come across with scales having various "structures", as is the case of pentatonic scales containing a variable number of notes, from 4 up to 32.

What increases that much the number of notes involved is the existence of many alterations between notes, partly due to speech inflexions, as is the case of vocal traditions in Eastern countries, or as a result of string instruments like *santur*, that indeed include adherent notes between mainstream ones.

Practically, this means that the well-known piano interface of seven white and five black keys per octave is altered as shown in Figure 7.

Indeed, musicians refer to the "well tempered clavier" as the prevailing interface for Western music being shaped since the Bach era. For most people this is equivalent to the easily recognizable piano Interface on the left of Figure 7. However, for many people outside the prevailing realm of Western societies, such an interface would be considered as a meager contribution and its contempt would be remedied by the interface on the right.

What makes things worse, is the advent of chromaticism (Politis et al., 2015b), that demands alterations not only in the number of notes per octave, but most importantly, in the intervals between main notes. Indeed, the move towards global music cannot ignore the fact that most Eastern traditions dip well into chromaticism. Therefore, keyboards that can reproduce scales with microtonal distributions are essential for the multimedia sonification of global music. Thus far this was not easily achieved: the lack of appropriate keyboard interfaces has not allowed the penetration of electronic music to Eastern traditions, continuing therefore the rift between East in West.

There is hope that soon this miscalculation may be cured.

The Audiovisual Cabal: From Mobile Device Interfaces to High Quality Large Screens

During the last couple of centuries, music recordings and productions worldwide have accumulated in immense indeed collections of music resources, which lie interspersed in different media on earth. Several years ago, it would imagine impossible to organize suitably and make accessible to any interested user all this vast volume of music data.

Actually, the audiophile a generation ago relied on his own efforts to create a personal collection, which in most cases rarely surpassed the 5,000 limit for songs recorded in vinyl or cassettes. And of course, there was the radio, not exactly an on demand service, that made use of really large repositories that on average handled some 500,000 musical compositions per station.

Of course, the shift from vinyl recordings to CDs caused a qualitative leap to a great height for the human sensorium, since copies were undistinguished from the original recordings, but it did not ameliorate user interactivity, nor it did cure the distribution shortcomings of the music industry. Indeed, the audience was kept within its local artistic boundaries and could not elevate to more prominent features of music synchrony and diachrony.

However, with the advent of new technologies, the digitization of sound gave new perspectives and capabilities to the music community. The growth of Internet, the small (in size) digital music files, the disks of enormous capacity and the development of computer music led the scientists to focus their efforts in organizing great music collections, which are accessible from the Web. The Digital Music Libraries offer their users new ways of interaction with music repositories and music stores online. Some of the capabilities of Digital Music Libraries are: classification, filing and sharing of music, music information retrieval etc. (Margounakis & Politis, 2011)

A notable digital media player, created by Apple Inc., which can be used for organizing digital music and video files is iTunes. The application also comprises an interface for managing the popular devices of the same company: iPod and iPhone. Hence, it has played a vital role for the revolution of mobile device interfaces that has led to notable, structural changes in the audiovisual industry bases. Moreover, iTunes has the capability of connecting to the online iTunes Store via Internet for purchasing and downloading of music, videos, TV series, applications, iPod games, audio books, several podcasts and ringtones. If we consider strictly music, then iTunes is a "digital jukebox" for organizing, sharing and listening to music (Voida et al., 2005).

Although iTunes is considered to be the most popular example of a music repository, according to the dominant business model for music distribution, YouTube is viewed more than 500-million times a day and has become one of the most spectacular success stories of the Internet in recent years. But the dazzling influence of the video file sharing website YouTube.com may have only just begun, after the site promoted ways of interaction that observers say could revolutionize the music industry and threaten even the online music giant iTunes (Margounakis & Politis, 2011).

YouTube's popularity has been based on the facility it offers users to post short home videos, usually of about five minutes, on the site, which other users can view, link to and share. Indeed, this is the key element for the alteration of music industry: mobile devices that are equipped with high quality cameras can record many musical events, that otherwise would slip into oblivion. Of course, high quality audiovisual events recorded with professional equipment, and duly broadcasted serve as the basic supply mechanism for YouTube and similar hubs. However, the ever-ameliorating process of capturing digitally all public events that have music investment has given an unparalleled breadth for digitally imprinting nearly every music performance in our planet!

Indeed, it is surprising, an exception to the general rule, if a music event is not present in YouTube! And what's moreover, there seems to be no copyright violation, since many of these uploads are recorded by mobile devices held by assembled spectators.

To present some other revolutionary moments of the canvas, it is noteworthy to mention Internet-radio.

Radio (along with television) has been one of the most powerful popular media during the last decades. Its evolution into the Internet world led to the development of *Internet Radio*. Internet Radio is also known as web radio, net radio, streaming radio or e-radio. Internet Radio actually serves at the transmission of radio sound through the web, however with audio and video format broadcasts, for the ones who can receive in both formats. New tools and applications serve as interactive media that tend to cure the traditional radio station handicap, that the user (as in traditional radio) has little control on the transmission process.

Internet Radio is becoming more and more popular since many e-radio stations provide for free news, sports, interviews and all kinds of music to the users, as in the traditional radio stations. Apart from the online versions of the actual traditional radio stations, many amateur e-radio stations create a great variety of music selections to the users worldwide.

It is obvious, that this way of streaming is bread and butter for mobile device interfaces, which may well complement their ubiquitousness with the potential for on-line transmission and reception (Ting & Wildman, 2002).

What is interesting is that the high capacity in broadband services shifts the online audience from simple listeners to music emissions to become viewers of music. So, in technological terms on-line servers streamline less mp3 files than their audiovisual equivalent: mp4, mpeg, avi and so on. With regard to synaesthesia, viewers receive more complete sense impressions, since video streaming of the staged events excites more strong feelings of enthusiasm, exhilarating experiences related with the perception of stylized movements, lighting and colors, gestures, and joggling pirouettes.

Again, this revolution would be unfinished, if it did not engage the conjugate of mobile device viewing, the big screen, in high-definition spectacle screening. It is obvious that had not this advance occurred, mp3 alone could not keep the public plugged in.

For the scope of this article, the envisaged scope is focused on the mobile device potential. Amidst exhaustion, however, and sharply falling profits, it is highly predictable that the smartphone industry will couple with the big-screen industry and seek ways to wirelessly broadcast crisp images and videos from mobile devices to the closest monitors available. In brief, music promotion will be connected with the advances of the mobile device industry and seemingly will be hovered by its audiovisual success stories: not easily a music clip will not be accompanied by its video variants.

Connecting Audio and Visual Devices: Reasoning Expediency

The digital playground of appliances, cameras of various sizes and potential, head-lights, robotic lighting equipment, sound devices of variable sizes and capacity mingling with powerful synthesizers seems to be forming the tools of the trade pursuing to reshape entertainment and music performance. Therefore, the notion of interconnection is not restricted to MIDI interface; instead, it seeks new road maps to correlate and consistently engage types of equipment that were thus far placed on separate trails.

If it is difficult for MIDI like protocols to engulf the variety of scales and alterations that exist in the global scene of ethnic music it is even more ambitious to correlate it with visual effects. The eminent shortcomings in representing aurally the exact pitches provide hindrance in mingling video streaming and lighting with audio in real time.

However, the "future" is technologically present: as seen if Figure 8 a variety of hi-tech audiovisual devices is used already in practice by professionals associated in recording visually striking performances. What is left for scientists, either in academia or within the industry, is to instigate a MIDI like protocol involving audio and video events in a synchronized, parameterized manner.

Figure 8. Combining audiovisual tools and services for visually striking performances. Left: The audiostream within the DJ's laptop music library. Audio streams are accompanied with robotic lighting streams. Center: A visual effect that cannot be performed by the DJ. It has the form of a "visual" loop. Right: The DJ is bypassing programmed effects and improvises according to the public's mood.

As it is perceived, music reproduction it is not a mere subject of interconnection and functioning. From this point and onwards the technological developments give further possibilities for the stage director: he can record all kinds of movement along with its attributes (musical, theatrical, audiovisual,...) and reuse them, the very same way that audio engineers take advantage of loops. Further more, if wireless devices are used, not only the stage set up overload is significantly reduced, but also the possibility of handling the system from distance is given, with what ever implications remote handling and interaction may bring to the world of performing arts.

In large area events, as is the case of massive crowd concerts and spectacles, the floor of the stage is equipped with sensors of various technologies. We distinguish three major approaches, thus far, in translating the mood, aesthetics and artistic content that streamed:

1. **Motion Sensors:** In practice wearable technology, stage based sensors, laser harps, and similar.
2. **Remote Controlled Sensors**: Video streams, infra red beams, laser lightings, exploited holography, stimulated emissions, LED technology and many more.
3. **Internet or Mobile Telephony Network Extensions:** Remote voting, opinion probing, mood sensing via tweets, distant users' reciprocal reaction and similar.

The wide use of mobile and portable devices has exasperated heavy cost reductions, when Internet technologies are involved, has changed the dominant business model and motivates for a different, altered type of participation which promotes more active engagement between performers, stage directors, producers and the general public.

Gradually, protocols that govern the exchange, transmission and synchronization of data electronically between devices flow in, guaranteeing a steady stream of audiovisual data. As a result, streams of big multimedia data production systems flood the WWW entertainment highway.

ACHIEVING EFFICIENT INTERACTIVITY

Human-Machine Interaction plays a crucial role for the performing arts, as increasingly performers and engineers find themselves in stringent communication with equipment that demands very short response times for task completion. Moreover, it binds artistic performance, which engages creative skills with strict machine configurations, and therefore it relates computer programs that intervene in artistic design in a manner quite different from the approach thus far utilized in classic Human-Computer Interaction (Preece et al., 2002). Typical HCI approaches hence have disadvantages when pairing expressive normality with precision and detail to accomplished stage standards (Miranda & Wanderley, 2006).

When implementing an interactive technological environment, four levels of influence are clearly distinguished:

1. The "translation" system successfully materializing the transformation from one form to the other; for example, a sequence of dancing steps may well and according to the musicological rules be interpreted to instrumental sound.
2. When the human factors of a performance understand how their movements and their activity on stage alters the functional characteristics of the performance.
3. When the whole technological environment functions in such a way that the public comprehends the interaction taking place, without having been previously informed on the performed function.
4. When the audience itself may alter the flow of the presentation; for example the overt movements of the public may redirect the sequence of events thrilling the climax of a concert.

For interactive performances, a split second is more or less the margin of tolerance for the audience; in practice, the time gap between the movements of the performers on stage and the response of the audiovisual supporting mechanism marks the smoothness of presentation. If the audience perceives the faintest inconsistency, usually as a time lag in synchronization, then the impression of retardation in movement is felt. Even worse, if these inconsistencies accumulate, the spectators begin thinking about the performance's intellect, that physical movements are inconsistent or irrelevant with the supporting audiovisual environment.

All these advances are not irrelevant with the new face of music. The term Digital Musical Instruments (aka DMI) characterizes the twofold of modern instrumentation which has two major characteristics: a) an interface that recognizes and accordingly interprets human movements, and b) a digital unit for the production of sound. These two units are independent in their technological development and yet so closely interconnected in their strategic mapping. In traditionally musical instruments this twofold segregation is nearly impossible (Wanderley & Batier, 2000).

The term "mapping" usually describes the mathematical process of correlating the elements of one dataset with those of another. In computer music mapping is often correlated with algorithmic composition, where a parameter characterized by an array of musical attributes may well climax to a crescendo of some kind or transform itself to another parameter controlling other aspects of the performance (Winkler,1998).

One of the issues that professionals have to solve when producing highly interactive audiovisual performances is the following: how the components that comprise musical skill may be mapped with visual effects and human motion? As the notion of interactive performance, which is so old yet so new, conveys to a new meaning involving machine automation, the multiplicity of technological parameters puzzles DJs, VJs, directors and programmers, for which design principles should prevail for an effective and efficient interactive performance.

More and more producers sum-up to the conclusion that there is not a particular technology per se that impacts the synaesthesia of the audience, but rather a combination of them. The triggering signals for example may be beams of light, on-stage visual effects, or computer-controlled audio effects.

However, music is not a mere collection of audio effects. Music perception involves highly complex events and successions, which usually are depicted as a musical score. Although this form of representation is rather incomplete in describing stage parameters, at least it provides the exact time parameters for event handling.

Increasingly, optical effects controllers, regulators and programming elements in the form of plug-ins are attached to the cue list forming a formidable interaction environment elaborating an extravaganza of lights, sound and music

Performing Arts: Tools and Technologies

Technological means have been used in the entertainment sector quite a while. In contemporary staged performances, the more complicated and realistic the production is, the more it depends on the upright support of machinery and equipment for its realization. Supported activities may range from detailed coordination of time lapsed musical events, up to complex operations when the interaction with the audience is encountered.

The use of largely automatic equipment is widely encountered: moving scenery, robotic lighting and audiovisual effects propel sensory impression and stimulate more active participation. However, although digital technology is advanced within the music industry, the Human-Machine Interaction part is rather lagging behind. What has not been incorporated with smoothness in staged performances is expression normality, exactness and detail that can be deployed in parallel with the music score, and accordance with the properties of human sensing.

Take laser music interfaces, for instance. They were presented first by G. Rose back in 1977. Since then, many variants have been produced varying is size, operability and interconnectivity. Pioneers in this field are B. Szainer, Y. Terrien and P. Guerre (Wiley & Kapur, 2009), who has manufactured the first MIDI compatible Laser Harp, and J. Jarre, the renowned French composer.

Laser Harp is musical instrument that produces music by deploying laser beams instead of strings. In Figure 9 an optoelectronic custom Laser Harp is shown. Nine green lasers constitute the performing interface of the instrument. This harp is equipped with a MIDI interconnection that drives a computer multimedia system that actually produces the sound. Indeed, more professional experimental devices have been produced, like the one demonstrated by Endo, Moriyama and Kuhara (Endo et al., 2012). For instance, by loading plug-ins that have different samples, a variety of effects is invoked that can produce a wide range of musical sounds. It can also trigger video or still image projection, though this characteristic is the early stages of its development.

For laboratory experimentation, laser harps can base their operation on Arduino cards, which are able to recognize when the laser beam is interrupted, and accordingly they can produce suitable notes for a prescribed music pattern. Such systems inherently endorse evolution in interaction practices. In Figure 9 is depicted the way that Arduino based arrays of optoelectronics can operate on proj-

Figure 9. Arduino programming elements forming a laser harp
Image cropped from Arduino users' forum

ects deploying prototypes of microcontrollers for the USB-MIDI interface, firmware and software, which can read and write MIDI events to/from the Arduino.

These interfaces are not the only ones monopolizing the field. For many decades electronic musical instrument could be played without physical contact using Theremin like devices. These controllers can produce music by playing tones generated by two high-frequency oscillators and the pitch controlled by the movement of the performer's hand toward and away from the circuit.

Based on this tradition many variants of the Laser Harp come to light. One of them is Roland's D-Beam and another is Termenova, i.e. a Theremin like device combined with laser beams and sensors like Airstick, that use IR detectors (Hasan et al., 2002; Franco, 2005).

Termenova adds degrees of control to the reproduction of music: by combining the Laser Harp with Theremin like devices, it allows the recognition of the height in which the laser beam is interrupted by the user's hand, and therefore extra characteristics may be added to the playing interface. Even further, Laser Harp may become Tweet Harp by incorporating to the performing array the possibility for Text-To-Speech reproduction with Internet feedback (Dahl et al., 2011).

Indeed, this potential has not been fully vitalized, since the wide public's intervention via the Internet is most times manually processed, indeed limiting massive participation.

It seems that musical interaction design, especially for large audiences or via the Internet has a road map ahead to convey. Perhaps the dissemination of sensor-based devices, like smartphones, wearable devices, remote sensors, radars (for detecting presence, direction or distance), floor sensors (capable of measuring capacitance, changes to the local electric field caused by a person or any other conductive object coming near them), infrared equipment and many others will change the attitude of the participating public to a more active role than cheerlead.

CONCLUSION

Rich content, cropping out of high quality multimedia environments is pouring out of broadcasted musical performances that can easily reach TV quality standards.

The reproduction and the transmission of lively staged audiovisual works through broadcasts and the Internet are of great importance for the formation of a global public sphere of entertainment. Amidst serious concerns about the rampaging of the multimedia industry due to extensive intellectual property violation, the mass media community hopes for a better future by amassing with the Internet and stockpiling a new generation of performances, that surpass in richness what has been uploaded thus far.

This way they plan to provoke worldwide attraction, and further more, build up their business models for its financial exploitation. Needless to say, that contemporary models do not rely only on sales of audiovisual material, which recently has become a "virtual" commodity rather than a tangible artifact (CD, DVD, Blue-Ray), but on distribution techniques, and even more, on advertisement.

Apart from broadcasting, the ease of access attracts growing number of users to the Internet highways. They can enjoy ubiquitously music streams not only by watching TV, but also by using their smartphones and other portable devices.

It seems that a new era in the form and format of music has just begun.

REFERENCES

Aikin, J. (Ed.). (2003). *Software Synthesizers, San Francisco*. Backbeat Books.

Cangeloso, S. (2012). *LED Lighting -Illuminate your World with Solid State Technology - A Primer to Lighting the Future*. O-Reilly - Maker Press.

Cook, P. (1999). *Music, Cognition and Computerized Sound, an Introduction to Psychoacoustics*. Cambridge, MA: MIT Press.

Cook, P. (2002). *Real Sound Synthesis for Interactive Applications*. A. K. Peters. doi:10.1201/b19597

Cox, C. (2003). Versions, Dubs, and Remixes: Realism and Rightness in Aesthetic Interpretation. In Interpretation and its Objects. Rodopi.

Cox, C., & Warner, D. (2007). *Audio Cultures, Readings in Modern Music*. Continuum.

Dahl, L., Herrera, J., & Wilkerson, C. (2011). TweetDreams: Making Music with the Audience and the World Using Real-Time Twitter Data. In *Proceedings of Proceedings of the 2011 Conference on New Interfaces for Musical Expression NIME2011*.

Endo, A., Moriyama, T., & Kuhara, Y. (2012). Tweet Harp: Laser Harp Generating Voice and Text of Real-time Tweets in Twitter. In *Proceedings of Proceedings of the 2012 Conference on New Interfaces for Musical Expression NIME2012*. University of Michigan.

Field-Selfridge, E. (1997). *Beyond MIDI*. Cambridge, MA: MIT Press.

Fox, M., & Kemp, M. (2009). *Interactive Architecture*. Princeton Architectural Press.

Franco, I. (2005). The Airstick: A Free-Gesture Controller Using Infrared Sensing. In *Proceedings of the 2005 Conf. on New Instruments for Musical Expression*.

Graham-Knight, K., & Tzanetakis, G. (2015). Adaptive Music Technology using the Kinect. In *Proceedings of the 8th ACM International Conference on PErvasive Technologies Related to Assistive Environments*.

Hasan, L., Yu, N., & Paradiso, J. (2002). The Termenova: a Hybrid Free-Gesture Interface. In *Proceedings of the 2002 Conference on New Instruments for Musical Expression*.

Margounakis, D., & Politis, D. (2011). Music Libraries - How Users Interact with Music Stores and Repositories. In I. Iglezakis, T.-E. Synodinou, & S. Kapidakis (Eds.), *E-Publishing and Digital Libraries - Legal and Organizational Issues*. Hershey, PA: IGI-Global.

Miranda, E., & Wanderley, M. (2006). *New Digital Musical Instruments: Control and Interaction Beyond the Keyboard*. Middleton, WI: AR Editions.

Noble, J. (2009). *Programming Interactivity*. O'Reilly.

Ouzounian, G. (2007). Visualizing Acoustic Space. *Musiques Contemporaines*, *17*(3), 45–56. doi:10.7202/017589ar

Politis, D., & Margounakis, D. (2010). Modelling Musical Chromaticism: The Algebra of Cross-Cultural Music Perception. *IJAR*, *2*(6), 20–29.

Politis, D., Margounakis, D., Tsalighopoulos, G., & Kyriafinis, G. (2015a). Transgender Musicality, Crossover Tonality, and Reverse Chromaticism: The Ontological Substrate for Navigating the Ocean of Global Music. *International Research Journal of Engineering and Technology, 2*(5).

Politis, D., Piskas, G., Tsalighopoulos, M., & Kyriafinis, G. (2015b). variPiano™: Visualizing Musical Diversity with a Differential Tuning Mobile Interface. *International Journal of Interactive Mobile Technologies*, *9*(3).

Preece, J., Rogers, Y., & Sharp, H. (2002). *Interaction Design: Beyond Human-Computer Interaction*. Wiley & Sons.

Schubert, E. (2004). Modeling Perceived Emotion with Continuous Musical Features. *Music Perception*, *21*(4), 561–585. doi:10.1525/mp.2004.21.4.561

Ting, C., & Wildman, S. (2002). The economics of Internet radio. In *30th Research Conference on Communication, Information and Internet Policy*.

Voida, A., Grinter, R., Ducheneaut, N., Edwards, W., & Newman, M. (2005). Listening in: Practices Surrounding iTunes Music Sharing. In *Proceedings of the SIGCHI Conference on Human Factors in Computing Systems*. ACM Press. doi:10.1145/1054972.1054999

Wanderley, M., & Battier, M. (Eds.). (2000). *Trends in Gestural Control of Music*. Ircam – Centre Pompidou.

Wiley, M., & Kapur, A. (2009). Multi-Laser Gestural Interface - Solutions for Cost-Effective and Open Source Controllers. In *Proceedings of Proceedings of the 2009 Conference on New Interfaces for Musical Expression NIME2009.*

Winkler, T. (1998). *Composing Interactive Music – Techniques and Ideas Using Max.* MIT Press.

Yeo, W., & Berger, J. (2005). Application of imagesonification methods to music. In *Proceedings of the International Computer Music Conference (ICMC2005).*

Zhang, Z. (2012). Microsoft Kinect Sensor and its Effect. *IEEE MultiMedia, 9*(2), 4–10. doi:10.1109/MMUL.2012.24

KEY TERMS AND DEFINITIONS

Arduino: It is an open-source computer hardware and software company, project and user community that designs and manufactures microcontroller-based kits for creating interactive electronic projects. Arduino is synonym for promoting a platform rather than specific products. Many other makers and software producers promote their products easily recognizable as based on the Arduino platform. Programming and interconnection takes place using the Wiring language, which relies on C++ like libraries to implement control over a range of electronic devices. Also languages like Max/MSP, PureData, Processing and SuperCollider are supported. The first two are specializing on music production.

Eurovision Song Contest: Most often simply referred to as *Eurovision*, it is the most influential worldwide TV song competition. Running since 1956, primarily among the member countries of the European Broadcasting Union (EBU), it has attracted massive online audiences, that in recent years surpass the 500,000,000 threshold. Apart from live viewing, it is influential via its own repository www.eurovision.tv or YouTube, extending the saga of a truly multinational and multilingual complex contest, that triggers audiences well beyond the European sphere of influence. Broadcasted to countries like USA and China that do not participate, it has caused interest as far as Asia or Australia; the latter was allowed to compete as a guest entrant for the 60th anniversary of the event in 2015.

Laser Harp: It is an electronic musical user interface and a laser lighting display for on stage performances. It projects several laser beams - which of course cannot produce music, but when a beam is being interrupted it sends MIDI messages to a sound generating unit, computer or a synthesizer, that undertakes sonification.

Mash-Up: Recording created by merging digitally, mastering and synchronizing instrumental tracks with vocal tracks from two or more different songs.

Mastering: Taking advantage of original movies, recordings, or multimedia elements from which copies of artistic work ready for distribution are made.

Multimedia Design: Technological development has multiplied and diversified the vectors for creation, production and exploitation for texts, images, sounds and videos. High quality compound productions of such elements, distributed via the internet, in various formats, become focal points for increasingly high interaction from the Learning Community. The design of such products is promoting multimedia learning.

Rich Content: Videos along with texts, sounds, animations and videos have emerged as a dominant media for entertainment and education purposes. Rich content relies on high quality audiovisual visual components. A key element, however, in most cases, is interaction.

Theremin: More of family of interrelated devices, it owes its name to the Russian physicist L. Theremin (anglicized form of L. Termen) who in 1919 invented an influential RF instrument, having recently once again come back to the music spotlight. Theremins are played without being touched. They use two antennas, one for controlling pitch and the other for adjusting intensity. As a hand moves towards the vertical antenna, the pitch gets higher. As it comes nearer the second, the horizontal antenna, volume decreases.

ENDNOTE

1 The rotating Eurovision Song Contest is a paradigm of its own kind: it attracts global audiences of about 1 billion every year, commencing from the national selections stage of songs and artists for its participating country, till the culmination of the main event, and it seems that it has become the equivalent of athletic big happenings like Olympic Games, World Cups and Grand Prix megastar events. Its annual cost is indeed extravagant taking into consideration that each one of the 40 participating countries organizes its own selection event.

Chapter 8
Music in Video Games

Dimitrios Margounakis
Aristotle University of Thessaloniki, Greece

Ioanna Lappa
Hellenic Open University, Greece

ABSTRACT

The industry of video games has rapidly grown during the last decade, while "gaming" has been promoted into an interdisciplinary stand-alone science field. As a result, music in video games, as well as its production, has been yet a state-of-the-art research field in computer science. Since the production of games has reached a very high level in terms of complication and cost (the production of a 3-d multi-player game can cost up to millions of dollars), the role of sound engineer / composer / programmer is very crucial. This chapter describes the types of sound that exist in today's games and the various issues that arise during the musical composition. Moreover, the existing systems and techniques for algorithmic music composition are analyzed.

INTRODUCTION

Sound is a very important part in a video game. It helps the player to integrate into the game and the character. By the term audio we refer to all the sound elements that make up a game: sound effects, dialogues, songs, background music and interface sounds. Depending on the type or the mechanics of the game, there is a different

DOI: 10.4018/978-1-5225-0264-7.ch008

relationship between all these elements. Nevertheless, these elements contribute to the experience enjoyed by the player when playing a game.

In the video games sound is vaguely referred to as "interactive", "adaptive" and "dynamic". However, there have been efforts to separate these three concepts. Interactive is the sound that happens as interplay to the player's moves. When the player presses a button, the character, for example, will shoot and then a certain sound will be heard, which is going to happen each time the player shoots. On the other hand, the adaptive sound does not interfere with the player's moves, but adjusted according to changes that occur in the game, such as the music in the video game Super Mario Brothers (Nintendo 1985), which while playing in a steady rhythm, changes when the time finishes. The term "dynamic" sound includes the above two conditions. So is the sound that interacts on player's actions, but also the flow of the game.

In a video game, players react in proportion to the sounds they hear apart from the image. There are games that are based on sound, and are ideal for players with visual impairments. Such games create an environment in the player's mind, which uses different sounds produced to move through the game. One such example is the game Papa Sangre (2010). It is a sound game in which the player moves in 5 castles trying to avoid monsters in order to collect musical keys. Monsters react to sounds produced by the player, if they run or push an object, so the player learns to listen carefully as moves in the game, and pays attention to all sounds.

Figure 1. Game surroundings in Papa Sangre
Source: Papa Sangre (2010)

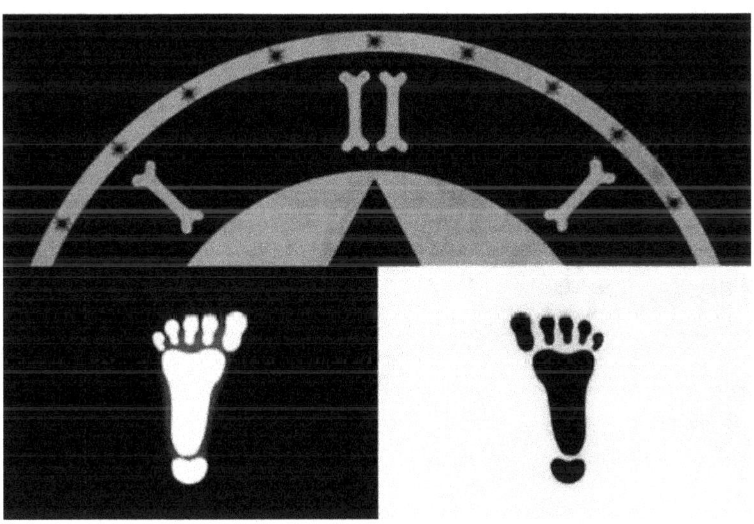

Contrariwise, in games that combine sound and image, an inseparable relationship is created: sound makes us see a picture differently, and this in turn makes us listen the sound differently etc. The console Atari 2600, released in the late 1970s, had very poor graphics and audio capabilities. The pictures looked like large pixel pieces with result that if someone that was out of the game saw them, would be unable to make sense. On the other hand, most sounds were very hard and had nothing to do with natural sounds. However, when combined sound and image, acquired meaningful game. So we can understand that short bursts in the game Combat (1977) is actually cannon blasts, and the hollow noise that sounds continuously is a moving tank.

There are two types of sounds in such games: the ones that are created by the player when they press a button and the ones that are based on the algorithm of the game, such as sounds that are heard at certain points of the game and build on timers within the code. The sounds created by the player are always interactive, and the sounds based on events of the game can be interactive or non-interactive. The rationale for interactive sounds is to be repeated, i.e. when the player makes the same move, the same sound will be heard. This helps the player to connect the sound with motion and essentially helps him while playing the game. Of course this can work negatively, when a sound is heard too many times in the game, especially when the player faces difficulties at some point in the game and is forced to spend a lot of time on it. Therefore sometimes there are different sounds stored on the soundtrack of the game which are selected randomly and relate to the same player's move. But

Figure 2. Combat (1977): In the game appear two tanks moving between walls

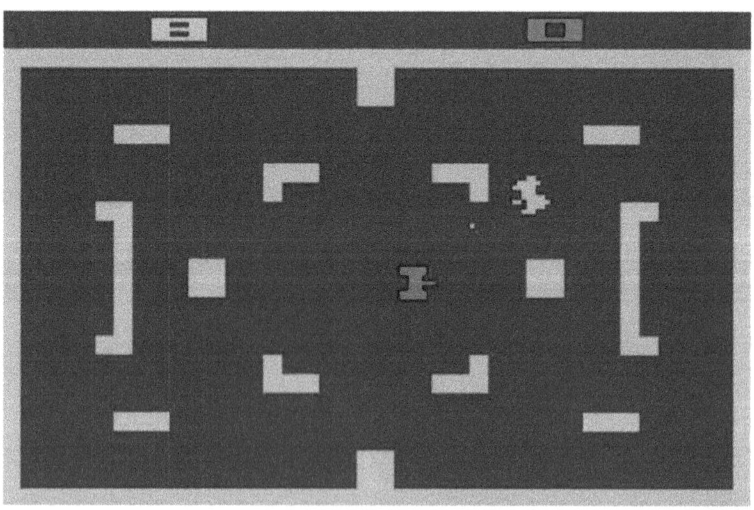

when it comes to music that is heard in the background of the game, this is not repeated endlessly, but there are built-in timers to turn off after a certain time. There are sounds in a game based on moves made by the player, but are connected to the onset of movement, such as the video game Heavy Rain (2010). That means that there may be a little motion-audio mismatch. For example, when the player closes a door slowly, the sound might stop one second before the completion of movement. However, such a discrepancy is not considered important, if this is not something that affects the development of the game.

How does the player interact in a game video? The events, actions and timings in a game video are unpredictable, and occur in real-time as the player moves through the game. Therefore all the elements that compose the music of the game will also have to evolve in real time. But the problem here is this: How can the designer of the game predict the duration of the sound if the movement the player makes is unpredictable? For this reason, many sound designers to video games believe that the solution to this problem is the synthesis of music and not fragmented sounds.

Apart from the sound effects in a video game, many games contain mostly dialogues or alternate texts and dialogues depending on the plot. In such games the player can adjust the playback speed of the dialogue, or even to regulate to some extent the timbre of the voice. Such a possibility as is the adaptation of the voice is very important in games where the player can choose the appearance of the character, creating an avatar. According to surveys where the possibility is given to us to create a character we tend to make it by using as a standard our own self. This way the player creates a character that can recognize, thus they will want to choose the character to sound like them. Games like mySims (2007) and The Sims 3 (2009), have a voice "slider" enabling players to adjust the tone to their avatar. Where there is not this possibility, many players argue that it is preferable to not have a voice at all, than to have a "wrong" one. In other games texts and dialogues alternate, depending on the plot, or specific text options can be given for the player to choose, and in accordance with evolving flow of the game.

In some video games there are mechanisms that enable the player to play a musical instrument in the game, or even add their own music using a podcast song or composing one of their own. The Lord of the Rings Online: Shadows of Angmar (2007) gives the possibility to the players, as they acquire musical instrument, to enter "music mode" which uses an ASCII keyboard, and play songs in real time. Another example is the Guitar Hero (2005) in which players use a guitar-shaped controller, pretending to play a bass or a guitar. Players match notes on the screen with the colored buttons on the controller, trying to score points and keep the audience excited.

Figure 3. Mass Effect 3: Dialog wheel in which appear three answers "I knew it / What's going on? / That's obvious"

Figure 4. Screenshot from the game Guitar Hero (2005)

EMOTIONAL ASPECTS OF HUMAN-COMPUTER INTERACTION IN VIDEO GAMES

A certain thing is that the whole environment of a virtual world in an interactive video game has to trigger certain feelings and emotions on the player to enhance the experience of gaming. One tool to achieve this goal is, of course, sound. Theories on psychoacoustics and research findings on human audio and music perception can be applied in order to have the desirable auditory result.

Each player understands the game's world in his/her own way, and lots of factors contribute to this. For sure, the player's experience, memories and expectations are some of these factors. But the game itself should lead them to certain feelings, according to the interaction, the events occurring at a certain time and the communication with other players and the environment itself. It has been proposed that a player forms a specific Game Ego within the game, during a process of re-identification (Wilhelmsson, 2006). The Game Ego is primarily a bodily based function that enacts a point of being within the game environment.

Sound has a very important function within games and can affect the player's Game Ego. Music is used to set game atmosphere and pace, and sound effects are used to give feedback to the player on actions and environmental change (Hendrikx, et. al. 2013). Although there is considerable resistance to algorithmic compositions from musicians and the general public (Edwards 2011), a variety of procedural techniques have been used in video-games. The most common way to obtain procedural sound is by using rule-based systems (Farnell 2007). However, the question that arises is "How deeply into the player's mind can algorithms go through, in order to affect the player's feelings?".

Munday (2007) analyzes the effect of music on the player in three levels:

1. **Environmental**: How music supports the perception of a gameworld. Taking into account the global power of music on listeners, we can observe that somber music can darken a sunny picture, whereas no end of sunny pictures can ever lighten somber music (Whalen 2004).
2. **Immersion**: How music supports the player's involvement in the game. For immersion to occur, the activity or stimulus has to be sufficiently engaging to block out the normal sense impressions of one's surroundings (Munday 2007).
3. **Diegetic**: How music supports a game narrative.

MUSIC COMPOSITION FOR VIDEO GAMES

Issues of Nonlinearity in Music Composition

The fact that in video games, the music production does not occur in a linear way, but is unpredictable and progresses in real time, makes the synthesis of it difficult. The smooth transition from a music signal (cue) to another plays an important role to the sequel of the game, as an unfortunate transition can create the opposite effect, and the game can lose some of its quality. Therefore many different types of transitions from one music label to another are used.

In the first video games that appeared, usually in games 8 and 16-Bit, the move was a direct link between the two cues, creating sudden interruption between the tracks, which was quite annoying for the player.

The most common technique is a quick fade out of the first signal and then the immediate start of the next (fade in). Even though this technique can be sharp, as the speed of fade. Another common technique is to use a sharp sound between the two cues. Since most abrupt transitions commonly found in battles, such sounds can be easily combined with gunfire, cross swords sounds etc.

A few more attempts have been made for successful transitions, more effective, but it is much more demanding for a composer because of nonlinearity. For example, some games use cue-to-cue variations, i.e. when a new cue is required, the current sequence may play for another measure or until there is a slowing-down of the tempo (downbeat), and then starts the next cue. The greatest difficulty in such changes is the time delay created. If for example in a game, the player received a sudden attack, it may take a few seconds until the change in the music cue happens. Nevertheless, it is a technique that is increasingly used as composers write hundreds of music clips for games, to reduce this switching time, and also to make their music more flexible.

Other methods include the synthesis of music in layers, i.e. music divided into musical instruments which may at any time be removed or added. This helps the changes in musical signals, but does not work on dramatic changes in a game.

Changes in musical matters do not only constitute the only difficulty for a video game music composer. The nonlinearity in games has many implications on how a game sounds overall. As we have mentioned, there are 5 types of sound in a game. Specifically, dialogues and sound effects of a battle for example, are mid-range, resulting if there are many such sounds there is a risk of creating a fuzzy sound. For example, if the character of the game is outdoors talking to another character and also has to listen to a distant sound (e.g. a shot) the result will be incomprehensible.

Another problem is the multi-player games. For example, if a game is designed to change cues when the player's health reached a bottom, what happens when a player is healthy and the other not? Or if an audible signal is designed to start at a certain point of the game, will it happen when they reach both players at this point, or only one?

Procedural Music in Video Games

Based on the degree of procedural processing the music of video games, the algorithms are divided into two categories: transformational algorithms and generative algorithms. The transformational algorithms have less impact on the size of the data but affect the overall structure. A phrase for instance can have many notes which can change the tone or some phrases can be restructured into a song, while the actual words do not change. Also, in a sentence can be added instruments. On the other hand, the generative algorithms to increase the total size of the music data as the basic audio materials are created. Due to the difficulty composition of procedural music games, most of the algorithms that control the music in games are transformational and not generative.

With transformational algorithms there are many possibilities in a game. For example instruments can be added or removed, or the rhythm of the music can be changed.

Lately, the use of recombinatorial music or in other words open form is increasing. The sequences or music tracks are left to chance or the musician. The difficulty here is that there is no one to make the decision about the order of the playback, and so data are already scheduled and the order is controlled by an algorithm. The structure of the composition is produced by a computer or by the player, therefore, although the sequence is random, but the tags are not generated algorithmically.

Another form of transformational algorithm uses smaller changes in pre-programmed musical sequences, based on parameters such as repetitions / loops, definitions start/expiry point, etc. In this way the composer creates music sequences and then ranks them depending on which quotes They will play continuously, what will change, what instruments will rotate etc. For example, in a battle, a musical instrument can be used to indicate a successful move and another when the player receives a hit, or as culminates the battle to change the tone music.

While a game cannot predict the player's movements through rotations of music can create an illusion. In the example above, the music could change depending on the player or the enemy's health:

"IF player's health is more than enemy health, THEN play WINNING music. IF player's health is less than enemy health, THEN play LOSING music.

There have been many studies on the definition of algorithmic music production, according to Wooler et al. Peter Langston provides the algorithm "riffology" in which the computer selects the parameters according to their potential weight as which song melody will be played, how fast and how loud it will be played, what notes will be skipped, where a pause will enter etc. To select the next chorus, the program randomly selects (for example, depending on the musical scale). For choosing which note will be eliminated or replaced with another, a dynamic possibility is created, which starts at a low price, increasing to the maximum in the middle of a solo and drops again at a low price at the end of the solo. A solo is unclear at first, stationary in the middle and culminates at the end. So the result is a perpetual improvisation on a musical accompaniment. (Langston, 1986)

Because video games follow a particular scenario and strategy, types of senior procedural music are not used frequently. However, in some cases, due to the abstract nature of the game, procedural music has been used. For example, in Spore, the music has been created in Pure Data and consists of many small samples which compose the soundtrack. All melodies and rhythms are produced by certain rules (for example, a sequence can be used by notes of the same scale). Players can create their own music or music collections by using rhythmic sequences. However, there are mechanisms that limit the capabilities of the players, so that no drastic changes will be made.

With the rise of online multiplayer games, new possibilities have been created concerning procedural music, since the sheer number of the associated players can influence the music.

Dynamic Music Systems

Over the years, various musical dynamic systems have been developed. Several of those are already used in games. Given below, an overview of such systems.

Vertical Sequencing

It is one of the oldest and most common techniques and is running with the play of multiple tracks simultaneously. Each fragment contains a portion of the total music. The intensity of the tracks changes independently and dynamically, depending on the state of the game. This changes the style of play and tension is created in a battle for example. Figure 5 shows an example of vertical repeat sequence. The 4 boxes are 4 different tracks during playback. The graph shows the evolution of the game in time. As we see the curve reaches a high intensity only briefly, compared to the baseline level. One of the advantages of this system is that it can react very quickly

Figure 5. Vertical resequencing

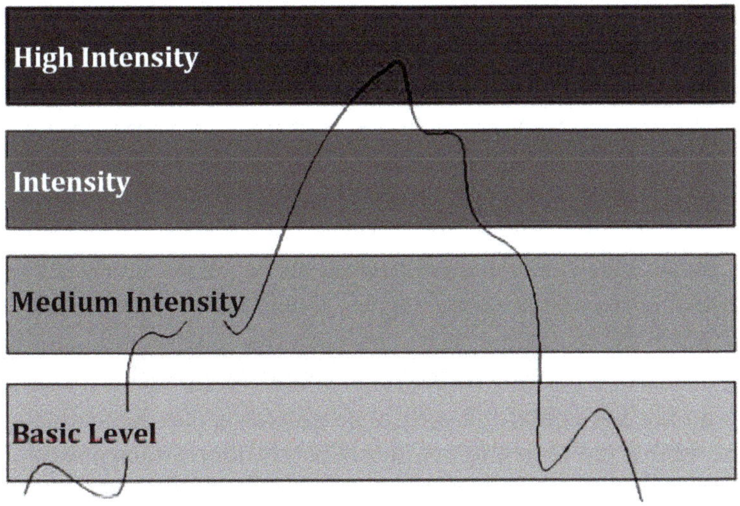

and change the mix in milliseconds, since the only thing that changes is the intensity. In contrast, the greatest disadvantage is failure to adapt the composition during playback. While it has created a dynamic mix, the composition has been made in advance, so when a piece follows a harmonious progress, all the other tracks that will be played with it should match.

Horizontal Resequencing

While the vertical resequencing involves a variety of music tracks that play simultaneously, horizontal resequencing reshapes many extracts or cells (namely audio files of a few seconds) which follow one another (horizontally). These networks grow very easily as we add music. (see Figure 6)

Figure 6. Horizontal resequencing

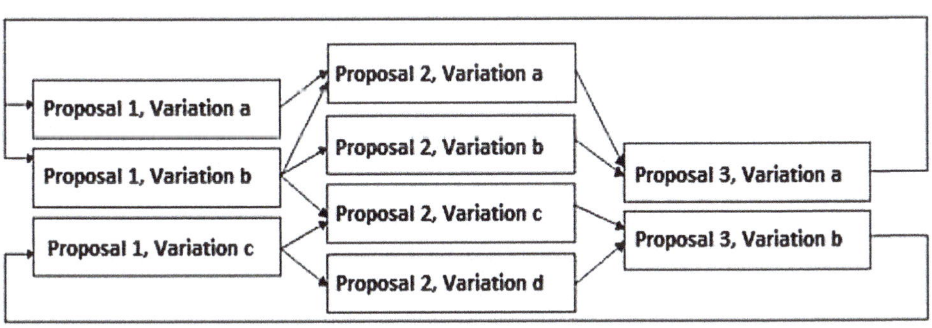

Unlike vertical resequencing, horizontal is expandable. If a soundtrack should support a continuous transition from one composition to another piece, then all we have to do is to write 2-3 transition cells. That way we can create a music network. This happens in games like Killzone 2 (Guerilla Games, 2009) and Killer Instinct (Rare, 2013). One common difficulty is how long should each cell last. Because we can change musical direction by moving to a new cell, the length of the cells should be covered in a realistic range. Neither too big nor too small to create the melody. Figure 7 shows that the cells follow one another. The fifth cell has not been selected yet, because the system has not reached the end of the fourth cell yet. For the performance of horizontal resequencing, we should know that we cannot cut a cell, by starting playback of another, but to regulate the cells according to the reverb. Respectively, if a cell has accelerated, we cannot choose the next cell just before the transition. The horizontal and vertical resequencing, are not mutually exclusive and may be used at the same time. Admittedly this does not happen often because of the increasing difficulty in musical compositions.

Agent Based System

This system consists of several independent entities called agents. The agents do not replace the horizontal or vertical resequencing, but can improve the decision-making process and control of an audio system that is dynamic and consists of several components. Such a system can control more than audio, such as lighting, artificial intelligence etc. Each agent is responsible for one part of the sound. For example, an agent can monitor sound when there's a threat in the game, and another to monitor sound for the highest score. Both agents can make decisions independently and either supplement or oppose each other. This way the most unpredictable soundtracks

Figure 7. Cell Network

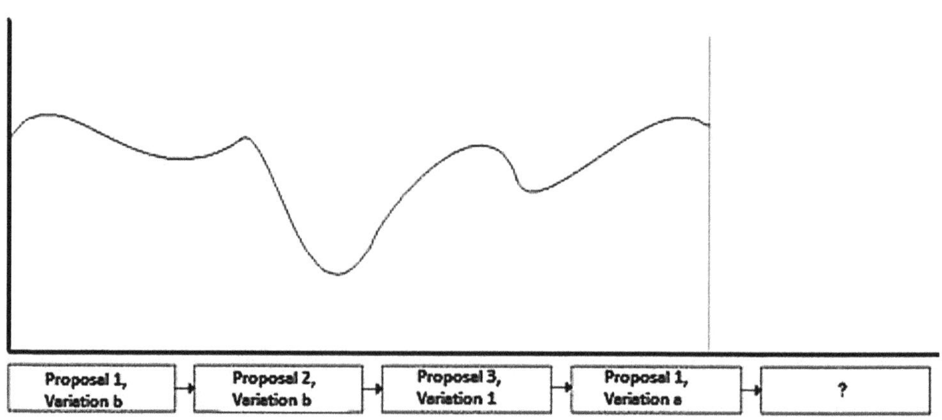

are created. We can namely give the general direction of the whole system, but we cannot know precisely every action. This results in not knowing whether the choices made by the agents are those that should be made.

Mixing in Real Time

There are systems like RUMR System that use different effects like reberbs and delays which change as the music plays. In SSX (EA 2012) it usually happens when the players do sports and get up or fall to the ground. The main disadvantage of mixing in real time is primarily based on techniques DSP. This means that the bigger (heavier) the effect the faster the CPU will run out.

TECHNIQUES FOR ALGORITHMIC MUSIC PRODUCTION

Algorithmic composition (also referred to as "automated composition") refers to the process of using some formal process to make music with minimal human intervention (Alpern, 1995). Following below, techniques for algorithmic music production which combined are used in various applications such as random play in music games.

Stochastic Binary Subdivision

This is a technique designed to create a rhythmic set of drums, since it was observed that most techniques for random music production fail because the metric structures are heard wrong. The complete notes are divided into halves, quarters, eighths, sixteenths etc. Although sometimes the notes are divided in triplets, rarely they are divided again in triplets. Thereby, 'random' rhythms that adhere to a model binary subdivision are created. (See Figure 8).

Figure 8. divvy ()

```
divvy(ip, lo, hi)
struct instr *ip;
{
      int mid = (lo + hi) >> 1;

      ip->pat[lo] = '|';
      if ((rand() % 100) < ip->density && hi - lo > ip->res) {
            divvy(ip, lo, mid);
            divvy(ip, mid, hi);
      }
```

The digital drum and melody program creates musical rhythms according to the technique shown in Figure 8. The divvy () shown in Figure 8 is the heart of the ddm (digital drum & melody). The instr structure contains amongst others, the density, namely the possibility that the division to the next level will occur, the res, i.e. the smaller note that can be created and the pat, a character string in which the beat generated stored. Figure 9 shows a typical input file for the program. The first column is the code that will be sent to the drum machine so as the sound of drums to be heard, the second column is the density, the third is the res, the fourth is the duration of the sound in 64ths, the fifth column relates to how loud is the sound, and the sixth concerns which MIDI channel will the sound be played on.

Figure 10 shows the output of the DDM in 2 forms. The first shows the results of counting errors (debugging) for all subdivisions and the second shows two musical measures with the final result. The '!' Indicates a subdivision where a drum «wants» to play and '#' show that will be played in reality. Priority is given to the musical instrument that appears earlier in the input file, so the bass drum BD (boot) even though all instruments wanted to play at this point. Similarly TOM3 drum is heard after 8 notes, having priority over the cymbals HHO (hi-hat).

"Riffology"

Creates free improvisations based on a model of human ones. In this model the basic unit used is the riff, a very small snippet of melody, which joined in time to create solos. The idea for the name of this algorithm came from the band guitarists. One of the most popular techniques that followed was to tie together several riff and play them at high speed, so what played a major role was good technique and riff repertoire, and not much thinking. This algorithm generates random selections of a specific weight for aspects such as what riff from the repertoire will be played,

Figure 9. Input file for DDM

```
45:75: 2:0: 96:1          BD
52:75: 4:0: 96:1          SD
57:50: 8:0:120:1          HHC
51:50: 8:0: 64:1          RIM
48:67: 8:0: 80:1          TOM3
54:70: 8:0: 64:1          CLAP
55:75: 8:0: 64:1          COWB
59:50:16:0: 80:1          HHO
53:67:16:0: 72:1          TOM1
```

Figure 10. Output file for DDM

```
A2  #...............................#............................... BD
E3  !...............#...............!...............#............... SD
A3  !...............................!............................... HHC
Eb3 !............................................................... RIM
C3  !.......#.......!...............!.......#.......!............... TOM3
Gb3 !...............................!.......!.......!.......#....... CLAP
G3  !...............................!.......!.......!.......!....... COWB
B3  !.......!.......!...............!............................... HHO
F3  !...............................!...#...!...#...!...#...!...#... TOM1
```

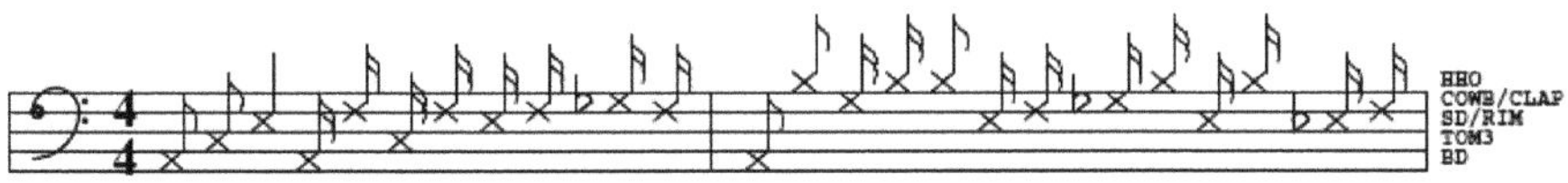

on what speed, what intensity, etc. These options are based on the model of an easy guitarist without imagination. Main which is illustrated in Figure 11 determines the number of meters, classifies the random number creator in the current year, sets the playback speed to 16 (2tempo = 21 eighths per measure entailing sixteenth), and enters a loop to create each measure. Inside the loop determines whether to change the rate at which you play the riff (20, 21, 22, i.e. eighths, sixteenths and thirty-second) measures the “energy” which will play the riff and then enters an interior loop which selects the riff to be played using the command pickriff () (see Figure 12).

Figure 11. Riffology main

```
main(argc, argv)
char   *argv[];
{
       int numbars, i, tempo, rpb, dur, energy, r, riff;

       numbars = argc > 1 ? atoi(argv[1]) : 2;     /* how many bars? */
       srand((int) time((long *) 0));              /* seed rand() */
       tempo = 1;                               /* initially 2 riffs / bar */
       for (i = 0; i < numbars; i++) {
              if (tempo > rand() % 3)                    /* play slower? */
                     --tempo;
              else if (tempo < rand() % 3)               /* play faster? */
                     tempo++;
              rpb = 1 << tempo;                    /* set riffs per bar */
              dur = BARLEN / (NPR * rpb);          /* calc note duration */
              energy = ecalc(i, numbars);          /* how energetic? */
              for (r = 0; r < rpb; r++) {
                     riff = pickriff();            /* pick next riff */
                     play(riff, dur, energy);      /* play it */
              }
       }
}
```

Figure 12. pickriff() command

```
riff = (rand() % 32767) % Numriffs; /* don't trust rand() */
if (Lstn == 0)                      /* no last note, so */
      return(riff);                 /* anything will do */
dn = abs(Lstn - Riffs[riff * NPR]); /* note distance */
if (dn == 0)                        /* we don't like 0*/
      dn = 6;
if (dn < min) {                     /* save best so far */
      bestr = riff;
      min = dn;
}
```

Figure 13 shows the command ecalc () that calculates the "energy", videlicet the guitarist's enthusiasm playing his solo. Starts dynamically, falls during the solo and up again as they approach the end. Depending on the value of ecalc (), is decided whether all the notes of the riff will be played or whether to repeal some (replacing them with the other or holding time above the previous note)

Key Phrase Animation: Intermediate Melodic Lines

This is a technique originally used by the animation designer and later by professional graphic designers. The designer draws the first frame containing the ends of the movement or appearance / disappearance of an object. These are the key frames. After the intermediate frames are generated by interpolating the key frame. This way the designers could define the largest part of the motion and then let less experienced designers to make the rest of the job with the intermediate frame. If we replace the key frames with musical phrases, and then interpolate tonalities and timings between the notes, then we have a musical version of the original technique. With this technique we benefit from the reduction of work after leaving the computer to do the hard work of intermediate phrases, but the result is different and unexpected when it comes to melodies. The program "kpa.c" creates a simple linear interpolation using the command interp () to create the synchronization between a phrase and speed. (See Figure 14).

Figure 13. ecalc() command

```
if (3 * i < numbars)          /* first third, rests increase */
      return(100 - (90 * i)   / numbars);
else if (3 * i > 2 * numbars) /* last third, decreasing rests */
      return(40 + (90 * i)    / numbars);
return(70);                   /* middle third, maximum rests */
```

Figure 14. interp() command

```
interp(b, e, step, numsteps)                 /* linear interp step/numsteps
                                             'twixt b & e */
long b, e;
{
      register int i, hadj;
      hadj = numsteps / 2;
      if (b <= e)
            i = ((e - b) * step + hadj)        / numsteps;
      else
            i = ((e - b) * step - hadj)        / numsteps;
      return(b + i);
}
```

Given the tone must have discrete values, due to limitations of the MIDI data; there is a limit on how soft will move tonicity be. Interference with several intermediate tends to produce static effects, unless the initial and final phrases have large difference in tonality, or if used 12-ketone scale.

Fractal Interpolation

With the international term fractal in Mathematics, Physics and in many other sciences we call a geometric pattern that is repeated unchanged in infinite magnification, often referred to as "infinitely complex". Fractal is presented as a "magic figure" which whenever it becomes magnified any part of it continues to show an equally intricate design with partial or complete repetition of the original. Many composers have tried to use fractal structures in music, taking advantage of the self-similarity that exists in some structures, which appear at different zoom levels. The Koch snowflake is an example of such a structure. The Koch flake can be constructed starting with an equilateral triangle, and then retroactively changing any part of the line as follows: divide each line segment into three segments of equal length, we design an equilateral triangle that has the middle portion of step 1 as base and facing outwards, and then remove the portion of the line is the base of the triangle from step 2.

The algorithm for the Koch snowflake is decisive, that each option is identical to the previous one. If the algorithm is changed so that they can make some random selections, then the result will look more "natural". Figure 15 shows the flake koch after 4 insertions (to the left) and the right is the same result except that each section of line was replaced by 4 rows, in which their direction was selected randomly (facing in or out).

Figure 15. Creating Koch flake

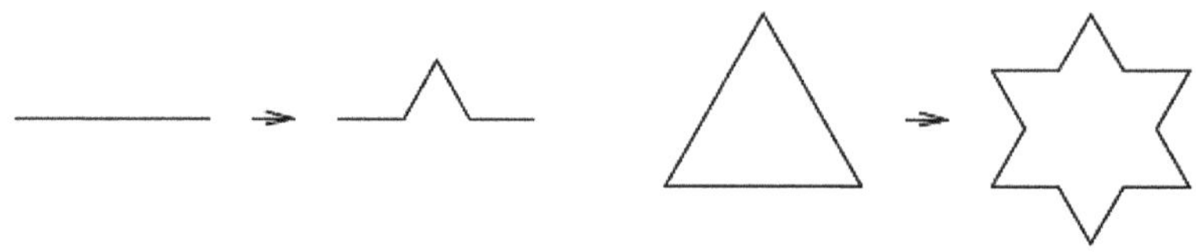

The "fract.c" program interferes with notes in a melody, through a pseudo-random pattern. Interference recursively subdivide the intervals between the notes until the desired resolution and then introduces new notes. The parameter "ruggedness" is what determines the relationship of time and maximum tonal shift for each new note. With this parameter to 1, the maximum shift is half tone. Generally the maximum displacement is: +/- ruggedness * dt, wherein the dt is measured in quarters. Therefore total displacement is delimited independently from the analysis of the subdivision. For example, with value "ruggedness" equal to 2, a melody may deviate at most an octave in a 4/4 measure.

Expert Novice Picker

It is a technique that uses specific information on the mechanics and techniques of the five-string banjo, for synthesizing orchestral tracks. Banjo is a stringed instrument that consists of a hollow cylindrical body with a diaphragm of the animal skin or plastic. From the body extends the neck, with 5 strings extending from the tuning keys until the bridge and one of the strings 5 extends only 2/3 of the neck. There are

Figure 16. Koch flake

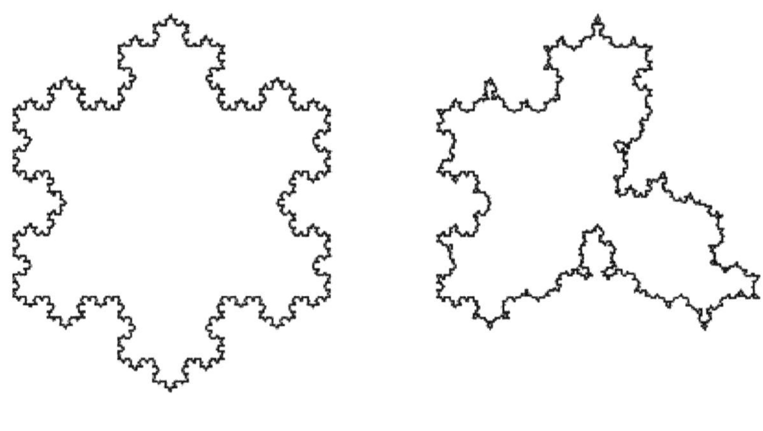

two ways one can play the banjo: one is to hit the string with the fingertips of his right hand and pulling the string with the thumb, and the other one is pulling the string with the thumb, the forefinger and the medium, in which we normally wear plastic or metal pens. In both ways, the left hand chooses the chords by pressing the strings to the neck of the banjo, among the carvings.

In the second way of playing the banjo, mentioned above the right hand follows specific sequences, the most common of them is the 8 notes played with variations of three fingers. It is very rare to use the same finger for two consecutive notes, because it is easier to alternate fingers. The most common pattern is the following: thumb, index, fourth finger, thumb, index, fourth finger, thumb, fourth finger. These mechanisms impose restrictions on melodies that can be played. Therefore, they can be produced at once, up to 5 notes, where the left hand can be stretched to about 5-6 frets, and sequences with the same chord notes are slower and sound different from that sequences which alternate strings. A program based on this technique follows a chord progression and generates improvisation, choosing the position of the left hand with small displacements, and then choosing which strings will hit through a set of standards for the right hand. The program exports the results in MPU format files and tablatures. Figure 18 shows the output file from such a program. The chords of the song are not typical for a five-stringed banjo, yet the result is quite reliable.

Figure 19 shows the same passage of the program, but in tablature. This format is designed generally for stringed musical instruments, therefore at the top there are some indications: TUNING line shows us how the instrument is tuned (there seems to be a 5-chord instrument). In the case of the banjo is tuned to G4 G3 Bb3 D3 D4, in order from fifth to the first chord. The NUT line shows that the fifth chord is smaller than the others by 5 frets. The SPEED line is showing us that there are 16 lines of data per meter. The following lines begin with the indication of the fingers (T-thumb, I-index, M-middle, R- fourth finger, P-small finger), following the ap-

Figure 17. Pentachord banjo

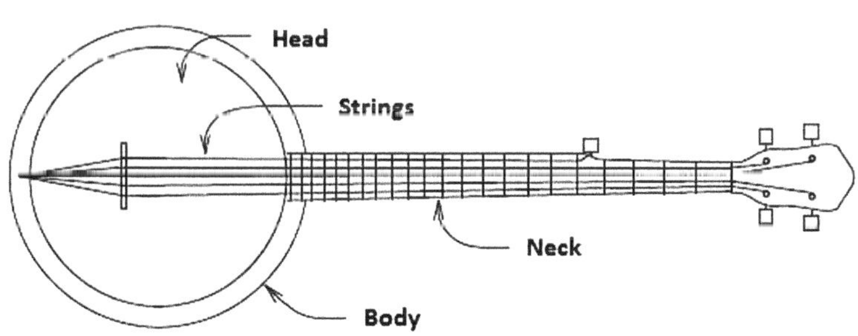

Figure 18. Staff notation – output file (an example for banjo)

Figure 19. Tablature

```
#TUNING    67 50 55 58 62
#NUT        5  0  0  0  0
#SPEED     16
T           |  |  0  |  |   Gm          T      |  |  0  |  |   Gm
I           |  |  |  0  |               I      |  |  |  2  |
M           |  |  |  |  0               M      |  |  |  |  0
T           |  5  |  |  |               T      0  |  |  |  |
I           |  |  |  0  |               I      |  |  |  2  |
M           |  |  |  |  0               M      |  |  |  |  0
T           |  5  |  |  |               T      0  |  |  |  |
M           |  |  3  |  |               M      |  |  |  |  1
T           0  |  |  |  |               T      |  5  |  |  |
I           |  |  7  |  |               I      |  |  |  0  |
M           |  |  |  0  |               M      |  |  |  |  0
T           |  5  |  |  |               T      |  |  0  |  |
I           |  |  7  |  |               I      |  |  |  0  |
M           |  |  |  0  |               M      |  |  |  |  0
T           0  |  |  |  |               T      |  5  |  |  |
M           |  |  |  4  |               M      |  |  |  0  |
T           |  |  8  |  |   Adim        T      |  4  |  |  |   D7
I           |  |  |  8  |               I      |  |  0  |  |
M           |  |  |  |  0               M      |  |  |  0  |
T           |  8  |  |  |               T      |  |  2  |  |
I           |  |  8  |  |               I      |  |  |  4  |
M           |  |  |  |  0               M      |  |  |  |  4
T           0  |  |  |  |               T      |  |  2  |  |
M           |  |  |  8  |               M      |  |  |  |  0
T           0  |  |  |  |               T      |  |  5  |  |
I           |  |  |  5  |               I      |  |  |  0  |
M           |  |  |  |  0               M      |  |  |  |  0
T           |  7  |  |  |               T      |  |  5  |  |
I           |  |  |  0  |               I      |  |  |  0  |
M           |  |  |  |  0               M      |  |  |  |  0
T           |  |  5  |  |               T      |  4  |  |  |
M           |  |  |  0  |               M      |  |  |  0  |
                                        T      |  5  |  |  |   Gm
```

pearance of five lines for the strings and on these numbers indicating the fret that the chord will stop (with the indication "0" pointing an open string). The other characters in our side show when the chord is changing.

CONCLUSION

Video games are so much more than another means of expression, in the sense that a fictional world is created in which the player creates stories and raises his imagination. Sound is an integral part of this world. By presenting and analyzing various techniques and models, this chapter gave an approach of existing technology for algorithmic music production. However, as video games are constantly evolving, scholars are currently focused on the research of real-time music production for video games. Thus, there is still much to be said and discovered in this research field.

REFERENCES

Alpern, A. (1995). *Techniques for Algorithmic Composition of Music.* Hampshire College.

Collins, K. (2007). An Introduction to the Participatory and Non-Linear Aspects of Video Games Audio. In S. Hawkings & J. Richardson (Eds.), *Essays on Sound and Vision* (pp. 263–298). Helsikini, Finland: Helsinki University Press.

Collins, K. (2009). An Introduction to Procedural Audio in Video Games. *Contemporary Music Review, 28*(1), 5–15. doi:10.1080/07494460802663983

Collins, K. (2013). *Playing with Sound: A Theory of Interacting with Sound and Music in Video Games.* MIT Press.

Edwards, M. (2011). Algorithmic composition: Computational thinking in music. *Communications of the ACM, 54*(7), 58–67. doi:10.1145/1965724.1965742

Farnell, A. (2007). An introduction to procedural audio and its application in computer games. In *Proceedings of the Audio Mostly (AM07) Conference.*

Frishert, S. (2013). Implementing Algorithmic Composition for Games. Utrecht School of the Arts, Department of Art, Media and Technology.

Hendrikx, M., Meijer, S., Van Der Velden, J., & Iosup, A. (2013). Procedural content generation for games: A survey. *ACM Transactions on Multimedia Computing, Communications, and Applications, 9*(1), 1–22. doi:10.1145/2422956.2422957

Langston, P. (1989). Six Techniques for Algorithmic Music Composition. In *Proceedings of the ICMC 1989.* The Ohio State University.

Munday, R. (2007). Music in Video Games. In J. Sexton (Ed.), Music, Sound and Multimedia: From the Live to the Virtual. Edinburgh, UK: Edinburgh University Press.

Whalen, Z. (2004). Play Along - An Approach to Videogame Music. Game Studies: The International Journal of Computer Game Research, 4(1).

Wilhelmsson, U. (2006). What is a Game Ego? (or How the Embodied Mind Plays a Role in Computer Game Environments). In M. Pivec (Ed.), *Affective and Emotional Aspects of Human-Computer Interaction* (pp. 45–58). IOS Press.

KEY TERMS AND DEFINITIONS

Algorithmic Composition: The process of using some formal process to make music with minimal human intervention. In other words, algorithmic composition is the use of a rule or procedure (algorithm) to put together a piece of music. Such "formal processes" have been familiar to music since ancient times. The title itself, however, is relatively new—the term "algorithm" having been adopted from the fields of computer science and information science around the halfway mark of the 20th century. Computers have given composers new opportunities to automate the compositional process. Several different methods of doing so have developed in the last forty years or so.

Dynamic Music: In video games, dynamic music is where specific events cause the background music to change. Dynamic music was first used in the video game Frogger by Konami (1981), where the music would abruptly change once the player reached a safe point in the game. Many of LucasArts' games used the iMUSE dynamic music system, from Monkey Island 2onwards and including games like Dark Forces, Star Wars: TIE Fighter, Full Throttle and Grim Fandango. The iMUSE system is notable in that it segues seamlessly between different pieces of music rather than having an abrupt cut.

Interactive Games: Video games that support communication. Human communication is the basic example of interactive communication which involves two different processes: human to human interactivity and human to computer interactivity. Human-Human interactivity is the communication between people. Today's standards for interactive games are very high (in terms of graphics and sound quality) and include the following characteristics: 1. Multi-player support, 2. Online support, and 3. Hardware interfaces support. Starting in the late seventies, players and designers quickly took advantage of the capabilities offered by the Internet to build complex online social worlds where people could meet and play. In recent web, hundreds of thousands of players interact in massively multiplayer online interactive games

Koch Snowflake: A mathematical curve and one of the earliest fractal curves to have been described. It is based on the Koch curve, which appeared in 1904. Apart from its use in graphics design, many composers have tried to use such fractal structures in music, taking advantage of the self-similarity that exists in some structures.

Music Sequencer: A device or application software that can record, edit, or play back music, by handling note and performance information in several forms.

Nonlinearity: A relationship which cannot be explained as a linear combination of its variable inputs. Nonlinearity is a common issue when examining cause-effect relations. Such instances require complex modeling and hypothesis to offer explanations to nonlinear events. Nonlinearity without explanation can lead to random, unforecasted outcomes such as chaos.

Procedural Music: Music generated by processes that are designed and/or initiated by the composer. Procedural generation is not something new and games have been using it for a long time to generate worlds, randomise item drops, or create unique characters, but it's very rarely used for music. This is because the human ear is trained from a very early age to accept certain structures, harmonies and frequencies as "musical" and trying to get a machine to choose which of all these is going to be musical to the ear is a difficult task. Properties like instrument, tempo, base scale, structure, etc. can all be set as "seeds" for the random generator and a complete musical piece can be created from that. Obviously, how it sounds will vary greatly as there are a vast number of algorithms out there that can be used and an infinite number of variations (as well as programing skills!) on them.

Riff: A brief, relaxed phrase repeated over changing melodies. It may serve as a refrain or melodic figure, often played by the rhythm section instruments or solo instruments that form the basis or accompaniment of a musical composition.

Section 3
Legal Action and Jurisprudence

Chapter 9
A Cloudy Celestial Jukebox:
Copyright Law Issues Concerning Cloud-Based Storing and Sharing Music Services

Pedro Pina
Polytechnic Institute of Coimbra, Portugal

ABSTRACT

Cloud computing offers internet users the fulfillment of the dream of a Celestial Jukebox providing music, films or digital books anywhere and when they want. However, some activities done in the Cloud, especially file-sharing, may infringe copyright law's exclusive rights, like the right of reproduction or the making available right. The purposes of the present chapter are to briefly examine how digital technology like p2p systems or Cloud computing potentiate new distribution models, how they allow unauthorized uses of copyright protected works and to point out solutions to reconcile the interests of rightholders and consumers so that the benefits from digital technology can be enjoyed by all the stakeholders in a legal and balanced way.

DOI: 10.4018/978-1-5225-0264-7.ch009

INTRODUCTION

In 1994, Goldstein predicted the celestial jukebox, described as a system by which subscribers around the world could rapidly and cheaply connect to "a vast storehouse of entertainment and information through a home or office receiver combining the powers of a television, radio, CD and DVD player, telephone, fax, and personal computer" (2003, p. 187). Instead of getting access to corporeal supports of copyrighted works through traditional distribution channels like physical mail, consumers would be able to download stored copies of copyright protected works and to reproduce them wherever they had an internet connection. Exclusive rights granted by copyright law, once erected regarding the analog world, should be extended to every corner where they have value, which, from the rightholders' point of view, would compensate the lowering of prices derived from the reduction of transaction costs wrought by digital technology.

In the most part, Goldstein's predictions turned out to be pretty accurate, since the celestial jukebox's digital delivery model exists and is working today, with digital services provided by traditional suppliers of creative content, like record labels, book publishers or film studios, but also directly by individual suppliers like authors deviating from the formers' activities. In fact, the emergence of digital technology, primarily the internet, has created the possibility of a free and global flow of informational contents that was reflected in the metaphor of the information highway and, soon, the economic facet of this inter- relational digital structure was revealed and online markets and e-commerce were developed. However, informational cybermarket revealed some problems concerning the immaterial and intellectual nature of its products, like music, movies, digital books or software, as some important realities like file-sharing, p2p or cloud computing, which were not anticipated by Goldstein, have put into stress in a much more dramatic way than the one foreseen the traditional delivery model protected by copyright law exclusive rights.

From the perspective of rightholders, a vast amount of digital creative content escaped from their control, since it started to flow and to be distributed without previous authorization and remuneration, decreasing the incentive to create.

For that reason, the European Commission declared in the Green Paper on Copyright in the Knowledge Economy that

A high level of copyright protection is crucial for intellectual creation. Copyright ensures the maintenance and development of creativity in the interests of authors, producers, consumers and the public at large. A rigorous and effective system for the protection of copyright and related rights is necessary to provide authors and producers with a reward for their creative efforts and to encourage producers and publishers to invest in creative works (2008, p. 4).

The purposes of the present chapter are to examine how digital technology like p2p systems or cloud computing potentiate new distribution models, how they allow unauthorized uses of copyright protected works and to point out solutions to reconcile the interests of rightholders and consumers so that the benefits from digital technology can be enjoyed by all the stakeholders in a legal and balanced way.

CLOUD BASED STORING AND SHARING MUSIC SERVICES

The traditional delivery model of the creative industry needs copyright protection to thrive. In fact, from an economic point of view, creative and aesthetic copyrightable contents, being informational and immaterial goods, are public goods. The consumption of an informational good by one person doesn't exclude the possibility of consumption by others, which means that they are non-rivaled goods.

Furthermore, without regulation, no one can be excluded from using the referred goods, which means that they are non-excludable goods. The identified characteristics are emphasized in the digital world as the positive externalities created by the free flow of copyrighted content information increase disproportionately, to the disadvantage of creators and rights' holders. That is the general justification for public regulation of the intellectual creations' market where intellectual property law is presented as an instrument used to fictionalize scarcity, since it gives the rightholders the economic exclusive right of the works' exploitation, excluding others from it without proper authorization (Pina, 2011, p. 303).

If copyright law was seen as an instrument to lock-up creative information, the internet was proclaimed as an environment where, following Brand's famous slogan, information wants to be free. And that is so, according to Brand,

because it has become so cheap to distribute, copy, and recombine...too cheap to meter. It wants to be expensive because it can be immeasurably valuable to the recipient. That tension will not go away. It leads to endless wrenching debate about price, copyright, 'intellectual property', the moral rightness of casual distribution, because each round of new devices makes the tension worse, not better (1985, p. 49, e 1987, p. 202).

Moreover, creative contents and information flowing on the internet not only wanted to be free but also appeared to be liberated from *de facto* rightholders' control and from judicial reaction (Boyle, 1997).

With digital technology, sharing data, namely creative content, was now possible amongst users regardless of traditional intermediaries and without rightholders' authorization.

The clash between copyright and technology is not recent. In fact, technology has always been an essential element for copyright regulation. Since copyright regards the protection of intellectual aesthetic creations or, in other words, immaterial goods, the externalization of the intellectual creation needs the mediation of a physical support which may transform and evolve according to the available technology. The referred considerations are the basis for the well-known Kantian dichotomy between *corpus mysticum* and *corpus mechanicum* (Kant, 1996, pp. 437-438), regarding the copyrighted creative and immaterial expression that is revealed by the *corpus mechanicum* that technology permits, like books, cassette, cd's, dvd's, etc. Different from real property rights, copyright is not a tangible right, but an intangible *sui generis* property right over intellectual creations that can be embodied in tangible objects like the ones mentioned.

Copyright itself was born with the advent of printed press and every time technology permitted new objects to embody intellectual creations, copyright problems arise and adaptation was needed. That happened with audio records, with the piano roll or with video records, with the broadcast of works via radio and television, expanding the ways creative content could be exploited by authors or others rightholders and the scope of copyright protection so that the new uses could be reserved to them.

Parallelly, technology gave consumers new means to reproduce works, like home audio or video cassette recorders, making unauthorized private copies to ulterior consumption or sharing among family and friends.

Digitization brought the possibility of experiencing works without a corporeal fixation, reducing the need of corporeal objects to experience copyrighted works and has favored an enormous, global and almost uncontrolled flow of intangible information, including copyrighted content, which easily escapes from rightholders' control. According to the U. S. Department of Commerce's Internet Policy Task Force,

As was predicted in the 1990s, the Internet has proved to present both an exciting opportunity and a daunting challenge for copyright owners. At the same time that it has opened a vast range of new markets and delivery methods, it has given consumers unprecedented tools to reproduce, alter and immediately transmit perfect digital copies of copyrighted works around the world, and has led to the rise of services designed to provide these tools. Today these include p2p file-sharing services and cyberlockers – which have a range of legitimate uses but also have become major sources of illegal content (2013, p. 38).

Technological progress has permitted the establishment of genuine parallel economies based on counterfeiting and some non-commercial uses, such as the exchange of digital files through p2p networks which have grown to such an extent that they are competing with the normal exploitation of works and challenging established commercial models (Geiger, 2010, p. 4).

The architecture of p2p systems promotes a distributed and decentralized network that enables a computer to find files directly on the hard drive of another network connected device without the need for central servers, making it very hard for rightholders to control the unauthorized exchange of files containing protected works. As a result, each user can be a consumer and a supplier of files simultaneously.

Cloud computing, which can be defined as "a model for enabling convenient, on-demand network access to a shared pool of configurable computing resources (e.g., networks, servers, storage, applications, and services) that can be rapidly provisioned and released with minimal management effort or service provider interaction" (Mell & Grance, 2009), has been getting more and more widespread recently. A cloud storage and share infrastructure, especially in the case of Software-as-a-Service (SaaS) where platforms like iCloud, Amazon Cloud Drive, SkyDrive or Dropbox can be included, allows users to store files containing texts, music, movies or photos on remote cloud servers, to access them whenever and wherever they want and to share such files within a synchronized format.

Like p2p systems, Cloud storage is also meant to be a sharing platform, but has a different architecture and creates new users' behaviors. As Gervais and Hyndman (2012) clearly state,

pre-Cloud, the Internet was used to transport data and allow hundreds of millions of individual and corporate computers on which content was stored to exchange using their Internet identity (an IP address). Switching from this connection paradigm, in which the Internet was essentially a network connecting computers, to an amalgamation paradigm, where user computers and devices are merely tools used to access private and commercial content amalgamated on server farms operated by major intermediaries (p. 55).

Amongst the services provided to their clients, Cloud Storage providers may offer digital personal lockers, synchronizing, sharing or matching functionalities. The Cloud service provider offers a remote memory space allowing users to duplicate the contents of their digital library on all digital devices. Users start by uploading digital content, copyright protected or not, to the Cloud and, afterwards, they have the possibility to stream or to download the stored content to any other device by means of synchronization services associated to sales, such as Google Play or Apple's AppStore. In these cases, the user buys the copyrighted content and automatically stores it on the Cloud so that it can be accessed, by acts of downloading or streaming on multiple devices. But the user can also upload contents that were previously obtained without rightholders' consent, *e. g.*, in p2p platforms. Moreover, the user may permit access to a specified file from the Cloud digital library to others, distributing and sharing it without the knowledge and the authorization of the rightholder.

Moreover, when the user uploads files, matching services, like iTunes' Match, scan the user's computer to determine which files are stored there and, after finding a match in the provider's database, gives that user access to an equivalent provider's file containing the same work. In that process, iTunes matches song titles with those in its database, but reportedly it can also determine whether each song on the user's computer was originally an iTunes download, ripped from a CD or acquired (presumably illegally) via

peer-to-peer (p2p) networks. If and when this occurs, a list is generated on Apple's servers matching the user's iTunes account with a specific number of p2p acquired songs (Gervais and Hyndman, 2012, p. 55). Cloud storage providers offering matching services are, therefore, means to turn legal works obtained without rightholders authorization.

The question to be answered is to know if every unauthorized use of copyrighted works in the Cloud must be considered an infringement.

COPYRIGHT IN THE CLOUD

Copyright is today recognized as a human right and not just as a mere economic privilege on the exploitation of intellectual aesthetic creations. In Article 27 of the Universal Declaration of Human Rights, after the proclamation that "[e]veryone has the right freely to participate in the cultural life of the community, to enjoy the arts and to share in scientific advancement and its benefits", it is granted by § 2 that "[e]veryone has the right to the protection of the moral and material interests resulting from any scientific, literary or artistic production of which he is the author".

Similarly, the International Covenant on Economic, Social and Cultural Rights provides in its article 15, § 1, that

States Parties recognize the right of everyone: (a) To take part in cultural life; (b) To enjoy the benefits of scientific progress and its applications; (c) To benefit from the protection of the moral and material interests resulting from any scientific, literary or artistic production of which he is the author.

It is not a matter of happenstance that copyright is granted the dignity of a fundamental right side by side with the other fundamental right of access to cultural and scientific information. As it is noted by Akester,

the rights that underpin access to information and copyright protection are linked within a perpetual cycle of discovery, enlightenment and creation. Freedom of expression, information, science and art promotes this cycle and, as such, is not only an essential element of man's spiritual freedom and of a democratic society, but also vital for the existence of a dynamic and self- renewing environment of information, knowledge and culture (2010, p. 2).

None of the mentioned provisions defines the content of copyright's protection: whether, amongst other possible models, the authors' or rightholders' interests must be protected by assigning them an exclusive private right or by giving them a direct public reward for their works. Truly, the option for the exclusive right's model is only taken in specifically oriented copyright normative instruments. That option is clearly drawn in Article 1, Section 8, Cl. 8, of the Constitution of the United States of America – the first to recognize copyright –, according to which the "Congress shall have power [...] to promote the progress of science and useful arts, by securing for limited times to authors and inventors the exclusive right to their respective writings and discoveries". But even in the bodies of copyright law that are not founded in the classic common law utilitarian perspective, the holder's right to exclusive economic exploitation of copyrighted works is considered the core of the granted protection. At the international level, the holders' exclusive rights of exploitation is provided in the Berne Convention for the Protection of Literary and Artistic Works, in the Universal Copyright Convention, as revised at Paris on July 24, 1971.

Consequently, the exclusive rights had to be foreseen by each contracting state's national legislation. Pursuant to most copyright laws, rightholders are granted moral rights, like the right to paternity or the right to integrity of the work, and also the exclusive patrimonial rights to reproduce, to distribute or to communicate their works to the public or to authorize such usages. For such reason, by rewarding or incentivizing authors to create, protection of authorship and copyright are seen as indispensable means to the private and free production of cultural and scientific works without the risks of public censorship that are inherent to a system of public subsidies.

The reproduction right is foreseen in Article 9 (1) of the Berne Convention as the core of patrimonial rights in the following terms: "Authors of literary and artistic works protected by this Convention shall have the exclusive right of authorizing the reproduction of these works, in any manner or form".

Considering that the normal exploitation process depends on the consumption by the public, exclusive rights of communication to the public, of broadcasting and of public performance were also predicted in articles 11 and 11bis of the identified Convention.

With the advent of digital technology and with the lesser need of a corporeal fixation of the copyrighted work, copyright protection was extended to that intangible reality by several international treaties and digital copyright national laws – from the Agreement on Trade Related Aspects of Intellectual Property Rights (TRIPS) or the World Intellectual Property Organization (WIPO) Copyright Treaty and the WIPO Performances and Phonograms Treaty, at the international level, to the Digital Millennium Copyright Act (DMCA), in the USA, or the Directive 2001/29/EC of the European Parliament and of the Council of 22 May 2001 on the harmonisation of certain aspects of copyright and related rights in the information society (Infosoc Directive), in the European Union, followed by subsequent transpositions into member state laws.

Initially, there was a legal uncertainty regarding the nature of acts of online transmission when users access the works from a place and at a time individually chosen by them and whether such uses were covered by traditional exclusive rights. WIPO Copyright Treaty enlarged the exclusive right of communication to the public and created the new making available right to cover such reality.

The making available right is foreseen in article 3 (2) of the Infosoc Directive, whose recital 24 clarifies that such right should be understood as covering all acts of making available such subject-matter to members of the public not present at the place where the act of making available originates, and as not covering any other acts. It should be made clear, according to recital 25, that all rightholders recognized by the Directive should have an exclusive right to make available to the public copyright works or any other subject-matter by way of interactive on-demand transmissions and that such interactive on-demand transmissions are characterized by the fact that members of the public may access them from a place and at a time individually chosen by them.

The faculties that Cloud services providers offer their clients may conflict with some of the exclusive rights granted by copyright law.

As it was mentioned above, users, after uploading digital copyrighted content to the Cloud have the possibility to download the stored content to any other device. The referred act may, in theory, collide with the reproduction right foreseen in Article 9 of the Berne Convention, since, as it was agreed in the WIPO Copyright Treaty:

The reproduction right, as set out in Article 9 of the Berne Convention, and the exceptions permitted thereunder, fully apply in the digital environment, in particular to the use of works in digital form. It is understood that the storage of a protected work in digital form in an electronic medium constitutes a reproduction within the meaning of Article 9 of the Berne Convention.

Moreover, when the user shares copyright content by granting access to specific folders or files where it is stored to third parties, such action may be considered copyright infringement by violation of the making available right. Since the technological possibility must be provided by the Cloud service provider, this internet service provider will not be considered no longer a simple host exempted from responsibility as it allows users to infringe the exclusive rightholders' right of distribution and of making the work available online.

Thai is to say that a copyright maximalist view may impede the legal and regular existence of the Cloud, subtracting its benefits in disadvantage of the public and of the dissemination of knowledge.

LIMITATIONS ON COPYRIGHT: THE OTHER SIDE OF THE COIN?

Before the digital era copyright found a relatively reasonable internal balance between holders' and users' interests considering the recognition by law of some limitations to the powers granted to the formers.

Firstly, objective limitations defining the copyright scope were foreseen, granting protection only to the original exteriorization of ideas and not to the ideas themselves: in short terms that is what the idea- expression dichotomy is all about.

Furthermore, copyright protection is time-limited, which means that, once it has exceeded its term, the work enters into the public domain and the exclusive rights cease.

Additionally, copyright acts normally preview exemptions or limitations on exclusive rights, allowing free usages of copyrighted works, like fair use or fair dealing in common law copyright systems or, in the continental European systems, the statutory exemptions expressly listed in legal instruments, combined with the three-step test rule foreseen in the Berne Convention.

The fair use doctrine is codified at 17 U.S.C. § 107. It is foreseen as a defense which consists in limitations on holders' rights for purposes such as criticism, comment, news reporting, teaching (including multiple copies for classroom use), scholarship, or research. In determining if a use is fair, some factors must be considered, such as:

1. The purpose and character of the use, including whether such use is of a commercial nature or is for nonprofit educational purposes;
2. The nature of the copyrighted work;
3. The amount and substantiality of the portion used in relation to the copyrighted work as a whole; and
4. The effect of the use upon the potential market for or value of the copyrighted work.

The fair use defense is, therefore, appreciated *a posteriori*, which creates uncertainty and insecurity to copyrighted works consumers over the legality of their unauthorized actions. In fact, the judgment on the extension and the substantiality of the original work's portion that is used can only be made on casuistic terms, which increases "the economic risk inherent in relying on the doctrine — not to mention the up- front costs of defending a lawsuit or seeking a declaratory judgment" (Hayes, 2008, p. 569).

In the European Union, the Infosoc Directive, foresaw in Article 5, no. 2, for future transposition by member States, a list of mandatory exceptions to reproduction rights, to the right of communication to the public of works and to the right of making available to the public other subject-matter that are basically regarded to educational or scientific purposes, but that also includes "reproductions on any medium made by a natural person for private use and for ends that are neither directly nor indirectly commercial, on condition that the rightholders receive fair compensation".

After predicting the mentioned exhaustive list of limitations on exclusive rights, the Infosoc Directive foresaw the existence of limits on the recognition of limitations, since they shall only be applied in certain special cases which do not conflict with a normal exploitation of the work or other subject-matter and do not unreasonably harm the legitimate interests of the rightholder. The Infosoc Directive imposes that limitations must fulfill the requirements of the three-step test, although this test, in its original sense, predicted in Article 9 (2) of the Berne Convention, was only a sort of general clause of internal limitations on exclusive rights that should be respected by national legislators when predicting limitations on copyright.

In fact, according to the identified provision, a use of copyrighted content shall only be considered free in certain special cases that don't conflict with a normal exploitation of the work and don't unreasonably prejudice the legitimate interests of the author. This solution is also predicted in article 10 of the WIPO Copyright Treaty, in article 13 of the Agreement on trade-related aspects of intellectual property rights (TRIPS).

Senftleben (2004) points out that, in its origins, the three-step test formula reflected a compromise between the formal and harmonized recognition of the holders' reproduction right and the preservation of existing limitations in different national legislations. The option that was then taken consisted not in enumerating exhaustively a list of existing free uses, but in the formulation of a general clause and abstract criteria that, "due to its openness, [...] gains the capacity to encompass a wide range of exceptions and forms a proper basis for the reconciliation of contrary opinions" (p. 51).

However, contrary to its original purpose, the three-step test was introduced by article 5 (5) of the InfoSoc Directive, in a rather curious manner: the test was presented as a restriction to the exhaustive list of limitations of the exclusive rights over the work granted to the holders, which leaves short space to implement limitations and free uses.

Furthermore, Article 6 (4) of the InfoSoc Directive expressly admits the possibility of escaping from copyright law and its exceptions to contract law, since Member States only have to ensure that rightholders take appropriate measures to make available to beneficiaries the means of benefiting from those exceptions or limitations in the absence of voluntary measures, including agreements between rightholders and other parties concerned at the limitations.

The provision of copyright limitations was made in a minimalistic way, which creates a legal system where, in theoretical terms, creative information is locked-up by rightholders.

EXTERNAL LIMITATIONS ON COPYRIGHT

If, in the past, copyright law kept internally a balance between divergent rights and interests, the current copyright legal system combined with contract law "may override copyright's escape valves – the idea- expression dichotomy, fair use, statutory exemptions – which are as much a part of copyright as are the exclusive right's themselves" (Goldstein, 2003, p. 170).

It is, however, "an historical constant that when internal limitations are missing, external limitations emerge" (Ascensão, 2008, p. 55). That idea reflects the growing trend to recognize the role of external limitations on copyright on the protection of the public interest as the strengthening and thebexpansion of this branch of law has put it in collision with other fundamental rights of similar or greater importance. If users's interests can't find satisfactory protection inside the boundaries of copyright law, they will seek it outside in other branches like privacy law or directly in fundamental liberties such as freedom of expression and access to knowledge.

Freedom of expression and information is a human right guaranteed by Article 19 of the Universal Declaration of Human Rights (UDHR).The scope of protection includes the freedom to hold opinions without interference, the traditionally protected feedom of speech, and also the freedom to seek, receive and impart information and ideas through any media and regardless of frontiers.

The European Convention on Human Rights also protects freedom of expression and information in its Article 10, but expressly declares that

the exercise of these freedoms, since it carries with it duties and responsibilities, may be subject to such formalities, conditions, restrictions or penalties as are prescribed by law and are necessary in a democratic society, in the interests of national security, territorial integrity or public safety, for the prevention of disorder or crime, for the protection of health or morals, for the protection of the reputation or rights of others, for preventing the disclosure of information received in confidence, or for maintaining the authority and impartiality of the judiciary.

In fact, freedom of expression and information is not an absolute right, since it can be constrained when it collides with rights of similar dignity. That is precisely the case of copyright. However, copyright may work as a restriction to freedom of expression only as a means to promote more expression, by creating incentives to creation. If the protection is so enlarged that copyright becomes an end itself and not a means to promote the public interest, then it will work against its basic purposes. According to Torremans (2004), the

Human rights framework in which copyright is placed does [...] put in place a number of imperative guidelines: copyright must be consistent with the understanding of human dignity in the various human rights instruments and the norms defined therein; copyright related to science must promote scientific progress and access to its benefits; copyright regimes must respect the freedom indispensable for scientific research and creative activity; copyright regimes must encourage the development of international contacts and cooperation in the scientific and cultural fields (p. 8).

There are not many relevant cases where courts had to decide conflicts between copyright and freedom of expression. The internal perspective on admitted limitations or exceptions still is the prevalent. As Guibault states,

statutory limitations on the exercise of exclusive rights are already the result of the balance of interests, carefully drawn by the legislator to encourage both creation and dissemination of new material. The protections of fundamental freedoms, of public interest matters, and of public domain material forms an integral part of the balance and, as a consequence, these notions should not be invoked a second time when interpreting statutory copyright limitations (1998, p. 1)

Nevertheless, some courts started timidly to adopt the external perspective although limited to exceptional cases. According to Hugenholtz (2001), one of the most preeminent copyright scholars in Europe, in France, a

Paris Court reminded that Article 10 ECHR is superior to national law, including the law of copyright, and then went on to conclude that, in the light of Article 10, the right of the public to be informed of important cultural events should prevail over the interests of the copyright owner (pp. 357-358).

Since both rights have equal dignity, a practical concordance must be found on an *ad-hoc* basis, but it will be very difficult to freedom of expression to override copyright, in cases where property rights in information are merely exercised to ensure remuneration, and the flow of information to the public is not unreasonably impeded (Singh, 2010, p. 15).

Privacy law may have a more relevant paper as an external limitation on copyright in the Cloud environment. However, such role is more visible in the field of copyright enforcement than in the substantive copyright law.

Directive 2004/48/EC of the European Parliament and the Council of 29 April 2004 on the enforcement of intellectual property rights (Enforcement Directive) does not only apply to infringements committed on a commercial scale, although some provisions like articles 6(2), 8(1) and 9(2) are only applicable in such cases. But even the concept of "commercial scale" proposed by the Directive is vague: in Recital (14) it is stated that acts carried out on a commercial scale "are those carried out for direct or indirect economic or commercial advantage; this would normally exclude acts carried out by end-consumers acting in good faith." There is no definition of the concepts of economic advantage or good faith, which may bring several interpretation problems, especially because in recital (15) it is recognized that the Directive should not affect substantive law on intellectual property and, consequently, the exclusive rights to distribute the work or to make it available to the public, which leaves space to a maximalist interpretation of the concept of commercial scale (Pina, 2015, p. 61).

In Article 6, paragraph 1, of the "Enforcement" Directive it is stated that:

Member States shall ensure that, on application by a party which has presented reasonably available evidence sufficient to support its claims, and has, in substantiating those claims, specified evidence which lies in the control of the opposing

party, the competent judicial authorities may order that such evidence be presented by the opposing party, subject to the protection of confidential information. For the purposes of this paragraph, Member States may provide that a reasonable sample of a substantial number of copies of a work or any other protected object be considered by the competent judicial authorities to constitute reasonable evidence.

In face of this provision, it seems correct to conclude that the European legislator assumed that collecting IP is a lawful rightholder's behavior if functionally directed to subsequent copyright enforcement, since in the context of p2p networks it will be the adequate means to present "reasonable evidence." Such assumption could also be supported by Article 8, paragraph 3, of the Infosoc Directive, which provides that "[m]ember States shall ensure that rightholders are in a position to apply for an injunction against intermediaries whose services are used by a third party to infringe a copyright or related right." In fact, the European Union solution was influenced by the US notice and take down solution provided for in the DMCA, § 512,(c)(3), and (h)(1), which grants the rightholders the right to "request the clerk of any United States district court to issue a subpoena to a service provider for identification of an alleged infringer." Such request may be made by filing with the clerk one notification of claimed infringement that must be a written communication provided to the designated agent of a service provider that includes substantially, amongst other elements, the identification of the copyrighted work claimed to have been infringed, the identification of the material that is claimed to be infringing or to be the subject of infringing activity and that is to be removed or access to which is to be disabled, and information reasonably sufficient to permit the service provider to contact the complaining party, such as an address, telephone number, and, if available, an electronic mail address at which the complaining party may be contacted.

One of the most controversial provisions of the "Enforcement" Directive is article 8, paragraph 1, which creates, under the epigraph "Right to information," a broad *sub pœna* that permits intellectual property holders to easily obtain the names and addresses of alleged infringers.

The referred right to information absolutely essential to ensure a high level of protection of intellectual property as it may be the only means to identify the infringer. Nevertheless, it is not absolute: paragraph 3 (e) of article 8, expressly stipulates that paragraph's 1 provision "shall apply without prejudice to other statutory provisions which [...] govern the protection of confidentiality of information sources or the processing of personal data". European Union's concern over the protection of personal data is clearly manifested in recital 2 of the "Enforcement" Directive, where it is stated that, although the protection of intellectual property should allow the inventor or creator to derive a legitimate profit from his invention or creation and to allow the widest possible dissemination of works, ideas and new know-how, "[a]t the same time, it should not hamper freedom of expression, the free movement of information, or the protection of personal data."

One of the greatest obstacles that rightholders have been facing in this field is precisely the protection of personal data argument that is used by Internet Service Providers (ISPs), such as Cloud storage providers, for not disclosing their clients' identity. Given the contractual relationships established with the users, ISPs are the best positioned to give an identity to the IP address collected by the rightholder. Indeed,

ISPs have developed into a relatively new form of governance in cyberspace because they maintain a substantial amount of private, consumer information regarding users' online activities, and because they often control the transmission and distribution of requested information. For these reasons, many consider the ISP the principal repository for all identifying information regarding individual users and their Web activities. (Katyal, 2004, p. 311)

Privacy and personal data protection may be an hard obstacle for rightholders to identify infringers. European responses on the matter are inspired by a Germany Federal Constitutional Court (BVerfGE, 1983) ruling according to which,

in the context of modern data processing, the protection of the individual against unlimited collection, storage, use and disclosure of his/her personal data is encompassed by the general personal rights constitutional provisions. This basic right warrants in this respect the capacity of the individual to determine in principle the disclosure and use of his/her personal data [and consists in] the authority of the individual to decide himself, on the basis of the idea of self-determination, when and within what limits information about his private life should be communicated to others.

This perspective recognizes the right to privacy with a broader scope than the traditional United States law understanding of this right as "the right to be left alone" (Warren and Brandeis, 1890), imposing an obligation of no trespassing.

Following Ferrajoli's teachings on the distinction between rights and their guarantees (2001), it can be noted that, although a negative dimension is included in the scope of the right to communicational and informational self-determination, this right is conceptualized not only as a mere guarantee of the right to privacy, but as a true fundamental right with an independent meaning; this meaning consists in the recognition of the freedom to control the use of information (if it is personal), and in the protection against attacks arising from the use of such information" (Castro, 2005, pp. 65*ff.*).

Therefore, the right to communicational and informational self-determination reveals two autonomous but intrinsically linked facets. The first one has a defensive nature, similar to the guarantee for the secrecy of correspondence and of other means of private communication, and is built as a negative right that protects the holder against interference by the State or by individuals who are responsible for processing digital or analogical data or others. The second facet constitutes a positive right to dispose of your own personal information, a power of controlling it and determining what others can, at every moment, know about you (Castro, 2006, p. 16). That is to say, the holder does not only have the right to remain opaque to others but also the right to control the use of his/her personal data and establish the terms of its use by third parties. The right to communicational and informational self-determination is a true fundamental right, related to the development of the personality of each individual, established in article 8 of the European Union Charter of Fundamental Rights:

1. Everyone has the right to the protection of personal data concerning him or her.
2. Such data must be processed fairly for specified purposes and on the basis of the consent of the person concerned or some other legitimate basis laid down by law. Everyone has the right of access to data which has been collected concerning him or her, and the right to have it rectified.
3. Compliance with these rules shall be subject to control by an independent authority.

The Charter's legislator followed the tracks of the European Convention on Human Rights and the jurisprudence of the European Court of Human Rights, according to which "the State is not merely under the obligation to abstain from interfering with individuals' privacy, but also to provide individuals with the material conditions needed to allow them to effectively implement their right to private and family life" (Rouvroy/Poullet, 2007, p. 20).

At the European Union derivative law level, three directives directly regulate privacy matters: a) Directive 95/46/EC of the European Parliament and of the Council of 24 October 1995 on the protection of individuals with regard to the processing of personal data and on the free movement of such data; b) Directive 2002/58/EC of the European Parliament and of the Council of 12 July 2002 concerning the processing of personal data and the protection of privacy in the electronic communications sector (Directive on privacy and electronic communications); and c) Directive 2000/31/EC of the European Parliament and of the Council of 8 June 2000 on certain legal aspects of information society services, in particular electronic commerce, in the Internal Market (Directive on electronic commerce).

Through the mentioned directives, the European legislator created a legal framework to regulate the activity of electronic data collecting and subsequent treatment guided by the following principles:

1. The principle of lawful collecting, meaning that collecting and processing of data constitute a restriction on the holder's informational self-determination and are only permitted within the parameters of the law and, particularly, with the holder's knowledge and consent;
2. The finality principle, according to which data collecting and the data processing can only be made with a clearly determined, specific and socially acceptable finality that has to be identifiable in the moment when the activity is being executed;
3. The principle of objective limitation, meaning that the use of the collected data must be restricted to the purposes that were communicated to the holder, and must respect the general principles of proportionality, necessity and adequacy;
4. The principle of temporal limitation, which implies that data shall not be kept by more than the time needed to achieve the finality that justified the activity;
5. The principle of data quality, meaning that the collected data must be correct and up-to-date;
6. The principle of free access to data, according to which the holder must be able to know the existence of the collection and the storage of his/her personal data and, if he/she wants, to rectify, erase or block the information when incomplete or inaccurate; and
7. The security principle, under which the controller must implement appropriate technical and organizational measures to protect personal data against accidental or arbitrary unlawful destruction or accidental loss, alteration, unauthorized disclosure or access, in particular where the processing involves the transmission of data over a network (Pina, 2015, pp. 60-61).

As it is regulated in the European Union, the right to communicational and informational self- determination gives an individual the power to control all the possible usages of his/her personal data. Therefore, considering the need to respect the identified fundamental right, many constitutional doubts will stand when enforcing copyright in a noncommercial scale, which will be the case of the individual clients of Cloud services. Which is to say that only in case of criminal offenses the right to communicational and informational self-determination may be overridden to enforce copyright.

CONCLUSION

Cloud computing offers internet users the fulfillment of the dream of a Celestial Jukebox providing music, films or digital books anywhere and when they want. However, some activities done in the Cloud, especially file-sharing, may infringe copyright law's exclusive rights, like the right of reproduction or the making available right. It is true that traditionally copyright law was only applied in public spaces.

However in p2p platforms and in the Cloud some activities make fainter the distinction between what is private and what is public in the copyright field, since unauthorized file-sharing may have a significant impact in the normal exploitation of protected works.

As it was mentioned above, the present state of copyright law presents maximalist copyright protection and limited exceptions in favor of users in the digital world, particularly in the Cloud. Users' file-sharing activities and matching services, even when provided by licensed providers, may infringe copyright law exclusive rights od reproduction and of communication to the public, including the making available right. On the one side, such reality potentiated legal offer of Cloud storing and sharing services. However, on the other side, illegal file-sharing of copyrighted content, whether it is done in p2p platforms or in the Cloud, still exists and a large amount of works continues to flow without rightholders authorization and remuneration.

Furthermore, law in action shows how inefficient copyright enforcement can be, especially because it is difficult to identify infringers and, even when that is possible, privacy rights must be secured, unless the infringement occurs in a commercial scale and deserves criminal law protection.

Collecting data to identify infringers may be considered acceptable under the current state of European law only if such activity respects the collecting and treatment principles discussed above and the general principles of proportionality, necessity and adequacy. For instance, a solution that imposes on ISPs the obligation of filtering data content without a court previous decision where, on an ad-hoc basis, all the factual and normative elements are available, should not be acceptable. Otherwise, all private communications, lawful or not, would have to be monitored by ISPs and government agencies, which would certainly infringe the most basic foundations of a democratic society and the principles of technology and net neutrality.

Ironically, all the parts seem to be sufficiently satisfied with the referred cloudy state of things: rightholders have relevant revenues derived from the legal offer; infringing consumers are aware of the inefficiency of the copyright enforcement regime and continue to upload, download and share protected content without authorization.

The future will show if legal offer will be elastic and appealing so that a market-approach of the subject matter provides balance between rightholders and users interests or if the unlawful services grow, to the disadvantage of rightholders and the creation of new intellectual content, imposing a regulatory state solution like levies on broadband connections to compensate creators.

REFERENCES

Akester, P. (2010). *The new challenges of striking the right balance between copyright protection and access to knowledge, information and culture*. Intergovernmental Copyright Committee, UNESCO. Retrieved June 28, 2016, from http://unesdoc.unesco.org/images/0018/001876/187683E.pdf

Ascensão. (2008). Sociedade da informação e liberdade de expressão. In Direito da Sociedade da Informação, VII. Coimbra: Coimbra Editora.

Boyle, J. (1997). *Foucault in cyberspace: Surveillance, sovereignty, and hard-wired censors*. Retrieved June 28, 2016, from http://www.law.duke.edu/boylesite/foucault.htm

Brand, S. (1985). *Whole Earth Review*. Retrieved from http://www.wholeearth.com/issue--electronic--edition.php?iss=2046

Brand, S. (1987). *The Media Lab: inventing the future at MIT*. Penguin Books.

Castro, C. S. (2005). O direito à autodeterminação informativa e os novos desafios gerados pelo direito à liberdade e à segurança no pós 11 de Setembro. In *Estudos em homenagem ao Conselheiro José Manuel Cardoso da Costa, II*. Coimbra: Coimbra Editora.

Castro, C. S. (2006). *Protecção de dados pessoais na Internet. Sub Judice, 35*. Coimbra: Almedina.

Commission of the European Communities. (2008). *Green Paper Copyright in the Knowledge Economy*. Retrieved June 28, 2016, from http://ec.europa.eu/internal_market/copyright/docs/copyright--infso/greenpaper_en.pdf

Department of Commerce of the United States of America. (2013). *Copyright Policy, Creativity, and Innovation in the Digital Economy*. Retrieved June 28, 2016, from http://www.uspto.gov/sites/default/files/news/publications/copyright-greenpaper.pdf

Ferrajoli, L. (2001). Fundamental rights. *International Journal for the Semiotics of Law, 14*(1), 1–33. doi:10.1023/A:1011290509568

Geiger, C. (2010). The future of copyright in Europe: Striking a fair balance between protection and access to information. *Intellectual Property Quarterly, 1*, 1–14.

Gervais, D., & Hyndman. (2012). Cloud Control: Copyright, Global Memes and Privacy. *Journal of Telecommunications and High Technology Law, 10*, 53-92. Retrieved June 28, 2016, from http://papers.ssrn.com/sol3/papers.cfm?abstract_id=2017157

Goldstein, P. (2003). *Copyright's Highway: From Gutenberg to the Celestial Jukebox* (Rev. ed.). Stanford, CA: Stanford University Press.

Guibault, L. (1998). *Limitations Found Outside of Copyright Law – General Report. ALAI Studies Days*. Retrieved June 28, 2016, from http://www.ivir.nl/publications/guibault/VUL5BOVT.doc

Hayes, C. J. (2008). Changing the rules of the game: How video game publishers are embracing user-generated derivative works. *Harvard Journal of Law & Technology*, *21*(2), 567–587.

Kant, I. (1996). The Metaphysics of Morals. In *Practical Philosophy* (M. J. Gregor, Trans.). Cambridge University Press.

Katyal, S. (2004). The new surveillance. *Case Western Reserve Law Review*, *54*, 297–386.

Leval, P. N. (1990). Toward a Fair Use Standard. *Harvard Law Review*, *103*(5), 1105–1136. doi:10.2307/1341457

Mell, P., & Grance, T. (2009). *The NIST definition of cloud computing*. National Institute of Standards and Technology, Information Technology Laboratory. Retrieved June 28, 2016, from http://www.nist.gov/itl/cloud/upload/cloud-def-v15.pdf

Pina, P. (2011). Electronic Surveillance, Privacy and Enforcement of Intellectual Property Rights: A Digital Panopticon? In Cruz-Cunha & Varajão (Eds.), Innovations in SMEs and conducting e-business: Technologies, trends and Solutions (pp. 301-316). Hershey, PA: Business Science Reference.

Pina, P. (2015). File-Sharing of Copyrighted Works, P2P, and the Cloud: Reconciling Copyright and Privacy Rights. In Gupta. M. (Ed.), Handbook of Research on Emerging Developments in Data Privacy (pp. 52-69). Hershey, PA: Advances in Information Security, Privacy, and Ethics (AISPE) Book Series.

Rouvroy, A., & Poullet, Y. (2008). The right to informational self-determination and the value of self-development: Reassessing the importance of privacy for democracy. In *Reinventing Data Protection:Proceedings of the International Conference*. Berlin: Springer.

Senftleben, M. (2004). *Copyright, Limitations and the three-step Test. An Analysis of the Three- Step Test in International and EC Copyright Law*. The Hague: Kluwer Law International.

Singh, P. (2010). *Copyright and freedom of expression in Europe*. Retrieved June 28, 2016, from http://works.bepress.com/pankaj_singh/8

Torremans, P. (2004). Copyright as a human right. In Copyright and human rights: Freedom of expression, intellectual property, privacy. Kluwer Law.

Warren, S., & Brandeis, L. (1890). The right to privacy. *Harvard Law Review*, *4*(5), 193–220. doi:10.2307/1321160

KEY TERMS AND DEFINITIONS

Copyright: The set of exclusive moral and economic rights granted to the author or creator of an original intellectual work, including the right to copy, distribute and adapt the work.

Cloud Computing: A model for enabling convenient, on-demand network access to a shared pool of configurable computing resources (e.g., networks, servers, storage, applications, and services) that can be rapidly provisioned and released with minimal management effort or service provider interaction.

File-Sharing: The practice of sharing computer data or space on a network.

Limitations (On Copyright): A set of free uses of copyrighted works that escape rightholders control, mainly because of public interests related to research, study, freedom or speech or the respect for privacy rights.

Making Available Right: The exclusive right of a copyright owner to make available to the public copyright works or any other subject-matter by way of interactive on-demand transmissions and that such interactive on-demand transmissions are characterized by the fact that members of the public may access them from a place and at a time individually chosen by them.

Peer-to-Peer (P2P): A computer network designed so that computers can send information directly to one another without passing through a centralized server.

Private Copy: A copy of a copyrighted work that is made for personal and non-commercial use.

Reproduction (Right of): The exclusive right of a copyright owner to make copies of the original work.

Chapter 10
Employees' Protection:
Workplace Surveillance 3.0

Chrysi Chrysochou
Aristotle University of Thessaloniki, Greece

Ioannis Iglezakis
Aristotle University of Thessaloniki, Greece

ABSTRACT

This chapter describes the conflict between employers' legitimate rights and employees' right to privacy and data protection as a result of the shift in workplace surveillance from a non-digital to a technologically advanced one. Section 1 describes the transition from non-digital workplace surveillance to an Internet-centred one, where "smart" devices are in a dominant position. Section 2 focuses on the legal framework (supranational and national legislation and case law) of workplace surveillance. In section 3, one case study regarding wearable technology and the law is carried out to prove that national and European legislation are not adequate to deal with all issues and ambiguities arising from the use of novel surveillance technology at work. The chapter concludes by noting that the adoption of sector specific legislation for employees' protection is necessary, but it would be incomplete without a general framework adopting modern instruments of data protection.

DOI: 10.4018/978-1-5225-0264-7.ch010

The only realistic attitude of human beings living in such environments is to assume that any activity or inactivity is being monitored, analysed, transferred, stored and maybe used in any context in the future.[1] *(J. Cas, 2005, p. 5)*

INTRODUCTION

Surveillance in the workplace has generated increasing concern in the recent past. The shift from a non-digital to a technologically advanced work environment allowed employers to use sophisticated monitoring systems to control their employees' activity during their working hours, their breaks or in some exceptional cases even outside working hours. Although many of these practices may serve legitimate employer rights, such as ensuring productivity and quality control, they can also carry major implications for the employees' right to privacy and data protection. The current European and national legal framework deal with certain aspects of employees' monitoring in the workplace and their right to privacy and data protection. However, it is not clear whether current laws are adequate and efficient to balance the conflicting interests of employees and employers in a modern environment where the rapid development of electronic technologies facilitates deeper and more pervasive surveillance techniques in the workplace (Lyon, 1994, p. 35).

The Context of Surveillance

The discussion on surveillance started officially in the eighteenth century with the conception of *Panopticon*[1] by J. Bentham (Boersma, 2012, p. 302) and continued in the twentieth century with Orwell's vision of a society under the watchful eye of *Big Brother* (Orwell, 1949). Since then, many scholars have defined surveillance in several ways, taking into consideration the impact that information technology had on surveillance. M. Poster (1996), for example, referred to a "*Superpanopticon*", a surveillance system that facilitates decentralized and dispersed transmission of an individual's data through computers without his (sic) knowledge. For Gary Marx (2002), surveillance is "the use of technical means to extract or create personal data. This may be taken from individuals or contexts". Marx (2007) believed that the 21st century is the era of "the new surveillance"(op. cit., p. 89), a hidden, surreptitious but ubiquitous surveillance. This "*new surveillance*" is found in everyday life; smart video surveillance cameras are found in streets and buildings, smart phones and computers are equipped with locator chips; workers are constantly monitored at work when using their corporate computers and GPS-fitted company cars or through closed circuit TV (CCTV), e-mail and phone-tapping (Coleman et al, 2011, p. 20).

In this modern computerized version of surveillance, Lyon talked about the "disappearance of the body" (Lyon, 1994, p. 35) and Van der Ploeg about the "informatisation of the body" (2007, p.47), where biometric surveillance transforms the unique characteristics of an individual's body into identification tools (fingerprints, facial recognition and iris scan). In the employment context, surveillance is expressed through monitoring, a direct or indirect observation of employees' activities and behaviour at work (Phillips, 2005, p. 40). A few examples of this monitoring include e-mail and phone-tapping, video recording and biometric surveillance. But what prompted such employee monitoring?

Reasons Why Employers Monitor

In a general context, surveillance has existed almost for as long as work itself. Traditionally, surveillance had the form of physical supervision aiming to assess work performance. Due to technological developments nowadays, employers have adopted advanced surveillance systems to monitor their employees in order to reduce the cost of human supervision. The two main types of surveillance in the workplace are 'performance surveillance' and 'behavioural surveillance' Both surveillance types exist to prevent employee misconduct, corrupted or criminal actions and to protect the employer's property rights over his undertaking.

A 2004 UK survey on employee monitoring reveals that employers might lose money for not monitoring their employees at work[2]. According to a more recent survey, 64% of the employees spent time surfing the Internet and visiting non-work-related websites, such as Facebook and LinkedIn (*cyberslacking*)[3]. As a result many employers introduced monitoring policies to avoid the loss of employees' productivity and consequently, loss of profits. Another reason for monitoring is the detection and repression at an early stage of employees' corrupt activities, i.e. data and confidentiality breaches, infringements of intellectual property rights and espionage, to name but a few. Moreover, avoiding liability (known as *cyberliability*) for defamation, preventing harassment and discouraging pornography viewing are also important reasons for an employer to initiate workplace surveillance. While it seems that under the above-mentioned reasons employee surveillance is indispensable for preserving the work standards and improving customer service and employee productivity, there is one fundamental element which poses certain limits to this diverse monitoring of employees, namely, privacy.

The Context of Privacy

Privacy is a fundamental modern human right. Privacy was first designed to protect individuals from the state's unauthorized intrusions into their private sphere. Warren and Brandeis (1980) defined privacy as the "right to be let alone". While discussing privacy in work-related relations and surveillance settings, it would be useful to distinguish its three basic concepts that apply in the workplace: information privacy, communication privacy and personal data privacy (Hendrikx, 2002, p. 46).

In the past there was a tendency to believe that there was no privacy of employees in the workplace since their work environment was outside their private sphere of power, where the employer had a dominant position. However, the courts held that employees do have rights of privacy even when their operating environment is public, semi-public or private, such as the workplace (Hendrikx, op. cit.). This means that by signing an employment contract, employees are not trading a privacy waiver (Hendrikx, op. cit., p. 52). Nowadays, privacy is protected as such in international and European legal instruments[2] and on a national level in the constitutions of most industrialized countries as well as in their national legislation.[4] Privacy also encompasses the right to the protection of personal data which has evolved as an autonomous right itself[5]. Both rights coexist in work-related relations and provide employees with legal guarantees against employer monitoring which is described in detail in subsequent chapters.

The aim of this paper is to present the modern technological and legal regime in workplace surveillance regarding the qualitative shift to more sophisticated surveillance technologies that have already infiltrated or will infiltrate the work environment in the near future. Section 1, is concerned with the historical background (overview) of employee surveillance from the early times until now. Section 2, delves into the legal background of employee surveillance in a supranational and national context.

SURVEILLANCE 1.0, 2.0, 3.0

Surveillance 1.0

Workplace surveillance is not a new phenomenon. In fact, employees have always been monitored in capitalistic structured workplaces. Surveillance 1.0 indicates the early surveillance practices at work. Traditionally, the concept of surveillance in the workplace had the form of a physical invasion. Searches of cars and lockers, strip searches, drug, alcohol and genetic tests, performance and IQ tests, time-clock checks and physical supervisions are the most important methods of employee surveillance, some of which are still a common-but more limited-practice in work environments. Furthermore, telephones were undoubtedly among the first electronic devices used for monitoring purposes[6]. In the late '60s almost all of the major businesses around the world were connected to the telephone network and almost immediately initiated telephone (and voicemail) tapping, known as wiretapping (introduced in the 1890s) to monitor their employees at work and ensure quality services.

One of the oldest forms of employee surveillance is strip-searching. Employers normally search an employee when they have the suspicion of drug use at work, theft or weapon possession and other illicit activities[7]. They may also proceed to physical searches of cars, desk drawers and lockers. These cases are likely to be considered as an invasion of an employee's privacy. On the other hand, time monitoring (non-digital timekeeping) and physical supervision are generally considered to be good monitoring practices and non-invasive forms of surveillance. Employees are expected to be at work on time, respecting the working limits and completing their job in a productive and efficient way. This type of surveillance is not only expected by an employee but is also self-evident. Moreover, medical testing as part of employee screening, was first introduced in the USA. It was part of a general plan to improve workplace safety and develop a social control policy at the same time. Health data are considered to be sensitive personal data[8]. However, the idea of an unlimited and indiscriminate monitoring of the employees' sensitive data through medical testing has triggered several discussions and privacy concerns not only in the US but in Europe as well[9]. Given the broad scope of data that can be collected from blood, urine and genetic tests, employers should prove a specific relationship between these tests and the job's requirements to justify a lawful monitoring. The US Occupational Safety and Health Administration (OSHA), for example, requires medical monitoring in employees that are exposed to hazardous material and substances such as arsenic, benzene and cadmium[10]. On the other hand, medical monitoring could be used both on existing and prospective employees as a discrimination tool, dismissing existing employees or avoiding hiring prospective employees with certain illnesses or addictions.

Surveillance 2.0

'Surveillance 2.0' describes the new version of surveillance methods due to the development of technology and Internet connectivity. The development of the Internet has increasingly expanded the use of surveillance technologies in the workplace. One of the first and most popular uses of the Internet is the e-mail. It has been used not only as a means of communication, but also as an instrument of surveillance. An e-mail message is a (small) file which passes through a chain of linked computers, the so-called servers, to reach its final destination, the addressee (Blanpain et al, 2004, p. 225). During this process, an email can be intercepted by installing a program (software) on a local computer or server or by renting the same software from an Application Service Provider (ASP). As a result the employer can collect personal information on his employees as well as "traffic data"[11] infringing the employees' right to privacy (and correspondence) and data protection. E-mail monitoring may breach many of the European Convention's fundamental rights (Arts 8,9,10 ECHR), if it is not conducted lawfully. However, email monitoring has only marked the beginning of the era of surveillance 2.0, in which other more sophisticated means of surveillance emerged.

Since the first CCTV system was introduced in the 1970s, CCTV cameras have been dramatically developed, expanding their capabilities. Modern cameras have colour pictures, are capable of operating remotely and recognizing car plates (ANPR). According to a 2013 survey of the British Security Industry Association, there are almost 6 million CCTV cameras operating in the UK, 1 camera for every 11 citizens[12]. These numbers show that CCTV has been employed more widely in the UK than in any other country in the world. CCTV was first introduced in the workplace to protect the legitimate interests of both the employer (property rights) and the employee (health and security). The use of cameras at work was easily justified for security purposes. However, employees' persistent and ubiquitous monitoring could be far more difficult to justify. The use of cameras in the workplace must be transparent and proportionate and a balance between the employers' and employees' conflicting rights is required (Nouwt et al, 2005, p.341).

The most important change in employee surveillance in the workplace, however, came with the rise of social networking sites (SNSs), such as Facebook, Twitter and LinkedIn. SNSs are online, interactive, and password protected platforms allowing people to upload their own material, build their own profiles and communicate with each other. Employers usually use social networks as a recruitment tool; in addition, they can also be used to control their employees' behaviour at work and after work. There are cases of employee dismissals with the justification that employees were expressing negative opinions about their co-workers, their employers or the company they work in. Recently, there has been a tendency of employers asking their employees to reveal the user names and passwords of all of their network sites. This surveillance method may entail both privacy and data protection risks. Therefore in the UK, the Information Commissioner's Office (ICO) has advised employers not to ask their existing and would-be employees to disclose the usernames and passwords of their social network accounts, because such a practice may have privacy implications[13]. This new trend will be analysed in the next chapter.

Surveillance 3.0

Surveillance 3.0[14] is a metaphor to mark the transition to a new hybrid world where technology-and its rapid evolution-is strictly intertwined with human beings. Due to the exponential increase in smartphones and other "smart" devices during the last decade and the impressive changes in computing technology, the traditional static monitoring of employees has been transformed into ubiquitous surveillance.

Employees work using corporate smartphones and laptops. These devices store data and information about employees and are also equipped with GPS (global positioning system) chips, capable of tracking the geolocation of the holder. This information could be obtained and examined by the employer, especially when the fidelity of an employee is questioned or when the employee leaves the company. An employer in Virginia, USA, for example, installed a GPS tracking software on his drivers' smartphones to monitor their route and their productivity.

Recently, a new trend has been introduced in the workplace. The "Bring your own Device (BYOD)" trend started when employees insisted to using one device for both personal and business matters The impact that the BYOD trend had on employment relations is twofold. On the one hand, employees may use company business data that is stored in their personal devices in an abusive manner; this data may also be lost or misused by an employee. Employers should ensure that their employees do not process this data in an unfair, unlawful and excessive manner. On the other hand, by implementing security measures to control employees and the use of data stored in their personal devices, employers may take the risk for employee privacy and personal data infringement.

Furthermore, modern CCTV cameras, which have become 'smarter' and equipped with high definition technology and recording capabilities, have already replaced conventional ones. Taxi owners in Southampton (UK) have placed smart CCTV cameras in their vehicles and record all passengers' conversations to protect passengers' as well as drivers' safety and security[15]. However, technology did not stop there.

Radio Frequency Identification (RFID) technology is already widely used in many areas of everyday life (products, clothing, livestock and ID badges). RFIDs are tiny wireless microchips that are used to collect and transmit data from a distance, using a radio frequency band. This technology was commonly used to locate goods and livestock but during the last decade there are several reports of an excessive use of RFIDs in the workplace. A 2005 Report of RAND Corporation reported the extended use of RFID chips by large corporations in the US[16]. IBM's identification badges are embedded with RFID chips[17]; an Australian casino has implanted RFID in more than 80,000 uniforms; GMB workers have been wearing wristbands and rings with embedded RFID chips. Analogous cases have been reported in the UK, where Sainsbury's, Marks & Spencer and Tesco were faced with charges of using RFID tags and GPS to monitor their workers. In Mexico, eighteen officials were voluntarily subjected to RFID chip implants to automatically access specific restricted areas of the Mexican Attorney-General[18]. These cases generate privacy concerns in the employment relations and indicate that RFID chips will sooner or later be accepted as novel means of employee behaviour and performance monitoring, if they have not done so already. In Europe, the most recent chip implants took place in Sweden, where a new hi-tech office block called Epicenter gave the opportunity to its 700 employees to be voluntarily implanted with a radio-wave-emitting microchip in order to allow them open doors, swap contact details or use the photocopier, all at the wave of a hand[19].

Biometric technology, on the other hand, has been used in the workplace a bit longer. It has been defined by the International Biometric Group as: "The automated use of physiological or behavioural characteristics to determine or verify identity" (IBG). Iris scans, fingerprint checks, signature verification, voice and gesture recognition and computerised facial recognition systems are only a few examples of biometric technology. This technology is commonly used in national security agencies, in airports or in large corporations with high security standards. In Athens, Greece, for example, iris scan technology is used at the airport to offer access to workers in high-security areas (Greek DPA, Decision 39/2004). However, recently employers have been using biometrics to establish records of employee working hours (i.e. biometric "time clock" scans). A major concern about the use of biometric technology at work is that biometric data could be stored and linked to other personal data of employees, further processed and shared with third parties. The biggest fear related to biometrics, however, is that although they might seem secure, they have already been bypassed by some remarkably simple and fast techniques in the recent past. The most common technique is to print a copy of a high resolution photograph found in Google searches or in Facebook profiles and use employee's eyes by zooming in that photograph to bypass biometric authentication (iris scan)[20].

A new hybrid model of workplace monitoring has recently been introduced in the US: a combination of RFID technology and biometrics. RFID chips are incorporated into access cards which are filled with biometric information, such as fingerprints, and other personal information, such as photo ID, driver license and social security numbers. This card has several uses: it can be used as an access card, as a timekeeping card or as a tool to log on to a computer. The major risks of these monitoring methods are not only the safety and the specific use (processing) of the data collected, but also the privacy implications, especially in cases where employees are not aware of employer monitoring methods and policies.

The very recent achievements of technology have brought ubiquitous surveillance a step closer. Wearable technology has been developed exponentially during the last 5 years and has increasingly been promoted in the retail market. Fitness and health monitoring devices as small as a wristband (FitBit and Nike+), wearable cameras and mini-computers (Google Glass), smart clothing and watches (Apple iWatch, LG's G Watch) are only a small specimen of next generation technology. The BYOD trend in the workplace seems to be replaced by the "Bring your own wearable device" (BYOWD) trend. Virgin Atlantic airlines launched a 6-week trial of Google Glass and Sony Smartwatch technology in which its concierge staff will be using this wearable technology to deliver personalized and high quality customer service[21]. Tesco's workers in Ireland wear wristbands that count the time and the movements needed for an employee to complete his task at goods distribution facilities. Wearable technology may raise not only privacy concerns from an employer to an employee but it may also have an impact on other employees' privacy (sousveillance)[22]. New CCTV cameras embedded with facial recognition technology[23] and behaviour prediction technology are raising some concerns for the future as well.

Still, in Europe there are no indications of an extended use of these surveillance technologies in the workplace, but it is undeniable that this technology is set to become widespread in the forthcoming years. Google is already running a programme called "Glass at work", which aims to encourage companies and enterprises to build applications for Google Glass in the workplace[24]. Among the first certified partners of Google's programme are APX, Augmedix, Crowdoptic, GuidiGO and Wearable Intelligence. At the same time, according to a new white paper titled "Wearables Make Their Move to the Enterprise", Google's and Apple's competitor, Samsung, is crafting a policy to promote and encourage the use of its wearable technology (including the Gear S, Gear Circle and Gear VR) in the majority of businesses over the next year.[25]

It is difficult to predict under which justifications employers will introduce and impose this surveillance technology in the workplace, but it is certainly easier to expect a heated debate between employee privacy/data protection rights and employer property rights. Finding a balance in a technologically advanced environment will be a real challenge for both legislators and interpreters.

THE LEGAL FRAMEWORK OF WORKPLACE SURVEILLANCE

Supranational Legislation

Privacy

While privacy and data protection are considered to be two separate fundamental rights, in reality they are so strongly intertwined that the one complements another. On an international level, privacy is protected by the Universal Declaration of Human Rights (Art. 12, UDHR, 1948), the International Covenant on Civil and Political rights (Art. 17, ICCR, 1966) and the Council of Europe Convention 108 (Art. 9, ETS 108, 1981). In Europe, the right to privacy is codified in article 8 of the European Convention of Human Rights (ECHR). Furthermore, the Charter of Fundamental Rights of the European Union, having a binding effect since 2009, protects privacy in article 7 and data protection in article 8.

Privacy on a National Level

On a national level, privacy is protected as a fundamental human right in many jurisdictions. In Europe, privacy is recognised as a fundamental right and is protected by the constitutions of many European countries (i.e. Spain and Belgium) and by laws that govern social relationships, such as civil and labour laws. In most countries though, the right to privacy in employment relations is under the protective scope of civil or tort laws (i.e. Germany and Greece). Exceptionally, there are a few countries that have specific employment laws protecting the employees' right to privacy and data protection[26].

On the other hand, in the USA the right to privacy is only limited protected. The Fourth Amendment of the US Constitution does not create a privacy right *per se,* but it protects individuals from government arbitrariness and intrusions into their private sphere (4th Amendment, US Constitution). The protection of privacy is realized only against state intrusions and only in cases where an individual has *reasonable expectations to privacy*[27]. The Supreme Court, however, interpreting the Fourth Amendment, provided public employees with limited legal guarantees against unreasonable governmental intrusions[28]. This protection does not apply to private employees. Private employees are protected through state and Federal statutes (HIPAA and HITECH) and case law[29]. Although public and private employees are not protected by the same legal sources in the US, they both must have a reasonable expectation of privacy to activate this protection. As a result, legislation in Europe offers a higher level of data protection than in the US.

ECHR

The right to privacy, however, is not an absolute right. It is subjected to limitations and restrictions when other (fundamental) rights intervene. Such limitations exist in article 8 paragraph 2 of the ECHR. This paragraph states:

There shall be no interference by a public authority with the exercise of this right except such as is in accordance with the law and is necessary in a democratic society in the interests of national security, public safety or the economic wellbeing of the country, for the prevention of disorder or crime, for the protection of health or morals, or for the protection of the rights and freedoms of others (Art. 8 par. 2 ECHR).

This paragraph introduces three principles that lawfully restrict the right to privacy: legality, finality and necessity (and/or proportionality). The right to privacy can be restricted in cases where the protection of other rights or legitimate interests is indispensable (finality). These interests need to be in accordance with legal norms such as written or customary laws and case law (legality). In order to conclude that the right to privacy needs to be restricted for the protection of other equivalent rights or legitimate interests, a balancing of the conflicting rights is mandatory. This is the case in employment relationships where balance should be struck between the employees' rights and the employers' legitimate interests.

The principle of necessity includes both the principle of relevance, which means that the interference should be relevant to the envisaged interests, and the principle of proportionality, which refers to a balancing of rights. The principle of proportionality in particular, means that any interference with the right to privacy should be appropriate, necessary and reasonable for the intended objective. Paragraph 2 of article 8 ECHR, in general, refers to the interference of privacy with public authorities, but the European case law has extended human rights protection to private relations as well (ECtHR, Cases N° 30668/96, 30671/96, 30678/96). This is known and accepted in Europe as the notion of "third-party effect of fundamental rights" ("Drittwirkung").

European Court of Human Rights: Case Law

In *Niemitz v Germany* the court held -for the first time -that there is no difference between private life and working life, as the latter is an integral part of the former (Iglezakis et al, 2009, p. 253).[30] Munich District Court has issued a warrant to search the applicant's law office in the course of criminal investigations. The physical search of the applicant's office was held to be a violation of article 8 ECHR. Even though this case is not directly related to an employment relation, it is essential because the Court found no reason not to extend the notion of "private life" to the employment relations.

This decision opened the path to protection of privacy in the workplace against excessive surveillance.

The first decision of the European Court of Human Rights (ECtHR) regarding article 8 in the employment context, was in *Halford v the United Kingdom*[31], in which it held that the interception of Ms' Halford's telephone calls, made from both work and home telephones, was a violation of article 8. The Court concluded that calls made from a work telephone were covered by the notion of "*private life and correspondence*", the same as for calls made from home, therefore article 8 ECHR was applicable in this case. Subsequently, the Court noted that there were no specific restrictions in the use of the work telephone and no warning had been given to Ms' Halford that her calls would be liable to interception, and as a result, she was entitled to an expectation of privacy.

Article 29 of the Working Party summarised in three principles the outcome of the above mentioned ECtHR cases regarding article 8. The first principle is that employees do have a reasonable expectation of privacy at work, which is limited-but not totally eliminated-if employers introduce certain privacy policies. Secondly, any communication at work is covered by the secrecy of correspondence; and thirdly, the respect for private life is extended to the workplace so the employer is obliged to use legitimate surveillance methods.

As far as the first principle is concerned, the concept of a reasonable expectation of privacy seems to offer a stronger protection in Europe than in the US. That is mainly because in the US, employers can destroy employees' reasonable expectations of privacy simply by way of notice. US courts allowed this practice and in most cases found limited or no expectations of privacy where employers had a legitimate interest in employee monitoring. The reason why US employee privacy is left unprotected in most monitoring cases is that the protection of privacy in the US is dependent only on reasonable (privacy) expectations. Unlike in the US, in Europe it is impossible for an employer under EU law to destroy the employees' reasonable expectations to privacy by way of notice. That is because employees must offer their consent for any data processing in a specific, clear and voluntary manner.

In *Copland v the United Kingdom*, the Court held that monitoring violated applicant's right to 'private life and correspondence' (article 8 ECHR).[32] In particular, the (stateowned) College in which Copland was working was secretly monitoring her telephone, emails and Internet use to ensure that she was not using college services excessively for personal purposes. At that time, there was no statutory law authorizing that kind of monitoring, therefore it was held that telephone, email and Internet monitoring was not "*in accordance with the law*" (Art 8 par. 2 ECHR). The Court accepted that the plaintiff had "*a reasonable expectation of privacy*", provided that there was neither specific legislation nor a notice for monitoring. Even though the Court specifically mentioned that telephone, email and Internet monitoring may be considered "*necessary for a democratic society*" in specific cases and for legitimate purposes, it failed, however, to clarify the criteria according to which an employer is allowed to use these surveillance methods.

Data Protection

In Europe, there are no Directives or other community legislative acts that specifically protect personal data at work. In a general context, personal data are protected by two Directives: the (general) Data Protection Directive (DPD)[33] and the E-Privacy Directive[34].

The Data Protection Directive General Principles

The DPD covers the processing of personal data. Employers are considered to be data controllers and employees data subjects (Blanpain, 2002, p.13). Personal data[35] is defined in article 2(a) as \

any information relating to an identified or identifiable natural person; an identifiable person is one who can be identified, directly or indirectly, in particular by reference to an identification number or to one or more factors specific to his physical, physiological, mental, economic, cultural or social identity

(Art 2(a) of Directive 95/46EC). Any information about actual or prospective employees is considered to be personal data (Nielsen, 2010, p. 100). However, this Directive does not apply in cases where the processing of personal data occurs manually and for personal purposes (Art. 3(1), (2) of Directive 95/46EC).

In order for personal data to be legitimately processed the DPD sets out some principles and specific criteria in articles 6 and 7 respectively. Article 6 states that data has to be processed lawfully and fairly (Art. 6 (1) (a) of Directive 95/46 EC), according to law. Furthermore, the finality principle implies that personal data has to be collected for specific purposes (Art. 6 (1)(b) of Directive 95/46 EC). The principles of proportionality and relevance in article 6.1(c) state that personal data has to be relevant and adequate for the purpose for which it is collected. Only accurate data should be kept (Principle of accuracy, Art. 6(1)(d) of Directive 95/46 EC) under the guarantee of data quality and security (Arts. 16,

17 of Directive 95/46 EC). In conclusion, transparency is the last principle that the DPD sets in article 6 and implies that the data subject has the right to ask information from the data controller in relation to the data controller's identity and the purpose of the processing of his data (Arts 10, 11 of Directive 95/46EC).

Consent and Legitimate Interests

Article 7 provides the legitimations of the processing of personal data. The first one is the given consent of the data subject (Art. 7(a) of Directive 95/46EC) and the second one is the contractual freedom (Art. 7(b) of Directive 95/46EC). The compliance with a legal obligation and the need to protect the data subject's vital rights follow next (Art. 7(c), (d) of Directive 95/46 EC). The two last reasons that justify the processing of personal data are the public interest and the legitimate interests of the data controller or third parties[36]. It is important to clarify that the "legitimate interests test" sets up a balancing of rights and interests between the data controller and the data subject. The employees' consent and their –allegedly– contractual freedom are two criteria that have to be evaluated in each specific case, especially when the legitimate interests of the employer and his dominant position in the workplace limit the employees' autonomy and freedom of decision[37].

Article 8 also deals with the data subject's consent, stating that the processing of sensitive personal data is *prima facie* prohibited, except in cases where data processing is necessary in the field of employment or where the data subject explicitly gives his consent (Art 8(2) of Directive 95/46EC). It is difficult to define what constitutes "consent" in employment relations, where the dominant position of the employer is indisputable. In most Member States, "consent" is perceived as an exception to the prohibition of workplace monitoring (Blanpain, 2002, p. 104). In general, the DPD treats consent as a precondition for any data processing and such consent needs to be "*unambiguously*" given (Art. 7 (a) of Directive 95/46 EC). The word '*unambiguously*' seems to prevent employers from arguing that any monitoring (invasive or not) is justified because of an implied consent (Craig, 1999, p. 19). Article 29 WP argues that a worker should be able to refuse and withdraw his consent without any repercussions[38]. The employee's consent should only be considered when it is genuinely freely given and could be withdrawn without detriment. However, consent is implemented differently in the national laws of each Member State[39]. This means that its application in employment relations is also divergent and creates legal uncertainty across Europe. The question which may be raised is whether consent alone provides adequate safeguards to deal with worker's personal data in employment relations, especially when sensitive data (political or religious beliefs, health or sex life) (Nielsen, 2010, p.100) is processed and the answer would be rather negative.

The E-Privacy Directive

The E-Privacy directive protects communication privacy in public communications networks. It is applicable in cases of employee e-mail and internet monitoring in the workplace where the monitoring takes place in public communication networks, complementing the Data Protection Directive (DPD) mainly for specific types of personal data, including cookies, location and traffic data. Surveillance and interception of communications as well as traffic data are *prima facie* prohibited unless the data subject gives its consent (Art. 5 of E-Privacy Directive). Simply put, both the content and the traffic data of an email should not be intercepted, unless the employee has given his (sic) consent by signing, for example, a privacy policy. Interception of communications is lawful (without consent) when legally authorized for the prevention and detection of crime and the facilitation of criminal investigations (Art. 5, par. 1(b) of E-Privacy Directive).

Reforming the Data Protection Legislation

In 2004 the Commission came forward with a proposal to create a complementary data protection directive which would specify the rules governing data protection in the workplace[40]. This endeavour failed at an early stage and the preliminary draft of this new directive was never presented in the Commission for approval. This draft included provisions for employee data protection at the stage of recruitment and at the stage of termination of the employment relationship. Individualized drug and alcohol tests were accepted only where an employer had reasonable suspicions against an employee. Genetic testing was allowed under the explicit consent of the worker and only under specific circumstances. Behavioural and covert surveillance were lawful only for the investigation of criminal offences in the workplace. Worker's private emails were considered private correspondence and were protected from interception. This draft directive showed that a detailed (and more technical) regulation of data protection in the workplace was possible. The reason why this legislative endeavour failed is, on the one hand, the political differences of the involved parties and, on the other hand, the fact that the protection of employees' personal data at work was not a priority at that time.

On January 25, 2012 the European Commission introduced a comprehensive reform of the current EU data protection regime to boost privacy protection, achieve harmonization within Europe and present higher data protection standards. On March 12, 2014 the European Parliament approved the new General Data Protection Regulation (GDPR); however it has not been yet adopted by the Council. The GDPR will be binding to all Member States, intending to replace the "national patchwork" that the implementation of the former (still in effect) DPD created.

Under the proposed regime, data controllers will have increased obligations to provide information to data subjects regarding the processing of their personal data. In article 4(11) of the Regulation, a definition of biometric data is introduced for the first time in a legal document. The "right to be forgotten"[41] provides data subjects with the opportunity to demand from data controllers the permanent erasure of the data stored in their databases. Moreover, in article 20, novel provisions related to employee profiling are introduced. The same article covers methods of profiling ranging from using web analysing tools to building profiles via social network sites (SNSs). Responsibility and accountability when processing personal data will be increased with the adoption of the proposed Regulation (Art. 22 GDPR). Data processor will be obliged to notify their national data protection authorities of any data breaches as soon as possible (Arts.31, 32 GDPR)

The most important change that this new Regulation may bring to data protection law is, in our opinion, the strengthened consent regime. The GDPR provides a further clarification for consent. Consent has to satisfy some conditions in order for data processing to be lawful and Article 7 refers to these conditions. Consent will no longer be assumed, but has to be explicitly given (Art.7 (2) GDPR).The most questionable paragraph of this article, however, is paragraph 4 which states that "Consent shall not provide a legal basis for the processing, where there is a significant imbalance between the position of the data subject and the controller". Recital 34 refers to employment relations as one example of such imbalances. This paragraph has raised a discussion over the lawful processing in the employment context. The DG Justice on the one hand, upholds the opinion that this provision still retains consent as grounds for data processing in working relations but the final assessment of the validity or not of the given consent should be based upon the facts of each individual case. On the other hand, the German employers Federation BDA comments that this paragraph explicitly excludes consent from employment relations, without leaving room for examining each individual case. It seems that despite this new regulation, it is still difficult to define consent in a clear, understandable and strict manner. This difficulty clearly indicates that the balancing of rights cannot be carved in laws in an absolute way.

In addition, article 82 of the GPDR specifically refers to the processing of data in the employment relations. This article sets the minimum standards for Member States to adopt specific legislation on the processing of personal data in the employment context. They can complement the proposed legislation but not deviate from it. While this provision provides Member States with the opportunity to adopt specific legislation on data protection at work, there is still a risk to create a 'patchwork' of divergent national laws regarding data protection in the workplace. However, paragraph 3 of the same article seems to offer a solution to achieve a harmonised effect. It allows the Commission to adopt delegated acts to specify the criteria that each Member State sets for the processing of personal data. The Employment Committee in its Opinion proposed amendments regarding the minimum standards[42]. These amendments include rules on employee data, collected through video surveillance and surveillance of communications, medical examinations and covert surveillance. Nevertheless, it is believed that these extra rules are impossible to fit in just one article in a coherent manner and it would be even harder to keep this regulation updated as technology evolves. These issues should be addressed on a national level or with European complementary rules (hard or soft law). The latter solution seems more efficient to address issues related to employment and technology with uniformity, incorporating the validity of the acts issued by European Institutions at the same time.

The Current Legal Framework and Surveillance Technologies

Geolocation data (as defined in Art. 2(c) of the E-Privacy Directive) collected by employers through corporate mobile phones and computers, GPS technology and Wi-fi access points are covered by both the DPD and the E-Privacy Directives (in a complementary manner), provided that this data leads to the identification of specific employees and that the processing of the data takes place only after the employees' given consent. However, according to Article 29 WP and the CJEU, the collection of geolocation data is only justified in cases where the same results could not have been incurred by less intrusive means (test of proportionality)[43]. Article 29 WP suggested that employers cannot monitor the quality of their workers' driving by placing GPS devices in their vehicles. In the context of RFID technology, the DPD applies 'to the collection, the processing and the retention of personal data', only if the information collected can be related to identifiable employees. An unambiguously given consent is necessary for a legitimate processing of the data subject's personal information[44]. The use of RFID chips should also be proportionate to the employer's legitimate purposes and any data being processed should be disclosed to the data subject (employee). When RFID chips are connected to public communication networks, E-Privacy Directive 2009/136/EC is applied.

While most of employee monitoring methods at work are mainly covered by article 8 ECHR and the DPD or the E-Privacy Directive, the SNSs, on the one hand, and the very recent surveillance technologies at work (wearable technology and RFID chips for example), on the other hand, are causing legal ambiguities. When the DPD was first drafted before 1995, it did not have SNSs in its mind. However, the general character of the DPD includes SNSs in its protective scope. When a social network, such as Facebook, is not used by users solely for domestic purposes, the DPD is applicable (Art. 3 (2b) DPD). In particular, when organizations, such as businesses, schools and universities, use social networking sites for educational, organizational or social purposes then the DPD is also applicable. Furthermore, the DPD applies in cases where employees are using social networking sites on behalf of their employer (university, company etc) and not for domestic purposes. The most common use of personal data found in SNSs is for marketing analysis, staff monitoring or recruitment purposes[45]. The ICO has issued a report explaining in detail the specific cases to which the DPA applies when the processing of data takes place on social networking sites[46].

If first is ensured that the DPD is applicable in a specific case between an employee and an employer, then the next step is to examine if the processing of data is fair and lawful, adequate, proportionate, relevant and not excessive. It could be more easily justified (legally) for an employer to check an employee's personal account for posts against his legitimate interests rather than dismiss an employee based solely on his Facebook activity and posts. Under articles 17 and 20 of the proposed GDPR employee surveillance via SNSs will be strongly affected. The "right to be forgotten" will entail massive erasures of prospective candidates' personal data. As a result, background checks will be diminished. Profiling as part of employee evaluation or surveillance system could be restricted upon the employee's request. Although all the above-mentioned laws may bring a basic stability in the SNSs environment regarding personal data, it is necessary to introduce new, specific European or national laws in relation to SNSs and social media in general.

Wearable technology goes along with many challenges to privacy and data protection. To begin with, it is difficult to discern whose data are collected-the wearer's or third parties' data-. This distinction is important because in most jurisdictions data processing activities are justified when the data subject is providing his/her consent (or implied consent). The wearer or the user of the wearable device is more likely to provide his/her consent than a third party, who often may not be aware of such a recording or processing of his/her personal data. In addition, most data collected by wearable devices will necessarily fall within the meaning of sensitive personal data (for example fitness armbands or health wearables used at work in order for employers to have a health record of their employees at their disposal). That basically means that under the DPD, sensitive personal data could only be processed under specific circumstances and certain levels of protection as already been mentioned above (see Art.4 par. 5 DPA). It is not certain whether the current legal framework is sufficient to address the legal issues faced in the area of wearable technology in the workplace or not. However, it is necessary for the existing legislation to incorporate in the near future the technical and scientific progress of the last 20 years, including the area of wearable technology.

National Legislation

On a national level, workplace surveillance is regulated *'a priori'* by general or workplace-specific data protection laws and *'a posteriori'* by case law. All EU countries protect in general the right to privacy. Their legal systems usually include constitutional laws, civil laws, telecommunications and labour laws which are intended to apply in cases regarding the right to privacy at work. Portugal, for example, has a specific provision in its constitution referring to data protection (Constituição da República Portuguesa de 1976, art. 25) and Spain recognizes in its constitution the right to privacy (Constitution of 27 December 1978, BOE of 29 December). Furthermore, the Data Protection Directive 95/46/EC also applies to the employment relationship. However, this directive leaves a degree of uncertainty when applied in the employment context and its data protection rules are not always clear in work-related conflicts of rights. The main reason for this uncertainty is that the adoption of the DPD by the Member States took place gradually and it allowed a broad discretion in its transposition. The result was a partial consistency between Member States and certainly not identical or similar solutions. Therefore, the Data Protection Authorities of some member states have formulated codes of practice and opinions regarding some broad provisions of the DPD Directive in order to fill the gaps that are created when these rules or principles have to be applied in employment relationships and especially when electronic monitoring in the workplace is involved.

In general, it is rare for countries to adopt rules governing the right to privacy and data protection in the employment context (such as Finland and Greece). For example, Belgium has specific laws governing employee on-line privacy and Denmark has included specific provisions related to employee internet and email use in its Penal Code[47]. In many countries, employment law regulates some privacy issues in the workplace, although this law appears to be different from country to country.

Due to the rapid development of surveillance technology and its massive invasion into the workplace, the legislators have started reforming legislation that covers privacy and data protection in the workplace, focusing more on modern surveillance methods than traditional ones. The most technologically advanced country in the world, USA, has already proposed laws incorporating social media surveillance trends. In Europe, only Germany has proposed a new Bill that will make it illegal for employers to search prospective candidates and their profiles on social networks. This Bill intends to establish a balance between the rights of employees on privacy and personal data and the legitimate interests of the employer when recruiting. However, due to the new proposed GDPR, this Bill has to be revised and its entrance into force will be further delayed.

In the USA, legislation has been introduced against social media surveillance-policies in at least 28 States. The new laws state that employers are prohibited from asking their employees for username and password disclosures. In the same context, California passed a law in 2008 that prevents employers from compelling their employees to get an RFID chip implanted under their skin (Bill no. SB 362). In 2014, California lawmakers dropped the plan to pass a legislation (California Bill SB-397) allowing RFID chips to be implanted in drivers' licenses and state identification cards, while Michigan, New York, Vermont and Washington have already begun embedding these microchips in several documents that are connected and controlled by the Department of Homeland Security. The European response on RFID technology came a year later, when the European Commission issued a general Recommendation on RFID chips (Commission Recommendation 2009/387/EC), with privacy and data protection implications, calling industry and the various stakeholders to submit a protection framework to Article 29 WP. So far, no specific European legislation regarding RFID chips has been introduced.

The lack of workplace-related specific legislation on data protection has transformed case law in an important source of law for many countries, especially for issues concerning new surveillance technologies. National case law on employee surveillance is very limited so far. New surveillance methods in the workplace, such as surveillance via SNSs and RFID chips, have not been very prominent to date neither in national courts nor in national legislation. Similarly, case law has in the main not yet dealt with novel technologies and surveillance at work mostly because of their surreptitious character and the difficulty of evidence in courts.

CONCLUSION

Contrary to the U.S., in Europe the right to privacy is protected on constitutional level and by national legislation. The form and the means of protection may differ, but a sufficient level of privacy and data protection is granted, in accordance with the requirements of article 8 ECHR and the DPD. The DPD provides criteria to assess the lawfulness of data processing, that is, consent and its validity, the principle of proportionality, "the legitimate interests test", and other factors that influence the legality of the processing (information to the data subject, data retention periods and privacy policies), which should all be taken into consideration. This legislation should be interpreted in such a way as to show that the employment relationship does not imply a waiver by an employee of his right to privacy and data protection.

It is notable that many EU Member States have drafted opinions, codes of practice or specific national rules in order to make privacy and data protection in the workplace more specific, comprehensive and concrete. It is clear however, that Member States have not managed to address most issues concerning workplace surveillance (especially novel technologies) on a coherent and uniform basis. Consent, for example, is differently interpreted by Member States and therefore its application is problematic, especially in technologically advanced environments.

New technologies in some countries are dealt with by obsolete and general provisions, creating many ambiguities and legislative gaps. So, e.g., the use of RFID chips cannot be regulated solely through guidance or general recommendations; besides that, the complicated regime of biometrics or wearable technology cannot be regulated by recommendations of national data protection authorities. Legislation governing new technologies cannot be fragmentary, superficial and incomplete. This is because in a constantly changing environment, the law has to be the regulatory factor of technology, not lagging behind it.

In our view, the adoption of sector specific legislation for employees' protection would be incomplete without a general framework adopting modern instruments of data protection, such as privacy by design, data protection impact assessment, etc., and elaborating on key concepts such as consent. Furthermore, the protection of employees' privacy requires specific regulations, based on this general framework, which could be introduced by legislation, collective agreements, etc. Thus, guidelines or recommendations issued by national data protection authorities and interpreting general provisions of the law cannot efficiently resolve the intriguing problems of employees' privacy.

REFERENCES

BDA. (2012). *Appropriate modernization of European data protection*. Position on the draft European regulation on the protection of individuals with regard to the processing of personal data and on the free movement of such data ("general data protection regulation").

Blanpain, R., & Van Gestel, M. (2004). *Use and Monitoring of E-mail, Intranet, and Internet Facilities at work*. Kluwer Law International.

Boersma, K. (2012). *Internet and surveillance-The challenge of Web 2.0 and Social Media* (C. Fuchs, K. Boersma, A. Albrechtslund, & M. Sandoval, Eds.). Routledge.

Bryant, S. (1995). Electronic Surveillance in the Workplace. *Canadian Journal of Communication*, *20*(4), 505–525. Retrieved from http://www.cjc-online.ca/index.php/journal/article/view/893/799

Cas, J. (2005). Privacy in pervasive computing environments: A contradiction in terms. *IEEE Technology and Society Magazine*, *24*(1), 24–33. doi:10.1109/MTAS.2005.1407744

Coleman, R., & McCahill, M. (2011). *Surveillance and Crime*. London: Sage Publications.

Craig, J. (1999). *Privacy and Employment Law*. Oxford, UK: Hart Publishing.

Garrie, D. B., & Wong, R. (2010). Social networking: Opening the floodgates to "personal data". *Computer and Telecommunications Law Review*, *16*(6), 167–175.

Hazel, O. (2002). Email and internet monitoring in the workplace: Information privacy and contracting-out. *Industrial Law Journal*, *31*(4), 321–352. doi:10.1093/ilj/31.4.321

Hendrickx, F. (2002). On-Line Rights for Employees in the Information Society. In *Bulletin of Comparative Labour Relations 40-2000*. Kluwer Law International.

Iglezakis, I., Politis, D., & Phaedon-John, K. (Eds.). (2009). *Socioeconomic and Legal Implications of Electronic Intrusion*. Hershey, PA: IGI Global.

DG Justice. (2004). *Draft Directive concerning the processing of workers' personal data and the protection of privacy in the employment context, Article 5*. Author.

Kravets, D. (2013). California abruptly drops plan to implant RFID chips in driver's licenses. *Wired*. Available at http://www.wired.com/2013/09/drivers-licenserfid-chips/

Lyon, D. (1994). The Electronic Eye: The rise of surveillance society. Polity Press.

Marx, G. T. (2007). What's new about new surveillance? Classifying for change and continuity. In S. P. Heir & J. Greenberg (Eds.), *The Surveillance Studies Reader*. Maidenhead, UK: Open University Press.

McColgan, A. (2003). *Do privacy rights disappear in the workplace?*. Human Rights Law Review.

Nielsen, R. (2010). *Employment and ICT Law.* Stockholm Institute for Scandinavian Law.

Orwell, G. (1949). *Nineteen Eighty-Four*. Harmondsworth, UK: Penguin.

Retzer, K. (2013). Aligning corporate ethics compliance programs with data protection. *Privacy & Data Protection, 13*(6), 5–7.

Roth, P. (2006). *The Workplace Implications of RFID Technology*. Employment Law Bulletin.

Sahin, A. (2014). New EU data protection laws: European Parliament proposes restrictive data protection laws in Europe. *Computer and Telecommunications Law Review, 20*(2), 63–65.

Siau, K., Nah, F.-H., & Teng, L. (2002). Acceptable Internet use policy. *Communications of the ACM, 45*(1), 75–79. doi:10.1145/502269.502302

Taylor, L. (2014). Wearable technology: The regulatory challenges. *Computer and Telecommunications Law Review, 20*(4), 95–97.

Van der Ploeg, I. (2005). *The Machine-Readable Body: Essays on Biometrics and the Informatization of the Body*. Maastricht: Shaker.

Warren, S., & Brandeis, L. (1980). The right to privacy. *Harvard Law Review, 4*.

Whitcroft, O. (2013). Bring Your Own Device -protecting data on the move. *Privacy & Data Protection, 13*(4), 10–12.

ADDITIONAL READING

Christie, D. (2000). 'Employee surveillance'. *Emp. L.B.,* 38(Aug).

European Parliament. (2013). Study on the "Protection of personal data in work-related relations". Directorate-general for internal policies-Policy department, Citizen's rights and constitutional affairs. Available athttp://www.vub.ac.be/LSTS/pub/Dehert/491.pdf

International Labour Office (ILO). (1997). Code of Practice: Protection of workers' personal data, Geneva.

Lloyd, I. J. (2011). *'Information Technology Law* (6th ed.). Oxford University Press.

Monahan, T. (Ed.). (2006). *Surveillance and Security: Technological Politics and Power in Everyday Life*. New York: Routledge.

Murray, A. (2013). *'Information Technology Law: The Law and Society* (2nd ed.). Oxford University Press.

Opinion 13/2011 on Geolocation services on smart mobile devices', WP185, 16 May 2011

Opinion 15/2011 on the definition of consent', WP 187 13 July 2011

Working document on data protection issues related to RFID technology', WP 105, 19 January 2005

Wright, C. R. & Joseph Wilson. (2014). 'Using biometrics in the workplace'. 6 January 2014, available at http://www.lexology.com/library/detail.aspx?g=d7c35ceff112-4204-8dfb-9458369c0924

ENDNOTES

1. Panopticon was an architecture concept for prisons where prisoners were constantly monitored. This notion was later used metaphorically by Foucault to describe the disciplinary power and surveillance societies.
2. *OnRec*, 'Managing internet surfing not plain sailing for employers', 20 April 2004, available at http://www.onrec.com/news/news-archive/managing-internetsurfing-not-plain-sailing-for-employers.
3. C. Connen, 'Employees Really Do Waste Time at Work', *Forbes*, 17 July 2012, available at http://www.forbes.com/sites/cherylsnappconner/2012/07/17/employeesreally-do-waste-time-at-work/.
4. Such as in UDHR, 1948 and in ECHR, 1950 (into force 1953).

5 See European Parliament's 'Study "Protection of personal data in work-related relations", *Directorate-general for internal policies, Policy department: Citizen's rights and constitutional affairs*, 2013, p.15.

6 *New Technology in the Workplace 1900-1950, Exploring 20th century*, available at http://www.20thcenturylondon.org.uk/new-technology-work-place-1900-1950.

7 *Searches, Workplace Searches Workplace Fairness*, available at http://www.workplacefairness.org/searches?agree=yes.

8 See Article 8(1)DPD.

9 USA: HIPAA (1996) and HITECH (2009), EU: a breach of art.8 ECHR L.Brunn, 'Privacy and the employment relationship', *25 Hous. L.Rev*, Vol.25:389, p.406.

10 Boden et al, 'Company characteristics and workplace medical testing', *American Journal of Public Health, 1995, 85*(8), p.1070.

11 Information about the origin and the destination of the mail but not its content.

12 T. Wessing, 'Regulating CCTV use in the UK', March 2014, available at http://www.taylorwessing.com/globaldatahub/article_regulating_cctv.html.

13 D. McGoldrick, 'The limits of freedom of expression on Facebook and other social networking sites: A UK perspective', *HRLR*, 2013, 13:1, p.129.

14 As an analogy to "Web 3.0"; John Markoff suggested to name the third-generation Web: "Web 3.0". J. Markoff; "Entrepreneurs See a Web Guided by Common Sense", *The NY Times*, available at http://www.nytimes.com/2006/11/12/business/12web.html?pagewanted=all&_r=0.

15 This practice was prohibited after ICO's consultation for a breach of Data Protection Act. *BBC*, 'Recordings in Southampton taxis 'must be stopped', 25 July 2012, available at http://www.bbc.co.uk/news/uk-england-hampshire-18982854.

16 E. Balkovich et al, '9 to 5: Do You Know If Your Boss Knows Where You Are? Case Studies of Radio Frequency Identification Usage in the Workplace', *RAND Corporation*, 2005, p. 14, at http://www.rand.org/pubs/technical_reports/TR197.html.

17 *IBM*, 'IBM RFID Solution for Asset Tracking – location awareness and safety', Available at https://services.mesa.org/ResourceLibrary/ShowResource/3759e743a882-4442-8f1f-57fe246e3f35.

18 ILO, 'RFID chips in the Workplace', *World of Work Magazine*, No.59, 2007, p.17.

19 Rory, Cellan-Jones, "Office put chips under staff's skin", BBC news, available at http://www.bbc.com/news/technology-31042477.

[20] Thomas Fox-Brewster, "Hacking Putin's Eyes: How To Bypass Biometrics The Cheap And Dirty Way With Google Images" Forbes website available at http://www.forbes.com/sites/thomasbrewster/2015/03/05/clone-putins-eyes-usinggoogle-images/.

[21] SITA, 'Virgin Atlantic first in world to use wearable technology to serve passengers', 11 February 2014, available at http://www.sita.aero/content/VirginAtlantic-first-world-use-wearable-technology-serve-passengers.

[22] 'Sousveillance' is the recording activity by an individual using wearable or portable devices.

[23] People's faces are compared with photos of people stored in databases for identification purposes.

[24] Sophie Curtis, "Google announces first 'Glass at Work' partners'', 17 July 2014 available at http://www.telegraph.co.uk/technology/google/10905326/Googleannounces-first-Glass-at-Work-partners.html.

[25] See Samsung "Wearables Make Their Move to the Enterprise", available at http://samsungbusiness.cio.com/wearables-make-their-move-to-the-enterprise/.

[26] The Finnish Privacy Protection in Working Life Act (2001) and the Swedish Employment Protection Act (2008).

[27] This term is determined by society's views or by the views of a "reasonable" person. See *Katz v. United States*, 389 U.S. 347, 360-61(1967) J.P.Kesan, "Cyber-Woring or Cyber-Shrinking?, *Florida Law Review* 2002, 54,p.294.

[28] *O'Connor v. Ortega*, 480 U.S. 709(1987).

[29] Only California protects employees' (public and private) right to privacy in its constitution. J.R.Mignin, et al, 'Privacy issues in the workplace: A post-September 11 perspective', *Employee Relations Law Journal,*2002, *28*(1), p.9.

[30] *Niemitz v Germany* (1992) 16 EHRR,97.

[31] *Halford v the United Kingdom*; (1997) 24 E.H.R.R. 523.

[32] *Copland v. the United Kingdom*, No. 62617/00, 3 April 2007.

[33] Directive 95/46/EC of the European Parliament and of the Council of 24 October 1995 on the protection of individuals with regard to the processing of personal data and on the free movement of such data ;Official Journal L 281, 23/11/1995.

[34] Directive 2002/58/EC of the European Parliament and of the Council of 12 July 2002 concerning the processing of personal data and the protection of privacy in the electronic communications sector (Directive on privacy and electronic communications);Official Journal L 201, 31/07/2002.

[35] In Joined Cases C-141/12 and C-372/12, the CJEU held that the legal analysis of personal data it is not considered as personal data itself.

[36] See next paragraph about the definition of employees' consent. Art.7(f) is the so-called principle of proportionality. Art.7(e),(f) 95/46 EC.

[37] As defined in art.2(d), Directive95/46EC. M.Kuschewsky, 'Surveillance at the Workplace-how to avoid the pitfalls', *PDP 9 6 (8)*, 2009 p.9.

[38] Article 29 Data Protection Working Party, *Opinion 15/2011 on the definition of consent*, WP 187, 13.7.2011, p.12.

[39] Belgium excluded the use of consent in employment relations. The UK had not included these provisions. France and the Netherlands implemented these provisions as such.

[40] European Parliament, 'Study "Protection of personal data in work-related relations", Directorate-general for internal policies, Policy department: Citizen's rights and constitutional affairs, 2013, p.22.

[41] This term has raised a heated debate after the ruling of CJEU in Google Spain(C-131/12), available at http://curia.europa.eu/juris/document/document.jsf?text=&docid=152065&pageInd ex=0&doclang=en&mode=req&dir=&occ=first&part=1&cid=264438, where the Court found a legitimate reason for the erasure of data subject's personal data, basing its argument to the right to erasure(Article 12b) and the right to object(Article 14) of the DPD. This decision does create a precedent on the "right to be forgotten" but it cannot compel search engines to comply with any takedown request without a fair balancing of rights, unless a national authority asks them to. However, Google is willing to erase any data subject's personal data if asked to within European borders, excluding the erasure of data for the domain name google.com.

[42] European Parliament, 'Study "Protection of personal data in work-related relations", Directorate-general for internal policies, Policy department: Citizen's rights and constitutional affairs, 2013, p.67.

[43] Art.29 DP WP, 'Opinion 13/2011 on Geolocation services on smart mobile devices, 16 May 2011; WP 185, pp. 13, 18, 20.

[44] See European Commission, 'Recommendation on RFID chips', 2009/387/EC, OJEU, Section 11.

[45] The Google Spain case(C-131/12) CJEU is possible to affect the pre-employment background checks. E.Smythe, 'Will the 'right to be forgotten' ruling affect candidate background checks?', *The Guardian*, 25 July 2014, available at http://www.theguardian.com/media-network/media-networkblog/2014/jul/25/google-right-forgotten-job-prospects.

46 The DPD applies under the same conditions since both legislations incorporate the "non-domestic purpose" prerequisite.
ICO, 'Social Networking and Online Forums-when does the DPA applies', p.5, available at http://www.pdpjournals.com/docs/88110.pdf.

47 Belgium National collective agreement No.81 on the protection of workers' privacy with respect to controls on electronic on-line communications data and Danish Penal Code par.263.

Related References

To continue our tradition of advancing business and management research, we have compiled a list of recommended IGI Global readings. These references will provide additional information and guidance to further enrich your knowledge and assist you with your own research and future publications.

Abdullah, M., Ahmad, R., Peck, L. S., Kasirun, Z. M., & Alshammari, F. (2014). Benefits of CMM and CMMI-based software process improvement. In *Software design and development: Concepts, methodologies, tools, and applications* (pp. 1385–1400). Hershey, PA: Information Science Reference; doi:10.4018/978-1-4666-4301-7.ch067

Abu-Shanab, E., & Ghaleb, O. (2012). Adoption of mobile commerce technology: An involvement of trust and risk concerns. *International Journal of Technology Diffusion*, *3*(2), 36–49. doi:10.4018/jtd.2012040104

Adapa, S. (2013). Electronic retailing of prepared food in Australia. In K. Tarnay, S. Imre, & L. Xu (Eds.), *Research and development in e-business through service-oriented solutions* (pp. 280–292). Hershey, PA: Business Science Reference; doi:10.4018/978-1-4666-4181-5.ch014

Aklouf, Y., & Drias, H. (2011). An adaptive e-commerce architecture for enterprise information exchange. In *Enterprise information systems: Concepts, methodologies, tools and applications* (pp. 329–345). Hershey, PA: Business Science Reference; doi:10.4018/978-1-61692-852-0.ch202

Al-Nawayseh, M. K., Alnabhan, M. M., Al-Debei, M. M., & Balachandran, W. (2013). An adaptive decision support system for last mile logistics in e-commerce: A study on online grocery shopping. *International Journal of Decision Support System Technology*, *5*(1), 40–65. doi:10.4018/jdsst.2013010103

Related References

Al-Somali, S. A., Clegg, B., & Gholami, R. (2013). An investigation into the adoption and implementation of electronic commerce in Saudi Arabian small and medium enterprises. In *Small and medium enterprises: Concepts, methodologies, tools, and applications* (pp. 816–839). Hershey, PA: Business Science Reference; doi:10.4018/978-1-4666-3886-0.ch040

Al-Somali, S. A., Gholami, R., & Clegg, B. (2013). An investigation into the adoption of electronic commerce among Saudi Arabian SMEs. In M. Khosrow-Pour (Ed.), *E-commerce for organizational development and competitive advantage* (pp. 126–150). Hershey, PA: Business Science Reference; doi:10.4018/978-1-4666-3622-4.ch007

Alavi, S. (2013). Collaborative customer relationship management-co-creation and collaboration through online communities. *International Journal of Virtual Communities and Social Networking*, *5*(1), 1–18. doi:10.4018/jvcsn.2013010101

Alavi, S., & Ahuja, V. (2013). E-commerce in a web 2.0 world: Using online business communities to impact consumer price sensitivity. *International Journal of Online Marketing*, *3*(2), 38–55. doi:10.4018/ijom.2013040103

Alawneh, A., Al-Refai, H., & Batiha, K. (2011). E-business adoption by Jordanian banks: An exploratory study of the key factors and performance indicators. In A. Tatnall (Ed.), *Actor-network theory and technology innovation: Advancements and new concepts* (pp. 113–128). Hershey, PA: Information Science Reference; doi:10.4018/978-1-60960-197-3.ch008

Albuquerque, S. L., & Gondim, P. R. (2012). Applying continuous authentication to protect electronic transactions. In T. Chou (Ed.), *Information assurance and security technologies for risk assessment and threat management: Advances* (pp. 134–161). Hershey, PA: Information Science Reference; doi:10.4018/978-1-61350-507-6.ch005

Alfahl, H., Sanzogni, L., & Houghton, L. (2012). Mobile commerce adoption in organizations: A literature review and future research directions. *Journal of Electronic Commerce in Organizations*, *10*(2), 61–78. doi:10.4018/jeco.2012040104

Aloini, D., Dulmin, R., & Mininno, V. (2013). E-procurement: What really matters in B2B e-reverse auctions. In P. Ordóñez de Pablos, J. Lovelle, J. Gayo, & R. Tennyson (Eds.), *E-procurement management for successful electronic government systems* (pp. 87–113). Hershey, PA: Information Science Reference; doi:10.4018/978-1-4666-2119-0.ch006

Amer, M., & Gómez, J. M. (2010). Measuring B2C quality of electronic service: Towards a common consensus. In I. Lee (Ed.), *Encyclopedia of e-business development and management in the global economy* (pp. 135–143). Hershey, PA: Business Science Reference; doi:10.4018/978-1-61520-611-7.ch014

Amer, M., & Gómez, J. M. (2012). Measuring quality of electronic services: Moving from business-to-consumer into business-to-business marketplace. In E. Kajan, F. Dorloff, & I. Bedini (Eds.), *Handbook of research on e-business standards and protocols: Documents, data and advanced web technologies* (pp. 637–654). Hershey, PA: Business Science Reference; doi:10.4018/978-1-4666-0146-8.ch029

Andriole, S. J. (2010). Business technology strategy for an energy information company. *Journal of Information Technology Research, 3*(3), 19–42. doi:10.4018/jitr.2010070103

Andriole, S. J. (2010). Templates for the development of business technology strategies. *Journal of Information Technology Research, 3*(3), 1–10. doi:10.4018/jitr.2010070101

Archer, N. (2010). Electronic marketplace support for B2B business transactions. In *Electronic services: Concepts, methodologies, tools and applications* (pp. 85–93). Hershey, PA: Information Science Reference; doi:10.4018/978-1-61520-967-5.ch007

Archer, N. (2010). Management considerations for B2B online exchanges. In *Business information systems: Concepts, methodologies, tools and applications* (pp. 1740–1747). Hershey, PA: Business Science Reference; doi:10.4018/978-1-61520-969-9.ch105

Arduini, D., Nascia, L., & Zanfei, A. (2012). Complementary approaches to the diffusion of innovation: Empirical evidence on e-services adoption in Italy. *International Journal of E-Services and Mobile Applications, 4*(3), 42–64. doi:10.4018/jesma.2012070103

Arh, T., Dimovski, V., & Blažic, B. J. (2011). ICT and web 2.0 technologies as a determinant of business performance. In M. Al-Mutairi & L. Mohammed (Eds.), *Cases on ICT utilization, practice and solutions: Tools for managing day-to-day issues* (pp. 59–77). Hershey, PA: Information Science Reference; doi:10.4018/978-1-60960-015-0.ch005

Related References

Arikpo, I., Osofisan, A., & Eteng, I. E. (2012). Enhancing trust in e-commerce in developing IT environments: A feedback-based perspective. In A. Usoro, G. Majewski, P. Ifinedo, & I. Arikpo (Eds.), *Leveraging developing economies with the use of information technology: Trends and tools* (pp. 193–203). Hershey, PA: Information Science Reference; doi:10.4018/978-1-4666-1637-0.ch011

Aryanto, V. D., & Chrismastuti, A. A. (2013). Model for digital economy in Indonesia. In I. Oncioiu (Ed.), *Business innovation, development, and advancement in the digital economy* (pp. 60–77). Hershey, PA: Business Science Reference; doi:10.4018/978-1-4666-2934-9.ch005

Asim, M., & Petkovic, M. (2012). Fundamental building blocks for security interoperability in e-business. In E. Kajan, F. Dorloff, & I. Bedini (Eds.), *Handbook of research on e-business standards and protocols: documents, data and advanced web technologies* (pp. 269–292). Hershey, PA: Business Science Reference; doi:10.4018/978-1-4666-0146-8.ch013

Askool, S., Jacobs, A., & Nakata, K. (2013). A method of analysing the use of social networking sites in business. In *IT policy and ethics: Concepts, methodologies, tools, and applications* (pp. 794–813). Hershey, PA: Information Science Reference; doi:10.4018/978-1-4666-2919-6.ch036

Association, I. R. (2013). Enterprise resource planning: Concepts, methodologies, tools, and applications (Vols. 1–3). Hershey, PA: IGI Global; doi:10.4018/978-1-4666-4153-2

Azab, N., & Khalifa, N. (2013). Web 2.0 and opportunities for entrepreneurs: How Egyptian entrepreneurs perceive and exploit web 2.0 technologies. In N. Azab (Ed.), *Cases on web 2.0 in developing countries: Studies on implementation, application, and use* (pp. 1–32). Hershey, PA: Information Science Reference; doi:10.4018/978-1-4666-2515-0.ch001

Azevedo, S. G., & Carvalho, H. (2012). RFID technology in the fashion supply chain: An exploratory analysis. In T. Choi (Ed.), *Fashion supply chain management: Industry and business analysis* (pp. 303–326). Hershey, PA: Information Science Reference; doi:10.4018/978-1-60960-756-2.ch017

Baporikar, N. (2013). ICT challenge for ebusiness in SMEs. *International Journal of Strategic Information Technology and Applications*, *4*(1), 15–26. doi:10.4018/jsita.2013010102

Barbin Laurindo, F. J., Monteiro de Carvalho, M., & Shimizu, T. (2010). Strategic alignment between business and information technology. In M. Hunter (Ed.), *Strategic information systems: Concepts, methodologies, tools, and applications* (pp. 20–28). Hershey, PA: Information Science Reference; doi:10.4018/978-1-60566-677-8.ch002

Barjis, J. (2012). Software engineering security based on business process modeling. In K. Khan (Ed.), *Security-aware systems applications and software development methods* (pp. 52–68). Hershey, PA: Information Science Reference; doi:10.4018/978-1-4666-1580-9.ch004

Barnes, D., & Hinton, M. (2011). The benefits of an e-business performance measurement system. In N. Shi & G. Silvius (Eds.), *Enterprise IT governance, business value and performance measurement* (pp. 158–169). Hershey, PA: Information Science Reference; doi:10.4018/978-1-60566-346-3.ch011

Bask, A., Lipponen, M., & Tinnilä, M. (2012). E-commerce logistics: A literature research review and topics for future research. *International Journal of E-Services and Mobile Applications*, *4*(3), 1–22. doi:10.4018/jesma.2012070101

Bask, A., & Tinnilä, M. (2013). Impact of product characteristics on supply chains: An analytical literature review. *International Journal of Applied Logistics*, *4*(1), 35–59. doi:10.4018/jal.2013010103

Basu, S. (2012). Direct taxation and e-commerce: Possibility and desirability. In E. Druică (Ed.), *Digital economy innovations and impacts on society* (pp. 26–48). Hershey, PA: Information Science Reference; doi:10.4018/978-1-4666-1556-4.ch003

Beckinsale, M. (2010). E-business among ethnic minority businesses: The case of ethnic entrepreneurs. In B. Thomas & G. Simmons (Eds.), *E-commerce adoption and small business in the global marketplace: Tools for optimization* (pp. 187–207). Hershey, PA: Business Science Reference; doi:10.4018/978-1-60566-998-4.ch010

Beckinsale, M. (2011). eBusiness among ethnic minority businesses: Ethnic entrepreneurs' ICT adoption and readiness. In S. Sharma (Ed.), E-adoption and socio-economic impacts: Emerging infrastructural effects (pp. 168-189). Hershey, PA: Information Science Reference. doi:10.4018/978-1-60960-597-1.ch009

Bedini, I., Gardarin, G., & Nguyen, B. (2011). Semantic technologies and e-business. In E. Kajan (Ed.), *Electronic business interoperability: Concepts, opportunities and challenges* (pp. 243–278). Hershey, PA: Business Science Reference; doi:10.4018/978-1-60960-485-1.ch011

Beedle, J., & Wang, S. (2013). Roles of a technology leader. In S. Wang & T. Hartsell (Eds.), *Technology integration and foundations for effective leadership* (pp. 228–241). Hershey, PA: Information Science Reference; doi:10.4018/978-1-4666-2656-0.ch013

Belhajjame, K., & Brambilla, M. (2013). Ontological description and similarity-based discovery of business process models. In J. Krogstie (Ed.), *Frameworks for developing efficient information systems: Models, theory, and practice* (pp. 30–50). Hershey, PA: Engineering Science Reference; doi:10.4018/978-1-4666-4161-7.ch002

Benou, P., & Bitos, V. (2010). Developing mobile commerce applications. In M. Khosrow-Pour (Ed.), *E-commerce trends for organizational advancement: New applications and methods* (pp. 1–15). Hershey, PA: Information Science Reference; doi:10.4018/978-1-60566-964-9.ch001

Berisha-Namani, M. (2013). Information systems usage in business and management. In I. Oncioiu (Ed.), *Business innovation, development, and advancement in the digital economy* (pp. 48–59). Hershey, PA: Business Science Reference; doi:10.4018/978-1-4666-2934-9.ch004

Bermúdez, G. M., & Rojas, L. A. (2013). Model-driven engineering for electronic commerce. In V. Díaz, J. Lovelle, B. García-Bustelo, & O. Martínez (Eds.), *Progressions and innovations in model-driven software engineering* (pp. 196–208). Hershey, PA: Engineering Science Reference; doi:10.4018/978-1-4666-4217-1.ch007

Bernardino, J. (2013). Open business intelligence for better decision-making. *International Journal of Information Communication Technologies and Human Development*, *5*(2), 20–36. doi:10.4018/jicthd.2013040102

Berzins, M. (2012). Scams and the Australian e-business environment. In K. Mohammed Rezaul (Ed.), *Strategic and pragmatic e-business: Implications for future business practices* (pp. 156–175). Hershey, PA: Business Science Reference; doi:10.4018/978-1-4666-1619-6.ch007

Binsaleh, M., & Hassan, S. (2011). Systems development methodology for mobile commerce applications. *International Journal of Mobile Computing and Multimedia Communications*, *3*(4), 36–52. doi:10.4018/jmcmc.2011100103

Binsaleh, M., & Hassan, S. (2013). Systems development methodology for mobile commerce applications. In I. Khalil & E. Weippl (Eds.), *Contemporary challenges and solutions for mobile and multimedia technologies* (pp. 146–162). Hershey, PA: Information Science Reference; doi:10.4018/978-1-4666-2163-3.ch009

Blake, R., Gordon, S., & Shankaranarayanan, G. (2013). The role of case-based research in information technology and systems. In P. Isaias & M. Baptista Nunes (Eds.), *Information systems research and exploring social artifacts: approaches and methodologies* (pp. 200–220). Hershey, PA: Information Science Reference; doi:10.4018/978-1-4666-2491-7.ch011

Boateng, R., Heeks, R., Molla, A., & Hinson, R. (2013). Advancing e-commerce beyond readiness in a developing country: Experiences of Ghanaian firms. In M. Khosrow-Pour (Ed.), *E-commerce for organizational development and competitive advantage* (pp. 1–17). Hershey, PA: Business Science Reference; doi:10.4018/978-1-4666-3622-4.ch001

Bonfatti, F., Monari, P. D., & Martinelli, L. (2011). Business document exchange between small companies. In E. Kajan (Ed.), *Electronic business interoperability: Concepts, opportunities and challenges* (pp. 482–510). Hershey, PA: Business Science Reference; doi:10.4018/978-1-60960-485-1.ch020

Boucadair, M., & Binet, D. (2014). Issues with current internet architecture. In M. Boucadair & D. Binet (Eds.), *Solutions for sustaining scalability in internet growth* (pp. 1–16). Hershey, PA: Information Science Reference; doi:10.4018/978-1-4666-4305-5.ch001

Bouras, A., Gouvas, P., & Mentzas, G. (2009). A semantic service-oriented architecture for business process fusion. In I. Lee (Ed.), *Electronic business: Concepts, methodologies, tools, and applications* (pp. 504–532). Hershey, PA: Information Science Reference; doi:10.4018/978-1-60566-056-1.ch032

Braun, P. (2011). Advancing women in the digital economy: eLearning opportunities for meta-competency skilling. In *Global business: Concepts, methodologies, tools and applications* (pp. 1978–1990). Hershey, PA: Business Science Reference; doi:10.4018/978-1-60960-587-2.ch708

Brown, M., & Garson, G. (2013). Organization behavior and organization theory. In *Public information management and e-government: Policy and issues* (pp. 160–195). Hershey, PA: Information Science Reference; doi:10.4018/978-1-4666-3003-1.ch007

Brown, M., & Garson, G. (2013). The information technology business model. In *Public information management and e-government: Policy and issues* (pp. 76–98). Hershey, PA: Information Science Reference; doi:10.4018/978-1-4666-3003-1.ch004

Related References

Burete, R., Badica, A., Badica, C., & Moraru, F. (2011). Enhanced reputation model with forgiveness for e-business agents. *International Journal of Agent Technologies and Systems*, *3*(1), 11–26. doi:10.4018/jats.2011010102

Business Research and Case Center. (2011). *Cases on business and management in the MENA region: New trends and opportunities*. Hershey, PA: IGI Global; doi:10.4018/978-1-60960-583-4

Bwalya, K. J. (2011). E-commerce penetration in the SADC region: Consolidating and moving forward. In M. Cruz-Cunha & J. Varajão (Eds.), *E-business managerial aspects, solutions and case studies* (pp. 235–253). Hershey, PA: Business Science Reference; doi:10.4018/978-1-60960-463-9.ch014

Charbaji, R., Rebeiz, K., & Sidani, Y. (2010). Antecedents and consequences of the risk taking behavior of mobile commerce adoption in Lebanon. In H. Rahman (Ed.), *Handbook of research on e-government readiness for information and service exchange: Utilizing progressive information communication technologies* (pp. 354–380). Hershey, PA: Information Science Reference; doi:10.4018/978-1-60566-671-6.ch018

Chaturvedi, N. (2013). Collaborative web for natural resources industries. In *Supply chain management: Concepts, methodologies, tools, and applications* (pp. 601–614). Hershey, PA: Business Science Reference; doi:10.4018/978-1-4666-2625-6.ch035

Chen, C., & Yang, S. C. (2008). E-commerce and mobile commerce application adoptions. In A. Becker (Ed.), *Electronic commerce: Concepts, methodologies, tools, and applications* (pp. 826–836). Hershey, PA: Information Science Reference; doi:10.4018/978-1-59904-943-4.ch068

Chen, Q., & Zhang, N. (2013). IT-supported business performance and e-commerce application in SMEs. *Journal of Electronic Commerce in Organizations*, *11*(2), 41–52. doi:10.4018/jeco.2013040104

Chen, T. F. (2011). Emerging business models: Value drivers in e-business 2.0 and towards enterprise 2.0. In T. Chen (Ed.), *Implementing new business models in for-profit and non-profit organizations: Technologies and applications* (pp. 1–28). Hershey, PA: Information Science Reference; doi:10.4018/978-1-60960-129-4.ch001

Chen, T. F. (2011). The critical success factors and integrated model for implementing e-business in Taiwan's SMEs. In *Global business: Concepts, methodologies, tools and applications* (pp. 1109–1133). Hershey, PA: Business Science Reference; doi:10.4018/978-1-60960-587-2.ch416

Chew, E., & Gottschalk, P. (2013). Critical success factors of IT strategy. In *Knowledge driven service innovation and management: IT strategies for business alignment and value creation* (pp. 185–220). Hershey, PA: Business Science Reference; doi:10.4018/978-1-4666-2512-9.ch006

Chew, E., & Gottschalk, P. (2013). Strategic alignment and IT-enabled value creation. In *Knowledge driven service innovation and management: IT strategies for business alignment and value creation* (pp. 141–184). Hershey, PA: Business Science Reference; doi:10.4018/978-1-4666-2512-9.ch005

Chew, E., & Gottschalk, P. (2013). Theories and models of service-oriented firms. In *Knowledge driven service innovation and management: IT strategies for business alignment and value creation* (pp. 1–34). Hershey, PA: Business Science Reference; doi:10.4018/978-1-4666-2512-9.ch001

Chiang, L. (2010). Digital confidence in business: A perspective of information ethics. In M. Pankowska (Ed.), *Infonomics for distributed business and decision-making environments: Creating information system ecology* (pp. 288–300). Hershey, PA: Business Science Reference; doi:10.4018/978-1-60566-890-1.ch017

Chugh, R., & Gupta, P. (2011). A unified view of enablers, barriers, and readiness of small to medium enterprises for e-business adoption. In M. Cruz-Cunha & J. Varajão (Eds.), *E-business issues, challenges and opportunities for SMEs: Driving competitiveness* (pp. 291–312). Hershey, PA: Business Science Reference; doi:10.4018/978-1-61692-880-3.ch017

Clear, F., Woods, A., & Dickson, K. (2013). SME adoption and use of ICT for networked trading purposes: The influence of sector, size and age of firm. In *Small and medium enterprises: Concepts, methodologies, tools, and applications* (pp. 774–791). Hershey, PA: Business Science Reference; doi:10.4018/978-1-4666-3886-0.ch038

Connolly, R. (2013). eCommerce trust beliefs: Examining the role of national culture. In P. Isaias & M. Baptista Nunes (Eds.), Information systems research and exploring social artifacts: Approaches and methodologies (pp. 20-42). Hershey, PA: Information Science Reference. doi:10.4018/978-1-4666-2491-7.ch002

Cormican, K. (2013). Collaborative networks: Challenges for SMEs. In *Small and medium enterprises: Concepts, methodologies, tools, and applications* (pp. 1638–1653). Hershey, PA: Business Science Reference; doi:10.4018/978-1-4666-3886-0.ch083

Related References

Costante, E., Petkovic, M., & den Hartog, J. (2013). Trust management and user's trust perception in e-business. In *IT policy and ethics: Concepts, methodologies, tools, and applications* (pp. 64–83). Hershey, PA: Information Science Reference; doi:10.4018/978-1-4666-2919-6.ch004

Costin, Y. (2012). Adopting ICT in the mompreneurs business: A strategy for growth? In C. Romm Livermore (Ed.), *Gender and social computing: Interactions, differences and relationships* (pp. 17–34). Hershey, PA: Information Science Publishing; doi:10.4018/978-1-60960-759-3.ch002

Cox, S. (2013). E-business planning in morphing organizations: Maturity models of business transformation. In E. Li, S. Loh, C. Evans, & F. Lorenzi (Eds.), *Organizations and social networking: Utilizing social media to engage consumers* (pp. 286–312). Hershey, PA: Business Science Reference; doi:10.4018/978-1-4666-4026-9.ch015

Cruz-Cunha, M. M., Moreira, F., & Varajão, J. (2014). *Handbook of research on enterprise 2.0: Technological, social, and organizational dimensions*. Hershey, PA: IGI Global; doi:10.4018/978-1-4666-4373-4

D'Aubeterre, F., Iyer, L. S., Ehrhardt, R., & Singh, R. (2011). Discovery process in a B2B emarketplace: A semantic matchmaking approach. In V. Sugumaran (Ed.), *Intelligent, adaptive and reasoning technologies: New developments and applications* (pp. 80–103). Hershey, PA: Information Science Reference; doi:10.4018/978-1-60960-595-7.ch005

Dabbagh, R. A. (2011). E-business: Concepts and context with illustrative examples of e-business and e-commerce in education. In A. Al Ajeeli & Y. Al-Bastaki (Eds.), *Handbook of research on e-services in the public sector: E-government strategies and advancements* (pp. 450–462). Hershey, PA: Information Science Reference; doi:10.4018/978-1-61520-789-3.ch033

Demirkan, H., & Spohrer, J. C. (2012). Servitized enterprises for distributed collaborative commerce. In S. Galup (Ed.), *Technological applications and advancements in service science, management, and engineering* (pp. 70–83). Hershey, PA: Business Science Reference; doi:10.4018/978-1-4666-1583-0.ch005

Denno, P. (2013). Trade collaboration systems. In *Supply chain management: Concepts, methodologies, tools, and applications* (pp. 615–633). Hershey, PA: Business Science Reference; doi:10.4018/978-1-4666-2625-6.ch036

Djoleto, W. (2011). E-business efficacious consequences the etiquettes and the business decision making. In O. Bak & N. Stair (Eds.), *Impact of e-business technologies on public and private organizations: Industry comparisons and perspectives* (pp. 278–295). Hershey, PA: Business Science Reference; doi:10.4018/978-1-60960-501-8.ch017

Djoleto, W. (2013). Information technology and organisational leadership. In *Electronic commerce and organizational leadership: Perspectives and methodologies*. Hershey, PA: IGI Global; doi:10.4018/978-1-4666-2982-0.ch003

Djoleto, W. (2013). Cloud computing and ecommerce or ebusiness: "The now it way" – An overview. In *Electronic commerce and organizational leadership: Perspectives and methodologies* (pp. 239–254). Hershey, PA: Business Science Reference; doi:10.4018/978-1-4666-2982-0.ch010

Djoleto, W. (2013). eCommerce and organisational leadership. In Electronic commerce and organizational leadership: Perspectives and methodologies (pp. 99-121). Hershey, PA: Business Science Reference. doi:10.4018/978-1-4666-2982-0.ch005

Djoleto, W. (2013). eCommerce: An overview. In Electronic commerce and organizational leadership: Perspectives and methodologies (pp. 74-98). Hershey, PA: Business Science Reference. doi:10.4018/978-1-4666-2982-0.ch004

Djoleto, W. (2013). Empirical analyses of ecommerce: The findings – A mixed methodology perspective. In *Electronic commerce and organizational leadership: Perspectives and methodologies* (pp. 150–189). Hershey, PA: Business Science Reference; doi:10.4018/978-1-4666-2982-0.ch007

Djoleto, W. (2013). Future endeavours. In *Electronic commerce and organizational leadership: Perspectives and methodologies* (pp. 269–280). Hershey, PA: Business Science Reference; doi:10.4018/978-1-4666-2982-0.ch012

Djoleto, W. (2013). Information technology: The journey. In *Electronic commerce and organizational leadership: Perspectives and methodologies* (pp. 32–54). Hershey, PA: Business Science Reference; doi:10.4018/978-1-4666-2982-0.ch002

Doolin, B., & Ali, E. I. (2012). Mobile technology adoption in the supply chain. In *Wireless technologies: Concepts, methodologies, tools and applications* (pp. 1553–1573). Hershey, PA: Information Science Reference; doi:10.4018/978-1-61350-101-6.ch603

Related References

Duin, H., & Thoben, K. (2011). Enhancing the preparedness of SMEs for e-business opportunities by collaborative networks. In M. Cruz-Cunha & J. Varajão (Eds.), *E-business issues, challenges and opportunities for SMEs: Driving competitiveness* (pp. 30–45). Hershey, PA: Business Science Reference; doi:10.4018/978-1-61692-880-3.ch003

Dulai, T., Jaskó, S., & Tarnay, K. (2013). IOTP and payments protocols. In K. Tarnay, S. Imre, & L. Xu (Eds.), *Research and development in e-business through service-oriented solutions* (pp. 20–56). Hershey, PA: Business Science Reference; doi:10.4018/978-1-4666-4181-5.ch002

Dza, M., Fisher, R., & Gapp, R. (2013). Service-dominant logic and supply network management: An efficient business mix? In N. Ndubisi & S. Nwankwo (Eds.), *Enterprise development in SMEs and entrepreneurial firms: Dynamic processes* (pp. 376–389). Hershey, PA: Business Science Reference; doi:10.4018/978-1-4666-2952-3.ch021

Ehsani, E. (2011). Defining e-novation in action. In H. Pattinson & D. Low (Eds.), *E-novation for competitive advantage in collaborative globalization: Technologies for emerging e-business strategies* (pp. 58–74). Hershey, PA: Business Science Reference; doi:10.4018/978-1-60566-394-4.ch005

Ekong, U. O., Ifinedo, P., Ayo, C. K., & Ifinedo, A. (2013). E-commerce adoption in Nigerian businesses: An analysis using the technology-organization-environmental framework. In *Small and medium enterprises: Concepts, methodologies, tools, and applications* (pp. 840–861). Hershey, PA: Business Science Reference; doi:10.4018/978-1-4666-3886-0.ch041

Emens, S. (2010). The new paradigm of business on the internet and its ethical implications. In D. Palmer (Ed.), *Ethical issues in e-business: Models and frameworks* (pp. 15–27). Hershey, PA: Business Science Reference; doi:10.4018/978-1-61520-615-5.ch002

Eriksson, P., Henttonen, E., & Meriläinen, S. (2011). Managing client contacts of small KIBS companies: Turning technology into business. *International Journal of Innovation in the Digital Economy*, *2*(3), 1–10. doi:10.4018/jide.2011070101

Escofet, E., Rodríguez-Fórtiz, M. J., Garrido, J. L., & Chung, L. (2012). Strategic e-business/ IT alignment for SME competitiveness. In *Computer engineering: Concepts, methodologies, tools and applications* (pp. 1427–1445). Hershey, PA: Engineering Science Reference; doi:10.4018/978-1-61350-456-7.ch604

Eze, U. C., & Poong, Y. S. (2013). Consumers' intention to use mobile commerce and the moderating roles of gender and income. In I. Lee (Ed.), *Strategy, adoption, and competitive advantage of mobile services in the global economy* (pp. 127–148). Hershey, PA: Information Science Reference; doi:10.4018/978-1-4666-1939-5.ch007

Eze, U. C., & Poong, Y. S. (2013). The moderating roles of income and age in mobile commerce application. *Journal of Electronic Commerce in Organizations, 11*(3), 46–67. doi:10.4018/jeco.2013070103

Fehér, P. (2012). Integrating and measuring business and technology services in the context of enterprise architecture. In V. Shankararaman, J. Zhao, & J. Lee (Eds.), *Business enterprise, process, and technology management: Models and applications* (pp. 148–163). Hershey, PA: Business Science Reference; doi:10.4018/978-1-4666-0249-6.ch008

Feja, S., Witt, S., & Speck, A. (2014). Tool based integration of requirements modeling and validation into business process modeling. In *Software design and development: Concepts, methodologies, tools, and applications* (pp. 285–309). Hershey, PA: Information Science Reference; doi:10.4018/978-1-4666-4301-7.ch016

Fengel, J. (2012). Semantic alignment of e-business standards and legacy models. In E. Kajan, F. Dorloff, & I. Bedini (Eds.), *Handbook of research on e-business standards and protocols: Documents, data and advanced web technologies* (pp. 676–704). Hershey, PA: Business Science Reference; doi:10.4018/978-1-4666-0146-8.ch031

Ferreira, M. P. (2013). SMEs and e-business: Implementation, strategies and policy. In *Small and medium enterprises: Concepts, methodologies, tools, and applications* (pp. 97–117). Hershey, PA: Business Science Reference; doi:10.4018/978-1-4666-3886-0.ch006

Fluvià, M., & Rigall-I-Torrent, R. (2013). Public sector transformation and the design of public policies for electronic commerce and the new economy: Tax and antitrust policies. In N. Pomazalová (Ed.), *Public sector transformation processes and internet public procurement: Decision support systems* (pp. 32–57). Hershey, PA: Engineering Science Reference; doi:10.4018/978-1-4666-2665-2.ch003

Franquesa, J., & Brandyberry, A. (2011). Organizational slack and information technology innovation adoption in SMEs. In I. Lee (Ed.), *E-business applications for product development and competitive growth: emerging technologies* (pp. 25–48). Hershey, PA: Business Science Reference; doi:10.4018/978-1-60960-132-4.ch002

Fries, T. P. (2014). Reengineering structured legacy system documentation to UML object-oriented artifacts. In *Software design and development: Concepts, methodologies, tools, and applications* (pp. 749–771). Hershey, PA: Information Science Reference; doi:10.4018/978-1-4666-4301-7.ch036

Galinski, C., & Beckmann, H. (2014). Concepts for enhancing content quality and eaccessibility: In general and in the field of eprocurement. In *Assistive technologies: Concepts, methodologies, tools, and applications* (pp. 180–197). Hershey, PA: Information Science Reference; doi:10.4018/978-1-4666-4422-9.ch010

Gan, J., & Gutiérrez, J. A. (2011). Viable business models for m-commerce: The key components. In M. Cruz-Cunha & F. Moreira (Eds.), *Handbook of research on mobility and computing: Evolving technologies and ubiquitous impacts* (pp. 837–852). Hershey, PA: Information Science Reference; doi:10.4018/978-1-60960-042-6.ch052

Garito, M. (2012). Mobile business and mobile TV: Available technologies, future opportunities and new marketing trends. In E-marketing: Concepts, methodologies, tools, and applications (pp. 1240-1251). Hershey, PA: Business Science Reference. doi:10.4018/978-1-4666-1598-4.ch072

Ghobakhloo, M., & Zulkifli, N. (2013). Adoption of mobile commerce: The impact of end user satisfaction on system acceptance. *International Journal of E-Services and Mobile Applications*, *5*(1), 26–50. doi:10.4018/jesma.2013010102

Gill, A. Q., & Bunker, D. (2014). SaaS requirements engineering for agile development. In *Software design and development: Concepts, methodologies, tools, and applications* (pp. 351 380). Hershey, PA: Information Science Reference; doi:10.4018/978-1-4666-4301-7.ch019

Gimenez, J. (2014). Reflections of professional practice: Using electronic discourse analysis networks (EDANs) to examine embedded business emails. In H. Lim & F. Sudweeks (Eds.), *Innovative methods and technologies for electronic discourse analysis* (pp. 327–345). Hershey, PA: Information Science Reference; doi:10.4018/978-1-4666-4426-7.ch015

Gionis, G. A., Schroth, C., & Janner, T. (2011). Advancing interoperability for agile cross-organisational collaboration: A rule-based approach. In Y. Charalabidis (Ed.), *Interoperability in digital public services and administration: Bridging e-government and e-business* (pp. 238–253). Hershey, PA: Information Science Reference; doi:10.4018/978-1-61520-887-6.ch013

Gnoni, M. G., & Rollo, A. (2011). A content analysis for evaluating RFID applications in supply network management. In I. Mahdavi, S. Mohebbi, & N. Cho (Eds.), *Electronic supply network coordination in intelligent and dynamic environments: Modeling and implementation* (pp. 93–112). Hershey, PA: Business Science Reference; doi:10.4018/978-1-60566-808-6.ch004

Gonçalves, A., Serra, N., Serra, J., & Sousa, P. (2011). How to use information technology effectively to achieve business objectives. In M. Cruz-Cunha & J. Varajao (Eds.), *Enterprise information systems design, implementation and management: Organizational applications* (pp. 21–37). Hershey, PA: Information Science Reference; doi:10.4018/978-1-61692-020-3.ch002

Gordini, N., & Veglio, V. (2014). Customer relationship management and data mining: A classification decision tree to predict customer purchasing behavior in global market. In P. Vasant (Ed.), *Handbook of research on novel soft computing intelligent algorithms: Theory and practical applications* (pp. 1–40). Hershey, PA: Information Science Reference; doi:10.4018/978-1-4666-4450-2.ch001

Gottschalk, P. (2007). The CIO developing e-business. In P. Gottschalk (Ed.), *CIO and corporate strategic management: Changing role of CIO to CEO* (pp. 148–185). Hershey, PA: Idea Group Publishing; doi:10.4018/978-1-59904-423-1.ch007

Goutam, S. (2010). Analysis of speedy uptake of electronic and digital signatures in digital economy with special reference to India. In E. Adomi (Ed.), *Frameworks for ICT policy: Government, social and legal issues* (pp. 76–88). Hershey, PA: Information Science Reference; doi:10.4018/978-1-61692-012-8.ch005

Grieger, M., Hartmann, E., & Kotzab, H. (2011). E-markets as meta-enterprise information e systems. In *Enterprise information systems: Concepts, methodologies, tools and applications* (pp. 638–647). Hershey, PA: Business Science Reference; doi:10.4018/978-1-61692-852-0.ch306

grzonkowski, s., ensor, b. d., & mcdaniel, b. (2013). applied cryptography in Electronic Commerce. In *IT policy and ethics: Concepts, methodologies, tools, and applications* (pp. 368-388). Hershey, PA: Information Science Reference. doi:10.4018/978-1-4666-2919-6.ch017

Ha, H. (2012). Online security and consumer protection in ecommerce an Australian case. In K. Mohammed Rezaul (Ed.), *Strategic and pragmatic e-business: Implications for future business practices* (pp. 217–243). Hershey, PA: Business Science Reference; doi:10.4018/978-1-4666-1619-6.ch010

Ha, H., Coghill, K., & Maharaj, E. A. (2012). Current measures to protect e-consumers' privacy in Australia. In *Cyber crime: Concepts, methodologies, tools and applications* (pp. 1728–1755). Hershey, PA: Information Science Reference; doi:10.4018/978-1-61350-323-2.ch806

Halas, H., & Klobucar, T. (2011). Business models and organizational processes changes. In *Global business: Concepts, methodologies, tools and applications* (pp. 192–205). Hershey, PA: Business Science Reference; doi:10.4018/978-1-60960-587-2.ch113

Han, B. (2012). I play, I pay? An investigation of the user's willingness to pay on hedonic social network sites. *International Journal of Virtual Communities and Social Networking*, *4*(1), 19–31. doi:10.4018/jvcsn.2012010102

Harnesk, D. (2011). Convergence of information security in B2B networks. In E. Kajan (Ed.), *Electronic business interoperability: Concepts, opportunities and challenges* (pp. 571–595). Hershey, PA: Business Science Reference; doi:10.4018/978-1-60960-485-1.ch023

Harwood, T. (2012). Emergence of gamified commerce: Turning virtual to real. *Journal of Electronic Commerce in Organizations*, *10*(2), 16–39. doi:10.4018/jeco.2012040102

Heravi, B. R., & Lycett, M. (2012). Semantically enriched e-business standards development: The case of ebXML business process specification schema. In E. Kajan, F. Dorloff, & I. Bedini (Eds.), *Handbook of research on e-business standards and protocols: Documents, data and advanced web technologies* (pp. 655–675). Hershey, PA: Business Science Reference; doi:10.4018/978-1-4666-0146-8.ch030

Hill, D. S. (2012). An examination of standardized product identification and business benefit. In E. Kajan, F. Dorloff, & I. Bedini (Eds.), *Handbook of research on e-business standards and protocols: Documents, data and advanced web technologies* (pp. 387–411). Hershey, PA: Business Science Reference; doi:10.4018/978-1-4666-0146-8.ch018

Hoops, D. S. (2011). Legal issues in the virtual world and e-commerce. In B. Ciaramitaro (Ed.), *Virtual worlds and e-commerce: Technologies and applications for building customer relationships* (pp. 186–204). Hershey, PA: Business Science Reference; doi:10.4018/978-1-61692-808-7.ch010

Hu, W., Zuo, Y., Kaabouch, N., & Chen, L. (2010). A technological perspective of mobile and electronic commerce systems. In M. Khosrow-Pour (Ed.), *E-commerce trends for organizational advancement: New applications and methods* (pp. 16–35). Hershey, PA: Information Science Reference; doi:10.4018/978-1-60566-964-9.ch002

Hua, G. B. (2013). *Implementing IT business strategy in the construction industry*. Hershey, PA: IGI Global; doi:10.4018/978-1-4666-4185-3

Hua, S. C., Rajesh, M. J., & Theng, L. B. (2011). Determinants of e-commerce adoption among small and medium-sized enterprises in Malaysia. In S. Sharma (Ed.), *E-adoption and socio-economic impacts: Emerging infrastructural effects* (pp. 71–89). Hershey, PA: Information Science Reference; doi:10.4018/978-1-60960-597-1.ch005

Huang, J., & Dang, J. (2011). Context-sensitive ontology matching in electronic business. In E. Kajan (Ed.), *Electronic business interoperability: Concepts, opportunities and challenges* (pp. 279–301). Hershey, PA: Business Science Reference; doi:10.4018/978-1-60960-485-1.ch012

Hunaiti, Z., Tairo, D., Sedoyeka, E., & Elgazzar, S. (2010). Factors facing mobile commerce deployment in United Kingdom. In W. Hu & Y. Zuo (Eds.), *Handheld computing for mobile commerce: Applications, concepts and technologies* (pp. 109–123). Hershey, PA: Information Science Reference; doi:10.4018/978-1-61520-761-9.ch007

Hung, W. J., Tsai, C., Hung, S., McQueen, R., & Jou, J. (2011). Evaluating web site support capabilities in sell-side B2B transaction processes: A longitudinal study of two industries in New Zealand and Taiwan. *Journal of Global Information Management, 19*(1), 51–79. doi:10.4018/jgim.2011010103

Hunter, M. G. (2013). The duality of information technology roles: A case study. In C. Howard (Ed.), *Strategic adoption of technological innovations* (pp. 38–49). Hershey, PA: Information Science Reference; doi:10.4018/978-1-4666-2782-6.ch003

Huq, N., Shah, S. M., & Mihailescu, D. (2012). Why select an open source ERP over proprietary ERP? A focus on SMEs and supplier's perspective. In R. Atem de Carvalho & B. Johansson (Eds.), *Free and open source enterprise resource planning: Systems and strategies* (pp. 33–55). Hershey, PA: Business Science Reference; doi:10.4018/978-1-61350-486-4.ch003

Related References

Ingvaldsen, J., & Gulla, J. (2010). Semantic business process mining of SAP transactions. In M. Wang & Z. Sun (Eds.), *Handbook of research on complex dynamic process management: Techniques for adaptability in turbulent environments* (pp. 416–429). Hershey, PA: Business Science Reference; doi:10.4018/978-1-60566-669-3.ch017

Ingvaldsen, J., & Gulla, J. (2011). Semantic business process mining of SAP transactions. In *Enterprise information systems: Concepts, methodologies, tools and applications* (pp. 866–878). Hershey, PA: Business Science Reference; doi:10.4018/978-1-61692-852-0.ch320

Ioannou, M. (2013). Customer relationship management (CRM): A one-size-fits-all philosophy? In H. Kaufmann & M. Panni (Eds.), *Customer-centric marketing strategies: Tools for building organizational performance* (pp. 150–170). Hershey, PA: Business Science Reference; doi:10.4018/978-1-4666-2524-2.ch008

Islam, M. S., & Scupola, A. (2013). E-service research trends in the domain of e-government: A contemporary study. In A. Scupola (Ed.), *Mobile opportunities and applications for e-service innovations* (pp. 152–169). Hershey, PA: Information Science Reference; doi:10.4018/978-1-4666-2654-6.ch009

Jailani, N., Patel, A., Mukhtar, M., Abdullah, S., & Yahya, Y. (2010). Concept of an agent-based electronic marketplace. In I. Lee (Ed.), *Encyclopedia of e-business development and management in the global economy* (pp. 239–251). Hershey, PA: Business Science Reference; doi:10.4018/978-1-61520-611-7.ch024

Johns, R. (2011). Technology, trust and B2B relationships: A banking perspective. In O. Bak & N. Stair (Eds.), *Impact of e-business technologies on public and private organizations: Industry comparisons and perspectives* (pp. 79–96). Hershey, PA: Business Science Reference; doi:10.4018/978-1-60960-501-8.ch005

Joshi, S. (2013). E-supply chain collaboration and integration: Implementation issues and challenges. In D. Graham, I. Manikas, & D. Folinas (Eds.), *E-logistics and e-supply chain management: Applications for evolving business* (pp. 9–26). Hershey, PA: Business Science Reference; doi:10.4018/978-1-4666-3914-0.ch002

Kamal, M., Qureshil, S., & Wolcott, P. (2013). Promoting competitive advantage in micro-enterprises through information technology interventions. In *Small and medium enterprises: Concepts, methodologies, tools, and applications* (pp. 581–606). Hershey, PA: Business Science Reference; doi:10.4018/978-1-4666-3886-0.ch030

Kamel, S. (2012). Electronic commerce prospects in emerging economies: Lessons from Egypt. In *Regional development: Concepts, methodologies, tools, and applications* (pp. 1104–1115). Hershey, PA: Information Science Reference; doi:10.4018/978-1-4666-0882-5.ch604

Kamoun, F., & Halaweh, M. (2012). User interface design and e-commerce security perception: An empirical study. *International Journal of E-Business Research, 8*(2), 15–32. doi:10.4018/jebr.2012040102

Karakaya, F. (2012). Business-to-consumers ecommerce: How companies use the internet in marketing products and services to consumers. In N. Delener (Ed.), *Service science research, strategy and innovation: Dynamic knowledge management methods* (pp. 227–244). Hershey, PA: Business Science.

Karakaya, F. (2013). B2B ecommerce: Current practices. In *Supply chain management: Concepts, methodologies, tools, and applications* (pp. 497–510). Hershey, PA: Business Science Reference; doi:10.4018/978-1-4666-2625-6.ch029

Karimov, F. P. (2013). Factors influencing e-commerce growth: A comparative study of central Asian transition economies. In S. Sharma (Ed.), *Adoption of virtual technologies for business, educational, and governmental advancements* (pp. 1–17). Hershey, PA: Information Science Reference; doi:10.4018/978-1-4666-2053-7.ch001

Kart, F., Moser, L. E., & Melliar-Smith, P. M. (2010). An automated supply chain management system and its performance evaluation. *International Journal of Information Systems and Supply Chain Management, 3*(2), 84–107. doi:10.4018/jisscm.2010040105

Kelarev, A. V., Brown, S., Watters, P., Wu, X., & Dazeley, R. (2011). Establishing reasoning communities of security experts for internet commerce security. In J. Yearwood & A. Stranieri (Eds.), *Technologies for supporting reasoning communities and collaborative decision making: Cooperative approaches* (pp. 380–396). Hershey, PA: Information Science Reference; doi:10.4018/978-1-60960-091-4.ch020

Kerr, D., Gammack, J. G., & Boddington, R. (2011). Overview of digital business security issues. In D. Kerr, J. Gammack, & K. Bryant (Eds.), *Digital business security development: Management technologies* (pp. 1–36). Hershey, PA: Business Science Reference; doi:10.4018/978-1-60566-806-2.ch001

Kerr, D., Gammack, J. G., & Bryant, K. (2011). *Digital business security development: Management technologies*. Hershey, PA: IGI Global; doi:10.4018/978-1-60566-806-2

Kett, H. (2013). A business model approach for service engineering in the internet of services. In P. Ordóñez de Pablos & R. Tennyson (Eds.), *Best practices and new perspectives in service science and management* (pp. 228–236). Hershey, PA: Business Science Reference; doi:10.4018/978-1-4666-3894-5.ch013

Khurana, R., & Aggarwal, R. (2013). *Interdisciplinary perspectives on business convergence, computing, and legality*. Hershey, PA: IGI Global; doi:10.4018/978-1-4666-4209-6

Kim, G., & Suh, Y. (2012). Building semantic business process space for agile and efficient business processes management: Ontology-based approach. In V. Shankararaman, J. Zhao, & J. Lee (Eds.), *Business enterprise, process, and technology management: Models and applications* (pp. 51–73). Hershey, PA: Business Science Reference; doi:10.4018/978-1-4666-0249-6.ch004

King, K. P., & Foley, J. J. (2012). 21st century learning opportunities for SME success: Maximizing technology tools and lifelong learning for innovation and impact. In *Human resources management: Concepts, methodologies, tools, and applications* (pp. 731–752). Hershey, PA: Business Science Reference; doi:10.4018/978-1-4666-1601-1.ch045

Kipp, A., & Schubert, L. (2011). E-business interoperability and collaboration. In E. Kajan (Ed.), *Electronic business interoperability: Concepts, opportunities and challenges* (pp. 153–184). Hershey, PA: Business Science Reference; doi:10.4018/978-1-60960-485-1.ch008

Klink, S., & Weiß, P. (2011). Social impact of collaborative services to maintain electronic business relationships. In *Virtual communities: Concepts, methodologies, tools and applications* (pp. 2011–2040). Hershey, PA: Information Science Reference; doi:10.4018/978-1-60960-100-3.ch609

Koumpis, A., & Protogeros, N. (2010). Doing business on the globalised networked economy: Technology and business challenges for accounting information systems. In M. Cruz-Cunha (Ed.), *Social, managerial, and organizational dimensions of enterprise information systems* (pp. 81–92). Hershey, PA: Business Science Reference; doi:10.4018/978-1-60566-856-7.ch004

Kritchanchai, D., Tan, A. W., & Hosie, P. (2010). An empirical investigation of third party logistics providers in Thailand: Barriers, motivation and usage of information technologies. *International Journal of Information Systems and Supply Chain Management*, *3*(2), 68–83. doi:10.4018/jisscm.2010040104

Kritchanchai, D., Tan, A. W., & Hosie, P. (2012). An empirical investigation of third party logistics providers in Thailand: Barriers, motivation and usage of information technologies. In J. Wang (Ed.), *Information technologies, methods, and techniques of supply chain management* (pp. 272–288). Hershey, PA: Business Science Reference; doi:10.4018/978-1-4666-0918-1.ch016

Kumar, M. (2011). Role of web interface in building trust in B2B e-exchanges. In S. Chhabra & H. Rahman (Eds.), *Human development and global advancements through information communication technologies: New initiatives* (pp. 63–74). Hershey, PA: Information Science Reference; doi:10.4018/978-1-60960-497-4.ch005

Kumar, M., & Sareen, M. (2012). Trust theories and models of e-commerce. In *Trust and technology in B2B e-commerce: Practices and strategies for assurance* (pp. 58–77). Hershey, PA: Business Science Reference; doi:10.4018/978-1-61350-353-9.ch003

Kumar, M., Sareen, M., & Chhabra, S. (2013). Technology related trust issues in SME B2B e-commerce. In S. Chhabra (Ed.), *ICT influences on human development, interaction, and collaboration* (pp. 243–259). Hershey, PA: Information Science Reference; doi:10.4018/978-1-4666-1957-9.ch015

Kung, M. T., & Zhang, Y. (2011). Creating competitive markets for small businesses with new media and e-business strategy. *International Journal of E-Business Research*, *7*(4), 31–49. doi:10.4018/jebr.2011100103

Kuo, D., Wong, D., Gao, J., & Chang, L. (2013). A 2D barcode validation system for mobile commerce. In W. Hu & S. Mousavinezhad (Eds.), *Mobile and handheld computing solutions for organizations and end-users* (pp. 1–19). Hershey, PA: Information Science Reference; doi:10.4018/978-1-4666-2785-7.ch001

Kyobe, M. (2010). E-crime and non-compliance with government regulations on e-commerce: Barriers to e-commerce optimization in South African SMEs. In B. Thomas & G. Simmons (Eds.), *E-commerce adoption and small business in the global marketplace: Tools for optimization* (pp. 47–66). Hershey, PA: Business Science Reference; doi:10.4018/978-1-60566-998-4.ch003

Lawrence, J. E. (2011). The growth of e-commerce in developing countries: An exploratory study of opportunities and challenges for SMEs. *International Journal of ICT Research and Development in Africa*, *2*(1), 15–28. doi:10.4018/jictrda.2011010102

Lawrence, J. E. (2013). Barriers hindering ecommerce adoption: A case study of Kurdistan region of Iraq. In A. Zolait (Ed.), *Technology diffusion and adoption: Global complexity, global innovation* (pp. 152–165). Hershey, PA: Information Science Reference; doi:10.4018/978-1-4666-2791-8.ch010

Lee, I. (2012). B2B e-commerce, online auction, supply chain management, and e-collaboration. In *Electronic commerce management for business activities and global enterprises: Competitive advantages* (pp. 249–299). Hershey, PA: Business Science Reference; doi:10.4018/978-1-4666-1800-8.ch007

Lee, I. (2012). B2C online consumer behavior. In *Electronic commerce management for business activities and global enterprises: competitive advantages* (pp. 166–201). Hershey, PA: Business Science Reference; doi:10.4018/978-1-4666-1800-8.ch005

Lee, I. (2012). Introduction to e-commerce in the global economy. In *Electronic commerce management for business activities and global enterprises: Competitive advantages* (pp. 1–46). Hershey, PA: Business Science Reference; doi:10.4018/978-1-4666-1800-8.ch001

Lee, I. (2012). Mobile commerce. In *Electronic commerce management for business activities and global enterprises: Competitive advantages* (pp. 300–338). Hershey, PA: Business Science Reference; doi:10.4018/978-1-4666-1800-8.ch008

Lee, I. (2012). Online payment systems. In *Electronic commerce management for business activities and global enterprises: Competitive advantages* (pp. 340–365). Hershey, PA: Business Science Reference; doi:10.4018/978-1-4666-1800-8.ch009

Leonard, L. N. (2010). C2C mobile commerce: Acceptance factors. In I. Lee (Ed.), *Encyclopedia of e-business development and management in the global economy* (pp. 759–767). Hershey, PA: Business Science Reference; doi:10.4018/978-1-61520-611-7.ch076

Lertpittayapoom, N., & Paul, S. (2010). The roles of online intermediaries in collective memory-supported electronic negotiation. In *Electronic services: Concepts, methodologies, tools and applications* (pp. 1831–1847). Hershey, PA: Information Science Reference; doi:10.4018/978-1-61520-967-5.ch112

Li, L., Liu, C., Zhao, X., & Wang, J. (2011). Transactional properties of complex web services. In H. Leung, D. Chiu, & P. Hung (Eds.), *Service intelligence and service science: Evolutionary technologies and challenges* (pp. 21–34). Hershey, PA: Information Science Reference; doi:10.4018/978-1-61520-819-7.ch002

Li, X., & Lin, J. (2011). Call u back: An agent-based infrastructure for mobile commerce. *International Journal of E-Entrepreneurship and Innovation*, *2*(2), 1–13. doi:10.4018/jeei.2011040101

Liao, Q., Luo, X., & Gurung, A. (2011). Trust restoration in electronic commerce. In S. Clarke & A. Dwivedi (Eds.), *Organizational and end-user interactions: New explorations* (pp. 72–88). Hershey, PA: Information Science Reference; doi:10.4018/978-1-60960-577-3.ch003

Liberato, N. A., Varajão, J. E., Correia, E. S., & Bessa, M. E. (2011). Location based e-commerce system: An architecture. In M. Cruz-Cunha & F. Moreira (Eds.), *Handbook of research on mobility and computing: Evolving technologies and ubiquitous impacts* (pp. 881–892). Hershey, PA: Information Science Reference; doi:10.4018/978-1-60960-042-6.ch055

Lim, S. Y., & Wong, S. F. (2012). Impact of applying aggregate query processing in mobile commerce. *International Journal of Business Data Communications and Networking*, *8*(2), 1–17. doi:10.4018/jbdcn.2012040101

Lin, C., & Jalleh, G. (2013). Key issues and challenges for managing and evaluating B2B e-commerce projects within the Australian pharmaceutical supply chain. In *Supply chain management: Concepts, methodologies, tools, and applications* (pp. 1083–1100). Hershey, PA: Business Science Reference; doi:10.4018/978-1-4666-2625-6.ch064

Lin, C., Jalleh, G., & Huang, Y. (2013). E-business investment evaluation and outsourcing practices in Australian and Taiwanese hospitals: A comparative study. In K. Tarnay, S. Imre, & L. Xu (Eds.), *Research and development in e-business through service-oriented solutions* (pp. 244–266). Hershey, PA: Business Science Reference; doi:10.4018/978-1-4666-4181-5.ch012

Lin, C., Lin, H. K., Jalleh, G., & Huang, Y. (2011). Key adoption challenges and issues of B2B e-commerce in the healthcare sector. In M. Cruz-Cunha & F. Moreira (Eds.), *Handbook of research on mobility and computing: Evolving technologies and ubiquitous impacts* (pp. 175–187). Hershey, PA: Information Science Reference; doi:10.4018/978-1-60960-042-6.ch011

Liyanage, J. P. (2011). Copying with dynamic change: Collaborative business interfacing for SMEs under intergated eoperations. In M. Cruz-Cunha & J. Varajão (Eds.), *E-business managerial aspects, solutions and case studies* (pp. 136–147). Hershey, PA: Business Science Reference; doi:10.4018/978-1-60960-463-9.ch008

Related References

Liyanage, J. P. (2012). Hybrid intelligence through business socialization and networking: Managing complexities in the digital era. In M. Cruz-Cunha, P. Gonçalves, N. Lopes, E. Miranda, & G. Putnik (Eds.), *Handbook of research on business social networking: organizational, managerial, and technological dimensions* (pp. 567–582). Hershey, PA: Business Science Reference; doi:10.4018/978-1-61350-168-9.ch030

Loeser, F., Erek, K., & Zarnekow, R. (2013). Green IT strategies: A conceptual framework for the alignment of information technology and corporate sustainability strategy. In P. Ordóñez de Pablos (Ed.), *Green technologies and business practices: An IT approach* (pp. 58–95). Hershey, PA: Information Science Reference; doi:10.4018/978-1-4666-1972-2.ch004

Maamar, Z., Faci, N., Mostéfaoui, S. K., & Akhter, F. (2011). Towards a framework for weaving social networks into mobile commerce. *International Journal of Systems and Service-Oriented Engineering*, *2*(3), 32–46. doi:10.4018/jssoe.2011070103

Mahmood, M. A., Gemoets, L., Hall, L. L., & López, F. J. (2011). Building business value in e-commerce enabled organizations: An empirical study. In *Global business: Concepts, methodologies, tools and applications* (pp. 229–253). Hershey, PA: Business Science Reference; doi:10.4018/978-1-60960-587-2.ch201

Mahran, A. F., & Enaba, H. M. (2013). Exploring determinants influencing the intention to use mobile payment service. In R. Eid (Ed.), *Managing customer trust, satisfaction, and loyalty through information communication technologies* (pp. 288–309). Hershey, PA: Business Science Reference; doi:10.4018/978-1-4666-3631-6.ch017

Marimuthu, M., Omar, A., Ramayah, T., & Mohamad, O. (2013). Readiness to adopt e-business among SMEs in Malaysia: Antecedents and consequence. In S. Sharma (Ed.), *Adoption of virtual technologies for business, educational, and governmental advancements* (pp. 18–36). Hershey, PA: Information Science Reference; doi:10.4018/978-1-4666-2053-7.ch002

Mayes, P. (2014). Interactive advertising: Displays of identity and stance on YouTube. In H. Lim & F. Sudweeks (Eds.), *Innovative methods and technologies for electronic discourse analysis* (pp. 260–284). Hershey, PA: Information Science Reference; doi:10.4018/978-1-4666-4426-7.ch012

McGrath, T. (2012). The reality of using standards for electronic business document formats. In E. Kajan, F. Dorloff, & I. Bedini (Eds.), *Handbook of research on e-business standards and protocols: Documents, data and advanced web technologies* (pp. 21–32). Hershey, PA: Business Science Reference; doi:10.4018/978-1-4666-0146-8.ch002

Meredith, J., & Potter, J. (2014). Conversation analysis and electronic interactions: Methodological, analytic and technical considerations. In H. Lim & F. Sudweeks (Eds.), *Innovative methods and technologies for electronic discourse analysis* (pp. 370–393). Hershey, PA: Information Science Reference; doi:10.4018/978-1-4666-4426-7.ch017

Millman, C., & El-Gohary, H. (2011). New digital media marketing and micro business: A UK perspective. *International Journal of Online Marketing*, *1*(1), 41–62. doi:10.4018/ijom.2011010104

Mishra, B., & Shukla, K. K. (2014). Data mining techniques for software quality prediction. In *Software design and development: Concepts, methodologies, tools, and applications* (pp. 401–428). Hershey, PA: Information Science Reference; doi:10.4018/978-1-4666-4301-7.ch021

Misra, H., & Rahman, H. (2013). *Managing enterprise information technology acquisitions: Assessing organizational preparedness*. Hershey, PA: IGI Global; doi:10.4018/978-1-4666-4201-0

Mohammadi, S., Golara, S., & Mousavi, N. (2012). Selecting adequate security mechanisms in e-business processes using fuzzy TOPSIS. *International Journal of Fuzzy System Applications*, *2*(1), 35–53. doi:10.4018/ijfsa.2012010103

Möhlenbruch, D., Dölling, S., & Ritschel, F. (2010). Interactive customer retention management for mobile commerce. In K. Pousttchi & D. Wiedemann (Eds.), *Handbook of research on mobile marketing management* (pp. 437–456). Hershey, PA: Business Science Reference; doi:10.4018/978-1-60566-074-5.ch023

Molla, A., & Peszynski, K. (2013). E-business in agribusiness: Investigating the e-readiness of Australian horticulture firms. In S. Chhabra (Ed.), *ICT influences on human development, interaction, and collaboration* (pp. 78–96). Hershey, PA: Information Science Reference; doi:10.4018/978-1-4666-1957-9.ch004

Monsanto, C., & Andriole, S. J. (2010). Business technology strategy for a major real estate and mortgage brokerage company. *Journal of Information Technology Research*, *3*(3), 43–53. doi:10.4018/jitr.2010070104

Montes, J. A., Gutiérrez, A. C., Fernández, E. M., & Romeo, A. (2013). Reality mining, location based services, and e-business opportunities: The case of city analytics. In S. Nasir (Ed.), *Modern entrepreneurship and e-business innovations* (pp. 87–99). Hershey, PA: Business Science Reference; doi:10.4018/978-1-4666-2946-2.ch007

Moqbel, A., Yani-De-Soriano, M., & Yousafzai, S. (2012). Mobile commerce use among UK mobile users: An experimental approach based on a proposed mobile network utilization framework. In A. Zolait (Ed.), *Knowledge and technology adoption, diffusion, and transfer: International perspectives* (pp. 78–111). Hershey, PA: Information Science Reference; doi:10.4018/978-1-4666-1752-0.ch007

Movahedi, B. M., Lavassani, K. M., & Kumar, V. (2012). E-marketplace emergence: Evolution, developments and classification. *Journal of Electronic Commerce in Organizations, 10*(1), 14–32. doi:10.4018/jeco.2012010102

Mugge, R., & Schoormans, J. P. (2010). Optimizing consumer responses to mass customization. In C. Mourlas & P. Germanakos (Eds.), *Mass customization for personalized communication environments: Integrating human factors* (pp. 10–22). Hershey, PA: Information Science Reference; doi:10.4018/978-1-60566-260-2.ch002

Musso, F. (2012). Technology in marketing channels: Present and future drivers of innovation. *International Journal of Applied Behavioral Economics, 1*(2), 41–51. doi:10.4018/ijabe.2012040104

Mutula, S. M. (2010). Digital economy components. In S. Mutula (Ed.), *Digital economies: SMEs and e-readiness* (pp. 29–38). Hershey, PA: Business Science Reference; doi:10.4018/978-1-60566-420-0.ch003

Mutula, S. M. (2010). Trends and best practices in the digital economy. In S. Mutula (Ed.), *Digital economies: SMEs and e-readiness* (pp. 283–301). Hershey, PA: Business Science Reference; doi:10.4018/978-1-60566-420-0.ch017

Nachtigal, S. (2011). E-business: Definition and characteristics. In O. Bak & N. Stair (Eds.), *Impact of e-business technologies on public and private organizations: Industry comparisons and perspectives* (pp. 233–248). Hershey, PA: Business Science Reference; doi:10.4018/978-1-60960-501-8.ch014

Nah, F. F., Hong, W., Chen, L., & Lee, H. (2012). Information search patterns in e-commerce product comparison services. In K. Siau (Ed.), *Cross-disciplinary models and applications of database management: Advancing approaches* (pp. 131–145). Hershey, PA: Information Science Reference; doi:10.4018/978-1-61350-471-0.ch006

Nair, P. R. (2010). Benefits of information technology implementations for supply chain management: An explorative study of progressive Indian companies. In S. Parthasarathy (Ed.), *Enterprise information systems and implementing IT infrastructures: Challenges and issues* (pp. 323–343). Hershey, PA: Business Science Reference; doi:10.4018/978-1-61520-625-4.ch021

Ndou, V., Del Vecchio, P., Passiante, G., & Schina, L. (2013). Web-based services and future business models. In P. Papajorgji, A. Guimarães, & M. Guarracino (Eds.), *Enterprise business modeling, optimization techniques, and flexible information systems* (pp. 1–13). Hershey, PA: Business Science Reference; doi:10.4018/978-1-4666-3946-1.ch001

Ndou, V., & Sadguy, N. (2013). Digital marketplaces as a viable model for SME networking. In *Supply chain management: Concepts, methodologies, tools, and applications* (pp. 275–288). Hershey, PA: Business Science Reference; doi:10.4018/978-1-4666-2625-6.ch016

Ochara, N. M., & Krauss, K. (2012). Towards a collaborative e-business vision for Africa. In K. Mohammed Rezaul (Ed.), *Strategic and pragmatic e-business: Implications for future business practices* (pp. 396–414). Hershey, PA: Business Science Reference; doi:10.4018/978-1-4666-1619-6.ch018

Oncioiu, I. (2013). *Business innovation, development, and advancement in the digital economy*. Hershey, PA: IGI Global; doi:10.4018/978-1-4666-2934-9

Ondimu, K. O., Muketha, G. M., & Ondago, C. O. (2013). E-business adoption framework in the hospitality industry: The case of Kenyan coast. In K. Tarnay, S. Imre, & L. Xu (Eds.), *Research and development in e-business through service-oriented solutions* (pp. 225–243). Hershey, PA: Business Science Reference; doi:10.4018/978-1-4666-4181-5.ch011

Ovaskainen, M., & Tinnilä, M. (2013). Megatrends in electronic business: An analysis of the impacts on SMEs. In S. Nasir (Ed.), *Modern entrepreneurship and e-business innovations* (pp. 12–27). Hershey, PA: Business Science Reference; doi:10.4018/978-1-4666-2946-2.ch002

Özcan, O., & Reeves, K. A. (2011). The firm boundary decision for sustainability-focused companies. *International Journal of Applied Logistics*, *2*(2), 49–68. doi:10.4018/jal.2011040104

Öztayşi, B., & Kahraman, C. (2014). Quantification of corporate performance using fuzzy analytic network process: The case of e-commerce. In P. Vasant (Ed.), *Handbook of research on novel soft computing intelligent algorithms: Theory and practical applications* (pp. 385–413). Hershey, PA: Information Science Reference; doi:10.4018/978-1-4666-4450-2.ch013

Palmer, D. E. (2010). The transformative nature of e-business: Business ethics and stakeholder relations on the internet. In D. Palmer (Ed.), *Ethical issues in e-business: Models and frameworks* (pp. 1–14). Hershey, PA: Business Science Reference; doi:10.4018/978-1-61520-615-5.ch001

Pańkowska, M. (2014). Frameworks of IT prosumption for business development (pp. 1-347). doi:10.4018/978-1-4666-4313-0

Pelet, J. É., & Papadopoulou, P. (2013). The effect of e-commerce websites' colors on customer trust. In I. Lee (Ed.), *Mobile applications and knowledge advancements in e-business* (pp. 167–185). Hershey, PA: Business Science Reference; doi:10.4018/978-1-4666-1960-9.ch011

Pennington, R. (2012). Enhanced social presence through ebranding the consumer in virtual communities. In A. Kapoor & C. Kulshrestha (Eds.), *Branding and sustainable competitive advantage: Building virtual presence* (pp. 189–206). Hershey, PA: Business Science Reference; doi:10.4018/978-1-61350-171-9.ch012

Peslak, A. R. (2012). Industry variables affecting ERP success and status. *International Journal of Enterprise Information Systems*, *8*(3), 15–33. doi:10.4018/jeis.2012070102

Peterson, D., & Howard, C. (2012). Electronic payment systems evaluation: A case study to examine system selection criteria and impacts. *International Journal of Strategic Information Technology and Applications*, *3*(1), 66–80. doi:10.4018/jsita.2012010105

Pflügler, C. (2012). Fostering networked business operations: A framework for B2B electronic intermediary development. *International Journal of Intelligent Information Technologies*, *8*(2), 31–58. doi:10.4018/jiit.2012040103

Pillai, K., & Ozansoy, C. (2013). Web-based digital habitat ecosystems for sustainable built environments. In P. Ordóñez de Pablos (Ed.), *Green technologies and business practices: An IT approach* (pp. 185–199). Hershey, PA: Information Science Reference; doi:10.4018/978-1-4666-1972-2.ch011

Pinto, M., Rodrigues, A., Varajão, J., & Gonçalves, R. (2011). Model of funcionalities for the development of B2B e-commerce solutions. In M. Cruz-Cunha & J. Varajão (Eds.), *Innovations in SMEs and conducting e-business: Technologies, trends and solutions* (pp. 35–60). Hershey, PA: Business Science Reference; doi:10.4018/978-1-60960-765-4.ch003

Pires, J. A., & Gonçalves, R. (2011). Constrains associated to e-business evolution. In M. Cruz-Cunha & J. Varajão (Eds.), *E-business issues, challenges and opportunities for SMEs: Driving competitiveness* (pp. 335–349). Hershey, PA: Business Science Reference; doi:10.4018/978-1-61692-880-3.ch019

Polovina, S., & Andrews, S. (2011). A transaction-oriented architecture for structuring unstructured information in enterprise applications. In V. Sugumaran (Ed.), *Intelligent, adaptive and reasoning technologies: New developments and applications* (pp. 285–299). Hershey, PA: Information Science Reference; doi:10.4018/978-1-60960-595-7.ch016

Potocan, V., Nedelko, Z., & Mulej, M. (2011). What is new with organization of e-business: Organizational viewpoint of the relationships in e-business. In M. Cruz-Cunha & J. Varajão (Eds.), *E-business issues, challenges and opportunities for SMEs: Driving competitiveness* (pp. 131–148). Hershey, PA: Business Science Reference; doi:10.4018/978-1-61692-880-3.ch009

Potocan, V., Nedelko, Z., & Mulej, M. (2011). What is new with organization of e-business: Organizational viewpoint of the relationships in e-business. In M. Cruz-Cunha & J. Varajão (Eds.), *E-business issues, challenges and opportunities for SMEs: Driving competitiveness* (pp. 131–148). Hershey, PA: Business Science Reference; doi:10.4018/978-1-61692-880-3.ch009

Pucihar, A., & Lenart, G. (2011). eSME Slovenia: Initiative and action plan for the accelerated introduction of e-business in SMEs. In Global business: Concepts, methodologies, tools and applications (pp. 995-1022). Hershey, PA: Business Science Reference. doi:10.4018/978-1-60960-587-2.ch409

Quan, J. (2011). E-business strategy and firm performance. In *Global business: Concepts, methodologies, tools and applications* (pp. 56–66). Hershey, PA: Business Science Reference; doi:10.4018/978-1-60960-587-2.ch105

Quente, C. (2010). Brand driven mobile marketing: 5 theses for today and tomorrow. In K. Pousttchi & D. Wiedemann (Eds.), *Handbook of research on mobile marketing management* (pp. 468–483). Hershey, PA: Business Science Reference; doi:10.4018/978-1-60566-074-5.ch025

Qureshil, S., Kamal, M., & Wolcott, P. (2011). Information technology interventions for growth and competitiveness in micro-enterprises. In M. Tavana (Ed.), *Managing adaptability, intervention, and people in enterprise information systems* (pp. 106–137). Hershey, PA: Information Science Reference; doi:10.4018/978-1-60960-529-2.ch006

Rabaey, M. (2014). Complex adaptive systems thinking approach to enterprise architecture. In P. Saha (Ed.), *A systemic perspective to managing complexity with enterprise architecture* (pp. 99–149). Hershey, PA: Business Science Reference; doi:10.4018/978-1-4666-4518-9.ch003

Rahman, H., & Ramos, I. (2012). Trends of open innovation in developing nations: Contexts of SMEs. In H. Rahman & I. Ramos (Eds.), *Cases on SMEs and open innovation: Applications and investigations* (pp. 65–80). Hershey, PA: Business Science Reference; doi:10.4018/978-1-61350-314-0.ch004

Rahman, H., & Ramos, I. (2013). Implementation of e-commerce at the grass roots: Issues of challenges in terms of human-computer interactions. *International Journal of Information Communication Technologies and Human Development*, *5*(2), 1–19. doi:10.4018/jicthd.2013040101

Rajagopal, D. (2010). Customer value and new product retailing dynamics: An analytical construct for gaining competetive advantage. In *Business information systems: Concepts, methodologies, tools and applications* (pp. 1998–2014). Hershey, PA: Business Science Reference; doi:10.4018/978-1-61520-969-9.ch121

Rajagopal, D. (2010). Internet, reengineering and technology applications in retailing. In *Business information systems: Concepts, methodologies, tools and applications* (pp. 1324–1342). Hershey, PA: Business Science Reference; doi:10.4018/978-1-61520-969-9.ch082

Rajagopal, D. (2011). Marketing strategy, technology and modes of entry in global retailing. In *Global business: Concepts, methodologies, tools and applications* (pp. 1–27). Hershey, PA: Business Science Reference; doi:10.4018/978-1-60960-587-2.ch101

Rajagopal, D. (2012). Convergence marketing. In *Systems thinking and process dynamics for marketing systems: Technologies and applications for decision management* (pp. 274–290). Hershey, PA: Business Science Reference; doi:10.4018/978-1-4666-0969-3.ch011

Rajagopal, D. (2012). Product development and market governance. In *Systems thinking and process dynamics for marketing systems: Technologies and applications for decision management* (pp. 88–117). Hershey, PA: Business Science Reference; doi:10.4018/978-1-4666-0969-3.ch004

Rajagopal, D. (2012). Systems thinking and cognitive process in marketing. In *Systems thinking and process dynamics for marketing systems: technologies and applications for decision management* (pp. 170–197). Hershey, PA: Business Science Reference; doi:10.4018/978-1-4666-0969-3.ch007

Rajagopal, D. (2013). Pricing for new products. In *Marketing decision making and the management of pricing: Successful business tools* (pp. 56–74). Hershey, PA: Business Science Reference; doi:10.4018/978-1-4666-4094-8.ch003

Ramayah, T., Popa, S., & Suki, N. M. (2013). Key dimensions on B2C e-business: An empirical study in Malaysia. *International Journal of Human Capital and Information Technology Professionals*, *4*(2), 43–55. doi:10.4018/jhcitp.2013040104

Rambo, K., & Liu, K. (2011). Culture-sensitive virtual e-commerce design with reference to female consumers in Saudi Arabia. In B. Ciaramitaro (Ed.), *Virtual worlds and e-commerce: Technologies and applications for building customer relationships* (pp. 267–289). Hershey, PA: Business Science Reference; doi:10.4018/978-1-61692-808-7.ch016

Ratnasingam, P. (2010). The evolution of online relationships in business to consumer e-commerce. In M. Khosrow-Pour (Ed.), *E-commerce trends for organizational advancement: New applications and methods* (pp. 167–176). Hershey, PA: Information Science Reference; doi:10.4018/978-1-60566-964-9.ch010

Ratnasingam, P. (2010). The impact of e-commerce customer relationship management in business-to-consumer e-commerce. In M. Hunter (Ed.), *Strategic information systems: Concepts, methodologies, tools, and applications* (pp. 2099–2111). Hershey, PA: Information Science Reference; doi:10.4018/978-1-60566-677-8.ch132

Razavi, A. R., Krause, P., & Moschoyiannis, S. (2010). Digital ecosystems: Challenges and proposed solutions. In N. Antonopoulos, G. Exarchakos, M. Li, & A. Liotta (Eds.), Handbook of research on P2P and grid systems for service-oriented computing: Models, methodologies and applications (pp. 1003-1031). Hershey, PA: Information Science Reference. doi:10.4018/978-1-61520-686-5.ch043

Regazzi, J. J. (2014). *Infonomics and the business of free: Modern value creation for information services*. Hershey, PA: IGI Global; doi:10.4018/978-1-4666-4454-0

Riaz, N., & Rehman, M. (2013). Negotiation by software agents in electronic business: An example of hybrid negotiation. In E. Li, S. Loh, C. Evans, & F. Lorenzi (Eds.), *Organizations and social networking: Utilizing social media to engage consumers* (pp. 327–349). Hershey, PA: Business Science Reference; doi:10.4018/978-1-4666-4026-9.ch017

Roberti, G., & Marinelli, A. (2012). Branding identity: Facebook, brands and self construction. In F. Comunello (Ed.), *Networked sociability and individualism: Technology for personal and professional relationships* (pp. 147–168). Hershey, PA: Information Science Reference; doi:10.4018/978-1-61350-338-6.ch008

Rodrigues, D. E. (2012). Cyberethics of business social networking. In M. Cruz-Cunha, P. Gonçalves, N. Lopes, E. Miranda, & G. Putnik (Eds.), *Handbook of research on business social networking: Organizational, managerial, and technological dimensions* (pp. 314–338). Hershey, PA: Business Science Reference; doi:10.4018/978-1-61350-168-9.ch016

Roos, G. (2013). The role of intellectual capital in business model innovation: An empirical study. In P. Ordóñez de Pablos, R. Tennyson, & J. Zhao (Eds.), *Intellectual capital strategy management for knowledge-based organizations* (pp. 76–121). Hershey, PA: Business Science Reference; doi:10.4018/978-1-4666-3655-2.ch006

Rowley, J., & Edmundson-Bird, D. (2013). Brand presence in digital space. *Journal of Electronic Commerce in Organizations*, *11*(1), 63–78. doi:10.4018/jeco.2013010104

Rusko, R. (2013). The redefined role of consumer as a prosumer: Value co-creation, coopetition, and crowdsourcing of information goods. In P. Renna (Ed.), *Production and manufacturing system management: Coordination approaches and multi-site planning* (pp. 162–174). Hershey, PA: Engineering Science Reference; doi:10.4018/978-1-4666-2098-8.ch009

Sahi, G., & Madan, S. (2013). Developing a website usability framework for B2C e-commerce success. *International Journal of Information Communication Technologies and Human Development*, *5*(1), 1–19. doi:10.4018/jicthd.2013010101

Sainz de Abajo, B., de la Torre Díez, I., & López-Coronado, M. (2010). Analysis of benefits and risks of e-commerce: Practical study of Spanish SME. In I. Portela & M. Cruz-Cunha (Eds.), *Information communication technology law, protection and access rights: Global approaches and issues* (pp. 214–239). Hershey, PA: Information Science Reference; doi:10.4018/978-1-61520-975-0.ch014

Samanta, I., & Kyriazopoulos, P. (2011). Can global environment influence B2B relationships? In P. Ordóñez de Pablos, M. Lytras, W. Karwowski, & R. Lee (Eds.), *Electronic globalized business and sustainable development through IT management: Strategies and perspectives* (pp. 54–69). Hershey, PA: Business Science Reference; doi:10.4018/978-1-61520-623-0.ch004

Sambhanthan, A., & Good, A. (2012). Implications for improving accessibility to e-commerce websites in developing countries: A study of hotel websites. *International Journal of Knowledge-Based Organizations*, *2*(2), 1–20. doi:10.4018/ijkbo.2012040101

Sampaio, L., & Figueiredo, J. (2011). E-sourcing electronic platforms in real business. In M. Cruz-Cunha & J. Varajão (Eds.), *E-business managerial aspects, solutions and case studies* (pp. 185–205). Hershey, PA: Business Science Reference; doi:10.4018/978-1-60960-463-9.ch011

Seetharaman, A., & Raj, J. R. (2011). Evolution, development and growth of electronic money. In S. Sharma (Ed.), *E-adoption and socio-economic impacts: Emerging infrastructural effects* (pp. 249–268). Hershey, PA: Information Science Reference; doi:10.4018/978-1-60960-597-1.ch013

Sengupta, A., & Glavin, S. E. (2013). Predicting volatile consumer markets using multi-agent methods: Theory and validation. In B. Alexandrova-Kabadjova, S. Martinez-Jaramillo, A. Garcia-Almanza, & E. Tsang (Eds.), *Simulation in computational finance and economics: Tools and emerging applications* (pp. 339–358). Hershey, PA: Business Science Reference; doi:10.4018/978-1-4666-2011-7.ch016

Serpico, E., Aquilani, B., Ruggieri, A., & Silvestri, C. (2013). Customer centric marketing strategies: The importance and measurement of customer satisfaction – Offline vs. online. In H. Kaufmann & M. Panni (Eds.), *Customer-centric marketing strategies: Tools for building organizational performance* (pp. 315–357). Hershey, PA: Business Science Reference; doi:10.4018/978-1-4666-2524-2.ch016

Shareef, M. A., & Kumar, V. (2012). Prevent/control identity theft: Impact on trust and consumers' purchase intention in B2C EC. *Information Resources Management Journal, 25*(3), 30–60. doi:10.4018/irmj.2012070102

Sherringham, K., & Unhelkar, B. (2011). Business driven enterprise architecture and applications to support mobile business. In *Enterprise information systems: Concepts, methodologies, tools and applications* (pp. 805–816). Hershey, PA: Business Science Reference; doi:10.4018/978-1-61692-852-0.ch316

Shin, N. (2011). Information technology and diversification: How their relationship affects firm performance. In N. Kock (Ed.), *E-collaboration technologies and organizational performance: Current and future trends* (pp. 65–79). Hershey, PA: Information Science Reference; doi:10.4018/978-1-60960-466-0.ch005

Sidnal, N., & Manvi, S. S. (2010). Service discovery techniques in mobile e-commerce. In I. Lee (Ed.), *Encyclopedia of e-business development and management in the global economy* (pp. 812–823). Hershey, PA: Business Science Reference; doi:10.4018/978-1-61520-611-7.ch081

Sidnal, N., & Manvi, S. S. (2013). English auction issues in mobile e-commerce. In K. Tarnay, S. Imre, & L. Xu (Eds.), *Research and development in e-business through service-oriented solutions* (pp. 208–223). Hershey, PA: Business Science Reference; doi:10.4018/978-1-4666-4181-5.ch010

Singh, S. (2010). Usability techniques for interactive software and their application in e-commerce. In T. Spiliotopoulos, P. Papadopoulou, D. Martakos, & G. Kouroupetroglou (Eds.), *Integrating usability engineering for designing the web experience: Methodologies and principles* (pp. 81–102). Hershey, PA: Information Science Reference; doi:10.4018/978-1-60566-896-3.ch005

Söderström, E. (2010). Guidelines for managing B2B standards implementation. In E. Alkhalifa (Ed.), *E-strategies for resource management systems: Planning and implementation* (pp. 86–105). Hershey, PA: Business Science Reference; doi:10.4018/978-1-61692-016-6.ch005

Sood, S. (2012). The death of social media in start-up companies and the rise of s-commerce: Convergence of e-commerce, complexity and social media. *Journal of Electronic Commerce in Organizations, 10*(2), 1–15. doi:10.4018/jeco.2012040101

Soto-Acosta, P. (2010). E-business and the resource-based view: Towards a research agenda. In I. Lee (Ed.), *Encyclopedia of e-business development and management in the global economy* (pp. 336–346). Hershey, PA: Business Science Reference; doi:10.4018/978-1-61520-611-7.ch033

Sourouni, A. M., Mouzakitis, S., Kourlimpini, G., Askounis, D., & Psarras, J. (2010). Ontology-based registries: An e-business transactions' registry. In E. Alkhalifa (Ed.), *E-strategies for resource management systems: Planning and implementation* (pp. 106–117). Hershey, PA: Business Science Reference; doi:10.4018/978-1-61692-016-6.ch006

Srinivasan, S., & Barker, R. (2012). Global analysis of security and trust perceptions in web design for e-commerce. *International Journal of Information Security and Privacy*, *6*(1), 1–13. doi:10.4018/jisp.2012010101

Su, Q., & Adams, C. (2012). Consumers' attitudes toward mobile commerce: A model to capture the cultural and environment influences. In A. Scupola (Ed.), *Innovative mobile platform developments for electronic services design and delivery* (pp. 1–20). Hershey, PA: Business Science Reference; doi:10.4018/978-1-4666-1568-7.ch001

Swilley, E., Hofacker, C. F., & Lamont, B. T. (2012). The evolution from e-commerce to m-commerce: Pressures, firm capabilities and competitive advantage in strategic decision making. *International Journal of E-Business Research*, *8*(1), 1–16. doi:10.4018/jebr.2012010101

Swimm, N., & Andriole, S. J. (2010). Business technology strategy for an energy management company. *Journal of Information Technology Research*, *3*(3), 54–65. doi:10.4018/jitr.2010070105

Tadjouddine, E. M. (2011). E-commerce systems for software agents: Challenges and opportunities. In M. Cruz-Cunha & J. Varajão (Eds.), *E-business issues, challenges and opportunities for SMEs: Driving competitiveness* (pp. 20–29). Hershey, PA: Business Science Reference; doi:10.4018/978-1-61692-880-3.ch002

Taylor, P. R. (2014). Enterprise architecture's identity crisis: New approaches to complexity for a maturing discipline. In P. Saha (Ed.), *A systemic perspective to managing complexity with enterprise architecture* (pp. 433–453). Hershey, PA: Business Science Reference; doi:10.4018/978-1-4666-4518-9.ch013

Tella, A. (2012). Determinants of e-payment systems success: A user's satisfaction perspective. *International Journal of E-Adoption*, *4*(3), 15–38. doi:10.4018/jea.2012070102

Terjesen, A. (2010). Anonymity and trust: The ethical challenges of e-business transactions. In D. Palmer (Ed.), *Ethical issues in e-business: Models and frameworks* (pp. 40–57). Hershey, PA: Business Science Reference; doi:10.4018/978-1-61520-615-5.ch004

Tijsen, R., Spruit, M., van de Ridder, M., & van Raaij, B. (2011). BI-FIT: Aligning business intelligence end-users, tasks and technologies. In M. Cruz-Cunha & J. Varajao (Eds.), *Enterprise information systems design, implementation and management: Organizational applications* (pp. 162–177). Hershey, PA: Information Science Reference; doi:10.4018/978-1-61692-020-3.ch011

Toka, A., Aivazidou, E., Antoniou, A., & Arvanitopoulos-Darginis, K. (2013). Cloud computing in supply chain management: An overview. In D. Graham, I. Manikas, & D. Folinas (Eds.), *E-logistics and e-supply chain management: Applications for evolving business* (pp. 218–231). Hershey, PA: Business Science Reference; doi:10.4018/978-1-4666-3914-0.ch012

Tran, Q., Huang, D., & Zhang, C. (2013). An assessment method of the integrated e-commerce readiness for construction organizations in developing countries. *International Journal of E-Adoption*, *5*(1), 37–51. doi:10.4018/jea.2013010103

Tung, H., Kung, H., Lawless, D. S., Sofge, D. A., & Lawless, W. F. (2011). Conservation of information and e-business success and challenges: A case study. In M. Cruz-Cunha & J. Varajão (Eds.), *E-business managerial aspects, solutions and case studies* (pp. 254–269). Hershey, PA: Business Science Reference; doi:10.4018/978-1-60960-463-9.ch015

Unhelkar, B. (2011). *Handbook of research on green ICT: Technology, business and social perspectives*. Hershey, PA: IGI Global; doi:10.4018/978-1-61692-834-6

Unhelkar, B., Ghanbary, A., & Younessi, H. (2010). Collaborative business process engineering (CBPE) model. In B. Unhelkar, A. Ghanbary, & H. Younessi (Eds.), *Collaborative business process engineering and global organizations: Frameworks for service integration* (pp. 98–120). Hershey, PA: Business Science Reference; doi:10.4018/978-1-60566-689-1.ch004

Unhelkar, B., Ghanbary, A., & Younessi, H. (2010). Emerging technologies for business collaboration. In B. Unhelkar, A. Ghanbary, & H. Younessi (Eds.), *Collaborative business process engineering and global organizations: Frameworks for service integration* (pp. 37–64). Hershey, PA: Business Science Reference; doi:10.4018/978-1-60566-689-1.ch002

Unhelkar, B., Ghanbary, A., & Younessi, H. (2010). Fundamentals of collaborative business. In B. Unhelkar, A. Ghanbary, & H. Younessi (Eds.), *Collaborative business process engineering and global organizations: Frameworks for service integration* (pp. 1–36). Hershey, PA: Business Science Reference; doi:10.4018/978-1-60566-689-1.ch001

Van Huy, L., Rowe, F., Truex, D., & Huynh, M. Q. (2012). An empirical study of determinants of e-commerce adoption in SMEs in Vietnam: An economy in transition. *Journal of Global Information Management*, *20*(3), 23–54. doi:10.4018/jgim.2012070102

Vannoy, S. A. (2011). A structured content analytic assessment of business services advertisements in the cloud-based web services marketplace. *International Journal of Dependable and Trustworthy Information Systems*, *2*(1), 18–49. doi:10.4018/jdtis.2011010102

Vasconcelos, V., & Campos, P. (2012). The role of social networks in distributed informal information systems for innovation. In J. Varajão, M. Cruz-Cunha, & A. Trigo (Eds.), *Organizational integration of enterprise systems and resources: Advancements and applications* (pp. 60–75). Hershey, PA: Business Science Reference; doi:10.4018/978-1-4666-1764-3.ch004

Venkatraman, R., Venkatraman, S., & Asaithambi, S. P. (2013). A practical cloud services implementation framework for e-businesses. In K. Tarnay, S. Imre, & L. Xu (Eds.), *Research and development in e-business through service-oriented solutions* (pp. 167–198). Hershey, PA: Business Science Reference; doi:10.4018/978-1-4666-4181-5.ch008

Verkasalo, H. (2011). Analysis of the forces reshaping the mobile internet business. In M. Bartolacci & S. Powell (Eds.), *Interdisciplinary and multidimensional perspectives in telecommunications and networking: Emerging findings* (pp. 19–45). Hershey, PA: Information Science Reference; doi:10.4018/978-1-60960-505-6.ch003

Verma, A. (2013). Effects of phishing on e-commerce with special reference to India. In R. Khurana & R. Aggarwal (Eds.), *Interdisciplinary perspectives on business convergence, computing, and legality* (pp. 186–197). Hershey, PA: Business Science Reference; doi:10.4018/978-1-4666-4209-6.ch017

Walker, B., & Posey, E. (2013). Digital El Paso: A public-private business model for community wireless networks. In A. Abdelaal (Ed.), *Social and economic effects of community wireless networks and infrastructures* (pp. 94–111). Hershey, PA: Information Science Reference; doi:10.4018/978-1-4666-2997-4.ch006

Wan, Y., Clegg, B., & Dey, P. K. (2013). A framework for enabling dynamic e-business strategies via new enterprise paradigms and ERP solutions. In *Enterprise resource planning: Concepts, methodologies, tools, and applications* (pp. 1561–1595). Hershey, PA: Business Science Reference; doi:10.4018/978-1-4666-4153-2.ch083

Wang, F., Lupton, N., Rawlinson, D., & Zhang, X. (2012). EBDMSS: A web-based decision making support system for strategic e-business management. In P. Zaraté (Ed.), *Integrated and strategic advancements in decision making support systems* (pp. 265–284). Hershey, PA: Information Science Reference; doi:10.4018/978-1-4666-1746-9.ch019

Wenyin, L., Liu, A., Li, Q., & Huang, L. (2011). Business models for insurance of business web services. In H. Leung, D. Chiu, & P. Hung (Eds.), *Service intelligence and service science: Evolutionary technologies and challenges* (pp. 261–272). Hershey, PA: Information Science Reference; doi:10.4018/978-1-61520-819-7.ch014

Wiedmann, K., Reeh, M., & Schumacher, H. (2010). Employment and acceptance of near field communication in mobile marketing. In K. Pousttchi & D. Wiedemann (Eds.), *Handbook of research on mobile marketing management* (pp. 190–212). Hershey, PA: Business Science Reference; doi:10.4018/978-1-60566-074-5.ch011

Williams, J. G., & Premchaiswadi, W. (2011). On-line credit card payment processing and fraud prevention for e-business. In *Global business: Concepts, methodologies, tools and applications* (pp. 699–717). Hershey, PA: Business Science Reference; doi:10.4018/978-1-60960-587-2.ch312

Wilms, A., & Andriole, S. J. (2010). Business technology strategy for a specialty chemicals company. *Journal of Information Technology Research, 3*(3), 11–18. doi:10.4018/jitr.2010070102

Winkler, U., & Gilani, W. (2012). Business continuity management of business driven IT landscapes. In S. Reiff-Marganiec & M. Tilly (Eds.), *Handbook of research on service-oriented systems and non-functional properties: Future directions* (pp. 381–399). Hershey, PA: Information Science Reference; doi:10.4018/978-1-61350-432-1.ch017

Wollenberg, A. (2013). Optimizing international joint venture (IJV) ownership structures: A technology and knowledge transfer-linked productivity growth perspective. In B. Christiansen, E. Turkina, & N. Williams (Eds.), *Cultural and technological influences on global business* (pp. 142–164). Hershey, PA: Business Science Reference; doi:10.4018/978-1-4666-3966-9.ch009

Wood, A. M., Moultrie, J., & Eckert, C. (2010). Product form evolution. In A. Silva & R. Simoes (Eds.), *Handbook of research on trends in product design and development: Technological and organizational perspectives* (pp. 499–512). Hershey, PA: Business Science Reference; doi:10.4018/978-1-61520-617-9.ch027

Wresch, W., & Fraser, S. (2011). Persistent barriers to e-commerce in developing countries: A longitudinal study of efforts by Caribbean companies. *Journal of Global Information Management, 19*(3), 30–44. doi:10.4018/jgim.2011070102

Wresch, W., & Fraser, S. (2013). Persistent barriers to e-commerce in developing countries: A longitudinal study of efforts by Caribbean companies. In F. Tan (Ed.), *Global diffusion and adoption of technologies for knowledge and information sharing* (pp. 205–220). Hershey, PA: Information Science Reference; doi:10.4018/978-1-4666-2142-8.ch009

Xiao, X., Liu, Y., & Zhang, Z. (2012). The analysis of the logistics mode decision to e-commerce. *Journal of Electronic Commerce in Organizations, 10*(4), 57–70. doi:10.4018/jeco.2012100105

Xu, L. (2010). Outsourcing and multi-party business collaborations modeling. In K. St.Amant (Ed.), *IT outsourcing: Concepts, methodologies, tools, and applications* (pp. 558–577). Hershey, PA: Business Science Reference; doi:10.4018/978-1-60566-770-6.ch033

Xu, M., Rohatgi, R., & Duan, Y. (2010). Engaging SMEs in e-business: Insights from an empirical study. In *Business information systems: Concepts, methodologies, tools and applications* (pp. 115–134). Hershey, PA: Business Science Reference; doi:10.4018/978-1-61520-969-9.ch009

Yermish, I., Miori, V., Yi, J., Malhotra, R., & Klimberg, R. (2010). Business plus intelligence plus technology equals business intelligence. *International Journal of Business Intelligence Research, 1*(1), 48–63. doi:10.4018/jbir.2010071704

Yeung, W. L. (2013). Specifying business-level protocols for web services based collaborative processes. In A. Loo (Ed.), *Distributed computing innovations for business, engineering, and science* (pp. 137–154). Hershey, PA: Information Science Reference; doi:10.4018/978-1-4666-2533-4.ch007

Z arour, M., Abran, A., & Desharnais, J. (2014). Software process improvement for small and very small enterprises. In *Software design and development: Concepts, methodologies, tools, and applications* (pp. 1363-1384). Hershey, PA: Information Science Reference. doi:10.4018/978-1-4666-4301-7.ch066

Related References

Zerenler, M., & Gözlü, S. (2012). Issues influencing electronic commerce activities of SMEs: A study of the Turkish automotive supplier industry. In *Human resources management: Concepts, methodologies, tools, and applications* (pp. 1035–1055). Hershey, PA: Business Science Reference; doi:10.4018/978-1-4666-1601-1.ch064

Compilation of References

Aikin, J. (Ed.). (2003). *Software Synthesizers, San Francisco*. Backbeat Books.

Akester, P. (2010). *The new challenges of striking the right balance between copyright protection and access to knowledge, information and culture*. Intergovernmental Copyright Committee, UNESCO. Retrieved June 28, 2016, from http://unesdoc.unesco.org/images/0018/001876/187683E.pdf

Alberti, P. (1995). *The anatomy and physiology of the ear and hearing*. University of Toronto Press.

Alpern, A. (1995). *Techniques for Algorithmic Composition of Music*. Hampshire College.

Anderson, S. (2012). *Languages - a Very Short Introduction*. Oxford University Press. doi:10.1093/actrade/9780199590599.001.0001

Ascensão. (2008). Sociedade da informação e liberdade de expressão. In Direito da Sociedade da Informação, VII. Coimbra: Coimbra Editora.

Bagchee, S. (1998). *Understanding Raga Music*. Ceshwar Business Publications Inc.

Barbour, J. M. (1972). *Tuning and Temperament: a Historical Survey*. New York: Da Capo Press.

Barsky, V. (1996). *Chromaticism*. Harwood Academic Press.

BBC. (2012). *Wi-fi, dual-flush loos and eight more Australian inventions*. Retrieved from http://www.bbc.co.uk/news/magazine-20071644

BDA. (2012). *Appropriate modernization of European data protection*. Position on the draft European regulation on the protection of individuals with regard to the processing of personal data and on the free movement of such data ("general data protection regulation").

Beckerexhibits, 19th century. (n.d.). Concealed Hearing Devices of the 19th Century. *Deafness in Disguise.*

Beckerexhibits, 20th century. (n.d.). Concealed Hearing Devices of the 20th Century. *Deafness in Disguise.*

Bernays, M., & Traube, C. (2013). Expressive Production of Piano Timbre: Touch and Playing Techniques for Timbre Control in Piano Performance. In *Proceedings of the 10th Sound and Music Computing Conference (SMC2013)*, (pp. 341-346). Stockholm, Sweden: KTH Royal Institute of Technology.

Blackwell, D., Lucas, J., & Clarke, T. (2014). Summary Health Statistics for US Adults: National Health Interview Survey, 2012. *Vital and Health Statistics. Series 10, Data from the National Health Survey*, (260), 1–161. PMID:24819891

Blanpain, R., & Van Gestel, M. (2004). *Use and Monitoring of E-mail, Intranet, and Internet Facilities at work*. Kluwer Law International.

Bluetooth. (2015). *Bluetooth Technology Basics*. Academic Press.

Boersma, K. (2012). *Internet and surveillance-The challenge of Web 2.0 and Social Media* (C. Fuchs, K. Boersma, A. Albrechtslund, & M. Sandoval, Eds.). Routledge.

Boundless. (2016). The Vestibular System. *Boundless Biology*. Retrieved from https://www.boundless.com/biology/textbooks/boundless-biology-textbook/sensory-systems-36/hearing-and-vestibular-sensation-208/the-vestibular-system-786-12022/

Boyle, J. (1997). *Foucault in cyberspace: Surveillance, sovereignty, and hard-wired censors*. Retrieved June 28, 2016, from http://www.law.duke.edu/boylesite/foucault.htm

Brand, S. (1985). *Whole Earth Review*. Retrieved from http://www.wholeearth.com/issue--electronic--edition.php?iss=2046

Brand, S. (1987). *The Media Lab: inventing the future at MIT*. Penguin Books.

Brown, M., & Schenker, (1986). The Diatonic and the Chromatic in Shenker's theory of harmonic relations. *Journal of Music Therapy*, *30*(1), 1–33. doi:10.2307/843407

Bryant, S. (1995). Electronic Surveillance in the Workplace. *Canadian Journal of Communication*, *20*(4), 505–525. Retrieved from http://www.cjc-online.ca/index.php/journal/article/view/893/799

Cangeloso, S. (2012). *LED Lighting -Illuminate your World with Solid State Technology - A Primer to Lighting the Future*. O-Reilly - Maker Press.

Cas, J. (2005). Privacy in pervasive computing environments: A contradiction in terms. *IEEE Technology and Society Magazine*, *24*(1), 24–33. doi:10.1109/MTAS.2005.1407744

Castro, C. S. (2005). O direito à autodeterminação informativa e os novos desafios gerados pelo direito à liberdade e à segurança no pós 11 de Setembro. In *Estudos em homenagem ao Conselheiro José Manuel Cardoso da Costa, II*. Coimbra: Coimbra Editora.

Castro, C. S. (2006). *Protecção de dados pessoais na Internet. Sub Judice, 35*. Coimbra: Almedina.

Chouard, C., Mac Leod, P., Meyer, B., & Pialoux, P. (1977). Surgically implanted electronic apparatus for the rehabilitation of total deafness and deaf-mutism[in French]. *Annales d'Oto-Laryngologie et de Chirurgie Cervico Faciale*, *94*, 353–363. PMID:606046

Chouard, C., Meyer, B., Fugain, C., & Koca, O. (1995). Clinical results for the DIGISONIC multichannel cochlear implant. *The Laryngoscope*, *105*(5), 505–509. doi:10.1288/00005537-199505000-00011 PMID:7760667

Cochlear Nucleus. (2015). *The breakthroughs continue with the Nucleus® 6 System*. Retrieved from http://www.cochlear.com/wps/wcm/connect/us/home/treatment-options-for-hearing-loss/cochlear-implants/nucleus-6-features

Cochlear. (2015). *True wireless freedom*. Academic Press.

Coleman, R., & McCahill, M. (2011). *Surveillance and Crime*. London: Sage Publications.

Collins, K. (2007). An Introduction to the Participatory and Non-Linear Aspects of Video Games Audio. In S. Hawkings & J. Richardson (Eds.), *Essays on Sound and Vision* (pp. 263–298). Helsikini, Finland: Helsinki University Press.

Collins, K. (2009). An Introduction to Procedural Audio in Video Games. *Contemporary Music Review*, *28*(1), 5–15. doi:10.1080/07494460802663983

Collins, K. (2013). *Playing with Sound: A Theory of Interacting with Sound and Music in Video Games*. MIT Press.

Colton, R. H., & Estill, J. A. (1981). Elements of voice quality: Perceptual acoustic, and physiologic aspects. In J. Lass (Ed.), *Speech and Language: Advances in Basic Research and Practice* (Vol. 5, pp. 311–403). Academic Press. doi:10.1016/B978-0-12-608605-8.50012-X

Commission of the European Communities. (2008). *Green Paper. Copyright in the Knowledge Economy.* Retrieved June 28, 2016, from http://ec.europa.eu/internal_market/copyright/docs/copyright--infso/greenpaper_en.pdf

Cook, P. (1999). *Music, Cognition and Computerized Sound, an Introduction to Psychoacoustics.* Cambridge, MA: MIT Press.

Cook, P. (2002). *Real Sound Synthesis for Interactive Applications.* A. K. Peters. doi:10.1201/b19597

Cox, C. (2003). Versions, Dubs, and Remixes: Realism and Rightness in Aesthetic Interpretation. In Interpretation and its Objects. Rodopi.

Cox, C., & Warner, D. (2007). *Audio Cultures, Readings in Modern Music.* Continuum.

Cox, C., & Warner, D. (2007). *Audio Cultures. In Readings in Modern Music.* Continuum.

Craig, J. (1999). *Privacy and Employment Law.* Oxford, UK: Hart Publishing.

D' Angour, A. (2013). *Oxford classicist brings ancient Greek music back to life.* Academic Press.

Dahl, L., Herrera, J., & Wilkerson, C. (2011). TweetDreams: Making Music with the Audience and the World Using Real-Time Twitter Data. In *Proceedings of Proceedings of the 2011 Conference on New Interfaces for Musical Expression NIME2011.*

Department of Commerce of the United States of America. (2013). *Copyright Policy, Creativity, and Innovation in the Digital Economy.* Retrieved June 28, 2016, from http://www.uspto.gov/sites/default/files/news/publications/copyrightgreenpaper.pdf

Devine, A. M., & Stephens, L. D. (1994). *The Prosody of Greek Speech.* New York: Academic Press.

DG Justice. (2004). *Draft Directive concerning the processing of workers' personal data and the protection of privacy in the employment context, Article 5.* Author.

Djourno, A., & Eyries, C. (1957). Auditory prosthesis by means of a distant electrical stimulation of the sensory nerve with the use of an indwelt coiling. *La Presse Medicale, 65*(63), 1417. PMID:13484817

Edwards, M. (2011). Algorithmic composition: Computational thinking in music. *Communications of the ACM, 54*(7), 58–67. doi:10.1145/1965724.1965742

EmCAP. (2008). *Emergent Cognition through Active Perception.* FP6-IST project for Music Cognition (Music, Science and the Brain). Retrieved from http://emcap.iua.upf.edu

Endo, A., Moriyama, T., & Kuhara, Y. (2012). Tweet Harp: Laser Harp Generating Voice and Text of Real-time Tweets in Twitter. In *Proceedings of Proceedings of the 2012 Conference on New Interfaces for Musical Expression NIME2012.* University of Michigan.

Eshraghi, A., Nazarian, R., Telischi, F., Rajguru, S., Truy, E., & Gupta, C. (2012). The cochlear implant: Historical aspects and future prospects. *The Anatomical Record, 295*(11), 1967–1980. doi:10.1002/ar.22580 PMID:23044644

Fant, G. (1960). *Acoustic theory of speech production.* The Hague, The Netherlands: Mouton.

Farnell, A. (2007). An introduction to procedural audio and its application in computer games. In *Proceedings of the Audio Mostly (AM07) Conference.*

Fast-Facts. (2015). *Bluetooth Fact or Fiction.* Author.

Fels, S. (2004). Designing for intimacy: Creating New Interfaces for Musical Expression. *Proceedings of the IEEE, 92*(4), 672–685. doi:10.1109/JPROC.2004.825887

Ferrajoli, L. (2001). Fundamental rights. *International Journal for the Semiotics of Law, 14*(1), 1–33. doi:10.1023/A:1011290509568

Field-Selfridge, E. (1997). *Beyond MIDI.* Cambridge, MA: MIT Press.

Flanagan, J., Coker, C., Rabiner, L., Schafer, R., & Umeda, N. (1970). Synthetic voices for Computers. *IEEE Spectrum, 7*(10), 22–45. doi:10.1109/MSPEC.1970.5212992

Fox, M., & Kemp, M. (2009). *Interactive Architecture.* Princeton Architectural Press.

Franco, I. (2005). The Airstick: A Free-Gesture Controller Using Infrared Sensing. In *Proceedings of the 2005 Conf. on New Instruments for Musical Expression.*

Frishert, S. (2013). Implementing Algorithmic Composition for Games. Utrecht School of the Arts, Department of Art, Media and Technology.

Garrie, D. B., & Wong, R. (2010). Social networking: Opening the floodgates to "personal data". *Computer and Telecommunications Law Review, 16*(6), 167–175.

Geiger, C. (2010). The future of copyright in Europe: Striking a fair balance between protection and access to information. *Intellectual Property Quarterly, 1*, 1–14.

Gervais, D., & Hyndman. (2012). Cloud Control: Copyright, Global Memes and Privacy. *Journal of Telecommunications and High Technology Law*, *10*, 53-92. Retrieved June 28, 2016, from http://papers.ssrn.com/sol3/papers.cfm?abstract_id=2017157

Gianelos, G. (1996). La musique Byzantine. L'Harmatan.

Glinsky, A. V. (1992). *The Theremin in the Emergence of Electronic Music*. (PhD thesis). New York University, New York, NY.

Goebl, W., Bresin, R., & Galembo, A. (2005). Touch and Temporal Behavior of Grand Piano Actions. *The Journal of the Acoustical Society of America*, *118*(2), 1154–1165. doi:10.1121/1.1944648 PMID:16158669

Goldstein, P. (2003). *Copyright's Highway: From Gutenberg to the Celestial Jukebox* (Rev. ed.). Stanford, CA: Stanford University Press.

Gombosi, O. J. (1944). New Light on Ancient Greek Music. *International Congress of Musicology*. New York: Academic Press.

Graham-Knight, K., & Tzanetakis, G. (2015a). Adaptive Music Technology: History and Future Perspectives. In *Proceedings of the International Computer Music Conference*.

Graham-Knight, K., & Tzanetakis, G. (2015b). Adaptive Music Technology using the Kinect. In *Proceedings of the 8th ACM International Conference on PErvasive Technologies Related to Assistive Environments*.

Guibault, L. (1998). *Limitations Found Outside of Copyright Law – General Report. ALAI Studies Days*. Retrieved June 28, 2016, from http://www.ivir.nl/publications/guibault/VUL5BOVT.doc

Halaris, C. (1999). *Music of Ancient Greece*. booklet and CD.

Hardcastle, W. J., Laver, J., & Gibbon, F. (2010). *The handbook of phonetic sciences*. John Wiley & Sons. doi:10.1002/9781444317251

Harmonia Mundi. (1999). Musique de la Grece Antique. Booklet and CD, HMA 1951015, France.

Harris, R. (1993). *The linguistics wars*. Oxford University Press.

Hasan, L., Yu, N., & Paradiso, J. (2002). The Termenova: a Hybrid Free-Gesture Interface. In *Proceedings of the 2002 Conference on New Instruments for Musical Expression*.

Hayes, C. J. (2008). Changing the rules of the game: How video game publishers are embracing user-generated derivative works. *Harvard Journal of Law & Technology*, *21*(2), 567–587.

Hazel, O. (2002). Email and internet monitoring in the workplace: Information privacy and contracting-out. *Industrial Law Journal*, *31*(4), 321–352. doi:10.1093/ilj/31.4.321

Hendrickx, F. (2002). On-Line Rights for Employees in the Information Society. In *Bulletin of Comparative Labour Relations 40-2000*. Kluwer Law International.

Hendrikx, M., Meijer, S., Van Der Velden, J., & Iosup, A. (2013). Procedural content generation for games: A survey. *ACM Transactions on Multimedia Computing, Communications, and Applications*, *9*(1), 1–22. doi:10.1145/2422956.2422957

Hochmair, E., Hochmair-Desoyer, I., & Burian, K. (1979). Investigations towards an artificial cochlea. *The International Journal of Artificial Organs*, *2*(5), 255–261. PMID:582589

Hochmair, I. (2013). "The importance of being flexible" (PDF), Laske Foundation. *Nature Medicine*, *19*(10), 1–6. PMID:24100995

Howard, A. (1998, November 26). Hearing Aids: Smaller and Smarter. *New York Times*.

Idson, W. L., & Massaro, D. W. (1978). A bidimensional model of pitch in the recognition of melodies. *Perception & Psychophysics*, *24*(6), 551–565. doi:10.3758/BF03198783 PMID:751000

Iglezakis, I., Politis, D., & Phaedon-John, K. (Eds.). (2009). *Socioeconomic and Legal Implications of Electronic Intrusion*. Hershey, PA: IGI Global.

Jacobs, A. (1980). *The new Penguin dictionary of music*. Penguin.

Jenkins, L., Trail, S., Tzanetakis, G., Driessen, P., & Page, W. (2013). An Easily Removable, Wireless Optical Sensing System (EROSS) for the Trumpet. In *Proceedings of the 2013 Conference on New Interfaces for Musical Expression NIME2013*.

Juslin, P. (2000). Cue utilization in communication of emotion in music performance: Relating performance to perception. *Journal of Experimental Psychology. Human Perception and Performance*, *26*(6), 1797–1813. doi:10.1037/0096-1523.26.6.1797 PMID:11129375

Kant, I. (1996). The Metaphysics of Morals. In *Practical Philosophy* (M. J. Gregor, Trans.). Cambridge University Press.

Kapur, A., Lazier, A., Davidson, P., Wilson, R. S., & Cook, P. (2004). The Electronic Sitar Controller. In *Proceedings of the 2004 conference on New interfaces for musical expression.*

Katsanevaki, A. (2011). Chromaticism – A theoretical construction or a practical transformation? *Muzikologija*, *11*(11), 159–180. doi:10.2298/MUZ1111159K

Katyal, S. (2004). The new surveillance. *Case Western Reserve Law Review*, *54*, 297–386.

Kravets, D. (2013). California abruptly drops plan to implant RFID chips in driver's licenses. *Wired*. Available at http://www.wired.com/2013/09/drivers-licenserfid-chips/

Kullar, P., Manjaly, J., & Yates, P. (2012). *ENT OSCEs: A Guide to Passing the DO-HNS and MRCS (ENT)*. Radcliffe Pub, UK: OSCE.

Kyriafinis, G. (2005). *Cochlear implantation*. Publish City.

Lalwani, A. (Ed.). (2008). Current Diagnosis & Treatment in Otolaryngology: Head and Surgery. McGraw-Hill Medical.

Langscape - Maryland Language Center. (n.d.). University of Maryland.

Langston, P. (1989). Six Techniques for Algorithmic Music Composition. In *Proceedings of the ICMC 1989*. The Ohio State University.

Laver, J. (1994). *Principles of phonetics*. Cambridge University Press. doi:10.1017/CBO9781139166621

Lerdahl, F., & Jackendoff, R. (1983). *A generative Theory of Tonal Music*. Cambridge, MA: MIT Press.

Leval, P. N. (1990). Toward a Fair Use Standard. *Harvard Law Review*, *103*(5), 1105–1136. doi:10.2307/1341457

Levitt, H. (2007). Digital hearing aids: Wheelbarrows to ear inserts. *ASHA Leader*, *12*(17), 28–30.

Liem, C., Müller, M., Eck, D., Tzanetakis, G., & Hanjalic, A. (2011). The Need for Music Information Retrieval with User Centered and Multimodal Strategies. In *Proceedings of the 1st International ACM Workshop on Music Information Retrieval with User-Centered and Multimodal Strategies*. doi:10.1145/2072529.2072531

Lin, F., Niparko, J., & Ferrucci, L. (2011). Hearing loss prevalence in the United States. *Archives of Internal Medicine*, *171*(20), 1851–1853. doi:10.1001/archinternmed.2011.506 PMID:22083573

Lyon, D. (1994). The Electronic Eye: The rise of surveillance society. Polity Press.

Mac Leold, P., Pialoux, P., Chouard, C., & Meyer, B. (1975). Physiological assessment of the rehabilitation of total deafness by the implantation of multiple intracochlear electrodes. *Annales d'Oto-Laryngologie et de Chirurgie Cervico Faciale*, *92*(1-2), 17–23. PMID:1217800

MacConnell, D., Trail, S., Tzanetakis, G., Driessen, P., & Page, W. (2013). Reconfigurable Autonomous Novel Guitar Effects (range). In *Proc. Int. Conf. on Sound and Music Computing (SMC 2013).*

Machover, T. (1991). *Hyperinstruments: A Composer's Approach to the Evolution of Intelligent Musical Instruments*. Organized Sound.

Marazita, M., Ploughman, L., Rawlings, B., Remington, E., Arnos, K., & Nance, W. (1993). Genetic epidemiological studies of early-onset deafness in the US school-age population. *American Journal of Medical Genetics*, *46*(5), 486–491. doi:10.1002/ajmg.1320460504 PMID:8322805

Margounakis, D., & Politis, D. (2006). Converting images to music using their colour properties. In *Proceedings of the 12th International Conference on Auditory Display* (ICAD2006).

Margounakis, D., & Politis, D. (2012). Exploring the Relations between Chromaticism, Familiarity, Scales and Emotional Responses in Music. In *Proceedings of the XIX CIM Music Informatics Symposium* (CIM 2012). Trieste: Conservatory of Music "Giuseppe Tartini".

Margounakis, D., Politis, D., & Mokos, K. (2009). MEL-IRIS: An Online Tool for Audio Analysis and Music Indexing. International Journal of Digital Media Broadcasting. doi:10.1155/2009/806750

Margounakis, D., & Politis, D. (2011). Music Libraries - How Users Interact with Music Stores and Repositories. In I. Iglezakis, T.-E. Synodinou, & S. Kapidakis (Eds.), *E-Publishing and Digital Libraries - Legal and Organizational Issues*. Hershey, PA: IGI-Global.

Marx, G. T. (2007). What's new about new surveillance? Classifying for change and continuity. In S. P. Heir & J. Greenberg (Eds.), *The Surveillance Studies Reader*. Maidenhead, UK: Open University Press.

McColgan, A. (2003). *Do privacy rights disappear in the workplace?*. Human Rights Law Review.

Med-El. (2015). *The hearing implant company*. Retrieved from http://www.medel.com/about-Med-el/

Mell, P., & Grance, T. (2009). *The NIST definition of cloud computing*. National Institute of Standards and Technology, Information Technology Laboratory. Retrieved June 28, 2016, from http://www.nist.gov/itl/cloud/upload/cloud-def-v15.pdf

Meyer, L. (1956). *Emotion and Meaning in Music*. Chicago: University of Chicago Press.

Mills, M. (2011). Hearing Aids and the History of Electronics Miniaturization. *IEEE Annals of the History of Computing*, *33*(2), 24–44. doi:10.1109/MAHC.2011.43

Miranda, E., & Wanderley, M. (2006). *New Digital Musical Instruments: Control and Interaction Beyond the Keyboard*. Middleton, WI: AR Editions.

Munday, R. (2007). Music in Video Games. In J. Sexton (Ed.), Music, Sound and Multimedia: From the Live to the Virtual. Edinburgh, UK: Edinburgh University Press.

Nielsen, R. (2010). *Employment and ICT Law*. Stockholm Institute for Scandinavian Law.

Noble, J. (2009). *Programming Interactivity*. O'Reilly.

Odowichuk, G., Trail, S., Driessen, P., Nie, W., & Page, W. (2011). Sensor Fusion: Towards a Fully Expressive 3D Music Control Interface. In *Proceedings* of the *Communications, Computers and Signal Processing 2011 IEEE Pacific Rim Conference (PacRim)*. doi:10.1109/PACRIM.2011.6033003

Orio, N. (2006). *Music Retrieval: a Tutorial and Review*. Boston, MA: Now Publishers Inc.

Orwell, G. (1949). *Nineteen Eighty-Four*. Harmondsworth, UK: Penguin.

Ouzounian, G. (2007). Visualizing Acoustic Space. *Musiques Contemporaines*, *17*(3), 45–56. doi:10.7202/017589ar

Padgette, J., Scafone, K., & Chen, L. (2012). *Guide to Bluetooth Security. NIST Special Publication 800-121, Revision 1*. National Institute for Standards and Technology.

PCmagazine Encyclopedia. (n.d.). *Definition of 802.11*. Retrieved from http://www.pcmag.com/encyclopedia/term/37204/802-11

PCmagazine Encyclopedia. (n.d.). *Definition of Wi-Fi.* Retrieved from http://www.pcmag.com/encyclopedia/term/54444/wi-fi

Perez-Carrillo, A., & Wanderley, M. (2015). Indirect Acquisition of Violin Instrumental Controls from Audio Signal with hidden Markov Models. *IEEE/ACM Transactions on Audio, Speech, and Language Processing*, *23*(5), 932–940.

Perttu, D. (2007). A quantitative study of chromaticism: Changes observed in historical eras and individual composers. *Empirical Musicology Review*, *2*(2), 47–54.

Pina, P. (2011). Electronic Surveillance, Privacy and Enforcement of Intellectual Property Rights: A Digital Panopticon? In Cruz-Cunha & Varajão (Eds.), Innovations in SMEs and conducting e-business: Technologies, trends and Solutions (pp. 301-316). Hershey, PA: Business Science Reference.

Pina, P. (2015). File-Sharing of Copyrighted Works, P2P, and the Cloud: Reconciling Copyright and Privacy Rights. In Gupta. M. (Ed.), Handbook of Research on Emerging Developments in Data Privacy (pp. 52-69). Hershey, PA: Advances in Information Security, Privacy, and Ethics (AISPE) Book Series.

Pöhlmann, E., & West, M. L. (2001). *Documents of Ancient Greek Music.* Oxford, UK: Academic Press.

Politis, D., & Margounakis, D. (2003). Determining the Chromatic Index of music. In *Proceedings of the 3rd International Conference on Web Delivering of Music* (WEDELMUSIC '03).

Politis, D., Linardis, P., & Mastorakis, N. (2002). The arity of Delta prosodic and musical interfaces: A metric of complexity for "vector" sounds. In *Proceedings of the 2nd International Conference on Music and Artificial Intelligence* (ICMAI2002).

Politis, D., Margounakis, D., & Mokos, K. (2004). Visualizing the Chromatic Index of music. In *Proceedings of the 4th International Conference on Web Delivering of Music* (WEDELMUSIC '04).

Politis, D., Margounakis, D., Tsalighopoulos, G., & Kyriafinis, G. (2015). Transgender Musicality, Crossover Tonality, and Reverse Chromaticism: The Ontological Substrate for Navigating the Ocean of Global Music. *International Research Journal of Engineering and Technology, 2*(5).

Politis, D., Margounakis, D., Tsalighopoulos, G., & Kyriafinis, G. (2015a). Transgender Musicality, Crossover Tonality, and Reverse Chromaticism: The Ontological Substrate for Navigating the Ocean of Global Music. *International Research Journal of Engineering and Technology, 2*(5).

Politis, D., Piskas, G., Tsalighopoulos, M., & Kyriafinis, G. (2015b). variPiano™: Visualizing Musical Diversity with a Differential Tuning Mobile Interface. *International Journal of Interactive Mobile Technologies*, *9*(3).

Politis, D., Tsalighopoulos, M., Kyriafinis, G., & Palaskas, A. (2014). Mobile Computers, Mobile Devices, Mobile Interfaces: … Mobile Ethics?. In *Proceedings of the6th International Conference on Information Law and Ethics ICIL'14*. University of Macedonia.

Politis, D., & Margounakis, D. (2010). Modeling musical Chromaticism: The algebra of cross-cultural music perception. *International Journal of Academic Research*, *2*(6), 20–29.

Politis, D., & Margounakis, D. (2010). Modelling Musical Chromaticism: The Algebra of Cross-Cultural Music Perception. *IJAR*, *2*(6), 20–29.

Preece, J., Rogers, Y., & Sharp, H. (2002). *Interaction Design: Beyond Human-Computer Interaction*. Wiley & Sons.

Puckette, M. (1996). Pure Data: Another Integrated Computer Music Environment. In *Proceedings of the Second Intercollege Computer Music Concerts*.

Ramos, A., Rodríguez, C., Martinez-Beneyto, P., Perez, D., Gault, A., Falcon, J. C., & Boyle, P. (2009). Use of telemedicine in the remote programming of cochlear implants. *Acta Oto-Laryngologica*, *129*(5), 533–540. doi:10.1080/00016480802294369 PMID:18649152

Raphael, L., Borden, G., & Harris, K. (2007). *Speech Science Primer - Physiology, Acoustics and Perception of Speech*. Williams & Wilkins.

Retzer, K. (2013). Aligning corporate ethics compliance programs with data protection. *Privacy & Data Protection*, *13*(6), 5–7.

Roland, N., McRae, R., & McCombe, A. (2000). *Key topics in Otolaryngology*. Taylor & Francis.

Roth, P. (2006). *The Workplace Implications of RFID Technology*. Employment Law Bulletin.

Rouvroy, A., & Poullet, Y. (2008). The right to informational self-determination and the value of self-development: Reassessing the importance of privacy for democracy. In *Reinventing Data Protection:Proceedings of the International Conference*. Berlin: Springer.

Rowe, R. (2004). *Machine musicianship*. Cambridge, MA: MIT Press.

Sadie, S., & Tyrell, J. (Eds.). (2004). *New Grove Dictionary of Music and Musicians*. Grove.

Sahin, A. (2014). New EU data protection laws: European Parliament proposes restrictive data protection laws in Europe. *Computer and Telecommunications Law Review*, *20*(2), 63–65.

Schubert, E. (2004). Modeling Perceived Emotion with Continuous Musical Features. *Music Perception*, *21*(4), 561–585. doi:10.1525/mp.2004.21.4.561

Seashore, H. (1937). An objective analysis of artistic singing. In University of Iowa Studies in the Psychology of Music: Objective Analysis of Musical Performance (vol. 4). University of Iowa.

Senftleben, M. (2004). *Copyright, Limitations and the three-step Test. An Analysis of the Three- Step Test in International and EC Copyright Law*. The Hague: Kluwer Law International.

Shepard, R. (1999). Pitch, perception and measurement. In P. Cook (Ed.), *Music, Cognition and Computerized Sound*. Cambridge, MA: MIT Press.

Siau, K., Nah, F.-H., & Teng, L. (2002). Acceptable Internet use policy. *Communications of the ACM*, *45*(1), 75–79. doi:10.1145/502269.502302

Simmons, F. (1966). Electrical Stimulation of the Auditory Nerve in Man. *Acta Oto-Laryngologica*, *84*(1), 2–54. PMID:5936537

Singh, P. (2010). *Copyright and freedom of expression in Europe*. Retrieved June 28, 2016, from http://works.bepress.com/pankaj_singh/8

Sundberg, J. (1987). *The Science of the Singing Voice*. Northern Illinois University Press.

Sundberg, J. (1999). The perception of singing. In D. Deutch (Ed.), *The Psychology of Music* (2nd ed.). London: Academic Press. doi:10.1016/B978-012213564-4/50007-X

Swingler, T. (1998). The Invisible Keyboard in the Air: An Overview of the Educational, Therapeutic and Creative Applications of the EMS Soundbeam™. In *2nd European Conference for Disability, Virtual Reality & Associated Technology*.

Taylor, L. (2014). Wearable technology: The regulatory challenges. *Computer and Telecommunications Law Review*, *20*(4), 95–97.

Tenkanen, A. (2008). *Measuring tonal articulations in compositions*. MaMuX Computational Analysis Special Session, Paris, France.

Tindale, A., Kapur, A., & Tzanetakis, G. (2011). Training Surrogate Sensors in Musical Gesture Acquisition Systems. *IEEE Transactions on Multimedia*, *13*(1), 50–59. doi:10.1109/TMM.2010.2089786

Ting, C., & Wildman, S. (2002). The economics of Internet radio. In *30th Research Conference on Communication, Information and Internet Policy*.

Torremans, P. (2004). Copyright as a human right. In Copyright and human rights: Freedom of expression, intellectual property, privacy. Kluwer Law.

Traube, C., Depalle, P., & Wanderley, M. (2003). Indirect Acquisition of Instrumental Gesture based on Signal, Physical and Perceptual Information. In *Proceedings of the 2003 Conference on New Interfaces for Musical Expression NIME2003*.

Tzanetakis, G., Kapur, A., Schloss, A., & Wright, M. (2007). Computational Ethnomusicology. *Journal of Interdisciplinary Music Studies*, *1*(2), 1–24.

Updhayay, N. (2015). *Do You Have A Body Balancing Problem?* Your Ears Can Make You Look Drunk.

Van der Ploeg, I. (2005). *The Machine-Readable Body: Essays on Biometrics and the Informatization of the Body*. Maastricht: Shaker.

Voida, A., Grinter, R., Ducheneaut, N., Edwards, W., & Newman, M. (2005). Listening in: Practices Surrounding iTunes Music Sharing. In *Proceedings of the SIGCHI Conference on Human Factors in Computing Systems*. ACM Press. doi:10.1145/1054972.1054999

Wanderley, M., & Battier, M. (Eds.). (2000). *Trends in Gestural Control of Music*. Ircam – Centre Pompidou.

Wanderley, M., & Orio, N. (2002). Evaluation of Input Devices for Musical Expression: Borrowing Tools from HCI. *Computer Music Journal*, *26*(3), 62–76. doi:10.1162/014892602320582981

Warner, G., Thirlwall, A., Corbridge, R., Patel, S., & Martinez-Devesa, P. (2009). *Otolaryngology and head and neck surgery*. Academic Press.

Warren, S., & Brandeis, L. (1890). The right to privacy. *Harvard Law Review*, *4*(5), 193–220. doi:10.2307/1321160

Warren, S., & Brandeis, L. (1980). The right to privacy. *Harvard Law Review, 4.*

Wasowski, A., Skarzynski, P., Lorens, A., Obrycka, A., Walkowiak, A., & Bruski, L. (2010). Remote Fitting of Cochlear Implant System. *Cochlear Implants International, 11*(Supplement 1), 489–492. doi:10.1179/146701010X12671177318105 PMID:21756680

Wesarg, T., Kröger, S., Gerber, O., Kind, H., Reuss, S., Roth, J., & Laszig, R. et al. (2006). Pilot Study of Remote Measurement and Fitting of Cochlear Implant Recipients. In *8th EFAS Congress / 10th Congress of the German Society of Audiology*. Heidelberg, Germany: EFAS.

Wesarg, T., Wasowski, A., Skarzynski, H., Ramos, A., Gonzalez, J., Kyriafinis, G., & Laszig, R. et al. (2010). Remote Fitting in Nucleus Cochlear Implant Recipients. *Acta Oto-Laryngologica, 130*(12), 1379–1388. doi:10.3109/00016489.2010.492480 PMID:20586675

Wessel, D., & Wright, M. (2002). Problems and Prospects for Intimate Musical Control of Computers. *Computer Music Journal, 26*(3), 11–22. doi:10.1162/014892602320582945

West, M. L. (1992). *Ancient Greek Music*. Oxford, UK: Academic Press.

Whalen, Z. (2004). Play Along - An Approach to Videogame Music. Game Studies: The International Journal of Computer Game Research, 4(1).

Whitcroft, O. (2013). Bring Your Own Device -protecting data on the move. *Privacy & Data Protection, 13*(4), 10–12.

Wi-Fi Alliance Org. (2015). *Discover Wi-Fi Security*. Retrieved from http://www.wi-fi.org/discover-wi-fi/security

Wiley, M., & Kapur, A. (2009). Multi-Laser Gestural Interface - Solutions for Cost-Effective and Open Source Controllers. In *Proceedings of Proceedings of the 2009 Conference on New Interfaces for Musical Expression NIME2009.*

Wilhelmsson, U. (2006). What is a Game Ego? (or How the Embodied Mind Plays a Role in Computer Game Environments). In M. Pivec (Ed.), *Affective and Emotional Aspects of Human-Computer Interaction* (pp. 45–58). IOS Press.

Williamson, V. (2014). *You Are the Music: How Music Reveals What it Means to be Human*. Icon Books Ltd.

Winkler, T. (1998). *Composing Interactive Music – Techniques and Ideas Using Max*. MIT Press.

Yeo, W., & Berger, J. (2005). Application of imagesonification methods to music. In *Proceedings of the International Computer Music Conference (ICMC2005)*.

Yin, J., Wang, Y., & Hsu, D. (2005). Digital Violin Tutor: an Integrated System for Beginning Violin Learners. In *Proceedings of the 13th annual ACM International Conference on Multimedia*. ACM. doi:10.1145/1101149.1101353

Zhang, Z. (2012). Microsoft Kinect Sensor and its Effect. *IEEE MultiMedia*, *9*(2), 4–10. doi:10.1109/MMUL.2012.24

Index

M

N

O

P

R

S

T

V

W

www.ingramcontent.com/pod-product-compliance
Ingram Content Group UK Ltd.
Pitfield, Milton Keynes, MK11 3LW, UK
UKHW050418051026
15470UKWH00022B/1669

9 781522 502647